# THE ENVIRONMENT IN BRITISH PREHISTORY

# The Environment in British Prehistory

*edited by*

## I.G. SIMMONS
## M.J. TOOLEY

Duckworth

*First published in 1981 by*
*Gerald Duckworth & Co. Ltd.*
*The Old Piano Factory,*
*43 Gloucester Crescent, London NW1*

© *1981 by I.G. Simmons and M.J. Tooley*

ISBN 0 7156 1362 6 cased
ISBN 0 7156 1441 X paper

British Library Cataloguing in Publication Data

The environment in British prehistory.
  1. Man, Prehistoric – Great Britain
  2. Anthropo-geography – Great Britain
  I. Simmons, Ian Gordon
  II. Tooley, M J
  301.31'09361     GN805

  ISBN 0-7156-1362-6
  ISBN 0-7156-1441-X Pbk

*Photoset by*
*Specialised Offset Services Ltd., Liverpool*
*printed in Great Britain by*
*Redwood Burn Ltd, Trowbridge & Esher*

# Contents

# Plates

*( between pages 150 and 151)*

# Preface

The starting point for this book was the publication in 1974 of Professor Colin Renfrew's edited collection, *British Prehistory: A New Outline*. We noticed that only one of the contributors devoted any space to environmental issues and thought that a companion volume dealing exclusively with man's environment during British prehistory would be a useful book to compile. This work is then the outcome of our invitations to a number of scholars who agreed to write accounts of the environment structured not by the usual environmentally-based chronozones but by the conventional cultural divisions of British prehistory. Our hope is that archaeologists of many kinds who have felt the need for an 'environmental commentary' on their period may find it useful, and that this value will extend to undergraduate students of the subject who would like a little more detail than they find in the excellent beginning-level texts now becoming available to them. Our experience in meeting and working with amateur archaeologists suggests to us that they are becoming very interested in the environmental interactions of early man and so we hope that they too will enjoy this book.

We asked the contributors to consider the physical environment of man and to attempt to consider as many aspects as possible which impinged upon man: climate, soils, sea-level, animals and vegetation are given most space, and, where possible, there is a discussion of the changing landscape that was the home of these early communities. An essay on methods of palaeoenvironmental investigation precedes the accounts of each cultural period, and a brief statement on the relative environmental impact of the different cultural groups forms the tailpiece.

One of the many problems encountered by all the contributors in trying to develop the theme of the nature of the environment during each of the phases of British prehistory is the different length of each of them. For instance, the Palaeolithic includes at least two interglacial and glacial cycles, whereas the Bronze Age covers a relatively short period during part of what may well turn out to be an interglacial stage. The large-scale and repetitive changes of climate, sea-level, vegetation and animal communities of the former contrast with the subtle and slight changes of the latter. Such problems were exacerbated for our writers by the uneven spread of sites within the British Isles in which the evidence for environmental change is found within specifically archaeological contexts: the concatenation of evidence (even then lacking human skeletons) found at Star Carr ought to be paralleled for each culture and preferably for both Highland and Lowland zones: such sites would make a great difference to our ideas about man-environment relations. But the piecing together of smaller fragments of evidence is yielding discernible patterns and our contributors have tried to make these clear. Future multidisciplinary research on archaeological sites and their environs will surely fill in the foreground details in a picture still dominated by the less strongly defined background which has been painted by palaeobotanists, some of whom have been concerned, quite properly, with problems of regional vegetational history or historical phytogeography. Nevertheless, one thing seems clear: that our knowledge of man's impact upon the ecosystems of his environment grows in strength and variety as new evidence emerges, and that any deterministic ideas based on human societies as products of their natural environment are clearly outdated. Yet the environment as provider of resources and ultimate framework was (and is) always there. It seems preferable to think of a systems approach in which from time to time and place to place one component or another was a dominant influence in the system; combined with this is the idea of iteration in which there is a continuous interaction between human culture and environment, modifying both as time proceeds.

We have no illusions, though, that our synopsis is other than provisional. Between manuscript and submission to the press, some alterations can be made but thereafter little can be done to reflect new work which is appearing. The best we can say is that we represent the major strands of thinking at the time of going to press, and that users of the book will regard it as a context in which they can view new research as it appears. To the extent that we stimulate some interest in environmental archaeology, the sooner the material becomes outdated the more successful we shall have been.

We have adopted the current archaeological convention for radiocarbon dates: they are given in their uncalibrated form with the annotations bc/bp. Any calibrated dates are designated as BC. However, we have encouraged authors to include uncorrected dates even if they wish to make deductions on the basis of the application of a dendrochronologically-revised correction curve. We have not attempted to compile lists of all the environmentally relevant radio-carbon assays for each period: we do not see that such lengthy inventories would serve any purpose in this context.

The editors take this opportunity of thanking the contributors for their willingness to write these essays, and for their forbearance in putting up with our stream of queries, suggested alterations and requests for new paragraphs on yet another environmental factor. Caroline Grigson in particular should be especially mentioned for her willingness to adapt her archaeozoological knowledge to the structure not only of the book but to the patterns chosen by individual contributors. Much of the editing was carried out at Durham and Judy Turner often helped with ideas at difficult times. IGS would like to express to her and to Brian Roberts his grateful thanks for reading a draft of the tailpiece at very short notice, and, most of all, to co-editor Michael Tooley for undertaking not only a big share of the routine editorial work but for carrying out almost all the final tidying-up phase of the manuscript while IGS was changing jobs.

Grateful acknowledgment is made to the following authors and publishers for permission to reproduce figures in this book: Fig. 1.2, Director, Danish Geological Survey and Dr J. Troels-Smith. 1.4, Blackwell Scientific Publications Ltd. and Dr S.T. Andersen. 1.5, Professor A. van der Werff. 3.1, Dr M.J. Tooley and the Royal Geographical Society. 3.2, Dr M.J. Tooley and the editor of the Geological Journal. 3.3, Mr J.A. Taylor and the Council for British Archaeology. 4.1, Dr H.J.B. Birks and the Royal Society. 4.2, Dr F.A. Hibbert and Somerset Levels' Project. 4.3, Dr J.G. Evans and Academic Press. 4.4, Dr W. Pennington and Cambridge University Press. 4.5, Director, Danish Geological Survey. 4.6, Sir Harry Godwin and the editor of *Antiquity*. 4.7, Dr D. Walker and the Royal Society. 4.8, Professor F. Oldfield and the editor of *Geografisker Annaler*. 4.12, Dr W. Pennington and the Council for British Archaeology. 4.13, Dr F.A. Hibbert. 4.14, Dr F.A. Hibbert and the Council for British Archaeology. 5.1, Dr M.P. Kerney and the Royal Society. 5.2, Dr J. Turner and the Royal Society. 5.3, Professor I.G. Simmons and the editor of *New Phytologist*. 5.4 and 5.5, Institute of

British Geographers. 5.6, Professor G.W. Dimbleby and Oxford University Press.

Rosanna Tooley drew Figure 1.1 and Val Winchester drew Figures 1.3 and 3.3. Susan Holt redrew Figures 2.1, 2.2, 2.3, 2.4, 2.5, 2.6, 5.6 and 6.1. Dr P.A. GreatRex assisted by proof reading. The editors acknowledge this help with gratitude.

Bristol and Durham,                                          I.G.S.
July 1980                                                     M.J.T.

# *Contributors*

Professor I.G. Simmons, Department of Geography, The University, Bristol

Dr M.J. Tooley, Department of Geography, The University, Science Laboratories, South Road, Durham

Professor G.W. Dimbleby, Institute of Archaeology, 31-4 Gordon Square, London

Dr Caroline Grigson, Odontological Museum, The Royal College of Surgeons of England, 35-43 Lincoln's Inn Fields, London

Professor A.G. Smith, Department of Botany, University College, Cardiff

Dr H.M. Tinsley, 86 Topstreet Way, Harpenden, Hertfordshire

Dr J. Turner, Department of Botany, The University, Science Laboratories, South Road, Durham

J.J. Wymer, 17 Duke Street, Bildeston, Ipswich, Suffolk

# 1. *Methods of Reconstruction*

## M.J. TOOLEY

### Introduction

There are many specialist methods available that can be used to obtain data that are relevant to the reconstruction of early physical and biotic environments associated with prehistoric man. However, the information derived from the application of these methods is often difficult to interpret because the physical and biotic environments of early man differed considerably in scale and nature from those of the present. For example, the Mesolithic period in the British Isles lasted for about 5,000 years, during which time the land area available for hunting and migration contracted as the sea-level rose and England became isolated from the continent: in addition, the composition of the forests changed from a boreal aspect with birch and pine to an atlantic aspect with oak, elm, alder, ash and lime.

During the prehistoric period, man was a component of the biotic environment, participating in many diverse ecosystems, competing for food resources with herbivores and carnivores, and fuelling decomposer food chains. The balance in ecological systems that obtained during the prehistoric period is something that distinguishes this period from the historic period. However, as cultural and technological change occurred and cognition grew in the human community during the prehistoric period and, with an increasing rate, during the historic period, so food chains to it were shortened and biotic communities servicing it were simplified.

The present-day agricultural and industrial landscape of north-west Europe contains few niches in which natural plant and animal communities have survived unaltered, and from which analogues can be taken to interpret fragmentary fossil finds or fossil assemblages of plants and animals with any confidence. In the British Isles, the extensive riverine and coastal flood plain primeval forests of fen and carr have been progressively cleared following effective drainage, and before them the forests of oak, elm, lime and ash on the drier replacement slopes and interfluves. Fragments of oak forest survive, such as Wistman's Wood in the valley of the West Dart in Devon and in Keskadale and Birkrigg in the Lake District, although even these fragments are probably secondary. Whether primary or secondary, such fragments cannot serve adequately to interpret, in terms of vegetation composition and structure, micro- and macro-fossil plant assemblages from sites where deposits span the prehistoric period. Indeed, if we accept West's (1964) conclusion that present plant communities are temporary aggregations with no long history in the Quaternary, then the search for the modern analogue of fossil assemblages is a vain one. The resource potential for man of former plant communities may have been quite different from that which the identification of the nearest modern analogue from a fossil assemblage would permit. Watts (1973) has made the point that not only are plant associations ephemeral but also, in the past, quite different and often surprising associations commonly occurred. This may also apply to animal associations and biotic communities generally.

Furthermore, the fossil record is neither unbroken nor distributed evenly. It has to be assumed that conditions remain homogeneous or change continuously in one direction between sites where inter- polation is necessary. Correlation is as strong as the quality of the analytical data from each site.

Many single elements of prehistoric man's environment can be established directly or indirectly, but rarely is it possible to derive evidence of the nature, scale and complexity of whole ecosystems in which man participated. Only occasionally have sites been discovered, such as the early Neolithic Muldbjerg dwelling place at Aamosen in Denmark (Troels-Smith 1960b) and the Mesolithic site at Star Carr in the Vale of Pickering (Clark 1954) where extraordinarily rich fossil remains and a co-ordinated, inter- disciplinary research programme have allowed detailed palaeo- environmental reconstructions.

## Environmental elements and techniques

Elements of the prehistoric environment that can be established include climatic values and patterns, sea-level movements and coastal changes, the probable migration routes of plant and animal taxa, regional and local vegetation patterns, water depth and quality, soil types and slope stability, and food resources.

Some of these elements can be measured directly whereas others are derived indirectly. An example of direct measurement is the maximum altitude attained by sea-level and known as the marine limit. The extent and altitude of marine transgression and regression deposits, including beaches, can be recorded. An example of indirect measurement is climate: the value of climatic elements such as temperature and precipitation can be derived indirectly from a consideration of the presence or absence and the distribution of a particular plant or animal taxon. Such an inference is possible only if the present distribution of the taxon and those operationally significant factors affecting its distribution are known. Furthermore, it is necessary to assume not only that the taxon has not undergone genetic change, thereby affecting its potential ecological range, but also that the taxon occurred in the same or similar biotic association: perhaps the latter assumption can no longer be sustained in the light of the conclusions of West (1964) and Watts (1973).

The measurement of a particular element, in the first instance, refers only to the recording site. However, if many measurements are made, for example, in a coastal lowland, an estuary or a drainage basin then a common pattern of values may occur permitting generalisation. Some elements may occur at more or less the same time and affect extensive areas, such as the deposition of Fen Clay in the Fenlands or of Holland peat in the Netherlands. Other elements may be of local significance and occur at different times, catastrophically, such as landslips.

There are many assumptions, both explicit and implicit, in applying the techniques and interpreting the raw data that accrue. Upon these interpretations palaeoenvironmental reconstructions are based. Many techniques are now available and these have been applied with varying success to biogenic and minerogenic sediments of Quaternary age. Selection of appropriate techniques is an important initial stage and their application will often provide unequivocal data, permitting strongly supported reconstructions. For example, different micropalaeontological techniques need to be applied to the organic and inorganic sediments of the former tidal flat and lagoonal zones of the coast: pollen analysis of organic sediments has provided evidence of changing water quality and water depth, and of progressive and retrogressive succession of plant communities in coastal and near coastal situations; diatom analysis of minerogenic sediments has indicated the intensity of marine conditions and the position of the sedimentary environment within the former intertidal zone.

Evidence of climatic conditions during glacial and interglacial stages and interstadials has come from high latitude ice cores (Dansgaard *et al.* 1969; Epstein *et al.* 1970) from deep sea cores (Emiliani 1964; Shackleton 1977), from the distribution of periglacial phenomena, such as fossil ice wedges, polygons, stripes, pingos and cover sands (Williams 1975) from fossil Coleopteran assemblages (Coope 1975, 1977) and from pollen analysis (Zagwijn 1975). The characteristics and conditions of deposition of glacial sediments have recently been reviewed (Francis 1975). The techniques used include stratigraphic and granulometric analyses, macrofossil analyses of plant and animal remains and microfossil analyses, and are described in Faegri and Iversen (1964), Kummel and Raup (1965), Barber (1976) and West (1977).

It is not the purpose of this contribution to provide a repertorium of techniques that could be used in isolating data relevant to the reconstruction of glacial, interstadial and interglacial environments. The intention is to concentrate on those techniques that have been applied to interstadial and interglacial sediments. It is these sediments that occasionally contain either evidence of early man, or his artifacts, or more rarely human skeletons. To this end, stratigraphic analysis, the analysis of plant and animal macrofossils, pollen and diatom analyses and radiocarbon dating methods are considered, an indication of their strengths and limitations is given and some illustrations from the late Quaternary of the British Isles are provided.

### Stratigraphic analysis

The quality of the interpretative evidence, upon which environmental reconstruction is based, is as sure as the quality of the raw data collection in the field. Poor quality data at this stage will jeopardise the validity of any conclusion based both on these data and subsequent analyses. For these reasons consideration should be given to the type of sediment sampler, how the cores can be related spatially, and the method of recording the composition of the layers in the stratigraphic column.

*Methods of sampling*

Although there are many mechanical corers, using a hydraulic or percussive principle, such as the Land Rover-mounted Proline corer, a standard drilling rig, and the underwater corers, such as the Mackereth corer and the vibrocore, capital and recurrent costs are high, and most sampling is carried out using hand-operated samplers. Hand samplers include the Beus and Mattson Hiller-type peat sampler, the Russian peat sampler, the Dachnowski sampler and the gouge sampler, some of which are illustrated in Fig. 1.1. A very efficient, modified Livingstone corer which is used with a vibrator has been described by Merkt and Streif (1970). Other samplers are described and illustrated by Faegri and Iversen (1964), Barber (1976) and West (1968). The Hiller sampler, described by von Post and Granlund (1926), has been used for many years and samples adequately in all organic sediments, except those that are fibrous, such as unhumified *Sphagnum-Eriophorum* peat. It will not sample silts and sands adequately and clay is difficult to remove from the chamber. The outer tube of the Hiller scoops a 50 cm. high column of sediment into the chamber which is opened and closed by anticlockwise and clockwise rotation. The sediment is deformed, and structures are lost but no compression is recorded. As with other hand sampling devices, vertical drift during sampling may occur and results in contamination: this may be overcome by clamping the extension rods above a metal plate which serves as the surface datum from which depths are recorded and the surface altitude measured.

The Russian-type peat sampler was first described by Jowsey (1966) and modifications to the design described by Barber (1976) have resulted in a most versatile and robust sampler for all but the most intractable sediments. The sampler retrieves half-cores 50 cm. long and 5 cm. in diameter. The chamber is rotated 180° only against a plate which acts as an anchor at the sampling level. The half cores that are retrieved show very clearly the sedimentary structures and if the reverse side of the plate without the fin is used, the half core may be scooped from the plate inside a pvc tube split longitudinally and returned to the laboratory in polythene layflat tubing. From such half cores, samples for micropalaeontological and radiometric analyses may be taken. Again, the only possibility of contamination arises when drifting during sampling occurs. Also, if at all possible, the sampling level should be reached at the end of a

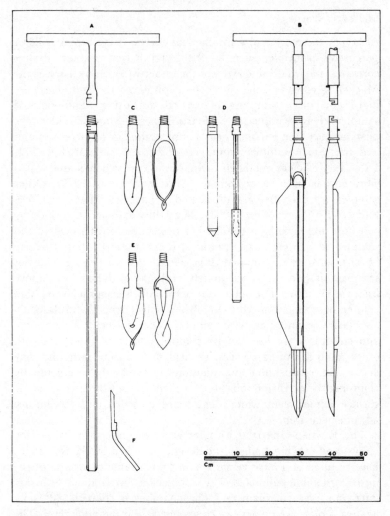

Figure 1.1. Hand sampling equipment used to obtain unconsolidated samples for stratigraphic analysis. A – Gouge sampler and scoop (F) to remove sediment from the chamber. B – Russian-type sampler. C – Clay auger. D – Dacknowski sampler showing boring position (left) and piston withdrawn for sampling (right). E – Sand auger.

continuous through-fall. The Russian-type sampler has been used in all types of biogenic sediment and in clays, silts and sands up to three metres thick: passage through the latter sediments can be effected by slight agitation of the sampler which results in spontaneous liquefaction of the sediment. The consequence often is that retrieval is difficult, and some sort of leverage on the handle is necessary, to break the friction on the chamber. A Farnell sleeve coupling is used to attach the sampler to the extension rods, and a wire attached to a metal ring on the sampler ensures that the sampler can be retrieved from depth in the event of rod failure or faulty coupling. The first rod needs to be shortened by 11 cm. to accommodate the distance between the top of the chamber and the first coupling: if a standard metre rod is used, then 11 cm. of sediment is lost between 50 and 61 cm. and all recorded depths below 50 cm. are deeper by 11 cm. This error can be overcome by measuring from the half metre marks on the extension rods to the sampling chamber. Russian-type samplers have been made in Sweden with a chamber length of 100 cm. and have proved successful in limnic sediments. In layered sediments with alternating organic and inorganic bands which are the typical sediments of the tidal flat and lagoonal palaeoenvironments, the chamber of the sampler may buckle and collapse as the result of stresses set up by the torque on the sampler. To a great extent this weakness has been overcome by using a heavier gauge stainless steel chamber, but this has been at the expense of the sample size. The Russian sampler may be used for routine stratigraphic analysis and for sample collection. For the former, the Russian has been superceded by the gouge sampler, which is the most efficient, robust and reliable sampler for reconnaissance surveys and routine analysis.

The gouge sampler is made by Eijkelkamp, Lathum in the Netherlands and is part of a set of equipment that includes a Dacknowski piston sampler, a sand and clay auger head, rods, spanners and spatula. The gouge sampler comprises a metre-long tube (22 mm inside diameter), split longitudinally, and sharpened and chamfered at the base. It has been used to sample alternating layers of organic and inorganic sediments up to eight metres in thickness. The sediment core is pushed through the chamber and out obliquely at the top as the sampler is pushed into the ground to the sampling level. There is some consolidation of the core and smearing when well-consolidated *limus* deposits are sampled. In common with other samplers, fibrous unhumified *turfas* are poorly sampled or badly compressed during sampling.

A network of sampling sites should be laid out across a bog or former lake bed, and the sampling sites related to each other by levelling. In some cases only the relative altitude of sampling sites is required, but usually levels should be related to the zero datum of the country, which is Ordnance Datum (Newlyn) in the United Kingdom (abbreviated to O.D. throughout). This is particularly important if altitudinal correlation is to be attempted of a persistent horizon over an extensive geographical area: for example, a marine transgression facies in one area may have a constant altitudinal range whereas elsewhere the same age facies may be recorded at a higher or lower altitude because of land uplift or subsidence. Ordnance Survey levelling data should be from the most recent geodetic re-surveying of the country, and Ordnance Survey bench marks should be the origin and destination of a levelling traverse: spot heights on maps should be avoided because they are not only established less accurately but also more subject to change.

Only when a complete stratigraphic survey of the area has been completed can a decision be made about the site with the most representative layers or the most complete sedimentary record, from which a core can be taken for laboratory analysis.

The spacing of the sampling sites will depend on the complexity of the stratigraphy. In some tidal flat and lagoonal areas, the sediments are sheet-like and homogeneous over extensive areas: in this case a sampling interval of 300 m. is sufficient. Locally, in the vicinity of former saltmarsh gullies and where a marine transgression reaches its landward limit, feathering into brackishwater and freshwater limnic sediments, the sampling interval must be increased to establish the detail of the feature.

In most cases the build-up of the bog or the stages of infill of a lake basin can only be established by sampling at regular intervals with the devices described. Occasionally, temporary excavations enable a detailed record of the layers to be made. Rarely is the excavation more than 5 m. deep, and there is a risk of rotational slipping and collapse if the sides of the excavation are not secured by a timber framework or piling. The excavation is usually made for engineering purposes, and both recording and sampling are difficult in the time the excavation remains open.

Shallow excavations are instructive and have not been employed as often in Quaternary geology as in archaeology. The excavation at Aamosen in Denmark was made for both purposes and provided rich data (for example Troels-Smith 1960b, Jørgensen 1963) for environmental reconstruction at the site.

*Description of sediment types*

Troels-Smith (1955b) has argued that 'the starting point of all stratigraphic studies, no matter how elaborate, must be the objective description and recording of sections as seen in the field'. It is important to describe the layers and their components before any genetic interpretation can be made. In practice, this distinction is often blurred, and a layer is characterised on the basis of the plant community that it is assumed generated the deposit. Hence, in the literature, sediment types such as 'fen peat', '*Alnus* carr peat' and '*Betula* carr peat' are found. Fen vegetation comprises grasses and sedges, such as *Phragmites, Molinia* and *Cladium*, with local flushes of bryophytes, such as *Sphagnum* and *Hypnum*, and locally trees and shrubs such as *Alnus, Betula, Salix* and *Rhamnus*. One would expect a fen peat to be markedly heterogeneous with leaves, twigs, branches, trunks and roots of woody plants set in a matrix of monocotyledonous or bryophyte peat. The term 'carr peat' begs the question whether or not a carr-type plant community existed at the time the peat was forming. Carr vegetation will be dominated by *Alnus* with *Salix* abundant and frequently *Betula*. A dense undergrowth of shrubs and herbaceous plants will also occur. The organic deposit formed will still be heterogeneous but with a marked increase of woody detritus material and woody roots.

There is further confusion because different workers employ different symbols for the same deposit, so that comparisons become impossible if only a stratigraphic diagram and not a description is available. Faegri and Gams (1937, in Faegri and Iversen 1964) established the principle that different types of deposit should be immediately recognisable from the symbols used: hence sediments such as gyttjas should be shown by intersecting lines, telmatic peats such as *Phragmites* and *Cladium* peat by vertical lines and terrestrial peats, such as *Sphagnum* and *Eriophorum* peat by horizontal lines. Thickening of the lines symbolising telmatic and terrestrial peats indicates degrees of humification. However, a comparison of Figure 3 in Faegri and Iversen (1964) and Figure 4.2 in West (1968) shows different practices: for example, West shows fen peat by horizontal lines, whereas Faegri and Iversen show it by vertical lines and reserve horizontal lines for terrestrial grass peat; *Eriophorum* peat is shown by West as broken, wavy, vertical lines, compared to the broken, wavy, horizontal lines of Faegri and Iversen. These differences have been transmitted to and amplified in the literature, so that no assumptions can be made about comparability of symbols and their meaning.

More than twenty years ago, Troels-Smith (1955b) attempted to overcome these difficulties by devising an objective scheme for the recording of the components of a layer in a stratigraphic succession. He stressed the need for objectivity in recording, arguing that a thorough knowledge of the components of a deposit precedes and does not follow inferences of origin.

Troels-Smith's scheme defines three elements that should be specified for each layer of stratigraphy identified; these are the components of the layer, the degree of humification and the physical properties of the layer.

Initially the layers comprising a section, for example, are identified and marked by slivers of wood every metre along the face of the section. At each metre point, successive samples of material 10 cm³ are cut from the peat face from top to bottom. The samples are broken horizontally and vertically, and the characteristics of the samples recorded: at this stage, 'it is essential to let imagination work upon the observations in an effort to see things which have not yet been demonstrated, and in particular to record objectively and faithfully everything found or observed independent of whether, at the time of excavation, it fits into present theories' (Troels-Smith 1960b).

The first element to be described is the composition of the layers. The layer may contain one or more components, the proportions of which are estimated on a 25% basis on a scale of 1 to 4, with 1 indicating 25% composition of the component and 4 100%. The slight presence of a component is indicated by a plus sign in the final formulation. The main components recognised are *turfa, detritus, limus, argilla* and *grana*: there are several accessory elements such as *testae molluscorum, stirpes* and *rudimenta culturae*. Symbols for *turfa* and *limus* according to Troels-Smith (1955b) are shown in Fig. 1.2.

*Turfa* is equivalent to the telmatic and terrestrial peat of Faegri and Gams, and is defined as the roots of woody and herbaceous plants, and the stumps, trunks, branches and stems if connected to the roots. *Turfa* also includes mosses. Different types of *turfa* may be recognised: *T. bryophytica* includes the remains of *Sphagnum* and *Hypnum* for example; *T. lignosa* includes the roots and stumps of woody plants and their trunks, branches and twigs if it can be demonstrated that they are connected to the roots and have not

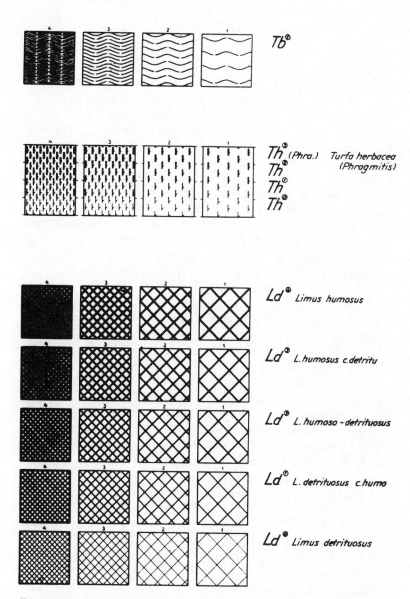

Figure 1.2. Symbols for some unconsolidated sediments according to Troels-Smith (1955b). *Tb* is *Turfa bryophtica; Th (Phra.)* is *Turfa herbacea (Phragmitis)* and *Ld* is *Limus*. The horizontal axis shows the proportion of the elements on a 25% (=1) scale. The vertical axis for *Th* shows the degree of humification of the element: $Th^0$ = no humification and $Th^3$ = well humified. The encircled superscript numbers for *Limus* indicate the proportion of humous substance in the matrix.

arrived at the sedimentary site as the result of drifting (*detritus*); *T. herbacea* includes the roots and rhizomes of herbaceous plants and their stems and leaves, if it can be shown that they are connected to the roots in the layer. Different types of *T. herbacea* can be recognised such as *Cladium turfa, Phragmites turfa* and *Molinia turfa.*

*Detritus* is made up of plant fragments that are unconnected to a root system. It comprises fragments of wood, bark, branches, and trunks, stems and leaves, fruits and seeds, all of which have either rained down onto the forest floor or been washed into a lake. *Detritus* is an allochthonous deposit compared with *turfa* which is autochthonous. Different types of *detritus* are recognised. *D. lignosus* is made up of fragments from woody plants; *D. herbosus* from herbaceous plants; and *D. granosus* from both woody and herbaceous plants in which the degree of disintegration is so great that assignment to either *D. lignosus* or *D. herbosus* is impossible.

*Limus* is a difficult deposit to individualise, for in many transitional deposits it consistitutes up to 25% of the matrix and may be taken for *Substantia humosa.* Essentially it is made up of small organic particles (often microscopic) arising from the productivity of lakes and the input of organic and inorganic material from the drainage basin. Different types of *Limus* are recognised: *L. detrituosus* is the product of more or less complete breakdown of the primary producers in a lake as well as plant fragments. If an excavated face is left for several hours *L. detrituosus* reveals itself by shrinking and cracking, and may become lighter in shade. *L. siliceus organogenes* is formed of the siliceous remains of plants such as grasses and diatoms: it feels like carborundum between the teeth, but the component cannot be determined without a microscope.

*Argilla* is a minerogenic sediment and falls within the clay fraction class. It is plastic when wet, unlike *Limus,* whose elastic qualities it lacks. *Argilla* may be rolled and turned into a circle without breaking. Two types of *Argilla* are recognised: *A. steatodes* with grains < 0.002 mm., it is plastic and dries as a hard, coherent mass; and *A. granosa* with grain sizes from 0.06 to 0.002 mm., once dried the surface of the mass can be rubbed away.

*Grana* is made up of macroscopic particles that can be seen with the naked eye. *Grana* lacks coherence, cannot be rolled when wet and crumbles when dry.

The class limits for *Argilla* and *Grana* size fractions are the same as those used for establishing the particle size distribution of a sediment specified by the British Standards Institution (1961). The largest size fraction allowed for in Troels-Smith's scheme is 6-20 mm. (*G. glareosa majora*) which is often exceeded in layers dominated by shingle or soliflucted deposits.

When the components in a layer have been identified and assigned a proportion on the 25% scale, the degree of humification and the physical properties of the layer are estimated.

Humification is estimated on a five point scale and refers to the degree of breakdown of the macrofossils that can be observed. Hence 0 on the scale indicates that the plant structure is unhumified and squeezing yields clear, colourless water; 4 indicates more or less complete humification and the peat may be squeezed through the fingers. Humification tests are applied to *turfa*, and the degree of humification is shown symbolically on the stratigraphic diagram by increasing the line thickness: unhumified deposits are represented by thin lines and humified deposits by thick lines. The humification test gives an indication of the degree of oxidation and breakdown of plant structure before burial, although post-depositional decay may occur if the rate of sedimentation is slow or if drainage and peat-cutting expose the deposit to oxidation. Degrees of humification are not applied to *Detritus* even though the constituents of both *D. lignosus* and *D. herbosus* may display varying degrees of disintegration. The reason for this is that the woody and herbaceous components of *Detritus* may undergo breakdown and oxidation *en route* to a sedimentation site.

Physical properties, such as the degree of darkness (*nigror*) of the layer, stratification (*stratificatio*), the elasticity (*elasticitas*) of the deposit, and the degree of dryness (*siccitas*) of the layer are all estimated on a five point scale. In addition, the colour of the layer is estimated according to the Munsell Color Scheme. The structure of the deposit is described, and the sharpness of the boundary between two layers is indicated on a five point scale.

The components, degrees of humification and physical properties of a layer may be summarised in an abbreviated form, thus:

Tb°4, Lc+, Ag +, *part. test. moll.* +
nig.3, strf.3, elas.4, sicc. 1‡, struct. fibrous, lim.sup.1.

This abbreviated notation from layer 3, 1.692-1.820 m. Gammelholm 28.9, Samsø, Denmark can be expanded into the following description: an unhumified fibrous bryophyte turfa, composed of *Scorpidium scorpioides* with fragments of ostracod valves, some rounded quartz grains and a silty shell marl fraction. The layer was dark, well-stratified, highly elastic, and saturated with water. The boundary layer was diffuse.

An example from Nancy's Bay, Lytham (see also Tooley 1978a) is given in Fig. 1.3 to show the stages in the construction of a stratigraphic diagram from an open excavation.

In this way all layers encountered in open sections and in samplers can be characterised. The descriptions of the layers then serve as a solid foundation for interpretation and correlation.

## Pollen analysis

Pollen studies in the British Isles, as in many other countries, have been pursued in two more or less mutually exclusive areas: the first is in aero-allergy studies and the second in correlation and the reconstruction of former vegetation types based on the analysis of fossil pollen assemblages. The contribution of aero-allergy studies, some of which are early in identifying pollen types (for example Blackley 1873) may have been underestimated, for they have considered the local and regional components of the pollen rain and its composition at recording stations, the contribution of pollen from entomophilous plants in the pollen rain and annual variations in pollen productivity (Hyde 1950a, 1950b, 1951, 1955, 1963; Hyde and Williams 1944, 1945), all of which are relevant considerations in pollen influx studies.

It is, however, in the analysis of fossil pollen assemblages from appropriate sedimentary environments, such as lakes and bogs, that data are obtained on the relative ages of the sediment, vegetational history, climatic change, changing hydrological relationships, the influence of prehistoric man on the vegetation and the development of prehistoric farming types, examples of which are given in the succeeding chapters. Although work in fossil pollen had been undertaken in Switzerland in the 1860s (Troels-Smith 1975), von Post (1916) was the first to make systematic analyses of fossil pollen in Southern Sweden and used the results not only for the correlation of deposits but also to elucidate changes in forest composition.

The application of pollen analytical techniques to sites in the British Isles began in the 1920s when Erdtman (1924) described analyses from 38 sites in north-west Scotland, the Outer Hebrides, and the Orkney and Shetland Islands. Subsequently, Erdtman

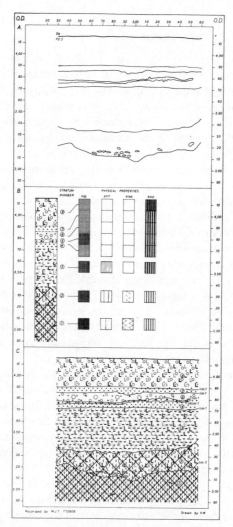

Figure 1.3. The stages in the construction of a stratigraphic diagram from the tidal flat and lagoonal zone of Nancy's Bay, Lytham, Lancashire using the notation of signatures described by Troels-Smith (1955b). A – Cross-section showing the main layers, numbered 1 to 8 in part B. The vertical axes show altitude in metres and centimetres in relation to Ordnance Datum, U.K. and the horizontal axis shows distance in metres and centimetres from the control point in Nancy's Bay. Da and P2.3 indicate that at 2.30m. from the control point in the excavation the stratigraphy was recorded and samples for pollen analysis taken. B – The stratigraphy recorded at Da, the strata recognised numbered 1-8 and the physical properties of the strata are shown. C – The stratigraphic signatures shown in part B are extended to the cross-section shown in part A.

(1928) extended this work to England, Wales and Ireland. Stimulated by the potentialities of pollen analysis, papers on the pollen content of sediments in south-west Lancashire (Travis 1926), on the Pennines (Woodhead 1929, Woodhead and Erdtman 1926) and north-east England (Raistrick and Blackburn 1931, 1932) appeared. But it was Godwin (1934a, 1934b) who described the method of pollen analysis and demonstrated its potential and the problems inherent in the method. He reiterated von Post's dual claim for pollen analysis as a chronological tool and as a key to former vegetation types and vegetational history.

Since the publication of these two seminal papers, pollen analysis has become instituted as a powerful means of establishing the nature of former environments and their direction of change, particularly during interglacial stages. Faegri and Iversen (1964) note that pollen analysis has been from the middle twenties the dominant method for investigation of late Quaternary development of vegetation and climate. The tenets established by von Post of correlation and regional parallelism of vegetation development are examined below in the light of recent developments in pollen analytical techniques.

Pollen analysis involves the isolation of pollen grains from successive levels in a sediment, using standard physical and chemical methods (Gray 1965, Faegri and Iversen 1964), their identification and enumeration. Each pollen taxon is expressed as a percentage of the pollen sum which will vary depending on the age of the deposits, the vegetation contributing to the pollen rain and the objectives of the pollen analytical investigation. Von Post (1916) was interested in the relative displacement of forest vegetation types and utilised a pollen sum that comprised the forest tree pollen, namely *Pinus, Betula, Picea, Alnus, Carpinus, Acer,* and *Fraxinus. Populus* would now be added to the list of tree pollen, although it was not identified in 1916. Von Post (1916) excluded *Corylus* from the pollen sum on the basis that it was a component of the shrub layer and only exceptionally forms a distinctive community in competition with the mixed oak forest. This view is contested by Faegri and Iversen (1964) who argue that hazel forms areas that flower profusely, and thus hazel should be regarded as part of the pollen sum. Percentages of the pollen of non-tree taxa can also be calculated and the sum usually comprises a summation of the tree pollen and non-tree pollen. The pollen sum used should always be indicated.

*Pollen diagrams*

A pollen diagram can be drawn to show the change in frequencies of pollen taxa at successive levels: depth is shown on the ordinate and frequency on the abscissa. A pollen diagram is made up of a series of pollen spectra which is the relative percentage frequencies of pollen taxa at successive levels. The form of presentation of pollen diagrams has varied considerably and there remains a diversity which makes comparison and correlation difficult in the absence of the numerical data upon which they are based. Von Post and Faegri and Iversen (1964) recommended the use of symbols for pollen and spore types for 'clarity and comparability' with other diagrams. But in the British Isles, since the early pollen diagrams of the 1920s and 1930s, most investigators have preferred the use of saw-edge diagrams or frequency histograms: thus, whilst clarity may have been gained, comparability has been lost with earlier diagrams from the British Isles and in general from northern Europe.

*Relative and absolute pollen frequencies*

Davis and Deevey (1964) have noted that pollen percentage values are interdependent and in traditional pollen diagrams, using percentage frequencies, changes in the number of one pollen taxon will elicit changes in the values of all other taxa. Von Post (1916) stressed the desirability of giving absolute pollen frequencies, but was unable to overcome the problem of different rates of sedimentation, upon which the calculation of absolute pollen frequencies would have to be based. The application of radiocarbon dating to a sequential series of samples in a core has allowed the calculation of annual pollen deposition rates: pollen concentration values may also be obtained as a measure of absolute pollen frequency by the addition of known quantities of exotic pollen to standard volumes of sediment prior to analysis (Matthews 1969; Stockmarr 1971). The application of absolute pollen frequency techniques to sediments older than ten thousand years has resulted in a fundamental revision of the chronostratigraphic subdivisions of the Late Devensian. Pennington (1975a) has compared relative pollen percentage frequency, annual pollen deposition rates and pollen concentration from Blelham Bog in the Lake District, and resolved the traditional tripartite division of Late Devensian cores into a sequence of chronozones closely correlated with the scheme from Norden (Mangerud *et al.* 1974). The identification and separation of the Bölling and Allerød interstadials on percentage frequency pollen diagrams has been obscure in the British Isles, but absolute frequency diagrams from Blelham Bog (Pennington 1975a) show pronounced minima in pollen concentration and annual deposition rates for warmth-demanding plants such as *Betula, Juniperus, Filipendula* and *Myriophyllum* throughout a narrow unit of stratigraphy now re-interpreted as the Older Dryas chronozone.

During the Flandrian Stage, although Sims (1973) notes the overall similarity of relative pollen frequency and absolute pollen diagrams in East Anglia, Pennington (1973a, 1975b) is able to deduce changes in environmental conditions from absolute pollen diagrams when relative pollen diagrams show little significant variation. For example, at Blea Tarn there are significant falls in the deposition rates of *Ulmus, Alnus* and *Corylus* more than a thousand radiocarbon years before the elm-decline (*c.* 5,000 bp), and not apparent in the diagram of relative pollen frequencies (Pennington 1970). The fall in deposition rates is interpreted as the consequence of a period of wet climate resulting in increased leaching and a decline in the base status of soils. Rather significantly this coincides with the culminating stage of a marine transgression in north-west England and an inferred climate deterioration (Tooley 1978a).

*Pollen zones*

Pollen diagrams can be zoned visually (Faegri and Iversen 1964) or numerically (Gordon and Birks 1972, 1974; Birks 1974). Zone boundaries drawn from conventional relative frequency diagrams, where the frequencies of tree taxa rise or fall sharply, do appear to correspond with boundaries established objectively using numerical techniques such as constrained single-link analysis and principal components analysis, except that, without weighting, the 'elm decline' is not registered consistently as a boundary using these methods.

The synchroneity of the zone boundaries over wide areas has important implications for correlation of phenomena such as vegetational history, climatic change, sea-level changes and cultural diffusion. The regional parallelism of vegetation has been the subject of discussion throughout Europe as well as in the British Isles. Godwin (1940a) described eight pollen zones and subzones, which, he concluded, were applicable to England and Wales. This conclusion was reinforced by radiometric dating of pollen zone

boundaries and Godwin (1960b) was able to state that 'the radiocarbon dates for pollen zone boundaries ... go some distance
towards showing that the pollen zones are not time transgressive'.
This conclusion is supported by Hibbert *et al.* (1971) and Hibbert
and Switsur (1976), but questioned by Smith and Pilcher (1973).
When comparing pollen zone boundaries that have been dated
radiometrically, there is the problem that sample thicknesses have
varied, thereby increasing or decreasing the age range of material
dated. Different types of material have been used for dating and
each one carries a different potential level of contamination and
error. Furthermore, investigators have differed in their recognition
of a significant frequency for taxa used in establishing pollen zone
boundaries: in some cases the commencement of the rise in
frequency is dated, in others the steeply rising curve and in others its
culmination. Smith and Pilcher (1973) have introduced into the
literature referring to British sites the useful criteria of the rational
and empirical limits of pollen taxa in pollen diagrams also referred
to by von Post (1916) and Nilsson (1952), to overcome the
inconsistent and subjective criteria used to establish pollen zone
boundaries. The rational limit is defined as the point at which the
pollen curve begins to rise to sustained high values, and the
empirical limit is defined as the point at which pollen of a particular
taxon becomes consistently recorded in consecutive samples, albeit
in low frequencies. Nilsson (1952) also identifies an absolute pollen
limit, in which the first presence of the pollen taxon is recorded. It is
important that the same part of the curve showing a change in
frequency of a pollen taxon at different sites is dated and that the
basis for calculating critical pollen frequencies is the same. It is also
clearly important to establish whether pollen zone boundaries are
synchronous or diachronous over small areas, such as England and
Wales, or Scotland.

A pollen zone, whose boundaries have been established by the
change in frequency of particular taxa, has been described as an
'Assemblage Zone, defined as a body of strata characterised by a
certain assemblage of fossils without regard to their ranges' (West
1970b). Godwin (1940a) defined five pollen assemblage zones and
five sub-zones. Subsequently, Hibbert *et al.* (1971) at Red Moss,
Lancashire, have applied the principles of biostratigraphic
subdivision where a complete pollen stratigraphical record for the
Flandrian Stage is available, and established six pollen assemblage
zones. The characteristics of these zones are shown in Table 1.1.

**Table 1.1. Biostratigraphic subdivision of the Flandrian stage in England and Wales.**

| Blytt-Sernander units | Godwin zones | Pollen assemblage zones | Characteristics | Chronozones | Date, years bp. commencement |
|---|---|---|---|---|---|
| Sub-Atlantic | VIII | | | | |
| Sub-Boreal | VIIb | f | *Quercus-Alnus* | FIII | $5010 \pm 80$ |
| Atlantic | VIIa | e | *Quercus-Ulmus-Alnus* | FII | $7107 \pm 120$ |
| | VIc | d | *Pinus-Corylus-Ulmus* | FId | $8196 \pm 150$ |
| | VIb | | | | |
| Boreal | VIa | c | *Corylus-Pinus* | FIc | $8880 \pm 170$ |
| | V | b | *Betula-Pinus-Corylus* | FIb | $9798 \pm 200$ |
| Pre-Boreal | IV | a | *Betula-Pinus-Juniperus* | FIa | (10250) |

Red Moss has been adopted as the type site for the Flandrian Stage (Hibbert and Switsur 1976) and therefore each bio-stratigraphic zone corresponds to a chronozone (West 1970b). Local pollen assemblages defined from pollen diagrams elsewhere in England and Wales can be correlated with the chronozones at the type site, often through regional pollen assemblage zones established in homogeneous geographical areas. In this way, pollen assemblages derived from pollen spectra from organic material adhering to archaeological finds or to bones, or short pollen diagrams from biogenic material intercalating marine clays from tidal flat and lagoonal coastal palaeoenvironments, may be assigned with some confidence to the chronozones of the type site and a relative age obtained. In practice, chronozone boundaries are dated radiometrically and this confers greater exactitude on the estimated age of the local pollen assemblage zone.

*Pollen analysis and vegetation*

In addition to the application of pollen analysis to correlation and relative chronology, pollen analysis can be used as a tool to elucidate the historical development of regional vegetation and flora and local plant communities.

The relationship of pollen frequencies to the plant communities and vegetation generating the pollen rain is complex. It has been a basic assumption in the interpretation of pollen diagrams that the relative pollen frequencies reflect the proportion of species in the regional vegetation at the moment of pollen sedimentation (Davis

1963). However, von Post (1916) had noted that the pollen diagram 'can only give trends of frequency changes between forest types. As long as we have no indices to express the relative pollen productivity of the various trees, nor to express the different degrees to which their pollen is dispersed we have no right to seek in the percentage figures an adequate expression of the composition of the forest communities'. Recent work on pollen productivity, pollen dispersal and pollen influx has made better attempts to relate pollen percentages or pollen concentration values to vegetation composition, and therefore derive a more accurate picture of former vegetation and vegetation changes from corrected pollen diagrams.

Tauber (1965) demonstrated that pollen transfer from terrestrial vegetation to a sedimentary site such as a lake depended on the size of the pollen grains, the season when the pollen was emitted, the structure of the vegetation surrounding the lake and the nature of the airflow within and above the plant communities. He deduced three components, each with a particular pollen spectrum, which contributed to the pollen influx to a lake: the first component was pollen derived from the trunk space, the second was pollen derived from above the canopy and the third was derived from scavenging of the air by rainfall. The size of the lake will affect the weighting of each component and any change in the position and composition of the littoral vegetation will affect the composition of the trunk space component reaching the lake basin. Recently Tauber (1977) has indicated that the trunk space component was generated within 200 m. of the lake, the above canopy component within 1000 m. of the lake and the rainout component within 200-400 m. of the lake. In addition to these components, pollen sedimentation on the lake floor would include a proportion of pollen brought into the lake by streams from the drainage basin. Indeed, Peck (1973) has demonstrated a large water-borne component arriving in a sedimentary basin, and shown that lake morphometry and extreme events such as flood discharges will affect the composition and number of pollen grains transported to the lake sediment. Clearly such empirical studies demonstrate the problems of interpreting the fossil pollen spectra in terms of vegetation in the drainage basin.

*The use of correction factors in pollen analysis*

Davis (1963) has suggested the use of 'R' values for correcting relative pollen frequencies. R is the ratio of a pollen taxon percentage to the percentage of the taxon in the vegetation, and is based on the contemporary relationship between pollen rain and vegetation composition. Davis was able to demonstrate that corrected pollen frequencies significantly deviated from relative pollen percentage frequencies and that deductions about vegetation and climate during the postglacial based on uncorrected data were suspect. Iversen (1947, in Andersen 1973) had suggested correction factors for pollen spectra from lakes and bogs that would permit a more accurate estimation of forest composition to be made. Iversen's values are similar to those proposed by Andersen (1970, 1973) for north European tree taxa based on empirical data from Denmark:

| | |
|---|---|
| *Quercus, Betula, Alnus, Pinus, Corylus, Taxus* | $1 \div 4$ |
| *Carpinus* | $1 \div 3$ |
| *Ulmus, Picea* | $1 \div 2$ |
| *Fagus, Abies, Populus* | $1 \times 1$ |
| *Tilia, Fraxinus, Acer* | $1 \times 2$ |

Andersen concludes that *Quercus* is likely to be over-represented in most pollen diagrams and that *Tilia* and *Fraxinus* are under-represented. The status of these taxa in postglacial forests will need revision in the light of the correction factors that have been proposed.

An example of applying correction factors to pollen spectra from Eldrup forest in Denmark is described by Andersen (1973). The pollen diagram (see Fig. 1.4) comes from a gyttja and peat-filled hollow in a forest of beech and oak. Figure 1.4A shows the preponderance of tree taxa over all other taxa during the period of biogenic sedimentation. Figure 1.4B shows the relative percentage frequencies of tree pollen, and Figure 1.4C the corrected tree pollen diagram. Inferences made from the corrected tree pollen diagrams on vegetation composition and structure differ fundamentally from inferences made from the uncorrected diagram. During stage II the uncorrected diagram indicates that oak (*Quercus*) dominated the forest, whereas the corrected diagram shows that oak was subordinate to lime (*Tilia*) in the forest. The fall of lime frequencies and the increase of oak are marked, but short-lived increase in birch (*Betula*) pollen frequencies in both the uncorrected and corrected diagrams indicates clearance by man and the destruction of the lime forest probably by fire, shown by the peak birch value. In stage IV, the uncorrected diagram suggests a forest with beech (*Fagus*) and oak as co-dominants, whereas the corrected diagram indicates that oak was subordinate to beech.

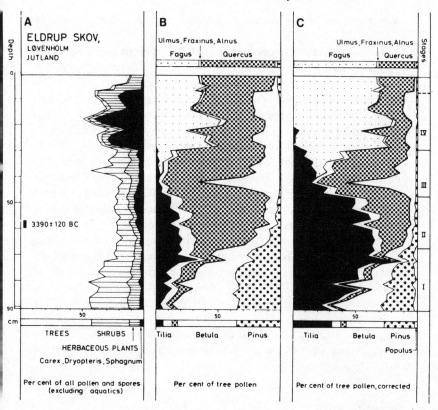

Figure 1.4. A pollen diagram from Eldrup Skov, Jutland, Denmark, showing A – The relative frequencies of the pollen of trees, shrubs, herbaceous plants and *Carex + Dryopteris + Sphagnum*. B – The uncorrected relative frequencies of tree taxa. C – The corrected relative frequencies of tree taxa. (Andersen 1973.)

Birks (1977), in a recent study, has demonstrated a good match between many corrected pollen percentages from pollen from surface samples at Ickenthwaite and the present-day forest composition within a 30 m. radius of the pollen sampling point. There are close matches between the predicted and observed values of *Pinus* (22.3% predicted value, cf. 22.3% observed value), *Quercus* (38.2% cf. 40.9%), *Corylus* (3.9% cf. 4.9%) and *Taxus* (1.2% cf. 1.8%). Of other tree taxa, *Betula* and *Fraxinus* are overestimated (6.3% cf. not present within 30 m. radius; 8.8% cf. 4.3%), and *Tilia* and *Fagus* are underestimated (not recorded in surface sample cf. 1.8%; 2.2% cf. 5.5%).

The correction factors are based on present-day vegetation patterns and pollen rain and it is assumed that contemporary analogues can be applied to fossil pollen assemblages and a more accurate index of forest conditions thereby derived. However, H.J.B. Birks (1973) has pointed out that R-values 'based on single points in space and time may not be applied with any great confidence to fossil spectra derived from different depositional situations'. Hence, R-values derived from present-day limnic sediments may be used to correct pollen curves from samples from limnic sediments, but care should be exercised in correcting curves from telmatic and terrestrial sediments. Furthermore, former plant communities and the pollen rain they generate may have no present-day analogues, particularly as climatic change, soil maturation and degradation and migrations of plants and animals from refugia during interglacial stages would permit a multiplicity of apparently unexpected permutations of association (West 1964, 1971). Watts (1973) has recorded from Gortian interglacial sediments in Ireland a forest assemblage comprising *Picea abies, Abies alba, Rhododendron ponticum, Ilex aquifolium* and *Taxus baccata*; at present, *Picea* is associated with severe winter climates whereas the rest are associated with an oceanic climate and mild winters.

*Soil pollen analysis*

In the context of many archaeological sites, suitable locations for pollen analysis, such as lakes or raised bogs, are not available, and it has been necessary to examine the pollen content of contemporary or fossil soils.

Fossil soils are often found beneath mounds, embankments, barrows, field banks and strip lynchets and in ditch fills. In a natural context they occur in sand dune systems where excavations reveal ephemeral palaeosols and are well-developed along the landward margin of sand dunes where sand has overblown the moss lands (see Tooley 1978a). Former saltmarsh soils buried by *Phragmites* peat have been identified in the tidal flat and lagoonal zones of low-lying coasts (Tooley 1978a).

One of the problems of soil pollen analysis is the interpretation of the pollen residue in the humus or mineral layers of the soil.

Dimbleby (1957) has shown that the composition of the pollen spectra depends on:

(i)    the leaching of pollen grains through the soil profile, so that grains of different ages become concentrated in one soil horizon, thereby 'blurring' the pollen record (J.G. Evans 1975)

(ii)   differential pollen preservation: soils with pH5 or less have good pollen preservation, whereas soils with pH6 or more are 'virtually useless for pollen analysis' (Dimbleby 1957, p.18)

(iii)  older, re-worked pollen from till may be incorporated into the pollen spectra as the till weathers and clay colloids are incorporated into the soil matrix

(iv)   in neutral or alkaline soils (mull) earthworms actively mix layers

Although Dimbleby (1957) concluded that there was no evidence of faunal mixing and that the pollen spectra showed broad features of past vegetational changes, Faegri and Iversen (1964) have stressed the complexity and difficulty of interpreting pollen diagrams from terrestrial soils, and Iversen (1969) has avoided the analysis of pollen from mull soils.

There is, however, one category of soils in which the problems enunciated do not apply: this is the mor soil. A mor is characteristically a fine-grained organic soil, with high acidities < pH6 and occasionally pH3.5 (e.g. Draved, Iversen 1969), a thin active layer, low biological activity, low decomposition rates and slow annual accumulation. Pollen preservation is excellent and leaching and mixing of particles are minimal. Iversen (1969) and Birks (1977) have demonstrated local vegetational successions initiated by man – the consequence of burning, clearance, ploughing and grazing from pollen analysis of mor soils.

Although it is no longer possible in pollen analysis to think in terms of a simple relationship between relative pollen frequency and vegetation composition, the technique may be used powerfully in correlation in small homogeneous regions such as drainage basins, particularly when a standard pollen diagram is available. Furthermore, the former composition of the vegetation and its changes may be approximated using absolute pollen frequencies and appropriate correction factors.

**Diatom analysis**

Analysis of the fossil diatom content of sediments gives an indication of water quality and depth during the period of sedimentation, and has been used to record the beginning and end of marine conditions in former lake basins in Sweden and Denmark (for example, Digerfeldt 1975; Iversen 1937) during the postglacial period and temperature changes of sea and lake water masses during the late-glacial period. Analyses have also been used to demonstrate changes in base status of freshwater lakes during the postglacial from eutrophic to oligotrophic conditions and the recent eutrophication caused by an influx of nutrients from farming activity and urban growth (for example, in the English Lake District, Round 1965, Pennington 1943, 1973b; Haworth 1969; in Lough Neagh, Battarbee 1973).

Diatoms are well-distributed and are found wherever there is sufficient light for photosynthesis and moisture. They are recorded in moist soils, on rocks and in lakes and the oceans within the photic zones. Fossil remains are found in *turfas, detritus* and *limus* deposits, and in the latter may characterise the deposit forming a heavy inelastic greyish-white deposit when moist, but chalky white and light when dry. It is known as diatomite, kieselguhr or *Limus siliceus organogenes*.

Diatoms are unicellular algae which may be free-floating (planktonic) attached (epiphytic) or bottom-living forms (benthonic). Some forms can live in the benthos and in the plankton and are known as tychoplankton. Others, such as *Melosira sulcata*, occur as a bottom-living form, as an epiphyte and in the plankton. The diatom cell is surrounded by a rigid, box-like structure of hydrated silica, which is resistent to destruction except by strong organic acids (Hendey 1964). The absence of diatoms from calcareous strata of Mesozoic age is attributed to solution in marine water with a high base status (Round 1965). Some clays and clay-gyttjas from tidal flat and lagoonal palaeoenvironments of Flandrian age are sometimes barren of diatoms, and these 'poverty phases' (Eronen 1974) are explained by the dissolution of the frustules. Battarbee (1973) has suggested that diatom dissolution contributes to the silica budget of Lough Neagh and may explain the difference between annual deposition on the lake floor and estimated production in the upper layers of the lake sediment.

The siliceous box or frustule enclosing the diatom cell is of a certain size, shape and patterning that permits identification, invariably to the species level. Hendey (1964) has summarised these characteristics that are the key to identification. The size of the frustule ranges from $4\mu$ to 1mm., though in British coastal waters size class limits of $40\text{-}200\mu$ are usual. The shape of the frustule varies. In general, circular or Centric and linear or Pennate diatoms can be recognised (Fig. 1.5) and the ratio Centrales: Pennales has been used to characterise freshwater quality and conditions of sedimentation (Miller 1964). Hendey (1964) has distinguished seven shape groups; linear, cuneate, cymbiform, carinoid, discoid, gonoid and solenoid. Each shape is reflected in the two halves that constitute the box or frustule. Each half comprises a valve, linked by a connective band or girdle. Dependent upon whether the top (valve) or side (girdle) of the frustule is larger, the diatom will sediment out with its large face uppermost; usually the valve face is seen. Running the length of each valve in pennate diatoms is a narrow split, interrupted in the central area by a thickening known as the central nodule and terminated at the poles by polar nodules: this split is called a raphe. Some diatoms possess pseudoraphes which are structureless spaces within the axial area.

As in pollen grain exines, the frustule is decorated by dots (Fig. 1.5D), reticulations (Fig. 1.5B) canals and ribs (Fig. 1.5F), the frequencies of which aid in identification. Hendey (1964) describes four ornaments. Puncta are dot-like markings, made up of small holes, irregularly scattered or in lines; areolae are reticulations which may be hexagonal, as in *Coscinodiscus* or linear as in *Pinnularia*; canaliculi are channels running through the cell wall and costae are ribs.

In shallow, inland seas, estuaries and the oceans, there are distinctive diatom assemblages, but because of occasional storm wave conditions or high river discharges, assemblages are often mixed. Ghazzawi (1933) has noted pelagic diatoms mixed with true littoral forms on the Isle of Man, and Hustedt and Aleem (1951) have recorded that diatoms on the mudflats near Plymouth are recruited from three sources: attached forms from rocky shores, pelagic forms, and freshwater forms from rivers and lakes.

Many diatoms are stenovalent and diatom assemblages permit of an assignment to a particular hydrographic regime. For example, Miller (1964) has identified five salinity groups: marine, euryhaline marine brackish, brackish, halophilous and freshwater. Marine diatoms (M) live in water with salinities of 30-40°/oo; Euryhaline

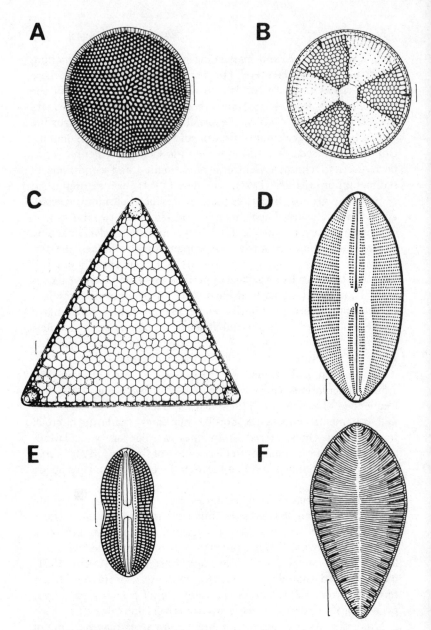

Figure 1.5. Drawings of centric and pennate diatoms from van der Werff and Huls (1958-1974). A – *Coscinodiscus excentricus* Ehrenberg. B – *Actinoptychus undulatus* (Bailey) Ralfs. C – *Triceratum favus* Ehrenberg. D – *Navicula lyra* Ehrenberg. E – *Diploneis didyma* Ehrenberg. F – *Surirella ovalis* De Brebisson. The scale in each case represents $10\mu$

marine brackish diatoms (MB) occur where salinities of 5-40°/oo are recorded and are able to tolerate wide salinity variations; Brackish diatoms (B) occur where salinities are 5-20°/oo; Halophilous diatoms (BF) occur in upper brackish water stages where salinities less than 5°/oo are recorded; Freshwater diatoms (F) are either indifferent to the chloride ion content of water or halophobus, and occur where salinities are less than 2°/oo. Van der Werff and Huls (1958-74) have identified seven groups according to the chloride ion concentration of the water; marine (M) > 17,000 mg. $Cl^-/1$: marine-brackish 10,000-17,000 $Cl^-/1$: brackish-marine (BM) 5,000-10,000 $Cl^-/1$: brackish (B) 1,000-5,000 $Cl^-/1$: brackish-fresh (BF) 500-1,000 $Cl^-/1$: fresh-brackish (FB) 100-500 $Cl^-/1$ and fresh (F) < 100 $Cl^-/1$. By grouping the diatoms identified in a layer into these classes a measure is obtained of the changes in water quality and the direction of change in a freshening or progressively saline succession. The application of this technique is invaluable in identifying the isolation contacts of marine transgression sequences and the varying marine influence during a transgression episode.

Fossil diatoms may be isolated from unconsolidated sediments using a standard preparation technique such as the one described by West (1968).

Once mounted, both unsieved and sieved fractions should be scanned at a magnification of about x800 and 'a careful qualitative analysis of the sample (made) to become acquainted with the forms occurring before beginning quantitative analysis' (Hustedt 1958, quoted in Miller 1964). Diatom identification should proceed using one of the standard keys (for example, Hendey 1964) and the floras (for example, Cleve-Euler 1951-3; Hendey 1964; Hustedt 1927-62; Van der Werff and Huls 1958-74).

The enumeration and presentation of diatom numbers counted follows many different forms and may be quantitative or qualitative.

In quantitative analyses, a decision must be made at the beginning to standardise the enumerations: in fossil sediments, diatom cells are rarely entire and may be fragmentary with only the central module area or apices present. Furthermore, the cell often separates into the two valves. Whole valves should be counted and divided by two to obtain numbers of individuals, whereas fragments, if they can be identified, should be accumulated as thirds or halves into whole valves. Alternatively, numbers of valves (half diatoms) can be counted and used as the basis for calculation (Miller 1964) and fragments can be expressed as percentages of whole valves

(Eronen 1974). The usual number of valves counted is 200, but Miller (1964) has demonstrated that as many as 2,000 valves need to be counted before the curve plotting number of taxa against number of valves counted levels out. Additional taxa recorded between 200 and 2,000 valves counted are often critical as indicators of climatic change. Diatom numbers can be expressed as percentages of the total number of valves or cells counted, or in frequency classes, or they can be grouped into ecological classes and shown as a summary diagram according to the salinity groupings. As with pollen percentages, so diatom percentages are interdependent, and in interpretations, large changes in frequency should not be unduly stressed but cognisance given to overall changes in the floral assemblage and the general succession (Eronen 1974).

Van der Werff and Huls (1958-74) have overcome this problem by recording numbers of species in a sample rather than numbers of valves of each species. The species composition of a sample is determined and all species that belong to the same chloride ion class are added together; this sum is then expressed as a percentage of the total number of species of that sample and a Marine-Brackish-Fresh (M-B-F) ratio diagram constructed (Du Saar 1978).

Interpretation of changing fossil diatom frequencies in limnic or estuarine sediments in terms of the living diatom assemblages that generated them is open to similar difficulties, encountered in relating pollen frequencies to former plant communities. Diatoms found in the surface sediment of the lake will be recruited not only from the plankton in the lake, but also from different habitats within the lake basin. However Haworth (1976) has suggested that in some cases the diatom composition of the living lake ecosystem is reflected in the relic diatom assemblage in the surface sediments.

Diatom analysis is a useful analytical tool to resolve changes in water quality in lakes and in tidal flat and lagoonal palaeoenvironments. Precise data may be obtained on the beginning and end of marine transgression episodes and on the changing base status of lakes, consequent upon vegetation change and soil maturation and prehistoric and historic farming activity in the drainage basins.

## Macrofossils

During site investigations, both plant and animal macrofossils are encountered and provide not only a record of the flora and fauna of the area, supplementing and refining the microfossil evidence, but also an index of changing environmental conditions.

*Plant macrofossils*

The occurrence of plant macrofossils in distinctive, repetitive layers in bogs was used at the end of the nineteenth century to explain the immigration of forest trees to northern Europe, the forest history and inferred climatic changes. The Blytt-Sernander climatic periods – Boreal (dry), Atlantic (humid), Sub-Boreal (dry and warm) and Sub-Atlantic (humid and cool) – derive from this interpretation (von Post 1916, Iversen 1973). Von Post argued that the most important information derived from plant macrofossils was the composition and structure of the local vegetation producing the macrofossils. But, in fact, the relationship between these two factors is complex and depends on the sedimentary site and its catchment. Plant macrofossils are encountered in sediments of lakes and bogs as well as in river estuarine sediments, sediments of shallow inland seas and sediments of continental shelf seas. The interpretation of macrofossil assemblages will vary with the size, nature and complexity of the catchment. Reid (1899) regarded peat mosses and lake deposits as unsatisfactory because of the lack of taxonomic variation: he preferred river alluvium particularly if the drainage basin contained a variety of habitats. The problem with such sites is the very real possibility of the incorporation of older material into contemporary sediments, making floral lists suspect and vegetation reconstructions difficult.

The problem of the relationship of a macrofossil assemblage to a specific plant community is similar to the problem in pollen analysis. Few empirical data are available that link contemporary assemblages in different sedimentary environments with the vegetation generating the plant remains. Where such data are available, H.H. Birks (1973) has demonstrated that environmental conditions can be reconstructed and interpretations based on pollen analytical evidence can be reappraised.

Plant macrofossils may be extracted from standard volumes of sediment in a wide-diameter core at successive levels or from free face excavations. The macrofossils can be extracted using standard procedures (Godwin 1956, Dickson 1970, West 1968) and comprise flowers, fruits, seeds, leaves, rhizomes, bud scales, wood, sporangia and megaspores. Many macrofossils are difficult to record quantitatively and, for example, leaves, flowers, wood fragments and charcoal may have to be recorded as present or on a qualitative scale (Walker 1966). Seed and fruit diagrams can be constructed and compared on a quantitative basis because the diaspores are of equal weighting. The diagram can show frequency histograms for each taxon, or the fruit and seed taxa may be grouped into habitat categories, such as dry land, aquatic and telmatic (Troels-Smith 1960b) to give an indication of changing water relations. Particular seed or fruit frequencies can be related to frequency changes in pollen diagrams allowing the resolution of a pollen taxon at the family level to its probable generic or species level. Huckerby and Oldfield (1976) suggest that low frequencies of Cupressaceae pollen at Bidart Plage, south-west France, may have been contributed by *Chamaecyparis* cf. *thyoides* for seed and leaf records coincide with pollen records. At Marbella, pollen frequency histograms at the generic level can be attributed to species on the basis of the macro-fossils present: for example, *Abies* pollen and *Abies alba* leaves, *Alnus* pollen and *Alnus glutinosa* fruit and *Vitis* pollen and *Vitis vinifera* fruit stones are recorded at comparable levels in the stratigraphy. Such concurrence of evidence strengthens the evidence of ecological site development in a way that was not possible when lists of plant microfossils were reported. By contrast, for example, Travis' (1926) list from the peat beds in the intertidal zone at Hightown cannot be related to the pollen diagrams from this site (Erdtman 1928, Tooley 1970) because no record of stratigraphic provenance is given for macrofossils.

Godwin (1956) notes that the record of a macrofossil establishes the presence of a taxon at a particular locality, whereas the record of pollen is equivocal: the presence of a pollen taxon may not be the consequence of long-distance transport. The presence of pollen grains with air sacs, such as *Pinus*, is often regarded as a result of long distance transport, particularly in sediments of Late Devensian age. Pennington (1970) has suggested (on the basis that no macroscopic remains of *Pinus* have been recovered from Late Devensian sites in north-west England) that the pine pollen frequencies of up to 20% may result from long distance transport. The opposite situation obtains for *Populus*: a catkin scale has been recovered from Windermere but no pollen has so far been recorded, yet at Rossall Beach (Tooley 1977) and at Red Moss in Lancashire (Hibbert *et al.* 1971) *Populus* pollen is recorded.

Watts (1973) succinctly summarises the role and status of plant macrofossil analysis and interpretation in environmental reconstruction:

> Macrofossils provide valuable subsidiary information to pollen diagrams. They permit accurate assessment of first local occurrence of invading species. They also allow a large range of species determinations to be made which are not possible with pollen. This permits more accurate and detailed statements to be made about species assemblages in the past than is possible by pollen analysis alone. However, macrofossils are much less suitable for statistical treatment than pollen influx data. In population studies, macrofossil analysis can only play a subsidiary role to pollen analysis.

*Animal macrofossils*

Animal macrofossils include bones, hair, nails, skin, coprolites from vertebrates, and shells, elytra, *inter alia* from invertebrates. Occurrences are sporadic, but are occasionally so rich in numbers and taxonomy that strong conclusions may be drawn about the fauna of a region, its climate and local vegetation, and, if the remains come from a butchering or midden site, the economy of prehistoric man. In the same way that the relative frequency of plant macrofossils recorded at prehistoric sites cannot be used to indicate the composition of forest communities because of bias for certain timbers (Godwin 1956), so bones from human food remains have a built-in cultural bias that hinders any climatic or environmental inferences being made (Ziegler 1973).

Ziegler (1973) has suggested that natural burial sites and the contents of owl pellets and carnivore droppings provide evidence for more reliable climatic reconstructions, and that fossil remains of extant animal species are preferable for study because present-day ecological requirements and ranges are known. Wallace (1876) used the same argument in justifying mammals as the basis for the recognition and extent of the zoogeographic realms of the globe ('the standard zoological regions'). Ziegler (1973) suggests that small mammals, amphibians, some reptiles, and freshwater fish are most sensitive indicators of local climatic conditions, and would serve, therefore, as useful indices of change.

Even natural burial sites contain ecological biases. The natural bestiaries are caves, freshwater river deposits and estuaries and lake sediments. Most cave deposits contain prey remains of carnivores.

Some caves, such as Joint Mitnor in south Devon (Sutcliffe 1960) were animal traps, containing probably a random representation of the fauna and an over-representation of carnivores and scavengers. Freshwater river and estuarine deposits contain mixed assemblages: fish and amphibians are well-represented together with fortuitous remains of terrestrial animals that drowned somewhere in the drainage basin. Because of the cycle of erosion and deposition in a drainage basin, closely related to secular variations in discharge and in sea-level, older alluvial deposits containing bone assemblages may have been eroded and incorporated with younger assemblages. In lake sediments, fish and amphibian remains are over-represented and sometimes contain vertebrate remains out of context. For example, at High Furlong, an elk (*Alces alces*) had foundered in a water-logged depression having been injured by an epipalaeolithic barbed point at some stage during the Allerød chronozone (Hallam *et al.* 1973), and in the intertidal zone of Hartlepool Bay, a human skeleton of Early Flandrian chronozone III age was recovered from a shallow burial in a lake mud (Tooley 1978b; Tooley, Mellars and Brothwell, in preparation).

Where well-stratified animal macrofossils occur in biogenic deposits, consistent environmental reconstructions may be possible. During the last interglacial, the Ipswichian, Stuart (1976) has indicated that many of the animal assemblages are associated with particular and characteristic vegetation types. Hence the mixed oak forest supported fallow deer, badger and bank vole, whereas the late temperate zone with more open woodland, probably dominated by hornbeam, witnessed a marked change in mammalian fauna with mammoth and horse the characteristic taxa.

A record of animal macrofossils provides not only an indication of the fauna and faunal changes but also a measure of the diversity of ecological systems. For the Quaternary of the British Isles, Stuart (1974) has shown how the fauna has changed and become progressively impoverished as one glaciation after another and the intervening interglacial high sea-level stands have eliminated one taxon after another or prevented re-immigration.

In addition to mammalian skeletal remains, two groups that have been well-worked are beetles and land snails, of which the latter particularly have provided evidence of environmental changes in archaeological associations.

Of the sub-fossil remains of insects, the beetles and weevils (Coleoptera) have been systematically analysed and the results interpreted in terms of environmental changes during the Quaternary, particularly the Devensian Stage.

There are many advantages in studying fossil Coleoptera (see Sparks and West 1972). Coleoptera are fairly common and are found in most terrestrial and freshwater habitats, including coastal ecosystems such as sand dunes and salt marshes. Although the beetle fauna of Britain is impoverished compared with the rest of Europe, there are about 3700 species (Coope 1977) and these occur widely; those species that have narrow ecological amplitudes (stenovalent species) are of particular value in palaeoenvironmental reconstructions. Some beetles are phytophages and live exclusively off particular plants: *Rhynchaenus quercus* feeds exclusively on oak (Shotton and Osborne 1965). Other beetles are carnivores and prey on each other, small vertebrates or fish: *Hydrophilus piceus* preys on aquatic insects and fish spawn (Hofmann 1908). Others feed on fungi, rotting plants, soil arthropods and colembola (Coope 1977).

In fossil sediments, beetles occur in terrestrial, telmatic and limnic deposits but extraction from silts and gyttjas is easier than from fibrous peats.

Coope (1977) has stated that speciation of beetles occurred during the Upper Tertiary, since which time there is little evidence of evolution. This morphological stability means that deductions about past environments can be made with some confidence because of the present-day coupling of distributions and environments. However, a disadvantage arises because lack of evolution means that as a group Coleoptera cannot be used for zoning in the Quaternary (Sparks and West 1972). Indeed Coope (1977) has noted that the list of species from the Nechells interglacial deposits and the Austerfield interglacial deposits are similar, yet on palynological grounds the former is referred to the Hoxnian and the latter to the Ipswichian interglacial.

Deductions about former environments using present-day distributions of colepteran species may not be valid. Even though it might be possible to demonstrate a high degree of fidelity in species association, Sparks and West (1972) have suggested that the present day restricted distributions of some species may be the consequence of man's activities, and Buckland and Kenward (1973) have indicated that beetle assemblages from Thorne Moor, Yorkshire, can be interpreted either as an indication of climate change or as a response to forest clearance.

Coope (1977) has maintained that the most significant

contribution that beetle analyses have made is in climatic interpretation. In interglacial stages the interpretation from the beetle assemblages concurs with that from the pollen assemblages. Coope concludes that the climatic optima of the Cromerian and Ipswichian interglacials were warmer than the Flandrian interglacial, whereas the Hoxnian was no warmer than today. The greatest discrepancy has arisen between the interpretation of beetle and pollen assemblages during the interstadials of the Devensian glaciation. During the Windermere interstadial, the beetle assemblages indicated a thermal maximum about 12,500 bp, well before the development of birch woodland inferred from the pollen record during the Allerød. However, the re-interpretation of the pollen analytical evidence from Blelham Bog in the Lake District (Pennington 1975a), indicating the maximum development of birch woodland during the Bölling interstadial, has made these two data sets more compatible.

In palaeoenvironmental reconstructions, mollusca share with beetles the advantage of occurrence in a great variety of deposits. Molluscan remains have been reported from terrestrial, telmatic and limnic sites, both in the marine and freshwater biocycle. Although finds are more widespread than for plant micro- and macro-fossils, they are unusual in non-calcareous sediments from which the exoskeletons, formed predominantly of calcium carbonate, are leached.

Mollusca often occur in large numbers and if preservation is good they can be identified to the species level. From the change in composition of the molluscan assemblage from level to level through a section, environmental changes can be inferred at the site. Molluscan assemblages are useful in establishing local site conditions, particularly if the assemblage includes stenovalent species. For example, *Pomatias elegans* (Miller) inhabits dry, friable, calcareous soils (Sparks and West 1972): its distribution is markedly southern, and in Britain and Europe its range has contracted since Flandrian II (Kerney 1968). This contraction may testify to a decline in temperature, but both Kerney (1968) and Sparks and West (1972) have warned against the use of mollusca as climatic indicators. Both mollusca and beetles are influenced by the microclimate of the local site rather than by macroclimatic variations registered in marine sediments and ice cores. Hence the local vegetation, slope, aspect and biotic factors will influence the molluscan distribution, and changes in the species composition of the assemblage may reflect ecological change rather than climatic change.

To aid the interpretation of local site assemblages, Sparks (1961) has identified ecological groupings of freshwater and land mollusca. He recognises four groupings of freshwater mollusca:

1. A 'slum' group comprising individuals that can tolerate or prefer poor water conditions, such as fluctuating water table or seasonally wet pools.
2. A catholic group comprising individuals that are euryvalent and can tolerate a wide range of wet habitats except the 'worse slums'.
3. A ditch group comprising individuals with a preference for clear slowly-moving water with rich, eutrophic aquatic plant communities.
4. A moving water group comprising individuals found in water bodies, streams and pools.

For land mollusca, Sparks (1961) identifies a marsh group, a dry land group, a woodland group and *Vallonia* spp. which may be used to indicate open conditions lacking woodland.

Mollusca can be used to indicate changes in water quality and water depth. Sparks (1961) has shown the change to brackish water conditions in Ipswichian interglacial sediments at Selsey, Sussex: here there is a considerable increase in the frequency of *Hydrobia ventrosa* and an increase in the frequency of the more salt-tolerant *H. ulvae* at the top of the diagram. Taken with the presence of a bivalve mollusc *Scrobicularia plana* (da Costa) inferences can be made about the location of the assemblage in the intertidal zone if it can be shown that the molluscs are in their living positions and have not been washed into the sedimentation site. In Morecambe Bay, Anderson (1972) has shown that *Hydrobia ulvae* is associated with fine-grained sediments and occurs at altitudes from +1.8 to +2.7 m. O.D. that is from the lower shore levels to just above Mean High Water of Neap Tides. Whether the data from Selsey can be interpreted in terms of position within the intertidal zone of the Ipswichian sea will depend on the provenance of the samples and their stratigraphic relationships. A salutary example can be given from north-west England. In Morecambe Bay, Anderson (1972) has reported that the maximum densities of *Macoma balthica* (Linné)

occur on a fine sand to silty substrate at altitudes of +1.82 to
+2.74 m. O.D. At the Altmouth, in south-west Lancashire, sub-
fossil remains of *M. balthica* occur at altitudes of +2.01 to +2.21 m.
O.D. mixed with *Cerastoderma edule* (Linné), *Barnea candida* (Linné)
and *Chlamys opercularis* (Linné). This assemblage is older than
4,545± 90bp (Hv-2679) which is the date on *Phragmites* peat above
the shell layer at +3.14 m. O.D. (Tooley 1970). From a superficial
comparison the conclusion would be that there has been little or no
change in altitude of the sea-level surface during Flandrian III.
However, the shell assemblage at the Altmouth includes the roots
and rhizomes of *Zostera* sp. and is set in a matrix of medium to coarse
sand. The shells, which are fragile, corroded and do not occur in
pairs, have been washed into the sedimentary site. The conclusion
follows that the assemblage is not *in situ* and probably represents a
fossil spring tide level. A comparison with the contemporary
MHWST level at Heysham of +4.57 m. O.D. shows that the relative
altitude of the sea-level surface has changed by at least 2 m. since the
latter part of Flandrian II. This interpretation supports Kerney's
conclusion that 'the basis of any analysis must depend on an understanding of stratigraphy and precise sampling.'

In an archaeological context, Evans (1972) has demonstrated how
land snails can be employed to elucidate local site conditions. At
Avebury (see Fig. 4.3), there is a buried soil beneath a henge dated
to about 2,000 bc. At the base of the section open woodland of
Flandrian I age is inferred. This was succeeded by dense forest of
Flandrian II age: open habitat taxa such as *Vallonia costata* are
reduced to 6% of the total. A period of forest clearance is inferred
from the increase in open habitat taxa such as *Vallonia* spp. and
*Pomatias elegans* which is found in shaded places, but where the
ground has been broken up. Finally, at the level of the buried turf
line, the molluscan assemblages indicate disforestation and no
successive forest regeneration: it is possible that initial arable
farming was replaced by grazing by sheep and cattle.

A strength of the analysis of molluscan assemblages lies in the
detail with which the local site conditions can be reconstructed.
Molluscs cannot be used with any confidence in establishing the
magnitude of climatic change, and they share with beetle
assemblages the unreliability of use as age indicators during the
Quaternary. This arises from the fact that molluscs show slow
evolution and in Britain 41 of the 57 indigenous Flandrian species
are known from pre-Anglian glaciation contexts (Kerney 1977).

## Dating

In palaeoenvironmental reconstructions a chronological framework is an essential requirement. The chronology may be relative or absolute. Relative chronologies place environmental changes and events in relation to one another without any indication of the duration of the change or event: all that may be deduced is that an event preceded or succeeded another event. Relative chronologies may be built up either by using marker horizons in stratigraphic series such as marine transgression facies, recurrence surfaces in raised and blanket bogs and ashfalls, or by using changes in the floral and faunal composition of sediments and magnetic intensity and declination measurements. Absolute chronologies may be established because some processes follow annual rhythmical patterns such as the addition, season by season, of wood with different cell structures to trees and shrubs (dendrochronology), whereas other processes involve geochemical changes that permit an age calculation to be made based on the known decay rate of the particular radioactive isotope (such as radiocarbon dating).

There are inherent uncertainties in all dating methods and each age estimate based on a relative or absolute chronology will lie within an envelope of uncertainty. Hence a local pollen assemblage zone may be referred to a regional pollen assemblage zone and a chronozone at a stage type site, but the nearest age estimate that can be made for the local pollen assemblage zone may be within a two thousand year envelope. Similarly, an illusion of time accuracy is bestowed upon radiocarbon dated samples all of which carry a standard error based on the statistical count of the residual radio-activity of the sample: hence a date of 5,250 ± 385 indicates that there is a 68% chance that the actual age of the material lies between the limits of 5,635 and 4,865 radiocarbon years age. There is also a chance that the actual age lies outside these limits.

To overcome the uncertainties and ambiguities of relative and absolute age datings in palaeoenvironmental reconstructions, it is necessary to use more than a single dating technique to ensure accuracy and test the validity of the date. It is unsafe to use a single radiocarbon date by itself without placing it in a chronological framework or without reference to stratigraphy or some other relative chronological framework. Michels (1973) has summarised such an approach:

A tightly knit stratigraphic sequence for which we have a sample from each level is not likely to be represented by a series of mean radiocarbon values that seriate perfectly. There will be a general trend from older to younger, which corresponds roughly to the stratigraphy, lower to upper, but the correspondence will very likely exhibit disturbing exceptions. By plotting the calculated standard deviation the overlap of the ranges of time for dating the samples from successive strata is likely to produce a more plausible time sequence with every date in the series fitting the stratigraphy.

Occasionally, this approach is not successful (for example Downholland Moss, West Lancashire, Tooley 1978a, 1978c), and dates have to be rejected, and explanations sought for inconsistent series of dates.

Three dating methods are described here: changes in the pollen flora of sediments, marine transgression surfaces and radiocarbon dating. Reviews of other dating methods are given in Brothwell and Higgs (1969), West (1977), Michael and Ralph (1971) and Michels (1973).

*Relative dating using pollen assemblages*

One of the early and continuing functions of pollen analysis, as described earlier (pp. 16, 17-20), is correlation. A unit of stratigraphy may be subdivided on the basis of changes in lithology or in pollen content. Changes in the frequency of pollen taxa, associations of pollen taxa and the pre-eminence of a pollen taxon permit the identification of pollen assemblage zones and zone boundaries. Assuming regional parallelism of vegetation development, pollen assemblage zones within that region may be assigned to the same relative time period and a relative chronology established. In this way a sequence of pollen assemblage zones may be recognised and different interglacial stages identified from the position in the succession or the presence of diagnostic pollen taxa.

Jessen and Milthers (1928) defined a series of climatic and vegetational changes that allowed interglacial stages to be recognised. The series comprises Arctic, Sub-Arctic, Boreal, Temperate, Boreal, Sub-Arctic and Arctic conditions. Iversen (1958) developed a model of climatic changes during an interglacial stage and the dynamic vegetational changes and soil cycles associated with them. The progressive and retrogressive development of ecosystems during interglacials is a persuasive model, substantiated by palaeoecological data. West (1970a) has elaborated and resolved the temperate stage of an interglacial into four zones with characteristic pollen assemblages:

Zone I.  Pre-temperate zone characterised by boreal trees such as *Betula* and *Pinus* and significant frequencies of heliophytes.

Zone II.  Early temperate zone characterised by mixed oak forest comprising *Quercus, Ulmus, Fraxinus* and *Corylus*.

Zone III.  Late temperate zone characterised by an expansion of forest trees such as *Carpinus, Abies* and *Picea* at the expense of mixed oak forest taxa.

Zone IV.  Post-temperate zone characterised by a reappearance and dominance of boreal elements such as *Betula, Pinus* and *Picea*. As the forest canopy opens, so dwarf shrubs, such as *Empetrum* and *Calluna*, make an appearance.

This framework permits reference not only to an interglacial stage but also to a period within the interglacial. Hence, the present interglacial, the Flandrian, is diagnosed by high *Corylus* frequencies in Zone I; the Ipswichian by high *Corylus* frequencies in Zone II and *Carpinus* in Zone III; the Hoxnian by high *Tilia* frequencies in Zone II, and *Abies, Picea, Carpinus* and *Pterocarya* in Zone III (West 1970a).

Valid correlation requires that over wide areas the effects of a transient climate, as recorded during the Quaternary era, are reflected in changing vegetation patterns. If this is the case, local pollen assemblage zones may be correlated with regional pollen assemblage zones and chronozones at the stage type site with some confidence. In the British Isles, where there are at present, as in the past, marked regional variations in vegetation, correlation with sites in different parts of the country is unsafe. Godwin (1940a) demonstrated a regional parallelism of vegetational development, pointed to the 'ancient and permanent character of this regional vegetational differentiation' and suggested that two or three regions in England and Wales could be distinguished and a separate scheme of forest history in each developed. Within these regions, correlations would be strong. Birks *et al.* (1975) concur in their conclusion and demonstrate that about 5,000 years ago the British Isles could be divided into three regions and two sub-regions: northern and eastern Scotland and western Ireland can be identified on the easis of abundant pine and birch; central and eastern Ireland, elm and hazel: England and Wales, alder and hazel. North and west

England recorded more oak and the south and east more lime. While, in general, the pollen maps for 5,000 bp. provide a visual summary for the pattern of forest vegetation and regional variations, additional pollen data will permit revision of the isolines. For example, *Quercus* values about 5,000 years ago on the Lancashire coast exceeded 32%, and rose locally to 57%, whereas this area is shown to have values less than 31%. Pine values locally exceed 15% in west Lancashire, whereas the isopollen map shows values less than 10%: these higher values are undoubtedly edaphically controlled and are associated with the distribution of a coversand, the Shirdley Hill Sands, in this area (see Tooley 1978a). However, awareness of local variation does not prohibit correlation which proceeds from the zonation of local pollen diagrams and the correlation of local and regional pollen assemblage zones.

*Relative dating using marine transgressions*

Correlation can also proceed from the recognition of marker horizons in stratigraphic series and a relative chronology established. Ash falls are important marker horizons in areas such as Iceland, New Zealand, Patagonia and north-west USA. There is some evidence for their occurrence synchronously and for sea-level minima to be associated with periods of volcanic activity (Schofield 1970). Marine transgression facies are recorded in appropriate sedimentary situations throughout the world, and there is stronger evidence for their synchronisation. In low-lying coastal areas in north-west Europe, lagoonal and tidal flat palaeoenvironments can be identified from the alternating layers of minerogenic and biogenic sediments. Landwards, the minerogenic layers of marine or brackish water origin feather into the organic sediments of the perimarine zone. The minerogenic layers were laid down during periods of marine transgression when sea-level was relatively higher. In north-west England, ten marine transgressions have been identified (Tooley 1974, 1976, 1978a, Huddart *et al.* 1977) and have the age limits shown in Table 1.2.

Marine transgressions with similar age limits have been proved elsewhere in north-west Europe (Sweden: Mörner 1969, Berglund 1971; Netherlands: Hageman 1969, Oele 1977; France: Ters 1973), and the results summarised in Figure 3.2 (Tooley 1974, 1976, 1978a). Morrison (1976) has analysed 500 radiocarbon dates from western Europe and identified sixteen marine episodes during the

**Table 1.2. Flandrian marine transgressions in north-west England (Tooley 1978a).**

| Lytham X | 830 − 805 years bp |
|---|---|
| Lytham IX | 1800 − 1370 .. .. |
| Lytham VIII | 3090 − 2270 .. .. |
| Lytham VII | 3700 − 3150 .. .. |
| Lytham VIa | 4800 − 4545 .. .. |
| Lytham VI | 5570 − 4897 .. .. |
| Lytham V | 5947 − 5775 .. .. |
| Lytham IV | 6710 − 6157 .. .. |
| Lytham III | 7605 − 7200 .. .. |
| Lytham II | 8390 − 7800 .. .. |
| Lytham I | 9270 − 8575 .. .. |

Flandrian Stage (*c.* last 10,000 years), comprising in most cases, a transgression and a regression stage. Of these episodes, the following correlations can be made with the marine transgressions from north-west England: Lytham I and Morrison's episode *b*; Lytham II and episode *c*; Lytham III and episode *d*; Lytham IV and episode *e*; Lytham V and episode *f*; Lytham VI and episode *g*; Lytham VIa and episode *h*; Lytham VII and episodes *j* and *k*; Lytham VIII and episodes *l* and *m*; Lytham IX and episode *o*.

Marine transgressions and the high sea-levels associated with them appear to be closely correlated with other global events, such as high latitude ice budgets, ocean water temperatures and climate. Fairbridge and Hillaire-Marcel (1977) have demonstrated a close relationship between these events and thereby demonstrate that marine transgressions associated with periods of high sea-level serve as important marker horizons in coastal areas.

Within areas of limited geographical extent, correlation of marine transgression marker horizons may proceed on the basis of altitude. Outside these areas, the horizons may now be recorded at higher or lower altitudes and reflect uplift or subsidence post-dating the horizon formation. However, the marine transgression facies or elevated shoreline may be followed and their limits mapped, and from this a relative age may be placed on a coastal prehistoric settlement site or the arrival of plant taxa in the course of immigration. Von Post (1916) demonstrated the arrival of thermophilous tree taxa in southern Sweden before the Littorina maximum, and Troels-Smith (1937, 1966) the relationship of Ertebølle settlement sites to Littorina transgression maxima. In the British Isles, Mesolithic coastal sites are closely associated with beaches, elevated in Scotland, close to sea-level in Cumbria, but well below sea-level and buried by Flandrian lagoonal and tidal flat sediments in Lancashire and elsewhere in southern England.

*Radiocarbon dating*

The most commonly used method to establish the 'absolute' age of a deposit during the prehistoric period has been radiocarbon dating. Radioactive carbon, present in the atmosphere as a gas and dissolved in the water in the ocean basins, is assimilated by organisms in the three biocycles – terrestrial, fresh and salt-water – to the extent that they are in equilibrium with the ambient radioactivity. At the moment of death assimilation ends, and disintegration of the radioactive isotope begins at a known rate. The half-life of the radioactive carbon isotope is given as 5,730 which indicates that in this unit time the organic material has lost half its specific C-14 radio-activity: in the succeeding 5,730 years, half of the remaining radioactivity is lost and so on. In the process of disintegration, carbon-14 returns to nitrogen-14 emitting a $\beta$-particle in the process. The number of $\beta$-emanations from modern carbon is about 15 counts/minute/gram, whereas carbon-14 which is 5,730 years old (the half-life) should emit about 7.5 counts/minute/gram (Michels 1973). The period of decay is finite, but there are physical limitations to the measurement of the residual radioactivity as the age of the sample increases. The initial carbon-14 content of organic material is very small (in living wood the ratio of C-12: C-13: C-14 is 98.5:1.5:1.07 x $10^{-10}$ (West 1968) and a sample 38,000 years old has a carbon-14 content only 1% of its original amount (Shotton 1967b). With a gas proportional counter, the limit to dating is 7 half-lives or 30,000-40,000 years; with liquid scintillation, in which the radioactive carbon is introduced as a liquid, such as benzene, the limit is 11 half-lives or about 60,000 years. The range of radiocarbon dating can be extended to 75,000 years using thermal diffusion isotopic enrichment of C-14 (Grootes 1978). In general, the older the sample is, the lower the $\beta$-emanations in unit time and the longer the counting time necessary. As the counting time increases, so there is an increase in the possibility of random decay, and the standard error on the mean date value is thereby increased. In younger samples, this also applies if the carbon content is low and counting time is increased.

Although the half-life of the radioactive carbon isotope has been determined to 5,730 ± 40 (Godwin 1962b), radiocarbon dating laboratories use Libby's original half-life of 5,568 years in reporting dates in *Radiocarbon*. A factor of 1.029 is necessary to convert all radiocarbon dates using the new half-life.

A more serious error in the radiocarbon timescale lies in the fact that radiocarbon years diverge from calendar years, and short-term oscillations (Suess' wriggles) can result in date ambiguities of up to 200 years. The discrepancy between radiocarbon years and calendar years has been demonstrated by dating wood samples for which an absolute age in calendar years has been established dendrochronologically (see, for example, Ralph and Michael 1970; Damon *et al.* 1970; Suess 1970). The calibration of the radiocarbon timescale indicates that during the last two thousand years the departure of radiocarbon years from calendar years was slight, whereas in the sixth millennium before present (present = 1950) the departure is as high as 869 years (from Table 1, Ralph and Michael 1970). In other words, radiocarbon dates are younger by about 14% of the true dates at this time. Radiocarbon dates can be corrected using the dendrochronologic calibration table of Damon *et al.* (1973) for the last eight millennia. However, if a radiocarbon-dated series of samples straddles the period from the eighth to the ninth millennium, then little can be served, at present, by recalibrating part of the series.

There are significant differences between the different series of tree-ring corrected radiocarbon time scales, and this has resulted in a lack of confidence in correcting from radiocarbon years to calendar years. Pearson *et al.* (1977) have demonstrated that there are additional factors contributing to the inaccuracy of radiocarbon measurements in the dating laboratory, such as the barometric pressure variation, and background variations with weight loss of the sample and purity. If these errors are overcome, the standard deviation of the count can be reduced to 25 years. Furthermore, Pearson *et al.* (1977) have indicated that their dendrochronological calibration, corrected for the additional laboratory errors, is smooth and not significantly different from a straight line. Calibration curves with marked deviations (Suess' wriggles) are not supported. The implications of the work of Pearson *et al.* is that it should be possible to produce not only an unambiguous, calibrated C-14 date, but also a date with a standard error whose 95% confidence limits yielded a range of 80 years.

West (1968) has ranked materials for radiocarbon assay in their preferred order for dating and Michels (1973) has listed sample sizes necessary for dating:

1. Charcoal 8-12 gm. dry weight.
2. Wood 10-30 gm.
3. Peat 10-25 gm.
4. Bone, 200-500 gm.
5. Shell, carbonate fraction 30-100 gm., conchiolin fraction 500-2,500 gm.

All these materials are subject to sources of error which have been reviewed by West (1968), Shotton (1967b, 1972) and Michels (1973). Contamination of a sample by old carbon can give an older date than the 'true' age and contamination by young carbon can give a younger age. The incorporation of older carbon will have the effect of ageing the sample from 400 years (5% contamination) to 1,800 years (20% contamination). The presence of modern rootlets will have the effect of reducing the age of the sample from 60 years (1% contamination) to 160 years (5% contamination) (Geyh 1969; Benzler and Geyh 1969). Streif (1972) has shown by examining and dating two fractions from the organic layers in the tidal flat and lagoonal zone of the Woltzeten area, Germany, that the root and rhizome fraction gave substantially younger dates than dates on the matrix in which the roots and rhizomes were embedded. Maximum age deviations of 845 ± 210 years were recorded. Streif (1972) concluded that only pretreated *Phragmites* and sedge peat samples, free of roots and rhizomes, were suitable for dating from tidal flat and lagoonal palaeoenvironments.

There is a delay in the transmission of carbon dioxide to the water in the ocean basins. For this reason, dates on shells or algae will be too old. Recently dead shell samples of known age give apparent radiocarbon ages of 200 to 500 years: Mörner (1969) has established a conversion factor of 305 ± 25 years for the Kattegat, and Berglund (1971) 60 ± 90 for the Baltic Sea. Geyh (1969) has noted that shells not in their living position and collected from the present beach yielded dates of 3,000-4,000 years bp.

Finally, Rafter (1975) has drawn attention to the fact that charcoal, which has acquired a primary importance for dating among archaeologists and is ranked first as a material for dating, is subject to post-depositional contamination. He recommended that three fractions from the sample should be dated and that larger pieces of charcoal were more reliable for dating than smaller pieces.

All materials collected for dating require a careful consideration of their provenance and likely contaminants. Such a consideration derives from a well-documented and recorded stratigraphic survey. Furthermore, some independent check on radiocarbon dates, such as pollen analysis of levels at and adjacent to the dated level, will be necessary for an objective assessment of the validity of the date. In order to build up a chronology of a series of naturally recurring events, it is preferable to date material from similar palaeoenvironments, rather than mix dates from shell, limnic deposits, telmatic and terrestrial peats (see Tooley 1978c).

## Conclusion

The acquisition of primary data upon which palaeoenvironmental reconstructions depend is a skilful, time-consuming and often tedious task. The results of this work are invariably partial and provide only a glimpse of part of a landscape which may or may not provide evidence of prehistoric man.

The primary data base must be sound if worthwhile interpretations and correlations are to be based upon it, and it is for this reason that stress has been given to stratigraphic analysis which is the starting point for all palaeoenvironmental reconstructions.

The diversity of physical, biological and chemical techniques involved in these reconstructions means that a number of specialists will participate, but the meeting point for the geographer, botanist, geologist and archaeologist is the field site where the stratigraphic succession can be examined and compatible sets of samples taken. The requirements of each specialist are slightly different, and rarely will a single set of samples suffice: the pollen analyst will need to know the stratigraphic succession in order to increase the sampling interval across boundary layers or to interpret discontinuities in the pollen frequencies; the archaeologist will need to know the relationship of a pollen diagram to the vertical distribution of artifacts in order to link evidence of cultural activities in the pollen curves to the concentration of artifacts.

It is essential that the results of one or two techniques applied to material from a single site do not serve alone as the basis for reconstructions. Stratigraphic analysis and a series of radiocarbon dates will provide a partial and sometimes erroneous picture of environmental changes. Radiocarbon dates require some means of independent corroboration and in England and Wales the establishment of regional pollen assemblage zones and chronozones has provided some means of corroboration. It is important to have some idea of the limitations of the data, in order to interpret them cautiously and reasonably.

In this chapter an attempt has been made to describe some of the techniques that have been used in palaeoenvironmental reconstructions, and to indicate ambiguities, inconsistencies and limitations in the primary data. Essentially, palaeoenvironmental reconstruction is the product of an interdisciplinary approach and the following chapters on each of the prehistoric periods draw on the results of a diversity of techniques and collaborative work to describe changing environmental patterns for each of these periods.

Grateful acknowledgements are made to Dr J. Troels-Smith for commenting on an early draft of this chapter and to Dr H.J.B. Birks for generously providing me with a copy of the paper he gave at the British Ecological Society's meeting in Lancaster in 1977.

# 2. *The Palaeolithic*

## J.J. WYMER

The environmental extremes produced by the advance and retreat of glacial ice over most of Britain are obvious. Between the extremes of actual glaciation and the climatic optima of interglacial periods was a complexity of transitional climatic patterns which all had different effects on the various geographical regions. Changing sea-levels, sub-aerial, fluviatile and marine erosion have constantly modified the landscape, either by gradual incessant wearing away of the rocks, or by catastrophic destruction. The shape of Britain at the beginning of the Pleistocene had little resemblance to that of today. Against this background of drastic change of every sort, it is worth remembering that the Palaeolithic inhabitants knew nothing of it: the land at any one time was, as far as they were concerned, the same. Even if climatic changes were rapid, on a geological scale, the inhabitants were unlikely ever to have modified their existence because of them within the memory of one generation to another. A curious hunter may well have noticed tree stumps inundated by the sea and pondered upon it. He may have reasoned that the sea had encroached on former land, but such phenomena fitted into no scheme and did not suggest that his world would alter around him. Change, to him, meant travel, as it still does to us. He lived in the environment he chose or to which necessity drove him. Our short study of the subject must emphasise the reciprocal nature of the problem: the effects of the ice age on the Palaeolithic population on one side, and the manner in which human groups adapted to different environments on the other. Therefore, some statement must first be made on the present stage of knowledge of Quaternary events in Britain, based for the most part on the interpretations of geological sediments and processes. Into this framework an attempt can be made to place the presence or absence of men. Where the evidence from particular sites is favourable we can then reconstruct, to the best of our ability, the type of settlement within the context of its environment. Slight clues, produced by purposeful excavation or study and analysis of excavated material and its associated sediments, may produce sufficient data to warrant speculation on the real purpose of archaeological investigation: that is to discover what type of society existed, and how it was organised within its environment.

The alternation of cold and warm climates during the Quaternary is irrefutable, but the number of alternations and the intensity of some of them is imperfectly known. The presence of boulder clay or till, outwash fans, moraines, eskers and other features all testify to ice. Separating or correlating the glacial stages represented by such deposits is by present methods, in the absence of suitable stratigraphy, difficult or impossible. Warmer periods are classified as interglacial or interstadial, and objectively defined by West (1968) following Jessen and Milthers (1928) on the basis of vegetational changes assessed from pollen analysis: an interglacial being a temperate period with a climatic optimum at least as warm as the Flandrian (postglacial; ie present 'interglacial'), and an interstadial either too short or too cold to permit the development of temperate deciduous forest as known in Britain. Turner and West (1968) recognise four distinct sub-periods of vegetational development in an interglacial:

Zone I.   Pre-temperate: dominated by *Betula* and *Pinus*.
Zone II.  Early-temperate: dominated by mixed oak forest.
Zone III. Late-temperate: dominated by late-immigrating trees such as *Carpinus* and *Abies*.
Zone IV.  Post-temperate: again dominated by *Pinus* and *Betula*.

These vegetational zones do not develop solely in response to climatic changes but also reflect a cycle of soil changes. Iversen (1958) describes the process from the period of maximum cold when no stable cover of vegetation can develop (cryocratic stage). The next stage is that when the ice retreats to leave immense areas of raw, basic or neutral mineral soils (protocratic stage). This is when the vegetational succession begins and the open landscape gives way to a more closed one. This has the effect of producing a basic or neutral soil reaction and, by the time the climatic optimum of the interglacial has been reached, fertile soils have developed. The forest becomes vigorous and dense (mesocratic stage) and this is the mixed oak forest of Zone II. In the last (telocratic) stage the soil becomes leached and podsols are produced, giving rise to open, heather-covered tracts of land.

Different interglacial periods are recognised by West on the basis of distinctive pollen assemblages (e.g. the Hoxnian interglacial, with *Hippophaë* in Zone IA (Late Anglian), abundance of *Tilia* in Zone H II, the late rise of *Ulmus* and *Corylus* in Zone H II, and the important *Abies* phase in Zone H III). West distinguishes four interglacials in the Middle-Late Pleistocene: Pastonian, Cromerian, Hoxnian, Ipswichian.

These terms have been adopted by the Geological Society (Mitchell *et al*. 1973) for national usage. Only in the case of the Hoxnian interglacial is there clear stratigraphical and botanical evidence for an unbroken sequence from full glacial to interglacial conditions, but tills have been identified as belonging to the following geological stages:

Anglian (between Cromerian and Hoxnian)
Wolstonian (between Hoxnian and Ipswichian)
Devensian (between Ipswichian and Flandrian = present)

Many other names have been used for local successions which may correspond, and Mitchell *et al*. (1973) is recommended for clarification in this respect. Correlations with Europe are still uncertain and it is generally thought to be unwise to use continental terminology. However, in a broad sense there is a general agreement between the Anglian, Wolstonian and Devensian with the Mindel, Riss and Würm of the classic Alpine chronology. In Britain there is no deposit or feature of glacial origin which can be certainly related to an earlier stage than the Anglian, although several lines of evidence (cool-loving flora and fauna, permafrost features) suggest earlier glacial periods existed but the evidence has been destroyed by later ones.

This basic framework is reliable, but does not pretend to be complete. The stages regarded as glacial, in particular, certainly include milder periods (interstadials) when parts of southern England would have been quite habitable. There were at least three such milder periods in the Devensian and, conversely, a relatively short period of intense cold (Late Devensian pollen Zone III Younger Dryas) after the last (Allerød) warmer one. This cold period is of great interest for Quaternary studies because it comes within the range of radiocarbon dating. It lasted little more than 500 years but in that time 7 m. of sand and gravel accumulated in the lower part of the River Gipping in Suffolk (Wymer *et al*. 1975) and Kerney (1963) has demonstrated extensive fans of chalky rubble and silt of this age beyond the coombs of the Kentish North Downs. Many periglacial features in S.E. England date to this time and it emphasises the great amount of change that can take place in a brief span of geological time. It also suggests that during the Pleistocene there could have been tens if not hundreds of such episodes, all of which could have had a profound effect on human occupation. This is not the place to consider European chronology, but the possibility must be remembered that an interstadial in Britain might have been an interglacial elsewhere. This raises the matter of duration and time. The development of thick forest cover is not just a matter of climate, but time. Coope has demonstrated the time lag between such vegetational development and climate by the study of beetles (Coope *et al.* 1961), which may be regarded as far more subtle indicators of climate than flora or mollusca. Warm-loving beetles may be found in conjunction with a woodland cover of pine, birch and willow which would otherwise indicate cooler conditions. Equally significant is his conclusion that, in part of the Devensian at least, northern species were 'suddenly' replaced by southern ones. This perhaps is more to do with theories of glaciation, but there would have been correspondingly rapid changes in environment which, on other lines of evidence, may not have been detected.

The major glaciation of Britain was during the Anglian, or at least the evidence remaining suggests this. Glacial ice reached North London and it is generally agreed that the Thames was diverted into its present valley by this ice which covered the whole of East Anglia. Certainly there is no evidence to show that ice ever reached as far south again in the succeeding Wolstonian and Devensian stages. Sparks and West (1972) put the limit of the Wolstonian ice to a nearly similar line, but more recent field work by the Institute of Geological Sciences convincingly demonstrates that much (they would say all) of this ice sheet is only a weathered version of the same till (Bristow and Cox 1973). Straw (1973) puts the Wolstonian ice only as far south, on the east side of Britain, as about Bury St Edmunds. The Devensian ice covered most of north-west England, Ireland and Wales, but not the Midlands. North Sea ice fringed the N.E. coast as far south as Norfolk. These are limits of the various ice-sheets and it must be realised that for a very long period of time (to be measured perhaps in tens of thousands of years) glacial conditions were probably much less extensive; interstadial deposits prove that they certainly were for some of it.

The Pleistocene is thus seen as a series of alternating cold and warm periods. Sometimes it was cold enough to produce a true glaciation, sometimes warm long enough to produce an interglacial. At other times permafrost dominated, or tundra or steppelike conditions in an interstadial.

Radiocarbon dating can only reach back as far as the Chelford interstadial of the Devensian (60,800 ± 1,500 bc GrN-1480) and many would regard a date of this order unreliable. There is no other proven method for obtaining absolute dates beyond this as, unfortunately, there are no volcanic sediments in the British Pleistocene to which the technique of potassium/argon dating can be applied. Uranium/thorium dates on bone from Clacton, Hoxne and Swanscombe (Szabo and Collins 1975) are in the expected order of time (100,000-300,000 years) but require corroboration. Dating must, at present, rely on indirect methods such as attempted correlations with dated sequences in Africa or elsewhere. A combination of several techniques, including palaeomagnetism, holds promise for the future. At present, the evidence from deep sea cores gives what seems to be the clearest indication of Pleistocene events. Oxygen isotope analysis of shell fragments from the cores, changes in carbonate content and abundance of foraminifera, enables an ocean temperature scale to be deduced. Extrapolation beyond radiocarbon dating produces a reasonably convincing time scale. There is a distinct pattern in the results (Emiliani 1968; Shackleton and Opdyke 1973) to suggest a swing from cold to warm conditions and back to cold in a fairly regular cycle of about 40,000 years from one peak to another. Hence an interglacial or glacial period might be expected to have a duration of *c*. 20,000 years. On independent evidence at Marks Tey the Hoxnian interglacial does appear to have a duration of about this length (Turner 1970, 1975). The Upton Warren interstadial complex in the Devensian stage is radiocarbon dated to around 40,000 years ago, which also fits in with this concept. However, the Chelford interstadial is thought to be around 60,000 years ago and this is out of step. The shortcomings are many when considered in critical detail, but taken broadly this may really be a Quaternary timetable. The late Percy Evans applied this principle of dating in his bold attempt to create a Pleistocene time-scale (P. Evans 1971). His comprehensive study encompasses a profound knowledge of the Pleistocene in Britain and elsewhere. It is not the final answer but is certainly more realistic than previous attempts, and a considerable advance on the initial brilliant application of the Milankovitch theory by Zeuner (1945). It would be more convincing if some method could be devised for correlating sections of the marine cores with terrestial deposits in Britain, but this may come.

If, with these reservations, we use the time scale derived by Evans, the Anglian Stage commenced about 320,000 years ago, the Hoxnian finished at about 200,000, and the Ipswichian commenced about 100,000. Similar assessments by Kukla (1977) would place the beginning of the Hoxnian at 400,000 and the date between oxygen isotope stages 9-10 as 330,000. These are probably more reliable estimations. When this order of time is compared to the numerous absolute dates obtained in East Africa, based on potassium argon and palaeomagnetic dating, it does seem extremely short. There are now several dates from around Lake Rudolf and the Omo Basin for early hominids and stone tools in the order of 2.5 to 3 million years (Fitch and Miller 1970). Revised dating of the KBS Tuff to 1.8 m.y. (Drake *et al.* 1980) suggests that these dates are too old. There are, of course, several ways of interpreting the evidence from deep-sea cores with arguments for both long and short chronologies. It remains the most intriguing problem in European Palaeolithic archaeology: is there really a gap of about 2 million years before people arrived here from Africa, or is our time scale all wrong? Was evolution on a much more parallel time scale? At present, it seems best to accept the shorter time scale for Europe and regard the inhabitants of Pleistocene Britain as immigrants with a cultural tradition inherited from elsewhere. There is nothing in the archaeological record to show that Britain was ever the world centre of cultural or economic innovation throughout the whole of the Palaeolithic period. The same can be said, perhaps, for Europe until the latter part of the Upper Palaeolithic.

It would be ideal to take the more extreme differences in climate (glacial, periglacial, boreal and temperate) one by one, consider the effect on the environment, and take British Palaeolithic sites individually and see how the population adapted. Unfortunately the number of sites where this type of information can be found is too scanty to allow it. It will be necessary to take the geological stages separately and see what evidence can be extracted from each one.

## Cromerian and earlier Stages

Until recently there was no incontrovertible evidence for any human occupation of Britain prior to the Anglian Stage. Some sites, such as

Kent's Cavern and Fordwich had good claim to be as old as this, but it could not be proved, even to the lax degree of 'proof' that archaeologists have to accept in order to get anywhere. Apparent worked flints and problematical bones from the Crags of East Anglia were frequently put forward as evidence for the presence of men in the Early Pleistocene (Moir 1927). Some of the claims were based on blatant absurdities, others need to be seriously considered. For the moment, this possible Early Pleistocene material must remain in suspension, but not forgotten.

The important site which has at last put back the beginnings of the Palaeolithic period in Britain is Westbury-sub-Mendip. The human evidence is restricted to a few struck flints found in cave sediments, associated with a Cromerian fauna (Bishop 1975). The sediments are regarded as downwash accumulations, so it is reasonable to regard the flints as having been derived only a short distance away from a cave mouth. The first clear record of human occupation in Britain is therefore at a cave. The climate was temperate, to judge by the fauna, including the rhinoceros *Dicerorhinus etruscus*, and preliminary pollen analyses. The flints include two small bifacial pieces which, in the opinion of Dr K.P. Oakley and the author, are probably Acheulian.

Kent's Cavern has produced several crude but distinctive hand-axes and the likelihood is that they are to be associated with the Cromerian fauna found in the same cave. Attempts to prove this association (Campbell and Sampson 1971) have not as yet been successful, but the site ranks high as a possibility for a second example of cave occupation during the Cromerian Stage.

On the basis of typology, Roe (1975) stresses the possibility that the stone-struck hand-axes from the high level gravels at Fordwich and Farnham are pre-Anglian. If so, their presence in south-east England precludes any cave occupation and they may represent the open sites which are almost certain to have existed. Similar so-called Abbevillian hand-axes occur at Yiewsley and in 'Ancient Channel' gravel between Caversham and Henley (Treacher *et al.* 1948; Wymer 1961). At this stage of the Pleistocene Britain was still part of the north-west European peninsula and even the low sea-level implied by the succeeding glaciation of the Anglian Stage is very unlikely to have produced even a temporary breach of the English Channel.

**Anglian and early Hoxnian Stages**

To the Anglian Stage belong the glaciations which produced the majority of the tills found in southern England, including the Northern Drift, the Cromer Till and the Lowestoft Till. There is nothing in the archaeological record to suggest there was any human occupation around the fringes of the ice sheet where periglacial conditions prevailed. This is hardly surprising but, as commented on above, there may well have been lengthy periods during the Anglian in which the climate ameliorated and human occupation would have been quite feasible, especially during the summer months. Recent work at Clacton-on-Sea (Singer *et al.* 1973) and at Swanscombe (Waechter and Conway 1969) has made it very difficult to reconcile the lower levels at either of these Clactonian sites with the Hoxnian Stage. In both cases there are reasons for thinking that at least part of the Clactonian material belonged to an earlier stage than the Hoxnian, and this could be nothing but the Anglian. Yet every other line of evidence (mammalian fauna, mollusca, pollen) points to a temperate climate, not a glacial one. The simplest explanation is that the time involved is some stage at the end of the Anglian; an interstadial prior to perhaps a final re-advance of Anglian ice. Ice may not have advanced as far south again as shown on Fig. 2.1 but it is interesting to record possible periglacial phenomena at Clacton-on-Sea (Gladfelter 1972) associated with the Lower Gravel. Likewise, at Swanscombe, there is a deposit at the base of the Lower Gravel which has been attributed to solifluction. In the latter case this could mean that the large numbers of flint artifacts in the Lower Gravel, together with faunal remains, may have been derived from surfaces pre-dating this possible cold-climate process. At both sites none of the occupation is thought to coincide with this phase.

Clacton and Swanscombe both epitomise the Palaeolithic preference for living beside wide stretches of water. At Clacton, the actual river bank was excavated, although the living surface on the dry land of the time beside it no longer remained. However, the numbers of artifacts and faunal remains increased towards the slope up to the original land surface and it is thought that this represents activity on the gravelly surface at the edge of the river at times of low water. The later occupation (represented by a much lesser amount of material in the overlying marl) took place, according to the pollen analyses, during the Hoxnian Ho.I Pre-temperate zone, although

ICE LIMIT
O    CAVE SITE
●    OPEN SITE

WESTBURY-
SUB-MENDIP

KENT'S
CAVERN

Figure 2.1. Distribution of pre-Anglian Palaeolithic sites. The only securely-
dated site is that of Westbury-sub-Mendip, Somerset. The association of
the crude hand-axes at Kent's Cavern with the Cromerian fauna is
unproven but most probable. The open sites shown qualify for inclusion
mainly on the insecure basis of archaeological typology. They are
Farnham, Surrey; Fordwich, Kent; Caversham-Henley Channel,
Oxfordshire; Yiewsley, London. The limit of Anglian ice is based on
West (1968).

this is disputed by West (personal communication). Mullenders (cited in Wymer 1974a) sees a completely forested landscape dominated by pine with less birch. Pollen from the 'freshwater beds', where Warren collected most of the original Clacton material including the famous wooden spear, indicate Ho.IIb (Early-temperate) (Turner and Kerney 1971) with a wooded landscape dominated by oak and alder. Seeds examined from earlier investigations suggested unwooded areas in the immediate locality. Mollusca from the same horizon indicate quiet water with some swamp. It is easy to see the advantages of such a riparian environment for hunters: fresh water, mammalian prey at the water's edge, edible molluscs (*Unio* sp.), water fowl, fish, flint cobbles in the river bed and thick forest nearby for shelter from the elements. There is no reason to think that their simple flint industry of chopper-cores and modified or unmodified flakes could not cope with all the butchering required and the working of wood for spears. Such a place was probably a living site in the real sense of the word. Settlement seems too grand a term for something that probably had nothing on the ground to mark it but trampled earth, old fires, discarded bones and a few heaps of flints. It also implies something more permanent. 'Home-base' is a more suitable term. The hunters must have travelled considerably and were aware of the superior knapping qualities of flint fresh from the chalk, as opposed to the local gravel cobbles, for a few such pieces were found among the spread of artifacts beside the water.

At Swanscombe, an almost identical environment is associated with the Clactonian material at the top of the Lower Gravel and within the Lower Loam. The molluscs at the base of the Lower Loam (Kerney 1971) indicate a mixture of reed swamp and fen habitats. Pollen shows a dominance of alder and pine, with some oak, hazel, birch and spruce. The mammalian fauna is also similar: Clacton fallow deer, red deer, straight-tusked elephant, giant ox, rhinoceros, bear. The flint industrial tradition is the same. Everything is so similar that it may not be fanciful to see these two sites as contemporary hunting grounds of one or more bands of Clactonian hunters.

## Hoxnian Stage

This interglacial was for a long time equated with the 'Great Inter-glacial'. The concept of a 'great' interglacial is no longer tenable.

Turner (1970) has calculated a duration for the Hoxnian Stage at Marks Tey, Essex, on the basis of laminations in the lake clay, of about 15,000-20,000 years, which fits neatly (too neatly?) into the estimated half-cycle of 20,000 years for an interglacial period, according to the Evans time scale (P. Evans 1971). Zeuner and others would put most of the hand-axe bearing flint gravels of Britain into this stage, and the Hoxnian is generally regarded as the apogee of the Acheulian Industry. When critically examined, there seems little to support this. I have argued that most of the coarse flint gravels of southern England, a lowland area, could only have been deposited under conditions different to the present day. Periglacial climate, with greatly increased volumes of annual melt-waters, would satisfy the conditions. Interglacial sediments in a valley such as the Thames would be restricted to fine sediments of clay, silt and sand, as they are today, and have been since Boreal times in the Flandrian at least. Only in the estuarine regions, such as off Southend, does gravel move and aggrade along the river bed, and few artifacts would be expected in such a situation. Therefore, if the hand-axe bearing gravels are not Hoxnian, and they are post-Anglian, and pre-Ipswichian, they can only be Wolstonian. However, there is positive evidence from Hoxne itself that hand-axes were being manufactured there in late Ho. IIc Early-temperate zone. The hand-axes in the gravels of rivers, such as the Thames, Wey, and Wiltshire Avon, generally 18-35 m. above present river levels, are clearly in a derived position. It seems most likely that some were derived from Hoxnian surfaces destroyed by the wholesale erosion during the Wolstonian Stage. Others, perhaps the majority, date to milder periods within that stage.

It has already been seen above that Clactonian industries are found in the Pre-(?) and Early-temperate zones of the Hoxnian. The earliest indisputable record for hand-axes in the Hoxnian is at Hoxne, where an Acheulian industry is found within the lake muds of Ho. IIc (West 1956). A similar industry has been excavated at a slightly higher level of the lake, on top of the alder carr of Ho. III Late-temperate zone. Here is clear evidence of a lakeside occupation, with all the advantages as briefly described at Clacton and Swanscombe, although flint may have been a little more difficult to find. This occupation appears to come at the end of a short phase of deforestation, at the start of which occurs the first evidence for the presence of man. The coincidence seems too great for chance, and man's accidental or intentional burning of the adjacent forest is the simplest and most attractive explanation. The same phenomenon is found in the pollen profile at Marks Tey: a deforestation phase at the end of Ho. IIc. There is no associated archaeological evidence at Marks Tey, although two hand-axes and a quantity of faunal remains have been found there, but their exact provenances are unknown. Intentional clearing of the forest to improve hunting grounds, as practised by Australian aborigines, may have been the reason for lighting fires. If it really was human activity, it seems more likely that the same practice was carried out in two different places rather than one mighty fire being responsible for both clearances. Animals hunted at this level in the Hoxne sequence, referred to as the Lower Industry, were mainly horse, deer and oxen, with some elephant and rhinoceros. Bones of water fowl and fish were also found.

Other archaeological sites of certain Hoxnian age are difficult to find in Britain. There were sites at Hitchin (Oakley 1947) also apparently a lakeside occupation, and another at Foxhall Road, Ipswich (Layard 1903, 1904, 1906), but in both cases the sites have not been firmly dated. Many other well-known Acheulian sites also have to be excluded as the evidence for their date is even more hazy. Others are included here under the Wolstonian Stage as the balance of the evidence is in favour of a date during that stage. However, at this point, it is pertinent to consider the prodigious quantity of hand-axes and other flint artifacts which occur in gravels such as the Lynch Hill Terrace of the Thames, virtually from the source to the estuary. Although these are in a secondary, if not tertiary, context, it seems unlikely that they have travelled very far from their place of use, otherwise they would have been rolled and abraded beyond recognition. The inference is that they represent the lithic litter swept off the river beaches, remaining from occupation during more clement periods. The distribution of this derived material in the Thames Valley is not quite as haphazard as might be thought, for a study of the distribution plans (Wymer 1968) shows a concentration of sites in regions such as Reading and Dartford where major tributaries join the Thames. This is just where wide, shallow sheets of water might be expected, and this was doubtlessly considered a favourable environment.

## Wolstonian Stage

This stage label will have to be more one of convenience than reality, for it is difficult if not impossible to be sure whether many of the individual sites really belong to this stage, or should be relegated to the Late Hoxnian or even the Early Ipswichian. For the purpose of this brief account there is no need to be unduly concerned, as it is the choice and manner of human habitation that require our attention. What is certain, is that this long period with its rather undefinable beginning and end saw very many changes in climate. Full glacial conditions certainly reached most of Britain, roughly north of a line from Suffolk to Bristol (Figs. 2.2 and 2.3), and periglacial conditions would have dominated south-east England for much of the time. For the first time, there is now a suggestion that people were coping with some of these severe environments. Not, of course, living on the glaciers, but penetrating into the periglacial tundra-like regions, presumably during the short but not harsh summers. Interstadial periods, lasting for some thousands of years, may have been more pleasant than a study of the pollen diagrams alone might indicate, in view of Coope's comments on beetles.

As might be expected, where it is possible to make some assessment of the environment of a particular site, there is again the Pleistocene hunter's preference for living beside water. The classic site is Swanscombe, as represented by the Middle Gravels. Whether it be of Late Hoxnian or Early Wolstonian interstadial date is of no consequence here. The Swanscombe skull and its associated Acheulian industry come from within the body of the Upper Middle Gravels, a fine, current-bedded sandy gravel consistent with a fast-flowing river, probably in flood. Excavations in 1955-60 (Wymer 1964) showed a distinct dispersal pattern of the hand-axes from a point in space which may have been the spot on the river beach that was littered with knapped flints, butchered animal bones and the body, or head at least, of Swanscombe Man. As at Hoxne, horse, deer and ox provided most of his food. Elephant and rhino were also fairly well represented. It is unlikely that the carcases of such large mammals would have been dragged very far so, apart from indicating dietetic preferences and hunting prowess, they also reflect the type of surrounding landscape: wide, open flood plains flanked by forest. Presumably this woodland was some distance from the riverside, for Kerney (1971) notes that woodland species of mollusca are absent, but others indicate damp, open grassland. He also points out that the mollusca from this level are strongly indicative of a cold climate, probably a cool, oceanic one. However, the interpretations are full of uncertainties, and it could be that the archaeological

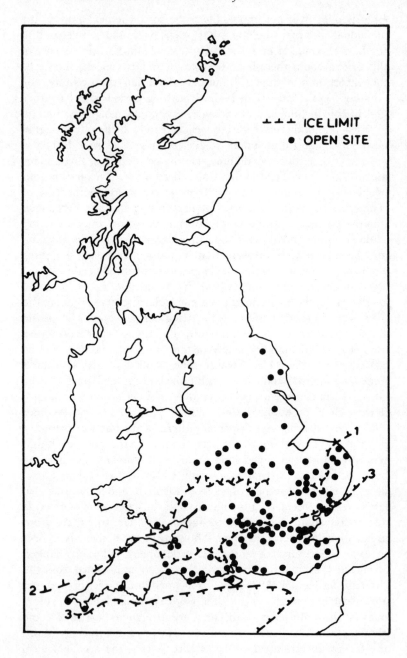

material was swept off its original place many thousands of years after it had been discarded, and thus the mollusca are not contemporary.

There is another group of Acheulian sites from the so-called 'Palaeolithic floor' of north-east London and Essex of Smith (1894). The famous sites were in the Stoke Newington area but attempts to find something similar in the district have, so far, been unsuccessful, in spite of methodical excavation and watching-briefs. However, a perfect example of this 'floor' as described by Smith, recently came to light during work on the M11 South Woodford bypass: a few hand-axes and flakes were found in a primary context at the top of gravel, covered by fluviatile silts and fine gravels (Wymer in press). The inference is, again, of Acheulian sites beside open water although, in this case, not a major river such as the Thames, but the precursor of the Roding.

Smith was also responsible for discovering the Acheulian sites of the Chilterns and here it is certain that Palaeolithic hunters were coping with an entirely different environment. These Chiltern sites, mainly around Caddington and Gaddesden Row (Smith 1916) are almost at the summit of the Chilterns, more than 150 m. O.D. At this stage of the Pleistocene a series of lakes and ponds existed on top of the impermeable clay-with-flints. These gradually became infilled with silt or 'brickearth', which has a loessic content. Such lakes may have been pre-glacial, and the loessic content is indicative of cold. However, unpublished work by R. Hubbard (personal communication) on pollen extracted from the brickearth, indicates temperate, interglacial conditions. Solifluction deposits, if not actual till, overlie this brickearth at various sites within this district. The data are conflicting, or apparently so, but it is incontrovertible that people were living at the top of the Chilterns, well away from any major river system.

Acheulian hand-axes have been found in several other

---

Figure 2.2. General distribution of some Palaeolithic sites represented by artifacts within sediments considered to be of Hoxnian or Wolstonian stages. Also included are a few surface finds of hand-axes unlikely to be earlier or later than these stages. No cave sites are known. The greatest concentrations, mainly of Acheulian industries, are in the Breckland area of East Anglia, the Lower and Middle Thames Valley and the Bournemouth and Southampton regions of the Hampshire basin. The limits of the Wolstonian ice sheets are shown as evaluated by (1) Straw (1973); (2) Sparks and West (1972); (3) Kellaway *et al.* (1975).

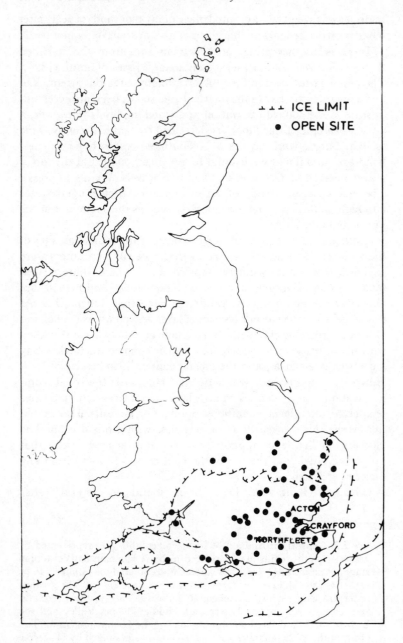

circumstances which, although it is impossible to reconstruct the climate and vegetation of the time, show that these hunters were not confined to river valleys. There are several sites on the North and Hampshire Chalk Downs, and even on the Wiltshire Downs around Hackpen Hill, where weathered and frost-shattered palaeoliths may be found in the sub-soil. A few occur on the surface of wide-gravel spreads such as the 'Silchester Stage' gravels west of Reading (Wymer 1974b). Whatever else, this presupposes that the vegetational cover was not so thick that movement was greatly hindered. This might mean the more open landscape of an interstadial or periglacial zone, but it does not mean to say that an interglacial climate is commensurate with total, dense impenetrable forest; the activities of browsing animals may have kept the chalk downs and other areas relatively clear of woodland. This is a factor likely to be underestimated when interpreting pollen diagrams.

The nearest evidence there is for the exploitation of marine resources by Acheulian hunters is the series of sites along the so-called 100 ft raised beach of Sussex (Calkin 1934). At Slindon and Eartham, hand-axes occur on top of the Slindon Sands, the date of which is problematical but probably Hoxnian. They are covered by chalky solifluction deposits. Numbers of unfinished hand-axes perhaps indicate that the visitors were more interested in the large quantities of available knapping material on the beach, rather than fishing or scavenging. It is hoped that current work by A.G. Woodcock will elucidate this problem.

There are two sites in the lower Thames valley near Gravesend which point to human activity during a very cold period: the Levalloisian site at Baker's Hole, Northfleet, and the proto-

---

Figure 2.3. Distribution of Levalloisian sites, based on Roe (1964). This is a very general distribution map which does not attempt to show all known sites, details of which may be found in Roe (1968). There are no cave sites.

There are very few rich Levalloisian sites in Britain and, for the most part, sites are represented by a few or even individual artifacts, usually in a derived context. The most prolific and useful sites are at Acton, Crayford and Northfleet. The stratigraphical evidence, where it does exist, indicates that this distinctive flint-working technique was not used until the latter part of the Wolstonian Stage. It also occurs in the Ipswichian and probably the Devensian. Ice limits for the later part of the Wolstonian glaciation are based on Straw (1973); Sparks and West (1972); Kellaway *et al.* (1973).

Levalloisian site at Purfleet. The detailed typology of the two industries is not our concern, but it is important that both of them were dependent on almost unlimited supplies of good quality flint. Levalloisian technique may just have been a particular method of flint-knapping practised by Acheulian people when confronted with a wealth of raw material. The Upper Chalk of this area is very rich in good flint, but under normal conditions most of it will be concealed by soil and vegetation. Erosion and other periglacial processes, however, could bare a chalk hillside and reveal flint in the quantities we are discussing. It is difficult to see how else men would have found the flint, for it seems too far-fetched to credit them with the facility for flint-mining. This could mean that these particular hunters were penetrating the Thames Valley almost on the edge of the ice-sheets. This theory is supported by the Coombe Rock which engulfed the Northfleet site, and the flooding which washed the Purfleet artifacts into a coarse, sandy gravel at the foot of the chalk hill.

The evidence for occupation of caves at this time is surprisingly non-existent, maybe because Wolstonian ice covered nearly all the limestone areas in the Highland Zone where caves could be found (Fig. 2.3).

## Ipswichian Stage

The Ipswichian interglacial has its typesite at Bobbitshole, Ipswich (West 1957), and is generally correlated with the Continental Eemian. It might be referred to as the Last Interglacial but, even here in such geologically recent time when the evidence might be expected to have survived so well that interpretations would be easier, there is much not yet understood. It has been suggested (Sutcliffe and Kowalski 1976) that two, or even three, different inter-glacials may be all masquerading as the Ipswichian. Certainly, the evidence for two must be considered seriously, mainly as it is so difficult to accept the possibility of two very different assemblages of large mammals in the same climatic zone of an interglacial and similar geographical contexts. The sites which emphasise this problem are those in the Lower Thames Valley at Ilford, Aveley and Trafalgar Square. At Ilford and Aveley, both attributed to the Ipswichian on palaeobotanical evidence (West *et al*. 1964; West 1969) there are plenty of mammoths and horses but no hippopotamus, whereas at Trafalgar Square, also attributed to the

Ipswichian, there are no mammoths or horses, but plenty of hippopotamus. There are several other 'Ipswichian' sites in Britain, including cave sites, with one or other of these faunal assemblages (Stuart 1976). The problem does not require amplification here, but has to be taken into account when referring to Ipswichian sites. For our purposes, the Ipswichian interglacial refers to an interglacial within the Ipswichian Stage, and any cold periods which may be shown as immediately preceding or succeeding such an interglacial but not necessarily belonging to the Wolstonian or Devensian Stages. In this way, it is possible to preserve the framework recommended by the Geological Society yet avoid the stultifying activity of wedging everything into preconceived pigeon-holes.

In lowland Britain, known Ipswichian sites are generally respresented by fine sediments in the lower reaches of major rivers. Accompanying mollusca and flora usually confirm that marsh, fen or dry flood-plain fringed quiet water and, in many cases, large numbers of mammalian bones testify to the presence of a rich fauna. This is just the type of environment that we have seen was so favoured by hunters throughout the Hoxnian and the Wolstonian, yet the number of rich archaeological sites associated with these Ipswichian sites is strangely very few. Ilford, Aveley and Trafalgar Square have yielded virtually nothing to suggest any association between the large numbers of faunal remains and Palaeolithic occupation or activity. There is a site near Cambridge at Barrington (Gibbard and Stuart 1975) with numerous hippopotamus, deer and oxen and only one possibly associated flake. There is nothing with the rich fauna of Grays, although the later brickearth at West Thurrock with mammoth, rhinoceros, ox or bison (Carreck 1976) may be the same as that which covered a Levalloisian site nearby. In East Anglia, the rich Stoke Bonebed (Layard 1920), recently re-investigated by the writer at Maidenhall, Ipswich, with plentiful mammoth and horse, but no hippopotamus, yielded just one broken flint flake. Rich mammalian sites in the valley of the Stour at Harkstead and Stutton have produced nothing at the former site and only a few pieces at the latter. Nor is there any other line of evidence to suggest hunters may have been responsible for the death of all these animals; no obvious signs of butchering, traces of fire, or apparent selection. J.G. Evans (1975), in his admirable survey of the archaeological evidence for the British Pleistocene, concludes that man was 'a creature of either interstadial environments or, when living within an interglacial, did so, at least in Britain, during the early or late stage of such a period, rarely in the middle'. This can be refuted for the Acheulian on the slender basis of the Hoxne Lower Industry, but it does appear to hold good for the Ipswichian as represented by the sites mentioned. The only rich archaeological site in the lower Thames Valley that is apparently Ipswichian and represents a waterside occupation is Crayford. Here, at the base of fine sediments (Kennard 1944), resting on gravel, was one of the famous Crayford 'working floors'. The rich associated fauna included mammoth, rhinoceros, horse, ox and deer as the commonest animals. The industry was a refined Levalloisian one, with an emphasis on elegant blades. Cordate hand-axes also appear to have been used. The climate was apparently cool at this site. There is no available pollen profile, but the land mollusca indicate open grassland. Sutcliffe (in Sutcliffe and Kowalski 1976) stresses that the rodent fauna from the *Corbicula* bed, which is above the Lower Brickearth which covers the archaeological site, is a typical assemblage of the 'penultimate' glaciation, i.e. Wolstonian. It includes an extinct form of ground squirrel, which was probably an animal of open grassland.

Another riverside site of Ipswichian date, with a similar fauna of mammoth and horse and no hippopotamus, is Brundon, Suffolk. Unfortunately, there is again no pollen evidence, and the reconstruction of the environment is dependent on the mammals and mollusca (Moir and Hopwood 1939). Stratum 4 was a clay or silt containing shells, and the top was considered to be a land surface. 17 species of land shells were identified by Kennard and prompted him to conclude that there was a total absence of marshes, 'while the adjacent land was grassland with a little scrub growth and certainly not woodland'. He thought the presence of *Belgrandia marginata* indicated a climate probably warmer than the present. This surface was apparently subject to floods and was eventually covered by thick beds of gravel, which may or may not be Devensian, but also contains flint artifacts and mammalian remains in a derived condition. The flint industry in the primary context is recorded as being unworn and unpatinated, although there is very little in the major collection at Ipswich Museum which accords with this description. However, those which do include some Levalloisian cores and flakes.

There is another group of sites along the Thames Valley which may fit into this stage and which could indicate a very different choice of living site. It is very difficult to fit them into any established chronology, but they are all more recent than the formation of the Lynch Hill and Taplow terrace gravels of the middle Thames Valley. Downstream, east of Maidenhead, these gravels are generally capped by varying degrees of silty clay, mapped and referred to loosely as brickearth. At West Drayton, Iver and Acton, especially, flint artifacts are found under or within the body of this sediment, generally patinated but otherwise in an unaltered condition. They appear to be in a primary context. There are no satisfactory results so far achieved from pollen, no associated mollusca or mammalian remains; there is nothing but the sediment itself. The brickearths have been studied by Hollin (1977) but with no conclusive results. They have been regarded as both fluviatile and colluvial. Particle size analysis isolates a loessic element and suggestions have been made that the sediment represents loess deposited in still water. The problem of having a sheet of still water higher than the Lynch Hill Terrace remains unexplained, especially as the brickearth spreads unconformably downwards over the lower terraces. Sparks and West (1972) regard this Thames Valley brickearth as loess, i.e. a wind-borne deposit. If this is accepted, there are two significant implications: it means that wide, open areas were inhabited by hunters at the time when the climate was cold, and that the sites were some distance from the actual river. If the flint artifacts represent anything more permanent than brief stops by bands of foragers, some form of constructed shelter would have been essential for survival if not minimum comfort. Levalloisian flakes and cores are found in the brickearth, also occasional hand-axes. A Late-Wolstonian/Early-Ipswichian date seems likely for much of this brickearth, but it is probably composite, and some may be earlier (? Stoke Newington area) and some may be of Devensian date (? Taplow).

The choice of an estuarine or marine environment is indicated by two important sites at Christchurch (Calkin and Green 1949) and Great Pan Farm on the Isle of Wight (Shackley 1973) (see Fig. 2.4). The industries may be described as British Mousterian of Acheulian tradition, with sub-triangular hand-axes and Levalloisian flakes. At Great Pan Farm, the artifacts are within beach sand which Shackley equates with the marine transgression responsible for the 7.5m. raised beach of the mainland. A Late Ipswichian date is inferred. Similar material at St Neots (Paterson and Tebbutt 1947) was in a low terrace gravel also containing mammoth, reindeer, woolly rhinoceros and horse. This gravel is unlikely to have

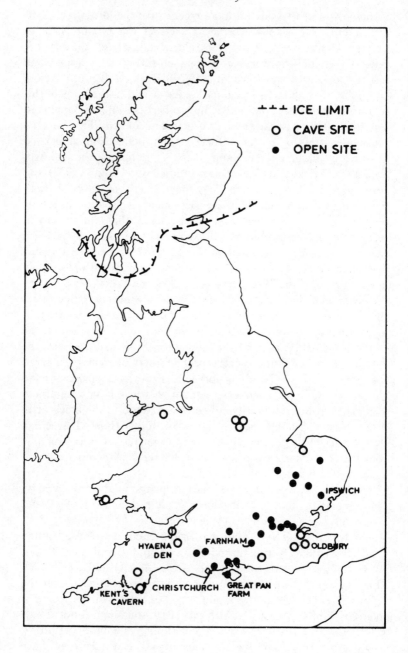

accumulated before the end of the Ipswichian.

Caves were certainly occupied at about this time, although the evidence is scanty. Kent's Cavern (Campbell and Sampson 1971) is the richest site of this type in Britain and there is an industry with cordiform and sub-triangular hand-axes in the cave earth. Pollen suggests a possible sub-arctic climate but, in the absence of controlled excavation in the past, it is impossible to know exactly how this relates to this Mousterian industry. However, it does confirm the use of caves by hunters at this time. Unfortunately, little more than this can be said about another rock shelter site in Kent, at Oldbury (Collins and Collins 1970).

## Devensian Stage

Several of the sites briefly noted in the previous section suggest that hunters were still occupying both open sites and caves even at times of harsh climate. The hardships of existing in cold or sub-arctic conditions may have been lessened, of course, by restricting visits to

---

Figure 2.4. General distribution of some sites of Mousterian industry of Acheulian Tradition, mainly based on the find-spots of flat-butted cordate (sub-triangular) hand-axes. Where there are any stratigraphical associations, Late Ipswichian to Early Devensian dates are indicated. Open circles are cave sites.

Sites featured:

(1) Cave sites: Pont Newydd, Clwyd; Coygan Cave, Dyfed; Hyaena Den, Wookey, Somerset; Kent's Cavern, Devon; Pin Hole, Cresswell Crags, Derbyshire; Robin Hood's Cave, Cresswell Crags, Derbyshire; Church Hole, Cresswell Crags, Derbyshire; Oldbury, Kent; Three Holes Cave, Torbryan, Devon; Uphill Down, Somerset.

(2) Open sites: Christchurch, Hampshire; Great Pan Farm, Isle of Wight; Holybourne, Hampshire; Warsash, Hampshire; Cams, Fareham, Hampshire; Fisherton, Wiltshire; Lake, Wiltshire; Farnham, Surrey; Sulhampstead Abbots, Berkshire; Marlow, Buckinghamshire; Swanley, Kent; Rochester, Kent; Ivy Hatch, Kent; Midhurst, Sussex; Creffield Road, Acton, London; Berrymead Priory, Acton, London; Wandsworth, London; Erith, London; Tilbury, Essex; Little Paxton, St. Neots, Huntingdonshire; North Wootton, Norfolk; Little Cressingham, Norfolk; Bramford Road, Ipswich, Suffolk; Sicklesmere, Suffolk; Lakenheath, Suffolk; Brandon Down, Suffolk.

The position of the limits of the Early Devensian ice sheet is shown in Scotland, but this is purely conjectural.

the most clement of the summer months. This infers a home-base elsewhere, in a more southerly temperate place, and the distances travelled by hunters should not be underestimated. However, this was not necessarily so, as will be discussed later. How long hunters remained, or continued to visit southern England once the Devensian ice sheets began to cover the Highland zone is unknown. Some of the sites already mentioned such as Christchurch and St Neots may belong more strictly to the Devensian than the Ipswichian Stage but, even so, the derived nature of the artifacts makes it impossible to be more precise. Fortunately, the sub-triangular hand-axe is one of the few distinctive Acheulian products that may be placed with some confidence into a time range of Ipswichian to Early Devensian, mainly on continental parallels. Small cordiform, triangular hand-axes and Levallois flakes are typical of this period. All that can be said is that such artifacts are occasionally found in the fillings of buried channels of rivers in south-east England, notably the Gipping in Suffolk and a few from the Thames. Whether this reflects a riparian distribution cannot be proved, but it seems likely.

The chronology of the Devensian Stage in Britain is not understood as well as it is in Denmark, Holland and Belgium, where eight interstadials are recognised. There is no site which shows the transition from the interglacial conditions of the Ipswichian to the glacial conditions of the Devensian, although the gravel of the type site at Four Ashes, Staffordshire, with its organic lenses (Morgan 1973) overlies a peat with a temperate flora considered Ipswichian (Shotton 1967a). Two periods have been recognised in the British Devensian Stage as interstadial, the Chelford and Upton Warren interstadials, probably centred around dates of 60,000 and 40,000 years respectively, on the basis of radiocarbon dating. There is also a Late Glacial interstadial at about 12,000 years, correlated with the Allerød. The Upton Warren interstadial (Coope *et al.* 1961) actually has several radiocarbon dates between 38,000 and 26,000 years and is thus usually referred to as the Upton Warren interstadial complex. Terrace deposits at Wretton, Norfolk (West *et al.* 1974) indicate a woodland biozone of birch and pine for the Early Devensian, whereas by the Middle Devensian, including the Upton Warren complex, there were herb biozones with 86-90% non-arboreal pollen. Much detail is available for many Devensian sites and a secure record of climatic, faunal and floral changes throughout the whole stage is becoming well established. It is also now clear that glaciers did not extend southwards to the limit as shown on Fig. 2.5 until the Late Devensian, *c.* 18,000 bp. It is also apparent that the changes from cold to warm were much quicker than warm to cold. It is both unfortunate and puzzling that there is a total absence of archaeological information at all these rich sites. As mentioned above, a few hand-axes of Mousterian type have been found in fluviatile sediments of Devensian age, but nowhere in useful contexts outside caves. The landscape certainly supported a varied fauna for much of the time, including reindeer, woolly rhino and mammoth, all favourite beasts of prey for hunters of this time. Conditions in the summer months in much of Britain would have been no worse than conditions tolerated elsewhere in Europe. Some suggestions for this relative lack of human activity are given below in the concluding summary.

If human activity was sparse in the Early and Middle Devensian, it was a little more prominent in the Late Devensian. Upper Palaeolithic occupation of numerous caves is well known, although there are no sites remotely comparable in richness to those of central France, northern Spain and central Europe. The origins of these peoples does not concern us here, but it is no longer considered wise to correlate British industries with their French counterparts. The British Upper Palaeolithic can be divided into earlier and later periods and, as might be expected, they would appear to be separated by an interval coinciding with the maximum extent of the Devensian ice sheet. The stratigraphic position of the early British Upper Palaeolithic is neatly demonstrated at Ffynnon Beuno and Cae Gwyn in North Wales by the till overlying the level with a bifacial point and a buskate burin (McBurney 1965). A mammoth carpal from the same cave has been radiocarbon dated to 16,045 ± 1,400-1,200 bc (Birm.-146) (Oakley 1971). At Kent's Cavern, a sample of unburnt tibia of woolly rhinoceros associated with an earlier Upper Palaeolithic industry has been radiocarbon dated to 26,205 ± 435 bc (GrN-6201) (Campbell and Sampson 1971). A date of 16,510 ± 340 bc (BM-374) was obtained from collagen separated from the leg of the famous human burial in the Paviland Cave on the Gower Peninsula (Oakley 1968). More recently, from the same cave, a date of 25,650 ± 1300 bc (BM-1367) has been recorded (Molleson and Burleigh 1978) from a *Bos* humerus. This date probably relates to the earlier Upper Palaeolithic industry there and equates well with Kent's Cavern. Earlier Upper Palaeolithic caves are also known in Devon, Somerset, Glamorgan

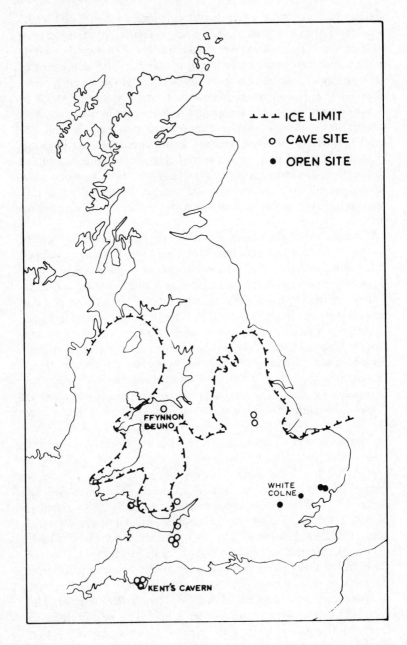

and Derbyshire (Fig. 2.5). A new survey of the whole of the British Upper Palaeolithic has been made by John Campbell (1977). A clear, concise account of this and earlier periods has been published by Mellars (1974). On the basis of radiocarbon dates alone it would appear that the earlier British Upper Palaeolithic stretched over a long period, and conditions are likely to have differed from one time to another. The evidence available at present is insufficient to place each known occurrence into its contemporary environment, but the more recent re-investigation of the Hyaena Den at Wookey Hole in the Mendips (Tratman *et al.* 1971) gives a picture which may be true for most of the sites. The part of the pollen profile from the Hyaena Den associated with the earlier Upper Palaeolithic shows that it was an open landscape (> 60% non-arboreal pollen) with patches of birch, pine, willow and juniper predominating among the trees. Clearly a cold environment, but with sufficient herbage to support a fauna of mammoth, woolly rhinoceros, horse, bison, reindeer, red deer and giant Irish deer.

The occupation of cave mouths and rock shelters in such an environment is understandable, but it seems odd that there are so few possible open sites in Lowland Britain for this period. The same people must have crossed large areas of lowland Britain to get to the margins of the highlands where there were suitable natural shelters, and it seems inconceivable that they did not camp somewhere or take advantage of the herds of animals that must have been present. The periglacial conditions on the fringe of the later ice sheet may well have disturbed the primary context of any such sites if they had existed, dispersed any artifacts and destroyed any faunal or other

---

Figure 2.5. Distribution of earlier Upper Palaeolithic sites. Cave sites indicated by open circles. Sites featured:

(1) Cave sites: Ffynnon Beuno and Cae Gwyn, Clwyd; Paviland Cave, Glamorganshire; Pin Hole, Cresswell Crags, Derbyshire; Robin Hood's Cave, Cresswell Crags, Derbyshire; Uphill Down, Somerset; King Arthur's Cave, Herefordshire; Hyaena Den, Wookey, Somerset; Badger Hole, Wookey, Somerset; Soldier's Hole, Wookey, Somerset; Kent's Cavern, Devon; Windmill Cave, Brixham, Devon; Bench Cavern, Brixham, Devon.

(2) Open sites: Broxbourne, Hertfordshire; Bramford Road, Ipswich, Suffolk; Constantine Road, Ipswich, Suffolk; White Colne, Essex.

The limit of the late Devensian ice sheet is shown, based on Sparks and West (1972). On radiocarbon evidence, it reached its maximum between about 18,000 and 15,000 years bp.

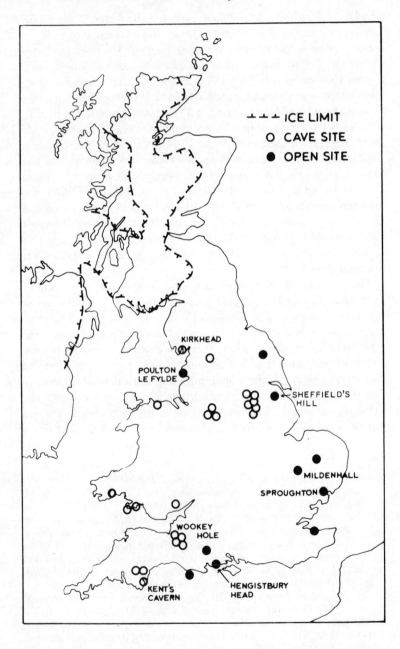

associated remains, but the virtual absence of any of the diagnostic artifacts of the period in Late Devensian sediments is puzzling. A few leaf-shaped bifacial points in or beneath river gravel in Suffolk and Essex (Moir 1930, Campbell 1977) are about the only pieces which qualify for possible acceptance as evidence for open sites.

It would seem that the country was unpopulated during the severe climate of the full Devensian glaciation from *c.* 18,000 to 15,000 years bp, but with the recession of the ice human activity is soon in evidence. Many of the caves occupied in the earlier phase of the British Upper Palaeolithic were reoccupied, and several others also for the first time (Fig. 2.6). There is a broadly similar distribution along the fringes of the Highland Zone, with nothing known north of Kirkhead Cave, Cumbria (formerly Lancashire). The richest sites are in Derbyshire and the Mendips but, as with the earlier phase, none of them is rich on continental standards. However, it would seem that this later British Upper Palaeolithic period was something distinctive to Britain and was an indigenous development through-out the Late Devensian (pollen Zones L-De I-III). Zone L-De II is usually equated with the Allerød mild period, and there is now much evidence to show that the final cold phase of Zone III was severe. These occupations need to be related to the complex climatic

---

Figure 2.6. Distribution of later Upper Palaeolithic sites. Open circles indicate cave sites. Sites featured:

(1) Cave sites: Kirkhead Cave, Lancashire; Victoria Cave, Settle, Yorkshire; Kendrick's Cave, Llandudno, Clwyd; Dowel Cave, Staffordshire; Fox Hole Cave, Staffordshire; Thor's Cave, Staffordshire; Anston Cave, Derbyshire; Ash Tree Cave, Whitwell, Derbyshire; Mother Grundy's Parlour, Cresswell Crags, Derbyshire; Church Hole, Cresswell Crags, Derbyshire; Pin Hole, Cresswell Crags, Derbyshire; Langwith, Derbyshire; Hoyle's Mouth, Dyfed; Paviland Cave, Glamorganshire; Cat's Hole, Glamorganshire; King Arthur's Cave, Herefordshire; Gough's Cave, Cheddar, Somerset; Sun Hole, Cheddar, Somerset; Aveline's Hole, Somerset; Soldier's Hole, Somerset; Three Holes Cave, Torbryan, Devon; Tornewton, Devon; Kent's Cavern, Devon; Wookey Hole, Somerset.

(2) Open sites: Flixton, Yorkshire; Sheffield's Hill, Scunthorpe, Lincolnshire; Poulton-le-Fylde, Lancashire; Cranwich, Norfolk; Mildenhall, Suffolk; Sproughton, Ipswich, Suffolk; Oare, Kent; Hengistbury Head, Hampshire; Portland Bill, Dorset.

The limits of the two Late Devensian ice re-advances are shown, based on Sparks and West (1972).

changes as outlined by Pennington's (1975a) study of the Late
Devensian sequences at Blelham Bog in Cumbria and Cam Loch in
Scotland. Kerney (1963) and Kerney *et al.* (1964) have
demonstrated the extent of solifluction and other periglacial
phenomena on the chalk downs of southern England at this time,
and large quantities of rock waste were scoured off the bare landscape into the rivers that had eroded deep channels in response to
the low sea-level of the Mid-Late Devensian. There were also
significant changes in the fauna. Stuart (1974) notes the absence in
the Late Devensian of the large mammals that were typical of the
Early and Middle Devensian: mammoth, woolly rhinoceros, bison,
lion. However, lion and woolly rhinoceros are recorded in the Black
Band of Kent's Cavern, associated with the later Upper Palaeolithic
and radiocarbon dated to 12,325 ± 120 bc (GrN-6203) and 10,230 ±
100 bp (GrN-6204) (Campbell and Sampson, 1971). Assuming
these are correct records, it is interesting to speculate that these
beasts may have last survived in Britain in this area and have been
slaughtered to extinction by later Upper Palaeolithic hunters.
Mammoth, woolly rhinoceros and lion certainly disappear from the
record about this time. Elk, horse, reindeer and red deer arrived in
large herds during the Late Devensian and, in their wake, other
groups of hunters. The discovery of a skeleton of elk at Poulton-le-
Fylde, Lancashire, associated with barbed bone points (Hallam *et
al.* 1973), within lacustrine detritus muds of L-De II age, attest
to hunting forays in the Fylde area of Lancashire, for which
there is virtually no other archaeological evidence. Similarly, at
Sproughton, Suffolk, barbed points have been found in L-De III
contexts (Wymer *et al.* 1975) and some of the Yorkshire barbed
points may also date to this period. It would seem that hunters were
active in Britain in spite of the severe climate, but it is reasonable to
assume they restricted their visits from the continent to the warmer
periods of the year. This could well be connected with seasonal
migrations of the animal herds. An open riverside site at
Sproughton, thought to be Late L-De III or Early Flandrian, is best
interpreted as a hunter's camp rather than any semi-permanent
settlement, but the long blade industry indicates very different
origins to the Creswellian and Cheddarian of the cave sites (Wymer
and Rose 1976). Other open sites with tanged points, such as
Hengistbury Head (Mace 1959) and a few other rare sites in south-
east England probably represent similar seasonal hunting forays for

yet other groups of hunters. It is against this background that the British Mesolithic developed.

## Conclusions

However tentative and indefinite the conclusions that can be made at individual sites, it is at least clear from the quantity of the evidence that Lower Palaeolithic hunters occupied a wide range of environments in a variety of climatic conditions. The banks of major rivers were unquestionably the preferred choice, whether it was during the mixed oak forest temperate zone of an interglacial (i.e. the later part of the Clacton-on-Sea sequence) or the cooler, more open landscape of an interstadial (i.e. Hoxne, upper industry). Similarly, lakesides were favoured in both warm (Hoxne, lower industry) and cold periods (? Caddington). Chalk downs were occupied at uncertain times and there is a little evidence for littoral activity. There is virtually nothing for the Highland zone of Britain but just how much this is a reflection of the distribution or destruction of the evidence by natural forces cannot be positively assessed. Perhaps the most surprising and significant consideration is the total absence of anything to show that caves were occupied during the long Wolstonian Stage. It is difficult to account for this as caves appear to have been regarded as favourable shelters prior to the Anglian and within the Devensian Stages. Neither is there any evidence for the use of caves during the Hoxnian Stage, although the necessity to do so may have been much less in these mainly milder periods. The answer to the lack of Wolstonian cave occupation may be connected with the severity of the glacial conditions. The limits of the Wolstonian ice-sheets shown in Figs 2.2 and 2.3 include the controversial English Channel glaciation (Destombes *et al.* 1975; Kellaway *et al.* 1975). If the latter is accepted, it is clear that only a small part of south-east England could have been occupied while glacial ice extended so far, and perhaps this was for the major part of the Wolstonian. It also implies that Britain was isolated from the continent in the latter part of this stage. The general distribution of artifacts (Figs 2.2 and 2.3) accords reasonably well with this interpretation. Levalloisian material (Fig. 2.3) lies outside the limits of the glaciated area except for a little between the Midlands and the Wash. Undifferentiated hand-axe and other industries of Hoxnian or Wolstonian age have a rather wider distribution (Fig. 2.2), especially from East Anglia to Yorkshire, well within the area of the Wolstonian ice-sheet. It may well be that some of this material is pre-Wolstonian but only at one site in Lincolnshire, Welton-le-Wold (Alabaster and Straw 1976) have Acheulian artifacts been found stratified beneath Wolstonian till. Any remaining sites in the more northerly part of England were probably destroyed by the passage of Devensian ice (cf. the distribution of material on Fig. 2.2 and the line of the limit of Devensian ice on Fig. 2.5).

The inference is that glacial ice, or the proximity of it, would have rendered the cave areas of England and Wales uninhabitable for most, if not all, of the Wolstonian Stage. Acheulian and Levalloisian occupation was probably restricted to late-summer hunting bands, or during the relatively short interstadials when ice retreat was minimal. In both cases, Palaeolithic people were coping with harsh environments. Shelter and fire must have been essential, but the evidence has yet to be found in Britain.

The suggestion that Britain was isolated from the continent by ice in the Late Wolstonian, and later by the high sea-level of the Ipswichian is supported by the archaeological evidence from northern France, where there is a much greater number of Levallois and Mousterian sites of 'Late Riss' and 'Riss-Würm' dates. It would explain the paucity of archaeological sites in Britain of Ipswichian date, a situation that may not have changed until the low sea-level of the Mid-Late Devensian once more joined Britain to the continent. The British earlier Upper Palaeolithic presumably arrived soon after the land was restored, and in view of the extreme conditions from about 18,000 bp, it is not surprising to find it in caves. Open sites of the period may have been destroyed by the periglacial conditions of the full glacial Devensian, but some may exist below the water-tables of the major rivers of southern England. There is a marked change in the variety of habitat occupied by later Upper Palaeolithic people as the ice sheets retreated.

In Table 2.1 a broad classification has been made to distinguish the flint industries of the different periods and environments. It would be satisfying to record a relationship between particular flint industries and certain climates or habitats, but it cannot be done, except perhaps with the Levalloisian. Where any evidence exists at all, the industry appears to be associated with a cold climate. Otherwise it would seem that hunters of all traditions during the Pleistocene were prepared to exploit almost any worthwhile habitat.

Table 2.1. Chart to indicate tentatively the environments preferred by hunters in Britain during the Middle and Late Pleistocene periods. A Acheulian, C Clactonian, L Levalloisian, MAT Mousterian of Acheulian Tradition, EUP Early Upper Palaeolithic, LUP Later Upper Palaeolithic

| GEOLOGICAL STAGE | | CAVES INLAND | CAVES MARINE | MAJOR RIVER VALLEYS | BESIDE LAKES | LITTORAL | ON HIGH GROUND |
|---|---|---|---|---|---|---|---|
| FLANDRIAN Warm / DEVENSIAN | L-DE III L-DE II L-DE I LATE MID EARLY | LUP Creswell Crags; EUP Hyaena Den; MAT Creswell Crags | LUP Kent's Cavern; EUP Kent's Cavern; Coygan Kent's Cavern | LUP Sproughton | LUP Poulton-le-Fylde | LUP Hengistbury Portland | |
| IPSWICHIAN Mainly Warm | | | | MAT Acton L | | MAT Breach Pan Farm | MAT Sulhampstead Abbots |
| WOLSTONIAN Mainly Cold | | | | L Crayford; L Northfleet; A Hoxne Swanscombe | Caddington | | A Caddington |
| HOXNIAN Warm | | | | | A Hoxne | | |
| ANGLIAN Mainly Cold | | | | C Clacton | | A Slindon | A N. Downs |
| CROMERIAN Mainly Warm | | A Westbury Sub-Mendip | A Kent's Cavern | A Fordwich | | | |

# 3. The Mesolithic

## I.G. SIMMONS, G.W. DIMBLEBY and CAROLINE GRIGSON

For the purposes of this essay, the Mesolithic period is taken to cover the period 10,000-5,000 bp, i.e. the years from the onset of the post-glacial amelioration of climate to the decline of *Ulmus* pollen which is usually coincident with the advent of Neolithic cultures. It comprises the chronozones Flandrian I and Flandrian II, which in turn include Zones IV-VIIa (Pre-Boreal, Boreal and Atlantic) of Godwin's (1940, 1975) scheme of pollen assemblage zones (see Tables 1.1 and 3.3.).

In environmental terms, the cultural period of the Mesolithic covers two rather different epochs. The first was one of rapid environmental change, when the withdrawal of the ice from Europe and North America brought in its train ameliorating climates, the replacement of open vegetation communities by forests (with attendant changes in the fauna), and rises in sea-level. This phase can be conveniently terminated at *c.* 7,500 bp with the final insulation of Britain from the European mainland. The second epoch was one of stability, with much of the British Isles covered with a mixed deciduous forest dominated by oak and a relatively warm and oceanic climate.

The study of the impact of human communities during these pre-agricultural phases is still subject to much accumulation of evidence and re-evaluation. For the period of rapid change, the possibilities of Early Flandrian 'overkill' of ungulates and of the encouragement of hazel (*Corylus avellana*) by man-set fire have been pointed out, but the evidence is as yet scanty. From the oak forest period (Flandrian II), the evidence that men manipulated parts of their habitat by means of fire is stronger, although most of the land probably remained untouched. The places where the effect was strongest appear to be the peripheries of the forest where the ecosystems were most fragile and hence most easily manipulated towards a different state. The margin most explored for evidence has been the upland edge of the forest but the coast may well have been another such tension zone although the evidence has often been buried if not destroyed by rises in sea-level. Perhaps 'fragile' in this context ought also to include the rapidly changing biota and habitats of Flandrian I, where ecosystems were under pressure from climatic change and possibly any additional stress from human activity might have produced shifts in vegetation and animal communities.

This chapter is in three main parts: a description of changes in sea-level and climate (I.G. Simmons), a study of the relations of soils, vegetation and man (G.W. Dimbleby), and a consideration of the natural fauna and its linkages with human activity (Caroline Grigson).

## Sea-level

During Mesolithic times, the level of the sea relative to the land changed drastically. Two forces were at work producing movements of the level of the seas around Britain: there was firstly the rise in the level of the seas caused by the melting of ice sheets and glaciers not only in northern Europe but also in North America and elsewhere in the world. The very rapid break-up of the Laurentide ice-sheet together with an unknown contribution from Antarctica released large volumes of water and thus contributed to rises in sea-level. However, such a process is not necessarily linear but subject to discontinuities which are caused by retardations or even reversals of the melting of large ice bodies. The changes in sea-level from such causes are said to be due to *eustatic* factors. Secondly, there are isostatic factors which are related to the rise of the land surface when released from the weight of a large body of ice or the fall of the land when a water load is applied (hydro-isostacy). The rate and magnitude of isostatic recovery is probably directly related to the weight of ice which was present, but in general terms the land rises rapidly at first and then more slowly: in north-west England Tooley (1974) shows the curve (Fig. 3.1) to decrease continuously from 8,000-5,000 bp after which it remains more or less static at 0.4 mm./yr. rise; at 8,000 bp the more relative rise was *c*. 8 mm./yr. Relative changes in sea-level therefore are the outcome of a 'race' between higher sea-levels caused by increased volumes of water in the oceans, and the lower sea-levels which would be the outcome of rising land masses. There is the further complication in Britain as elsewhere that isostatic recovery is not nationally uniform because of uneven loading of ice, Britain having been at the southern margin of the last glaciation. Data for relative changes of sea-level in northern Britain may therefore yield a slightly different picture from those for the south.

There is yet another element in the discussion. Two schools of thought have emerged on the nature of the change in sea-level during prehistoric times. They are both agreed that during Mesolithic times there was a considerable rise of relative sea-level, but they disagree about whether this was a continuous rise which can be depicted by a smooth curve, or an oscillating rise punctuated by small recessions, to be depicted by an interrupted curve. Details of the arguments are summarised by Jelgersma (1966); here the arguments of Tooley (1978a) and Mörner (1976) will be accepted and an intermittent rise of sea-level will be assumed.

The course of relative sea-level in Britain has been examined by several workers but some of this work has suffered from its lack of corroboration from adjacent European countries. Here we shall take as a record for Britain the course of change in north-west England described by Tooley (1974, 1978a) and then put this in the context of pan-British and pan-European correlations (Tooley 1974, Mörner 1976).

The evidence from north-west England is for an oscillating sea-level during the Flandrian Stage, accomplishing the final restoration of sea-level. The following oscillations in *relative* sea-level have been identified in west Lancashire (Fig. 3.1):

1. Relative sea-level rose rapidly from the end of Flandrian Ib until the middle of Flandrian Ic, at a rate of about 1.8 cm./yr, to a maximum altitude of −14.0m. O.D., from which altitude it then fell to an altitude of −15.2m. O.D.

2. During the latter half of Flandrian Ic sea-level rose by a metre or was stationary between 8,390 and 7,995 bp.

3. Shortly after 7,800 bp sea-level rose extremely rapidly to an altitude of −6.5m. O.D.

4. After 7,600 bp the rate of rise slackened to 0.3 cm./yr until 6,980 bp. During this period and the preceding one, the most extensive penetration by the sea occurred, landward of the present coast.

5. Sea-level fell after 6,980 bp, to about −4.3m. O.D., and there was an extensive removal of marine conditions in south-west Lancashire: on Downholland Moss, the removal of marine conditions extended over a surface greater than 2 km. in width.

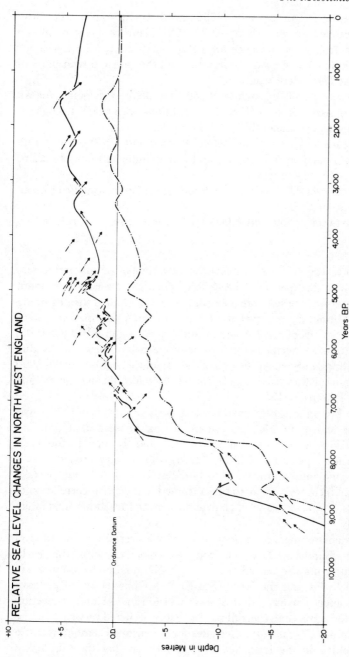

Figure 3.1. Relative sea-level changes in north-west England from 9,200 to 0 bp. The continuous line curve represents the relative movements of mean high water of spring tides, the pecked line curve represents mean sea-level, a reduction of 4m., based on the present difference between the two levels (Tooley 1974).

6. Sea-level rose between 6,800 and 6,300 bp over a metre and reached an altitude of −3.2m. O.D. During this general rise there is some evidence for a slight oscillation. The Lytham − Skippool Valley was inundated and the east and west parts of the Fylde were separated.

7. About 6,000 bp, sea-level fell and there is evidence for an extensive removal of marine conditions once again throughout south-west Lancashire and the Fylde.

8. Sea-level rose rapidly between 6,000 and 5,800 bp at a rate approaching 0.6 cm./yr, and a maximum altitude of −2.2m. O.D. was attained.

9. Sea-level fell between 5,775 and 5,500 bp to a nadir of about −3.4m. O.D.

10. Between 5,500 and 5,000 bp, sea-level rose at a rate of 0.5 m./yr.

This record shows the Mesolithic as a time of rapidly rising sea-level, with the period 7,800-6,980 bp as the time of maximum penetration of the sea from a low of *c.* −15.2m. O.D. at the beginning of the Mesolithic to a level of −4.64m. O.D. at 6,980 bp. There were further periods of rise between 6,800-6,300 bp and 6,000-5,800 bp, with retreat of marine conditions between each of these epochs, due to a falling sea-level. At the end of the Mesolithic period, 5,500-5,000 bp, sea-level was rising again but fell by 0.8m. during the earliest part of Flandrian III.

The British and European context of these periods of rise of sea-level is shown in Fig. 3.2, where it can be seen that a broad correlation across the rest of Britain and Europe is found, a conclusion repeated by Mörner (1976) who, however, relied upon a bristlecone pine calibration of C-14 dates. Thus the uneven effects of isostatic recovery appear to be subsumed in a general correlation of periods of relative sea-level change during the Mesolithic (and later) periods.

The environmental consequences of the overall rise in sea-level during Flandrian I which roughly coincides with the early Mesolithic may be viewed at two scales. Nationally, the formation of the Irish Sea and the North Sea-English Channel are of primary significance. The exact date of the final severance of land connection of the former is controversial but probably occurred very early in the Mesolithic. Thomas (1977) argues for a marine accompaniment to ice melting in the Irish Sea *c.* 19,000 bp so that there is a real

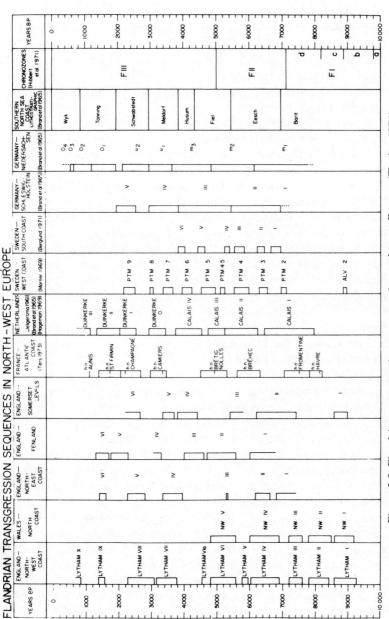

Figure 3.2. Flandrian transgression sequences in north-west Europe (Tooley 1976).

possibility that the Irish Sea formed then, but that isostatic recovery carried the land higher than the contemporary sea-level between about 18,000-10,000 bp. There is no doubt however that the Irish Sea was present again by 9,200 bp since the sea had penetrated Morecambe Bay. In the case of the North Sea the final severance of the eastern connection was probably around 7,800 bp (Kolp 1976) with the last land remaining along a line from Hull to the Dutch archipelago and Esbjerg in Denmark. These severances have obvious consequences in terms of human migration (and there is evidence from harpoon points dredged up from the Leman and Ower banks (Clark 1952) that this land bridge was occupied in Mesolithic times) but are also significant biogeographically. As Caroline Grigson points out in this chapter, several species which are absent from Ireland presumably spread too late to immigrate before the advent of higher sea-levels: the mole (*Talpa europea*), the common shrew (*Sorex araneus*), the beaver (*Castor fiber*), the aurochs (*Bos primigenius*), the elk (*Alces alces*) and the roe deer (*Capreolus capreolus*) are examples, and the brown hare (*Lepus europeaeus*) was introduced during historic times into Ireland, the Isle of Man and a number of Scottish Islands including Orkney and Shetland (Southern 1964; West 1968). Evidence for the wild cat, the wild boar and the beaver is absent or doubtful in prehistoric Ireland as it is for a number of smaller species.

Similarly, the immigration to England and Scotland of various continental species of plants was presumably prevented or retarded. The impoverished tree flora of Britain may be partly due to such a cause, as well as climatic factors: the failure of the spruce (*Picea abies*) to re-enter Britain in the postglacial period may be cited. None of these immigration failures prevented the assemblage of functioning ecosystems but they kept lower than was potentially possible the diversity of flora and fauna and hence possibly also the variety of biotic resources available to the inhabitants.

On a more local scale, the oscillations of sea-level must have affected the economy of Mesolithic inhabitants. Rises in sea-level would have meant the loss of familiar coastal settlement sites, but the penetration of marine conditions further inland brought their resources closer to those of the wooded interior of the country. On the other hand, lowering of sea-level, particularly in bays where even a small fall in sea-level would expose a lot of land, would yield new territory for the inhabitants. Initially this would perhaps contain few resources and mean further to go to the sea's edge. As such areas were colonised with broad-leaved shrubs however, they would have probably been a good habitat for deer and aurochs, particularly in winter. A detailed description of the sequence of plant colonisation of a newly uncovered area is given by Tooley (1978a).

## Climate

There is no doubt that the Mesolithic period saw the greatest amplitude of climatic change of all prehistoric periods except the Palaeolithic. From the sub-arctic conditions prevailing at the end of the Devensian or late-glacial oscillations, a rapid amelioration culminated in the postglacial 'optimum' or altithermal regime of the mid-Flandrian. The sources of evidence (discussed in detail in Sawyer *et al.* 1966, Lamb 1966, Lamb *et al.* 1966) point to this general trend: the story told by pollen analysis, macrofossil remains, oxygen isotope analyses of ocean-floor cores and the reconstruction of circulation patterns allows statements of a fair degree of confidence to be made about the climate of Britain at this time, although the data are of necessity rather general.

The changes in temperature experienced during the period are summarised in Fig. 3.3. By 8,000 bc the disappearance of ice from Britain allowed a very rapid amelioration, and the curve for the estimated average air temperatures climbs very rapidly from a yearly below-zero average in 8,000 bc to a period of sustained high temperatures around 12°C soon after 6,000 bc. Summer temperatures of an average of 16.5°C and over were established and persisted into the Neolithic. Thus summer temperatures were higher than the present average of 15.7°C: one of the sources of evidence for this is the occurrence of remains (not closely dated) of the pond tortoise (*Emys orbicularis*) in East Anglia. Its normal range is more southerly and continental and suggests the necessity of summer warmth in order to hatch the eggs in excess of what is now current in the British Isles. In the earlier part of the Mesolithic period, before 6,000 bc, Lamb *et al.* (1966) suggested that summers, although hot, would be short and that the rest of the year would be colder than at present. A generally more anticyclonic climate would bring less windy conditions. After 5,800 bc, the severing of Britain from the continent and its surrounding by the sea ameliorated winter temperatures to a probable level of about 2°C above those of today and increased the length of the spring and autumn seasons. The retreat from these 'altithermal' conditions appears to have come at

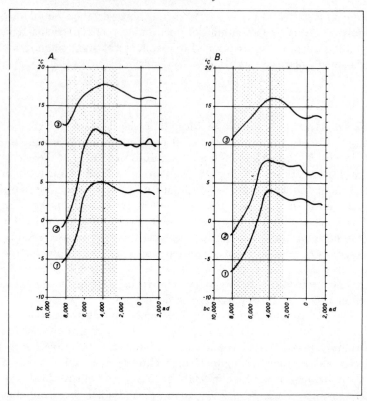

Figure 3.3. Estimated average air temperatures (A) in the Lowland Zone and (B) in The Highland Zone since 12,000 bp. Lapse rates range between 5.6°C and 7.6°C per 1000m., selected by Taylor (1975) as appropriate for 'Boreal' and 'Atlantic' phases. 1. Winter 2. Year 3. Summer.

about 3,400 bc (Frenzel 1966) and temperatures continued to fall for a millenium thereafter.

The division between a rather more 'continental' type of climate before 5,000 bc and a more 'oceanic' type after that date is reflected in estimates of precipitation: Lamb *et al.* (1966) suggest that yearly rainfall in the earlier times was 92-95% of the present averages and that the surplus water to be drained away was 89-94% of the present level: the difference being due to the evapotranspiration of the deciduous forest then accumulating. After 5,000 bc the rainfall increased and Taylor (1975) suggests that in the uplands 111% represents the deviation from current figures for precipitation. These of course are average figures: in the wetter part of the period deviations above the average must have produced times of very heavy run-off in spite of the blanket of forest which by then covered much of the country. More cyclonic conditions would have meant a windier climate especially in the Highland Zone. Early Mesolithic people lived therefore in a period of rapid climatic amelioration followed by a relatively continental period of climate; the late Mesolithic (*sensu* Mellars 1974) populations become identifiable at a period of increasing oceanicity although not until the end of their tenure (if the 3/4th millenium boundary was indeed their terminal date) did temperatures begin to decline. No inference of causality between climatic and cultural change is implied by these statements.

The data for climate during the Mesolithic do not permit many inferences about regional differentiation of regime. For the uplands, however, Taylor (1975) has corrected the data of Lamb *et al.* (1966) at an altitudinal lapse rate of 5.6-7.6°C per 1,000m. He argues that before the insulation of the British Isles climatic changes would have been retarded in the Highland Zone because of the truncation of the Gulf Stream off western Ireland. Altitudinally also, the effects of amelioration would have been slower to manifest themselves and this would have been no less true in the milder winters after the sea-level had cut off the British Isles. Then, west coast littorals must have been extremely mild in winter but are often backed by steeply rising land which would have had sharp lapse rates. The average air temperatures for 500m. in the Highland Zone and in lowland England during the Mesolithic have been estimated by Taylor (1975), and are given in Table 3.1.

Table 3.1. Average air temperatures : Highland Zone and Lowland England (°C).

|  | 6000 bc | 5000 bc | 4000 bc | 3000 bc |
|---|---|---|---|---|
| **Highland Zone (500m)** |  |  |  |  |
| July-August | 14.6 | 15.1 | 15.4 | 15.2 |
| Dec-Jan-Feb | 1.9 | 3.7 | 3.9 | 3.7 |
| **Lowland England** |  |  |  |  |
| July-August | 17.0 | 17.3 | 17.3 | 17.0 |
| Dec-Jan-Feb | 4.2 | 5.0 | 5.0 | 4.9 |

These figures (Taylor 1975) are approximate only: they probably contain errors of dating in the original data as well as in the inferences made from them. Taylor has also applied a calibration curve based on Olsson (1970), which can be ignored for the present discussion.

The most noticeable change in these figures is the rise of Highland Zone winter temperatures after 6,000 bc, presumably connected with the rise in sea-level; otherwise the difference is what would be expected given the assumptions about lapse-rates.

In the Cairngorms, investigations into fossil tree-lines (Pears 1968) have shown that the highest growth of *Pinus* forest was reached during Mesolithic times, probably just before 5,000 bc: then the mature trees reached as high as 2,600 ft. (792m.) and this is presumably indicative of optimal climatic conditions for *Pinus sylvestris*.

The consequences of the climatic conditions of the Mesolithic for tree growth and hence the extension of forests are dealt with later in the chapter. A few other results may also be mentioned. As permafrost declined in area and depth, water tables would have become lower and so in areas of unresistant rock there would have been landslips (Starkel 1966). The lower water tables may have contributed to a dry phase in lakes and ponds. In Flandrian Ic (Zone VIc in the Godwin scheme), evidence for a number of lowered water levels in freshwater impoundments has been found, e.g. at Hockham Mere (Godwin 1975), and in the Lake District, Pennington (1970) shows minerogenic layers in some, though not all, lake deposits. Where lowered lake levels occurred, the vegetation succession seems to have been:

Flandrian Ib : wet period – wet mire surface with willow-birch carr.

Flandrian Ic : dry period – dry mire surface with no willow; increase in pine and heather pollen suggest spread of them onto dry mires.

Flandrian II : wet period – mire surface flooded and lowered with alder carr.

The pollen evidence is paralleled by high-low-high sequence in the iodine content of lake sediments, which is interpreted by Mackereth (1966) as an index of precipitation. The Mesolithic would nevertheless have been a period of shrinkage of ponds and lakes: inorganic sedimentation would have been greatly reduced by the forest cover but organic sedimentation of muds and lake muds from fringing and bottom organisms would have gradually reduced the surface area of water. Streams too would have had progressively lowered silt loads and devoted much of their energy to deepening channels; but a contrary process might well have been the activities of beavers (*Castor fiber*) in damming streams and slowing stream flow as well as increasing the quality of still or slow-flowing water surface. Any forest recession, particularly after 5,000 bc, would have added to the silt burden of the streams and to the likelihood of floods, especially when above-average precipitation occurred.

Given the so-called 'postglacial' optimum of climate, it is not very surprising that the vegetation and animal communities changed very rapidly from their late-glacial condition: hunter-gatherer populations may therefore have been subject to stress from very rapid environmental change in the early Mesolithic but enjoyed a period of relatively static environments from 6,500 bc onwards in which to adjust to the resources of their surroundings.

## Vegetation and soils

In studying the ecology of this period it is imperative that all the important ecological factors which affect vegetation and soils should be taken into account. Man himself has been at times discounted as part of the ecosystems of the Mesolithic period on the assumption that it was not until agriculture was introduced that he had any detectable effect on the environment. This view begs two questions: firstly that the pre-agricultural way of life left the natural environment unaffected, and secondly that Mesolithic man's activities had no component that could come within the meaning of the word agriculture in its broadest sense. Smith (1970a) evaluated the available evidence that neither of these two assumptions can be taken for granted.

The interactions between man and his environment usually affect the vegetation in the first instance, and thereafter the soil. Similarly, these two elements are also those primarily affected by other forms of environmental change such as that of climate. In studies where hard and incontrovertible facts are relatively scarce, it is easy to give undue weight to one aspect or another in interpreting the scanty evidence. So, as an analytical approach and without in any way denying the essential unity of man and the ecosystem, it is helpful to look at a comparable situation where man is not present. This can be done by reference to an interglacial; it is now known that the different interglacials follow parallel trends, though differing in detail (see Chapters 1 and 2), and these trends may be compared with the trends of the Flandrian.

Table 3.2 shows schematically the ecological changes occurring

**Table 3.2. The terminology, soils, vegetation and flora of an interglacial cycle (Iversen 1958).**

|  | | The Interglacial Cycle | | |
| --- | --- | --- | --- | --- |
| *Characteristics* | *Cryocratic* | *Protocratic* | *Mesocratic* | *Telocratic* |
| Climate | Cold | Warm | Thermal maximum | Cooling |
| Soils | immature unstable, base-rich | fixed but transitional | brown earths | podsols and blanket bog |
| Vegetation | open herb and low shrub | park-tundra to light wood | closed deciduous forest | coniferous woodland and acidic heath |
| Floristic elements | arctic and alpine | residual arctic-alpine: steppe and S. European weeds and ruderals | woodland plants and thermophiles | recession of thermophiles |

through an interglacial period. The phases we are concerned with are the protocratic and mesocratic. (Compare with Table 3.3 in which a slightly different terminology is used for England and Wales.) It is immediately apparent that these two phases are strongly contrasting. The protocratic phase is a time of ameliorating climate, particularly reflected in rising temperatures, whilst the mesocratic phase is a period of stability of climate, vegetation and soils. The ecology of Mesolithic man can best be understood if it is appreciated that parallel conditions occurred in Flandrian I and II.

*Protocratic period*

The protocratic period is a period of change. The climate is ameliorating and in response plants are migrating in, though there may be considerable time-lags before they reach their full range (Smith 1965). Generally speaking, woodland is replacing open communities, and it can be expected that the trees themselves will be of increasing stature.

The appearance of tree birches (*Betula*), as opposed to the dwarf birch, is often regarded as the first manifestation of woodland conditions, but it should not be assumed that these tree birches had the stature of birch in this country at present. Where birchwoods still persist in Iceland, the height of the *Betula pubescens* is commonly

**Table 3.3. Terminology and chronology of the Holocene (Flandrian) in England and Wales.**

| Chronozones (Hibbert, Switsur and West 1971) (FIV) | Pollen assemblage zones. (Hibbert, Switsur and West 1971 West 1970) (Post-temperate) | Iversen (1958) (Cryocratic) | Climate | Blytt-Sernander climatic periods | Great Britain (Godwin 1940) | Ireland (Mitchell) |
|---|---|---|---|---|---|---|
| FIIIf | Late-temperate | Telocratic | Decreasing warmth | Sub-Atlantic<br>— 600 bc —<br>Sub-Boreal<br>— 3200 bc — | VIII<br>VIIb | IX<br>VIII |
| FIIe | Early-temperate | Mesocratic | Climatic Optimum | Atlantic<br>— 5500 bc — | VIIa | VII |
| FId<br>c<br>b<br>a | Pre-temperate | Protocratic | Increasing warmth | Boreal<br>— 7500 bc —<br>Pre-Boreal<br>— 8300 bc — | VI<br>V — 7000 bc<br>IV | VI<br>V — 7000 bc<br>IV |
| LDe I-III | | | | | I-III | I-III |

To be used in conjunction with Tables 1.1 and 3.2.

under 4m.; the trees have a shrub-like form and are associated with a rich herb layer. Another hardy early pioneer was the aspen (*Populus tremula*) which persisted throughout the Flandrian. However, details of its history are imperfectly known because its pollen is only picked up by the more sophisticated methods of pollen analysis (Godwin 1975). As tree size increases the light-demanding dwarf shrubs and herbs of small stature will be progressively eliminated. They will survive longest at higher altitudes as the tree-line gradually climbs the contours, and along the coasts. By the Boreal period of the Flandrian (Zones V and VI of the Godwin scheme) the tree cover was continuous at the lower altitudes, as shown by the insignificant representation of non-arboreal pollen in contemporary pollen analyses, with the exception of the type of place discussed on p.104. Simmons (1975b) has discussed the habitats occupied by man in the uplands in Flandrian I; his table (Table 3.4) summarises the evidence, and shows the succession of tree genera which characterised the forests. The lowland forests probably showed much the same sequence; there was apparently less distinction between lowland and upland at these times than is usually seen today. There were, however, differences of sequence in

Table 3.4. The habitats of Flandrian I in Britain.

| | Habitat | | | |
|---|---|---|---|---|
| Biota | leading to<br>Preforest ⟶ Forest | | Wetlands | Coast |
| Vegetation | *Empetrum* heath with tree and shrub thickets (*Pinus, Betula, Salix*) | *Betula-Pinus* followed by *Corylus, Ulmus, Quercus, Alnus, Tilia*, to mixed-oak forest in Flandrian II | Lakes with marginal veg. *Salix* carr.<br><br>Streams with steady regime | Inland penetration of salt-marsh, mudflats with rising sea-level |
| Large fauna | *Bos*<br>*Alces*<br>*Rangifer* | *Bos*<br>*Alces* } diminishing<br>*Rangifer*<br><br>*Cervus elaphus* } increasing<br>*Capreolus cap.*<br>*Sus* | Waterfowl<br>Fish<br><br>Salmonids | Seals<br>Mollusca<br><br>Crustacea |

The transition to forest was metachronous and would have arrived last in the uplands. Indeed, some uplands were probably never forested.

different parts of the country; pine (*Pinus*), for example, featured but little in the Cornish peninsula. The distribution maps for pine, birch and hazel (*Corylus*) published by Godwin (1975) show the regional fluctuations of these trees in Boreal times.

It is tempting to read into these forest successions ecological significance based on present-day relationships which were not necessarily applicable in the protocratic phase. For instance, it has been argued that the dominance of pine in Pollen Zone VI would have been associated with increased acidity and podsolisation of soils all over the country. In fact soils were probably more base-saturated at that time than their modern counterparts, and even today we can find pine growing successfully on calcareous soils (it is a common misconception that it 'likes' only acid soils), without any visually detectable development of an acidic soil profile. It also has to be remembered that the forest communities were probably quite different from those which are familiar today. Not only was pine abundant in Zone VI but so was hazel, and whilst it is difficult to prove they grew together (as they can do in southern Scandinavia today) the likelihood is that they did, in which case the effect of hazel litter would be to counteract the acidifying effect of the pine litter and help to preserve a mull type of humus. Species such as elm (*Ulmus*), lime (*Tilia*), and alder (*Alnus*), arriving late in the protocratic period, are species which favour mull humus and it seems probable that they found suitable soils for their growth except perhaps in Scotland.

It is difficult to obtain direct evidence of soil development during this period, so much of any assessment must be based on indirect evidence. In Table 3.2 the soils are described as fixed but transitional, indicating that the ground was no longer unstable as in the preceding cold phase, thus allowing true soil genesis to take place. In the early part of the protocratic period such a process would be slow, because the low temperatures would restrict both chemical and biological processes, but as the climate warmed up they would accelerate. There are figures for the time it takes for a soil to reach maturity under the present temperate conditions. These range from 1,500 years to 5,000 years or more (Jenny 1941), so proportionately longer times might be applicable to the protocratic phase. However, the duration of Flandrian I is only 2,800 years, so that at the end of this period some soils may still not have reached maturity; this would apply particularly to soils developing at the higher altitudes.

Iversen (1969) has drawn attention to what he terms 'retrogressive succession', i.e. the progressive acidification of soils in a moist temperate climate which can eventually result in such nutrient depletion of soils that it causes changes in the tree species. He has shown that this manifests itself most noticeably and most rapidly on base-poor parent materials, but as has been shown by Andersen (1961) the effect of this is not normally evident until the telocratic (or terminocratic) phase of the interglacial. This concept will be discussed further when considering the mesocratic phase, but it is clearly not a factor of general significance in the protocratic phase. It does, however, raise one point which may be important, which is that some ecosystems are more prone to degradation than others. These have been called fragile ecosystems because they are so easily disrupted. Ecosystems developed on base-poor soils are frequently in this category; others may be susceptible to influences such as drought, fire (or both together), and erosion. It is likely that there were fragile ecosystems even in this early stage of the Flandrian. A case in point may be the high level forest on Dartmoor revealed by Simmons' (1964) pollen analyses.

Such ecosystems tend to be prone to rapid fluctuations after disturbance of any of the major ecological factors, and it has already been seen that the protocratic period is one of change. It is to be expected, therefore, that such instability of vegetation and/or soils will be encountered naturally from time to time, but it is particularly likely to arise when man himself brings about changes in the ecological factors at work (see pp. 102-9 below).

*Mesocratic period*

The mesocratic period of the Flandrian lasted from about 5,500 to 3,200 bc, some 2,300 years. At its end, therefore, the duration of the Flandrian had been almost doubled. This represents a long period of dominance of the landscape by a mixed deciduous forest cover. Trees such as oak (*Quercus*), elm, alder and lime replaced the birches and pine at the end of the Boreal period, whilst the hazel still persisted, though not showing the marked abundance of the middle part of the protocratic period. In addition other species which characterised this forest were holly (*Ilex*), ash (*Fraxinus*) and ivy (*Hedera*). Their appearance in the pollen analyses of this period is a matter of interest because of their ecological significance. Ash is a light-demanding tree, and the fact that it is not represented abundantly (until farming came on the scene) probably confirms that the forest canopy was dense, as indicated by the very low non-arboreal pollen counts at many sites. This does not imply, of course, that the forest was impenetrable at ground level. The consistent occurrence of ivy, holly and hazel also has some significance regarding the state of the canopy; all three are able to survive beneath the canopy without flowering, so that their presence may not be reflected in the pollen analysis. It follows that their appearance in the pollen record implies that they were growing in conditions of good light. In the case of ivy this is probably explicable by the ability of the plant to climb into the canopy, for instance up a dead tree. Holly and hazel are thought of as shrubs, but this may be a misconception of the ecological potentialities of both these species. If allowed to do so both can reach a stature that would enable them to reach the canopy. In Wytham Wood near Oxford, old coppiced hazel which has been allowed to grow up is competing on equal terms with the dominant ash, and in the Staverton nature reserve in East Suffolk holly actually forms the woodland canopy.

The role of alder is also the subject of some speculation. It is often considered that the increase in the representation of alder must mean that the climate had become moister at the end of the Boreal period and that this pertained throughout the Atlantic period. There are other grounds on which we may judge the relative moistness of the climate, but as far as the alder goes, it is not solely a tree of wet soils; it can grow on relatively dry soils and it has been established with success on old well-drained heathland soils. It is possible that its abundance in the Atlantic period merely reflects the fact that in a vast continuous forest the microclimate beneath the canopy would be equable, with humidity constantly high, so enabling the alder to survive without suffering from seasonal water deficits.

No description of the forest of the Mesolithic period can be given that applies to the whole of England, let alone to Scotland and Ireland. Birks *et al.* (1975) have shown by isopollen maps the variation in the distribution of the main tree species over Britain about 5,000 years ago, variations which will reflect differences in ecological tolerances to climate and other factors. Soil differences especially may be expected to complicate the pattern even within any one isopollen area. Thus it has been argued by Morrison (1959) that in Ireland the elm, which is calcicolous, may have ousted sessile oak (*Quercus petraea*) as the dominant on the better soils. However, leaving aside such variations in detail, we can form some impression of what the mesocratic deciduous forest looked like.

At any given time in the mesocratic stage the trees present would have grown up in a forest milieu; they would therefore be tall, with long straight boles, the crowns forming a continuous high-level canopy. The associated shrub and ground vegetation would therefore be shade-tolerant and relatively sparse, so that movement through the forests would not be difficult. The biomass of the larger herbivores in this type of forest is not exceptionally high (Butzer 1972; Simmons 1975b), being restricted by the available fodder. The amount of light reaching the forest floor would have been a key factor. There are two phases of this type of ecosystem in which the limiting effect of shade is broken, namely in the annual vernal period, and in the regeneration phase. The so-called vernal aspect of deciduous woods is characterised by a vigorous growth of light-demanding perennial species, many of them herbs or rhizome geophytes which grow and flower early and have virtually completed their annual cycle by the time the canopy has reached full density. Examples of such plants are the bluebell (*Endymion non-scriptus*) and the wood anemone (*Anenome nemorosa*), but few of them seem to be of value as food either for man or the herbivores. The same is true of the regeneration phase. The death of a large dominant tree, or a gap created by lightning or windthrow, will allow the development of a rich shrub and herbaceous flora, as well as the establishment of the pioneer species (e.g. birch, ash) which will initiate a succession which will eventually close the gap. Not only is there more forage available for animals, but fruit and nut plants (e.g. currants (*Ribes*), brambles (*Rubus fruticosus*) and hazel), will flower and fruit. The few climbing plants of deciduous forests – ivy, honeysuckle (*Lonicera*) – will also take advantage of such temporarily improved light conditions, and may be carried to the canopy as the gap is closed.

By analogy with what we know of the ecology of the dominant trees in this mesocratic period, it would be expected that the soils of this period would be characterised by mull humus, normally associated with brown forest soils, or possibly *sols lessivés*, or the parent materials of poorer base status. Direct confirmation of this is difficult to obtain, but there are a few pointers. Havinga (1963), working on the pollen distribution in Dutch soils of this period, has shown that they are 'homogenised', that is, that the pollen was mixed throughout the humus layer, implying that soil faunal mixing was taking place, earthworms presumably being the predominant agents. Other indications of the presence of unpodsolised soils, whose modern descendants are strongly acid and have more humus, are reported by Romans and Robertson (1975), Dimbleby and Bradley (1975) and Proudfoot (1958a). In all these cases podsolisation has apparently occurred after the use of the land by prehistoric man. The changes which man brings about by forest clearance and land use have been discussed by Dimbleby (1962, 1976, 1978) and by Limbrey (1975) and need not be elaborated on here. It does not follow from this that all podsol profiles are secondary: there is clear evidence from countries such as Scandinavia and North America that on base-poor parent materials, temperate deciduous forest may be associated with a forest podsol. That this could apply in Britain in the Atlantic period is shown by the observations of Valentine (1973), who demonstrated that beneath fen peat, formed as the sea transgressed the low-lying land of Lincolnshire, there was a freely-draining iron-humus podsol, and he proved by pollen analysis that it had been associated with a mixed oak forest of Atlantic age.

Once again there is a reminder of the fact that even under the same general type of forest cover, differences in soil profile development can occur; in many cases it seems that the deciduous forest/brown earth complex was stable and persisted with little apparent change to the end of the mesocratic period; but under certain conditions, such as low base status, translocation of bases and sesquioxides could lead to the development of *sol lessivé* or podsol profiles. The stability of these compared with the brown soil is a matter which cannot be pursued here, but the possibility should be borne in mind that soils of this type are more susceptible to disturbances: i.e. they are part of a more fragile ecosystem.

Here, too, reference must be made to Iversen's (1969) concept of retrogressive succession; the longer the time scale, the greater will be the potential effect of leaching, and it is to be expected that detectable effects will show up first in soils of low base status, as he has in fact demonstrated. It has been shown by Rost (cited in Jenny 1941) that deciduous forest brings about decalcification and the translocation of sesquioxides considerably more rapidly than does a prairie vegetation. Clearly the deciduous forest is depleting the upper layers of the soil, and for an equilibrium to be achieved this has to be offset. This will normally be achieved through the action of deep roots bringing nutrients to the surface, but in a nutrient-poor medium leaching may exceed replacement. We are as yet ignorant of the nature of any balance which could be reached under such conditions, but it seems apparent that a podsol profile of some sort would develop. As is shown below, even within the mesocratic period, podsols of anthropogenic origin can develop on base poor soils that once had mull humus, but to put matters in perspective it should be pointed out here that not all podsols are of equal biological activity or nutrient potential. The acidity of forest podsols may be less by as much as a whole pH unit, and the rate of biological turnover much more rapid than in a man-made heathland podsol whose profile exhibited a similar appearance.

## The influence of Mesolithic man

Having outlined the broad trends of the development of plant-soil ecosystems through the protocratic and mesocratic phases of an interglacial we can now consider the Flandrian specifically from the point of view that in this particular interglacial human societies of Mesolithic culture were active through these two ecological phases. It is necessary, in order to do this, to consider how the capabilities and objectives of Mesolithic man exerted an ecological influence. This essay is not primarily concerned with the effect of the environment on the way of life of these people, though clearly the resources of the various environments determined where and how they lived. For instance it is now postulated that both in earlier and later Mesolithic times in northern England there was a seasonal transhumance with winter settlements in the lowlands (perhaps in places now beneath the sea) and summer quarters in the uplands of the Pennines or the North York Moors. The potential ecological impact of such people is accentuated, for the same bands are operating in two habitats differing in character and in spatial distribution.

The life style of the Mesolithic people was based on the exploitation of the native fauna, combined with some utilisation of the native vegetation (Clarke 1976). Testimony of the former comes from bone remains where preservation is adequate, and is inferred from the hunting tools possessed by these people; evidence of the use of the vegetation is even more indirect, since the plant remains are only preserved on sites that are waterlogged and therefore may only be typical of one phase of occupation, though the development of the tranchet axe, apparently a wood-cutting implement, suggests an increasing concern with felling in environments which had become closed forest. The existence of a proportion of open forest, or even of unwooded land, would have been of direct concern to people dependent on animals, particularly herbivores, and comparison with modern people following this type of existence shows that they do not merely accept the environment they find, but they try to mould it into a more favourable one for the animals on which they depend (Mellars 1975). It is important to stress that Mesolithic people had the equipment necessary to do this; especially they had the use of fire and it would be naive to imagine that fires would be started on a haphazard basis. It has been shown that after a burning the grazing and browsing potential of forest land is greatly increased and numbers of herbivores respond accordingly. This has been recently discussed in the context of the British Mesolithic by Simmons (1975b) and by Jacobi *et al.* (1976). It may be assumed that Mesolithic man would have observed the correlation between burning and the greater quantity and accessibility of his chosen animals; it may even be that the animals he selected were those which responded most to the use of fire. Jacobi *et al.* (1976) suggest that a strategy of regular burning, perhaps one tenth of a given area of range per season, would give the maximum advantages, bearing in mind that a degree of cover, as well as a supply of food, is part of the ecological requirement of most of the herbivores.

Such considerations take the use of fire by Mesolithic man out of the category of casual interference into that of the strategic use of fire as part of their way of life, and it helps to explain the apparent anomaly between the small numbers of people operating at any one time and the extensive influence which increasingly appears to have taken place. It also accords with the observations made in profiles covering this period that throughout the deposits charcoal fragments are found; Durno and McVean (1959), for example, suggest that at Beinn Eighe in north-west Scotland successive fires had led to progressive deforestation within the Boreal period: 'A Mesolithic presence in this area has not yet been established, perhaps because sites have not yet emerged by erosion of the blanket peat, as has happened elsewhere. It is significant that evidence of fire occurred during a period of supposed wetness in a strongly oceanic climate.' Smith (1970a) has discussed the view that the dominance of hazel in the Boreal period can itself be seen as the result of repeated burning; being a plant which coppices freely, hazel is not destroyed by fire (unless an intense ground fire develops) and so is able to sprout quickly and achieve the dominance that the pollen profiles show.

This Boreal preponderance of hazel pollen is without parallel in the protocratic phase of any of the previous interglacials.

The prevalence of open conditions is reflected in pollen analyses by the presence of light-demanding ruderals, such as ribwort plantain (*Plantago lanceolata*) and sorrel (*Rumex*), and grasses, plants that in later periods are associated with farming; they became far less common through the later part of the Boreal and into the Atlantic period. Therefore when they did occur they did so against the trend to increased forest cover, and moreover they seemed to represent short episodes that were quite quickly swallowed up in forest regrowth. This pattern certainly bears the mark of human disturbance. Another light-demanding plant which may respond to changes in the forest cover is heather (*Calluna*), and Radley *et al.* (1974) have shown that in the Southern Pennines an increase in the amount of heather pollen at the soil/peat junction is correlated with Mesolithic occupation; sites with no evidence of occupation do not show such a response in the heather curve. (It should not be assumed, however, that there was no human influence in places where no artifacts were found). Indeed if at the same time hazel is to be seen as a species which responded to human influence, the marks of man's influence may be stronger than generally believed. These changes could be primarily the result of fire; it is difficult to find any botanical evidence for this period to demonstrate the strength of grazing as an ecological factor. There is one finding, however, which may be connected with the actual feeding habits of the animals: the repeated occurrence of large concentrations of pollen of ivy, a low pollen producer, in archaeological sites of Mesolithic age (Simmons and Dimbleby 1974). There seems to be no natural explanation for such concentrations of ivy pollen, and the fact that they only occur on occupied sites lends support to the view that they are associated with human activity. The most likely explanation is that they arise from the feeding of ivy as a winter fodder to herbivores; it is an evergreen plant readily taken, especially by red deer, and since it flowers in the late autumn collection at this time would concentrate pollen where the material was stored or consumed. Troels-Smith (1960a) has given a similar explanation for concentrations of ivy pollen in Neolithic levels in Denmark and Switzerland and points out that it has been valued as fodder in historical times.

Such an argument supports a growing body of opinion that Mesolithic men in Britain were not just hunting the herbivore populations, but were sometimes exploiting them more intensively in what was perhaps some sort of husbandry, though this probably fell short of domestication. In France, Roux and Leroi-Gourhan (1965) have even suggested that in the late Mesolithic, animals such as domesticated sheep and cattle were being exploited and that forest clearances were made for their benefit. Clearly the view that Mesolithic man was merely another forest-dwelling species, having little effect on the ecosystem, is open to serious question. It is remarkable, nevertheless, that more direct evidence of any impact of husbanded herbivores is not found in the pollen record. Why, for instance, is there so little evidence, even on a local scale, of an elm decline in the Atlantic period? Elm is a very acceptable fodder tree to most browsing herbivores.

From what has been said it is apparent that Mesolithic man had both reason for and means of modifying his environment, and apart from such deliberate manipulation there would also be inadvertent impacts such as accidental or uncontrolled fires. The pollen evidence of clearances within the period (e.g. Simmons 1964, 1969b) shows that such influences were indeed exerted. We now have to consider whether these effects were more than simply ephemeral.

Jacobi *et al.* (1976), in their study of the Mesolithic occupation of the Southern Pennines, have shown that there was a concentration of sites in an altitudinal belt from 350m. to 500m. and that, at least in the late Mesolithic, this coincided with a reduction of forest cover, apparently through the use of fire. The presence of tree-stumps at higher altitudes shows that tree growth was indeed possible above this belt, but that the forest was replaced by hazel scrub or herbaceous communities. They even suggest that as Mesolithic pressures had probably operated throughout the whole of the protocratic period, the establishment of forest at higher levels as the colder climates ameliorated may have been prevented. There might be an explanation here of the fact that authorities differ about the height of the tree line in Britain in prehistoric times; climatologically there seems to be no reason why forest should not have reached up to 900m. in the Atlantic period (Dimbleby 1975), but over much of our uplands it does not seem to have occurred continuously above 600m. The importance of the forest margin for winter grazing and browsing for wild herbivores may contribute to pressure on the woody vegetation in this zone. With the extreme paucity of evergreen woody species in our flora (the value of ivy has already been mentioned) the plants which are likely to be sought are the smaller trees and bushes from which the bark can be stripped, and this will be more accessible at the forest margin than in the high forest itself. This type of browsing is soon lethal to the plants and could lead to rapid recession of the woodland. Further studies of the height of the tree-line in relation to the evidence of Mesolithic occupation are needed to test this hypothesis.

If forest was prevented from colonising these uplands, or was destroyed through Mesolithic activity, it may be asked why tree cover did not extend once the Mesolithic period ended, but Tallis (1975) points out that at these higher altitudes there was no break in use between Mesolithic and Neolithic times. Commonly, however, secondary soil deterioration took place in those environments with somewhat rigorous microclimatic conditions, especially at high altitudes. Acidification of the soil, the onset of blanket peat formation and the establishment of heathland or moorland, which had a high inherent risk of fire, produced conditions which discouraged tree growth and even brought about further recession of the forest.

## Site deterioration in the Mesolithic

The impact of Mesolithic man was on the dominant vegetation type at the local scale; this may amount to no more than the favouring of certain woody species (e.g. hazel) at the expense of others, or it may involve the replacement of the woody dominants by suffruticose chamaephytes or herbaceous species. These conditions may in fact succeed each other where anthropogenic pressure is maintained.

A change of this type involves some alteration in the soil/vegetation relationship, especially where trees give way to non-woody vegetation. The replacement of deep-rooting by more shallow-rooting dominants will initiate a trend towards soil acidification (Dimbleby 1962, 1975, 1976), and the effect of this tendency will be most marked in base-poor parent materials or where the local climate favours leaching as in high rainfall areas, like the uplands. Simmons (1969c) has estimated that $\frac{5}{8}$ of the land surface of England and Wales might potentially have been subject to such trends. Direct evidence of the appearance of soils of Mesolithic age is difficult to come by because at that time there was no construction of earthworks which could preserve such soils. Land surfaces of Mesolithic age are preserved beneath peat deposits (e.g. Cook's Study: Dimbleby 1969) or blown sand (e.g. Oakhanger: Rankine *et al.* 1960) but these surfaces are not absolutely protected from later pedogenic influences which may have modified the profile. It is therefore necessary to rely on indirect evidence, with the potential danger of circular argument. At Iping (Dimbleby 1965), for instance, pollen analyses show a dramatic change from hazel woodland to Callunetum, and it is to be expected that such a change would lead to the replacement of mull by mor humus and consequent acidification of the soil.

Acidification of a soil is not in itself damaging, unless it continues to the extreme. What is more significant ecologically is the change which may take place in the soil ecosystem; this may be accentuated by the operations that man himself carries out. The critical part of the soil ecosystem in this respect is the active soil surface. Here organic litter is being converted into a humus which is largely responsible for the soil structure. Mull humus, the result of active faunal and microbiological processes, produces a good crumb structure, but if this type of humus is replaced by a moder or mor type there is less incorporation of the organic matter with the mineral soil and a less stable structure results. If, additionally, the soil is burnt, exposed so that the humus is oxidised away, or trampled on, the structure is still further damaged.

Damaged soil structure may be the key to several forms of site deterioration which can be severe and permanent in some cases. The breakdown of soil structure today is commonly the precursor of erosion of one sort or another, and this appears to have been the case in the Mesolithic too. Simmons and Cundill (1974b) and Simmons *et al.* (1975) have demonstrated the occurrence of inwash stripes of mineral matter in accumulating peat of Mesolithic age; the responsibility of man for the movement of mineral soil into wet basin sites has not been critically examined and may be commoner than is generally believed. On light sandy soils in the drier lowlands Mesolithic levels are commonly covered by blown sand (as at Oakhanger and Iping, see above), and it is difficult to resist the conclusion that soil structure had been destroyed (probably by fire in these cases) allowing wind erosion to take place.

One of the most dramatic and most extensive environmental changes in this connection is the development of ombrogenous or blanket peat. The very word 'ombrogenous' in a sense begs the question, implying as it does that the determining factor in the development of such peat is the wetness of the climate. Clearly peat will only form in a wet climate, but there are many places in temperate latitudes with a heavier rainfall than that of upland

Britain but which do not carry peat; a good example is the coniferous rainforest of the Olympic Peninsula in Washington State (U.S.A.), which has a rainfall of 120-140in. (3,060-3,555mm.) per annum; the forest soil shows only incipient podsolisation and no sign of peat formation. The Great Smoky Mountains in the Appalachians have a temperature and rainfall regime not dissimilar to that of Britain and continuous forest persists at over 1,500m. altitude. Granted that such parallels cannot be close, the fact remains that the contrast between these regions and the British uplands is immense, seemingly beyond explanation merely on the grounds of climatic influence upon the vegetation. Does the difference lie in that much under-valued ecological factor, man himself?

There are two ways in which Mesolithic man could have influenced the onset of peat formation. The first has already been mentioned: the prevention by fire of the colonisation of higher land by trees. Jacobi *et al.* (1976) suggest that treelessness thus induced on flat uplands could have preceded the onset of blanket bog formation, though this may have been the culmination of a long period of human pressure on the land; the transpiration of a forest would be more effective at removing excess water than would herbaceous vegetation. Secondly we may note that Moore (1973, 1974) and Simmons and Cundill (1974a) have found that pollen of ruderal species usually associated with man's presence regularly occurs in small percentages at the base of blanket peat. Moore has linked this particularly to clearance by fire for the purpose of stock-grazing, and whilst his earliest records of human influence are Neolithic, the operations which are involved could have been carried out by Mesolithic man. E.E. Evans (1975) has pointed out that the surfaces of heavily grazed out-fields in Ireland become fibrous and compacted, leading to waterlogging, whilst Soulsby (1976) has evidence that peat formation in West Scotland was consequent upon soil deterioration under podsol-forming vegetation.

It is sometimes postulated that one stage in such a sequence may be that the soil first becomes podsolised, producing an impermeable iron-pan which then causes waterlogging. Certainly such pans can be virtually impermeable but whether they cause waterlogging or not depends upon the sub-surface configuration of the pan. Similarly, blanket peat is commonly found overlying soils which have no iron-pan development. Attention should therefore be concentrated on the state of the soil surface itself (Crompton 1952).

Proudfoot (1958) has observed that a sub-peat soil may be quite dry even when water is running out of the peat itself.

If climate were the prime factor in causing blanket bog to form, one would expect the basal layers to be datable to the transition from Boreal to Atlantic periods or to Atlantic time itself. Whilst this is true in some cases, it is not universally so, and in a number of cases they are attributable to the supposedly drier Sub-Boreal. In fact, as Radley *et al.* (1974) point out, on flat ground peat formation has started at any time from the Boreal-Atlantic transition, even as late as early medieval times. A human influence certainly seems to be involved in the early farming periods, and from what has been seen of the activities of Mesolithic man, it is apparent that he also had the propensity to exert similar ecological pressure which would have been crucial in particular circumstances.

**Fragile ecosystems**

This brings the discussion back to the question of fragile ecosystems. It was mentioned earlier that Mesolithic people apparently made seasonal migrations and so exploited a variety of habitats. We have discussed already the possible environmental interactions of these people at and above the tree-line; here the ecosystems are in tension (i.e. it is an ecotonal zone) so that a small influence is likely to have a major effect on the dominant plant species. This in turn may bring about soil changes, some irreversible. Such environments are in a somewhat precarious state, liable to be modified by small but persistent human influences: they are, to a greater or lesser extent, fragile ecosystems. The lowland forests, whether of the protocratic period or of the mesocratic, would be much less susceptible to change on a large scale. This is well illustrated by the pollen analyses of a late Mesolithic site at Addington (Dimbleby 1963); although this site was clearly occupied there was no detectable disturbance of the pollen spectrum that could be attributed to this occupation. On the other hand, the site of Iping (see above) is a lowland site in which Maglemosian people wrought a change from hazel woodland to heathland. The impact at the two sites may have differed, but the fact remains that a dramatic change took place at Iping; furthermore, it appears that forest conditions were not re-established even during the Atlantic period. Here there was an environment rendered fragile by the poverty and instability of its soil. It may be that the early impact of man on this site prevented the soil/vegetation complex building up the ecological stability apparent at the late Atlantic site of Addington, since both sites were on the Folkestone Sands.

In looking for the effects of Mesolithic man on the landscape, it is essential to consider the environment in space and time. The fragility of ecosystems may change with time, for ecological stability may develop, so that any later impact may have only a minor effect. On the other hand, trends such as retrogressive succession, especially if helped along by prolonged human influence, may lead to progressively greater fragility and susceptibility to rapid change. We are far from being able to forecast; the necessary evidence for more precise statements is far from complete: what is needed is many more observations of man-environment relationships in the Mesolithic period.

## Fauna

*Introduction*

In the early postglacial period Britain received what was to be the bulk of its present-day animal species. Britain was then a north-western extension of continental Europe and its late-glacial fauna was replaced by a wide spectrum of European forest animals. Some of the late-glacial animals survived, and still remain today as relicts in Ireland and Scotland and in the mountains of England and Wales. Ireland did not have this postglacial invasion as it had been cut off from Britain by the flooding of the Irish Sea and only received its animals by *ad hoc* means and so had and still has had a very impoverished fauna. Several hundred years later the British mainland suffered the same fate and was finally cut off from Europe. Consequently, its terrestrial and fresh water fauna are a little more sparse than that of other countries of north-western Europe, lacking, for example, the beech marten (*Martes foina* Erxleben), two species of white toothed shrew (both present in the Channel Islands and one on the Isles of Scilly) and several species of vole, including the common vole (*Microtus arvalis* Pallas), which is supposed to have been introduced into Orkney (Berry and Rose 1975), and which was identified in the Neolithic chambered tomb of Midhowe by Platt (1934).

Although most of the fauna arrived in a natural postglacial colonisation sequence before the flooding of the North Sea and the

Channel, some species arrived later, intentionally or accidentally introduced by man. Most of the Mesolithic animals survived in abundance for the entire prehistoric period (except for the elk and the aurochs), but many of them have died out in Britain since then, including the brown bear, the wolf, the beaver and the great auk; and others, which previously were widespread, are now rare and restricted in range. The evidence for the vertebrate fauna present in Britain during the Mesolithic and for its changes in response to environmental conditions is rather rough and ready. Most of it comes from the remains of animals found on archaeological sites and has, therefore, been 'culturally sieved', so caution has to be used in its interpretation. For example, wolf bones occur very sparsely on archaeological sites, and yet their wide distribution in time and space suggests that wolves were important members of the fauna. This also means that most faunal evidence comes only from the areas colonised by man and, of course, only from areas where site conditions are suitable for the preservation of bone, hence the almost total lack of knowledge of the fauna of the highland regions in Mesolithic times (E.E. Evans 1975).

There are, as far as can be ascertained, very few natural deposits in caves or fissures from which Mesolithic bones have been excavated. Practically the only evidence that is unassociated with man comes from isolated finds in peat – often of whole skeletons, but occasionally of horn alone (which can be preserved in acid bogs). Some of the more recent finds have been dated by stratigraphy, pollen analysis or radiocarbon dating; many others, particularly in Scotland, are of unknown date. Sometimes the presence or absence of an animal can be inferred from what is known about its general distribution in prehistoric or modern times. The absence of well stratified natural deposits of animal bones in the Mesolithic makes it impossible to reconstruct typical vertebrate faunas for its finer chronological divisions. On the other hand, as Mesolithic man was so dependent on his natural habitat the samples that he extracted for us do give a much more complete picture of the fauna of the period than can be obtained for any subsequent prehistoric period.

## Faunal changes in response to natural conditions

*Relict faunas from the late glacial*

In order to understand the significance of the postglacial fauna in the lives of the Mesolithic inhabitants of Britain and Ireland it is necessary to know something of the late-glacial fauna that it replaced. The fauna that arrived with the postglacial forests colonised a region of open country that was probably park tundra in southern Britain. This mid-latitude tundra had a large potential carrying capacity for herbivores and probably supported herds of reindeer and horse; aurochs, red deer and elk may have been present in the extreme south, though there is no osteological evidence for this, but in numbers of species the fauna of the Younger Dryas was very impoverished, lacking the bison, woolly rhinoceros, cave bear, cave lion, hyaena and giant deer (*Megaloceros*) of the earlier late glacial. For how long the tundra flora and fauna survived is unclear. Reindeer antler from Anston Cave in Derbyshire has been dated to 9,750 ± 110 bp, but this Pre-Boreal date has been questioned as the deposit was overlaid by sediments of the late-glacial type (Mellars 1974). A Pre-Boreal date gains credence, however, when the date from the reindeer antler in Gough's Cave of 9,920 ± 130 bp (Tratman, Switsur and Jacobi forthcoming) is considered. Many writers on the history of the British fauna state that there is evidence that reindeer survived late into the postglacial (for example, Butzer 1972). This opinion seems to be based on J. Ritchie's *The Influence of Man on Animal Life in Scotland* (1920). Ritchie's claim for reindeer survival comes from a few nineteenth-century finds of reindeer antlers in brochs (Smith 1869) which could well have been derived from earlier deposits. Ritchie also describes reindeer, lynx and other arctic animals found in the cave of Creag-nan-Uanb, Inchnadamph, Sutherland, but the Neolithic date suggested for the deposits is not reliably established.

In theory, Ireland and the other islands off the coast of England, Wales and Scotland received the bulk of their terrestrial fauna up to the time at which their connections with the mainland were at last severed by the rising sea-level, so their native animals should give us a picture of the fauna of the British Isles as a whole at that time. However, the distribution of animals can be such an erratic process that the presence of any particular species may not be significant: aquatic animals can often swim in salt as well as fresh water, terrestrial animals can usually swim, small mammals can be carried on floating wood, and, of course, animals can be moved across water intentionally or accidentally by man. Absence of particular species is, therefore, more telling when dealing with modern distributions. Louise Wijngaarden-Bakker (1974) in her admirable summary of

Irish mammalian history wrote, 'the absence of voles coupled with that of a number of palaeo-arctic woodland mammals (mole, weasel, roe deer) suggests that Ireland was not populated through the normal postglacial colonisation sequence'. The known absence of elk and aurochs and of some amphibians, snakes, and some other reptiles, as well as of the animals noted by Wijngaarden-Bakker, shows us that the last land bridge to Ireland must have been flooded in the earliest postglacial, certainly before the forest fauna reached the British side of the land bridge. Elk, aurochs and red deer are known to have been well established in England in the Pre-Boreal.

At the time of the last readvance of the Scottish ice, southern Britain and southern Ireland probably supported a limited mammalian fauna of which some members survived into the post-glacial in both areas (see Table 3.5). The formation of different subspecies in Ireland of stoat (*Mustela erminea hibernica* Thomas and Barrett-Hamilton), otter (*Lutra lutra roensis* Ogilby) and blue hare (*Lepus timidus hibernicus* Bell) (Dadd 1970) attest to their ancient isolation in Ireland and the widespread distribution of the pygmy shrew, and, less certainly, of the common fox, wolf, brown bear and common frog (*Rana temporaria* L), suggests that these species may have been in both Britain and Ireland for a very long time.

The other indigenous mammals of Ireland – that is those known to have been there in the early postglacial – might also have survived from the late glacial, but it seems more likely that most of them would not have lived through the cold conditions of the maximum readvance of the Younger Dryas ice, and that new populations of these animals (badger, polecat, red deer and pig) arrived in Britain in the early postglacial, and colonised Ireland at various subsequent times by one or more of the ways listed above. A few pig and red deer bones have now been identified from the earliest known Irish Mesolithic site (Mount Sandel Upper, 8,725 ± 115 bp (6,775 bc) ), and the economic emphasis of the site was definitely on fishing, with some fowling and hunting of the Irish blue hare, so red deer and pig were probably rare (Woodman 1978). To return to mainland Britain, the stoat, otter, blue hare, pygmy shrew, common fox and brown bear were probably late-glacial relics that flourished in the new conditions of the postglacial. The root vole (*Microtus oeconomicus* Pallas) which is now extinct in the British Isles, survived into the Mesolithic: the youngest reliable finds are from Dowel Cave and the Lea valley (Sutcliffe and Kowalski 1976). Among the birds the ptarmigan (*Lagopus mutus*) and capercailzie

Table 3.5. Terrestrial mammals of Ireland and Britain in the early postglacial.

| | Probable relict forms surviving from the late glacial | |
|---|---|---|
| | wolf *Canis lupus* L.†<br>otter *Lutra lutra* L.<br>brown bear *Ursus arctos* L.†<br>stoat *Mustela erminea* L.†<br>fox *Vulpes vulpes* L. (?later introduction) | ?horse *Equus* sp.†<br>pygmy shrew *Sorex minutus* L.<br>root vole *Microtus oeconomicus* Pallas†<br>blue hare *Lepus timidus* L.<br>reindeer *Rangifer tarandus* L.† |
| *Woodland species which arrived in Britain in the early postglacial* | | Present in Britain and absent from Ireland (some introduced into Ireland later) |
| | weasel *Mustela nivalis* L.<br>polecat *Putorius putorius* L. (polecat, or stoat, or weasel, as *Mustela* sp. present in Mesolithic)<br>? horse *Equus* sp.<br>roe deer *Capreolus capreolus* L.<br>aurochs *Bos primigenius* L.†<br>elk *Alces alces* L.†<br>common shrew *Sorex araneus* L.<br>water shrew *Neomys fodiens* Pennant<br>mole *Talpa europea* L.<br>hedgehog *Erinaceus europaeus* L.<br>wood mouse *Apodemus sylvaticus* L. (the only mouse known to have been present in Mesolithic, ?present in Irish cave sites) | yellow-necked field mouse *A. flavicollis* Melchior<br>red squirrel *Sciurus vulgaris* L. (?later introduction)<br>beaver *Castor fiber* L.†<br>brown hare *Lepus capensis* L.<br>voles. All voles were until recently absent from Ireland, and some may have been late arrivals in Britain.<br>water vole *Arvicola terrestris* L.<br>field vole *Microtus agrestis* L.<br>bank vole *Clethrionomys glareolus* Schreber: all are known early postglacial arrivals in Britain. |
| Present in Britain, and probably introduced into Ireland in early postglacial | | |
| badger *Meles meles* L.<br>pine marten *Martes martes* L.<br>wild cat *Felis silvestris* L. *<br>red deer *Cervus elaphus* L.<br>wild boar *Sus scrofa* L. | | |

(*Tetrao urogalus*) are glacial relicts in Scotland, and so, in western and northern Britain, is the red grouse (*Lagopus scoticus*), of which a slightly different form survives in Ireland, and which was probably present in the Mesolithic levels of Dowel Cave (Bramwell 1960).

## The postglacial colonisation from north-western Europe

The succession of the postglacial faunal colonisation of Britain is not known in detail. However the aurochs, elk, red deer, roe deer, beaver, pine marten, badger, hedgehog, mole, common shrew, the water vole (*Arvicola terrestris* L.), and possibly a woodland horse (*Equus* sp.) were quickly added to the surviving late-glacial animals; these postglacial arrivals are found at the early Mesolithic sites at Thatcham (King 1962a) and most of these animals, as well as the brown hare, were also present at Star Carr (Fraser and King 1954) at the end of the Pre-Boreal. Three rodents, *Apodemus sylvaticus* (woodmouse), *Clethrionomys glareolus* (bank vole) and *Microtus agrestis* (field vole) probably arrived during the Boreal period, and the yellow-necked mouse (*Apodemus flavicollis*) is known from Etche's Cave in Derbyshire in early postglacial levels (Sutcliffe and Kowalski 1976).

Because most of the sites from which faunal remains have been recovered are at lakesides, most of the birds found are marsh species; they include the crane (*Megalornis grus*) which is still an occasional vagrant to the British Isles, but which would have been a summer visitor in the Mesolithic. A probable identification of the white stork (*Ciconia ciconia*) which would also have been a summer visitor has been made. Many species of duck were here, including the golden-eye (*Bucephala clangula*) which is now a winter resident, but probably bred here in former times, and also grebes, divers, mergansers and lapwings. The buzzard (*Buteo buteo*) is recorded, as well as the barn owl (*Tyto alba*) and stockdove in Dowel Cave (Bramwell 1960). Most of the common woodland birds would

---

Table 3.5
Animals in bold type are known from the Mesolithic; others in light type are probable in the Mesolithic.
† Extinct in Britain and Ireland
* Extinct in Ireland
Irish information from Wijngaarden-Bakker (1974) and Woodman (1978). British information from Star Carr (Fraser and King 1954), Thatcham (King 1962a), King Arthur's Cave (Taylor 1927; Mellars 1974), Gough's Cave (Tratman *et al.* forthcoming) and MacArthur's Cave (Turner 1895). Most information on rodents from Sutcliffe and Kowalski (1976). Nomenclature from Brink (1973).

have been present, with sea birds on what are now the northern and western coasts. Primary fresh-water fish (that is those that do not migrate into the sea), for example pike (*Esox lucius* L.) and perch (*Perca fluviatalis* L.) would have been confined to those rivers draining into the northward extension of the great European river system: that is those meeting the sea on the southern half of the present east coast of Britain (Wheeler 1977). Salmonids and eels, which have a marine phase in their life histories, were probably present in rivers all over the country. The fauna was rich, varied and plentiful.

*Changes in animal species and numbers in the later Mesolithic*

Not surprisingly there seems to have been very little change in the vertebrate fauna of the Mesolithic period once Britain had been isolated from the continent, except for the apparent extinction of the elk which seems to have died out at around the end of the Boreal. Its habitat is marshy woodland, with much undergrowth, usually with birch trees and with pine bark available as a winter food. The drier climate of the late Boreal probably encouraged denser woodland and reduced the areas of open glades as well as the areas of marshes and lakes; the closed Atlantic deciduous forest, even though it came with wetter conditions, was probably equally unsuitable. As discussed below, the extinction of the elk may have been hastened by human activity.

Various attempts have been made to calculate the potential carrying capacity in terms of numbers or weights of ungulates and of other animals per given area of land in different types of habitat (particularly woodland), and to extrapolate the results backwards in time to the Mesolithic period (e.g. Mellars 1975; Simmons 1975a). This is probably impossible to quantify accurately, largely because the exact modern equivalents of the ancient Boreal and Atlantic forest of Britain no longer exist, because some of the Mesolithic species are extinct, and because human interference in modern habitats is rampant. However, it is clear that the carrying capacity of closed, Boreal, pine forests is much less than that of more open deciduous, or mixed deciduous woodland, and the same would probably have been true of the late Boreal pine forest of this country. The advent of such coniferous forests may have been enough to finish off the elk, but what effects it had on roe deer, red deer and aurochs are unknown. The closed deciduous forests of the Atlantic period may have been similarly inimical, but the aurochs at least were certainly very common at that time, as the many finds of skulls and skeletons dated to that period attest (Grigson 1978). The mammals identified for the first time in sites of the Atlantic period: the otter from MacArthur's Cave, Oban (Turner 1895) and the brown bear from King Arthur's Cave, Hereford (Taylor 1927; Mellars 1974) were certainly here in the earlier periods as well.

The birds identified from the late Mesolithic coastal sites in Scotland (Mellars, personal communication; Lacaille 1954) are obviously mostly seabirds. They include the great northern diver (*Gavia arctica*), no longer found in this country and probably a winter visitor during the Mesolithic, and the great auk (*Pinguinus impennis*, Plate 1), now extinct. Birds of open country and of woodland were also found.

The increased temperature of the sea water in the Atlantic period is attested by the presence in the estuarine clays and raised beaches of north-eastern Ireland of various species of molluscs which at the present time are found on more southerly and western shores of Ireland and England (Praeger 1888, 1896); all are, and were, uncommon and would have been of no economic importance. Similarly, Scharff (1907) notes that the range of the pond tortoise *Emys orbicularis* used to extend into Britain as its remains have been found in lake muds in East Anglia. He does not quote any dating evidence, but they probably come from about the time of the climatic optimum as shown for tortoise remains in Denmark by Degerbøl and Krog (1951).

Grey seals (*Halichoerus grypus* Fabricius), common seals (*Phoca vitulina* L.), rorqual (*Balaenoptera* sp.) and dolphin (*Delphinus* sp.) are known from the Scottish midden sites together with a variety of modern fish species. All the birds, shellfish and fish found on the east coast site of Morton Tayport B (Coles *et al.* 1971) are still present in the neighbourhood (see below) with the exception of the sturgeon (*Acipenser* sp.) which is only rarely found in British waters.

## Man and animals in Mesolithic times

### The early Mesolithic

The picture of the early Mesolithic economy in Britain is one of exploitation of the forest resources. This is hardly surprising as the early settlement seems to have been confined to southern and eastern England (Jacobi 1973) most of which had no shore at all in the Pre-Boreal and early Boreal times, being connected by land to the continent: across the Channel to France and across the southern part of the North Sea to the low countries and to Jutland. This exploitation was largely of ungulates, 'ambulatory stores of necessities' as Brinch Petersen (1973) has described them. Most sites of this period were by lakes and although lake-side settlements may have had advantages for fowling, for catching drinking ungulates, and for access to permanent water, there is very little evidence to suggest that they were used for fishing.

The fauna of the famous site of Star Carr has already been described above, and it gives us by far the most comprehensive picture of the economy of an early Mesolithic site in Britain. Clark (1954) estimates the importance of each species of ungulate found there in terms of its likely total carcass weight. Their descending order of importance is red deer, aurochs, elk, roe deer and pig, and from the figures he gives it is quite clear that all these animals were important in the diet, and that the economy of Star Carr was based on the exploitation of a spectrum of ungulate species.

There has been much speculation that red deer were the dominant food animals of the Mesolithic economy. The method used by Jarman (1972) to demonstrate this was to compare the total number of Mesolithic sites in Europe in which red deer are recorded with the numbers of sites on which other ungulates are recorded, and he found that red deer occur on more sites than any other ungulate. Jarman's results were recently recalculated by Woodman (1973-4) and showed a much less dramatic dependence on red deer than that claimed. If one uses Jarman's method on dated Mesolithic sites in Britain (as listed in Grigson 1978) 11 early sites have red deer, 9 have aurochs, 9 have roe deer, 7 have pig and 7 have elk. In the later sites 10 have red deer, 10 have aurochs, 9 have pig, and 6 have roe deer (there is no elk). This suggests that as well as the red deer all the other ungulates were of economic importance.

Ungulates and other animals were used not only for food, but as providers of other basic necessities: antler, bone, pigs' tusks and beavers' jaws for tools, teeth and whiskers for decoration, skins for clothing, bedding and possibly for covering huts and boats, leather for a variety of purposes, horns for carrying and storing liquids, sinews for use as thread, fat to be rendered for oil, and so on. There are also the antler frontlets at Star Carr which almost certainly had a ritual use (Plate 2). The fur-bearing animals found on early sites should not be forgotten, nor the birds. The use of a swan's wing as a baby's cradle in the cemetery at Vedbaek in Denmark (Albrethsen and Brinch Petersen 1976) is a reminder of the myriad of forgotten uses to which bits of animals may have been put. The use of dogs is discussed below.

Star Carr is usually thought of as a winter base camp of seasonally moving people (Clark 1972). The evidence used to arrive at this conclusion can be re-interpreted as it is based on the presence of the shed antlers of red deer and elk which could easily have been collected and stored from one season to another. The finding of unshed antler of roe deer is not usually quoted and complicates the picture by indicating summer occupation, and so do the bones of the crane (and probably also of the white stork) which would have been summer visitors. To demonstrate seasonality one needs not only definite evidence that a site was occupied at a particular season, but, equally important, evidence that it was *not* occupied at other seasons.

It seems likely that as well as living by lakes and rivers, people would have fished these inland waters, but there is strangely little evidence for this in Britain throughout the Mesolithic, although pike bones were found at Foxhole Cave (Bramwell 1971) and at Dowel Cave (Bramwell 1959). The almost complete absence of fish bones from the living sites of the 'hunter-fishers' is puzzling. As already mentioned, primary freshwater fish would have been confined to the rivers of the southern half of the east coast, but the lake at Star Carr was probably part of this system as it drained westwards into the river Derwent which is a northerly tributary of the Humber, and the Kennet, on which Thatcham and Wawcott are situated, drains into the Thames. However, in the case of Star Carr, it is thought that access for pike and other fish was prevented by a steep gorge above the lower reaches of the Derwent (Wheeler 1978). Pike bones preserve well, and although the bones of the secondary freshwater fish (salmonids and eels) are more fragile (Wheeler, personal communication), they survive in quantity in the Irish site of Newferry (Brinkhuizan 1977).

Tools that might have been suitable for fishing could also have been used for hunting, and there seems to be a dearth of specific fishing equipment (fish hooks, traps and weirs) in this country so far. Two barbed points were found side by side at Star Carr and may have been from a leister, but this is uncertain as the barbs faced outwards (Clark 1954, p.127). A barbed point found at Skipsea, Yorkshire, in 1903 is sometimes claimed as evidence for fishing as pike fins were later identified in an equivalent layer of silt several feet away (Godwin 1933), but bones, claimed to be those of a 'giant elk' *Cervus giganteus* (= *Megaloceros*?) and of reindeer, had been found with the barbed point, so even if these finds were truly contemporary (which would imply an unlikely survival date for the giant deer) the point might have been related to the mammals rather than to the pike. In Ireland, however, it was different, for there was extensive exploitation of salmonids and eels at Mount Sandel, and this contrast in economy may be real for, as already mentioned, there were probably no ungulates to hunt in Ireland apart from a very few red deer and wild boar.

*Changes at the time of the severance from Europe*

In the Boreal man spread into the western and northern parts of the British Isles (Jacobi 1976), including many upland regions. This colonisation of new areas was probably encouraged by the relatively low rainfall of the period when many erstwhile springs and lakes of the lowlands may have dried up, but perhaps more important was the effect of the rising sea-level, which culminated in the breaching of the North Sea land bridge and our final isolation from the continent; the land area of Britain was drastically reduced by the encroachment of the sea, particularly in the lowlying regions off the present East coast, but most of the rest of the country was also affected. This led not only to the penetration of dry land by new shoreline habitats (salt marshes, beaches, shingle bars, estuaries, drowned valleys, sand dunes, rocky shores and so on), but also to a large increase in the proportion of shoreline length to dry land area.

In the Atlantic period dense, mixed, oak forest spread over most of the country and was accompanied by increased rainfall and the development of new swamps and marshy areas, and while there is no evidence of a reduction in ungulate populations at that time (finds of aurochs in bogs are particularly numerous in the Atlantic) it may well be that their procurement became increasingly difficult. All this coupled with the likely increase in human population density seems to have forced man to exploit new ecological niches and ecotones, particularly those of the sea coast. Most of the known coastal sites are in the northern and western parts of the country, which is hardly surprising as the entire Mesolithic shore from Yorkshire south to Dorset is now under water, and the north-west of Britain has been uplifted.

*The later Mesolithic*

Its rich faunal remains make the shell midden of Morton Tayport B, Fife (Coles *et al.* 1971) as important to the study of economy in the Atlantic period as Star Carr was to the Pre-Boreal/Boreal interface. Its radiocarbon dates range from 6,382 ± 120 bp (Q-981) to 6,115 ± 110 bp (Q-928) (4,432 bc to 4,165 bc), and the site was probably an island at high tide. The faunal remains show the variety of habitats that were made use of by these late Mesolithic people: sandy, rocky, and muddy shores, both between the tide lines and below low water, and perhaps including the estuary of the nearby river Tay; inshore and deeper waters; the hinterland and rocky outcrops in the vicinity. The vast numbers of mollusc shells identified from the samples represent some forty species, all of which are still present in the area today. Numerically, *Cerastoderma edule* L. (the cockle) and *Macoma balthica* (L.), were the most important, and are found in intertidal mud and sand. *M. balthica* may indicate brackish water. Other molluscs are associated with intertidal rocky shores and vegetation, and yet others with offshore habitats which would only have been available at extreme low water springs, unless obtained by dragging or diving. Claws of the edible crab (*Cancer pagurus* Bell) were common. This crab migrates to deep water in winter, returning to shallow conditions in February.

Among the many very fragmentary fish bones, those of cod, haddock, turbot, salmonid and sturgeon were identified, with large cod far outnumbering the other species, this suggests that fishing took place in quite deep water by boat. The salmonids and sturgeon were probably caught in shallow water on their way to or from a river mouth. Eleven species of bird were found, mostly seabirds which would have nested on the rocky outcrops near the site. The guillemot (*Uria aalge*) was the most common, but may have been caught on the open sea.

The full range of ungulates (except the elk) was represented in small numbers of bones in the midden. The types of bones and tools found suggest that butchering was carried out at the site, after killing nearby. The absence of bones of marine mammals is notable. In spite of the huge numbers of molluscs present their estimated total meat weight was only equal to roughly one third of the meat supplied by vertebrates: in terms of consumable meat one aurochs is equivalent to a lot of cockles. The evidence for seasonality at Moreton Tayport B is inconclusive, but it is suggested that, as at

Star Carr, occupation was not continuous.

A similar use of sandy or muddy, and rocky shores as well as of the hinterland, is attested in the late Mesolithic sites of Blashenwell, Dorset (Reid 1896; Clark 1938), Westward Ho!, Devon (Churchill 1965; Jacobi, personal communication) and at Prestatyn, Flintshire (Clark 1938). Another area which shows how man used the full variety of available resources is the valley of the Forth where the carse clays, which were deposited during the marine transgression of about 6,000-4,000 bc, contain numerous skeletons of stranded whales. Antler implements have been found in the same deposits, one in close association with a whale skeleton, suggesting that good use was made of these chance strandings (Clark 1947).

There is a series of late Mesolithic (Obanian) sites on the west coast and islands of Scotland. Some were excavated in the last century and the surprisingly complete faunal analyses are summarised by Lacaille (1954). The sites, which are shell middens, contain small numbers of seals and whales, and the mainland sites have what seem from the reports to be bones of domestic animals – small cattle, small pigs and, possibly, goats. They are contemporary with the earliest Neolithic in the area which suggests some cultural overlap. A similar situation probably occurs with the late Mesolithic (Larnian sites) in Ireland. Recent, but not yet completed, excavations into Obanian sites on the island of Oronsay are yielding promising information on the seasonal use of the middens, mostly gained from the study of concretion layers on the otoliths of saithe (*Pollachius virens* L.) recovered from fine sieving of the deposits (Mellars 1978).

*The manipulation of animals and their environment*

In many organic sediments of Mesolithic age, evidence of fire has been found in the form of charcoal, and this is often accompanied by pollen spectra indicative of forest recession. It has thus been argued that woodland regenerating after burning would be particularly attractive to ungulates (Mellars 1975; Simmons 1975a). Although the overall carrying capacity for large herbivores might not increase, the abundant nutritious browse might help to concentrate animals so that they might be more easily killed. Such burnt-off areas would be especially attractive to elk (Bendell 1974) and it might be speculated that such a spatial concentration, combined with changing environmental conditions, led to 'overkill', and extinction, of the elk. These theories gain support if Britain is compared with Ireland, where there were neither elks, aurochs nor roe deer and probably few red deer and pigs, and so there could have been no economic dependence on ungulates. Various differences in the Irish Mesolithic are apparent (Woodman 1973-4); the settlement pattern is different, as there seem to be no sites in the Irish uplands from which ungulates would have been hunted, and there is a relative lack of hide processing tools like burins, scrapers and of tools made of antler. Equally important, there is an apparent lack of Mesolithic forest clearance, which points to a relationship between forest recession and ungulate exploitation on the British mainland in Mesolithic times.

The supposed preponderance of red deer in the Mesolithic of Britain and Europe, already mentioned, has been extended to suggest a close man-deer relationship amounting, if not quite to domestication, to herding at least, or to a controlled culling of these animals, but there is no direct evidence for this. The unexpectedly large amounts of ivy found in some Mesolithic pollen spectra have been explained as possibly indicating the use of ivy as fodder for red deer, but the authors of the paper describing this (Simmons and Dimbleby 1974) are at pains to point out that even if this were the case other species of ungulates would have been equally attracted to the ivy.

The reidentification of the Star Carr wolf bones as domesticated dog (Degerbøl 1961; Plate 3) caused rather a stir, but Mesolithic dogs (that is, domesticated wolves) are known from many other areas, particularly Denmark, and there are now records of Palaeolithic dogs both in the old and new worlds. It is quite clear that man first tamed wolves many thousands of years ago to aid him in hunting ungulates, and the process of domestication may have been carried on either continuously or intermittently over a very long period in many areas. The natural pack behaviour of wolves makes them ideally suited for a social relationship with man, and the manner in which wolves single out and hunt down their prey from an ungulate herd makes them very useful hunting companions. As well as at Star Carr dog bones have been found at Thatcham (King 1962a), at the Obanian site of the MacKay cave at Oban, Argyll (Lacaille 1954) and at two Larnian sites in Ireland (Wijngaarden-Bakker 1974), and dogs were probably present wherever man went throughout the Mesolithic. Observations on a bushman hunting excursion where one man with a pack of trained hunting dogs collected three-quarters of the meat and six men without dogs collected one quarter (Washburn and Lancaster 1968) point up the immense increase in efficiency allowed by the use of dogs. In general dogs would have been far too precious to eat, and their bones are usually present only in small numbers in domestic refuse, but presumably they could have been eaten in times of shortage. Dogs could also have been used as pack animals in this period, since as Laughlin (1968) remarks, 'women and dogs have been the principal beasts of burden since Palaeolithic times'.

## Epilogue

Even though Mesolithic societies were technologically simple, their usage of fire seems to have conferred on them the ability to alter their surroundings in a purposeful way. The changes they produced may also have been facilitated by the fragility of the ecosystems which they manipulated. Whether the effect of man was to initiate the acidification of upland soils by interfering in nutrient cycles and water balance, or whether it was to accelerate a natural process is not yet known.

The technological simplicity of Mesolithic cultures in the British Isles, together with a large volume of environmental information, means that it should soon be feasible to attempt rather more complex models of man-resources-environment relations than those based more narrowly on concepts derived from site catchment analysis (Clark 1972; Simmons 1975a). Given some more data from settlement sites about tools and food sources, the type of semi-quantitative modelling attempted for parts of the Danube valley by Jochim (1976) should be possible. If good ethnographic parallels can be used with care (e.g. Mellars, forthcoming) to suffuse such models with a critical imagination, then the chances are good of reconstructing the environmental context of the Mesolithic.

Caroline Grigson is grateful to all those who have patiently answered her queries and helped her with details of stratigraphy, especially F.R. Froome, J.J. Wymer, Roger Jacobi, Alwynne Wheeler (British Museum, Natural History), Peter Woodman, (the Ulster Museum), Paul Mellars (Sheffield University), Gale Sieveking (British Museum) and E. Brinch Petersen (Copenhagen).

# 4. *The Neolithic*

## A.G. SMITH (with CAROLINE GRIGSON, G. HILLMAN and M.J. TOOLEY)

### Introduction

The introduction of farming into a broadly forested countryside must surely have been guided to a large extent by the constitution of the vegetation cover. Neolithic man was presumably closely attuned to the subsistence potential of different vegetation types. He would, however, have been much less aware of the long-term degradation that his exploitation of that potential would bring about. While this degradation was on a much smaller scale than in subsequent periods its evidence remains for us to unearth and it will form one of the threads running through this account.

Except where modified by the activities of the Mesolithic populations, the constitution of the Atlantic vegetation of these islands would have reflected those two factors of prime importance to Neolithic man: climate and soil. The forests, for instance, would have varied in both species composition and in density of cover. The differentiation of the forest cover of Britain, as the Neolithic began, is well illustrated by the isopollen maps published by Birks *et al.* (1975), some of which are reproduced in Fig. 4.1. These maps are based on the constitution of the pollen rain immediately before the so-called 'elm-decline', a prominent feature of almost all British pollen diagrams which occurred around 3,000 bc. As might be expected, the isopollen maps show that large areas of the Scottish highlands were dominated by birch and pine. What is perhaps more revealing, however, is the importance of alder in the lowlands. While alder is known to be over-represented in pollen diagrams, the map illustrates one of the major problems facing the first farmers: it sets out for us those lowland areas of damp, heavy soils that would have been the most intractable.

The techniques available to the environmentalist in studying the past are in many ways rudimentary. The fossil remains of former

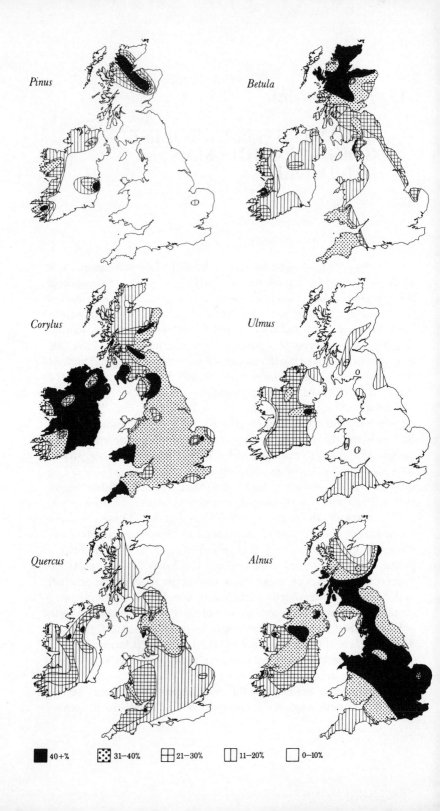

| ■ 40+% | ▓ 31–40% | ▦ 21–30% | ▤ 11–20% | ☐ 0–10% |

plant and animal communities are a very poor substitute for a time machine! While the aim of palaeoenvironmental studies may be a quantitative understanding of prehistoric plant and animal communities, it is this aspect that most often eludes us. Their intimate constitution and spatial distribution are extremely difficult to reconstruct. In addition, it is often tacitly assumed that the ecological preferences and climatic tolerances of organisms have not changed. There is no real way, however, of knowing whether or not this assumption is valid. Perhaps the area in which this is of most importance is the assessment of palaeoclimates. Not only may climatic tolerances have changed, the connection between climatic factors and the autecology of species is often imperfectly understood. In considering the Neolithic we shall encounter numerous instances where human activity could have brought about, or contributed to changes which might otherwise be considered to be climatic effects. The interactions between human and climatic factors have undoubtedly been complex. Moreover, the newer findings appear to be bringing about modification of the classical views on climatic change. This account will, therefore, stop short of recounting any quantitative reconstructions of climatic conditions during the Neolithic period.

Notwithstanding the limitations of environmental reconstruction, when it comes to environmental change we are in a much stronger position. We may not know the former environmental conditions with any precision, but we can often deduce the direction in which they changed. Above all, the Neolithic period was a period of change. Aside from any climatic effects, coastal areas, for instance, were affected in major ways by changes of relative sea-level. And man constantly modified his own environment. The rate of change, the rate of modification, is now becoming clearer than hitherto with the application of radiocarbon dating to environmental sequences. As a result, several classical ideas are being modified. Much remains

---

Figure 4.1. Isopollen maps for the British Isles. (After Birks *et al*. 1975.) These maps reflect the differentiation of forest cover as the Neolithic period began. They were prepared by drawing 'contours' for pollen percentages for the period just before the 'elm decline'; i.e. just before *c.* 3,000 bc. The maps are least reliable in the south-east of England where only a few sites have been investigated. The following tree taxa are shown: *Pinus*, Pine; *Betula*, Birch; *Corylus*, Hazel; *Ulmus*, Elm; *Quercus*, Oak; *Alnus*, Alder.

to be done, however, before we are within sight of any clear understanding of the multi-factorial and multi-dimensional relationships of Neolithic man with his environment. This chapter sets out to describe some contributions to such an understanding. This evidence comes largely from stratigraphic and biological analyses of relevant deposits, including occupation sites. In the occupation sites we find the direct, if only partial, evidence of Neolithic man's relationship with his biological resources. The chapter ends with some speculations and some of the questions that still need to be answered as we progress towards a greater understanding of how the agricultural revolution began to alter our landscape.

## Sea-levels (M.J.T.)

From the fourth to the first millenium bc the coasts of Britain were affected by three marine transgressions, consequent upon three periods of high sea-level. A marine transgression sequence has been identified for the Flandrian Stage in north-west England (Tooley 1974, 1978a). The type site for the sequence is Lytham, Lancashire. During the Neolithic period, three transgressions are recorded: Lytham VI, 3,620-2,947 bc; Lytham VIa, 2,850-2,595 bc; and Lytham VII, 1,750-1,200 bc.

Transgressions of similar age were underway in the Somerset Levels, along the south coast of England, in the Thames estuary, in the East Anglian Fenland and elsewhere in Britain. The pattern is similar in north-west Europe (Morrison 1976) and is the result of absolute changes in the sea-level surface that can be correlated with changes in mid-latitude climates and ice budgets (Aaby 1975; Fairbridge and Hillaire-Marcel 1977).

The extent of each transgression differs in each area and this is a consequence of regional or local factors such as continuing isostatic recovery in Scotland and tectonic downwarping in southern Britain. Hence, the extent and lithology of marine transgressions in the Fenlands have greater affinities with the Netherlands than with north-west England.

In the type area, Lytham VI transgression (3,620-2,947 bc) characteristically comprises a blue-grey marine clay and affected extensive areas in north Wales and north-west England. In south-west Lancashire tidal flat sedimentation occurred at 4.2 km.

landward of the present coast and in the south-west Fylde 3 km. landward of the present coast. The removal of marine conditions was equally extensive, and upon the gently-undulating, former tidal flats an autogenic plant succession was initiated: salt marsh communities with *Armeria* (thrift), *Artemisia* (sea wormwood) and *Plantago maritima* (sea plantain) gave way to brackish water reedswamps of *Phragmites* (reed) with pools containing *Ruppia*. These, in turn, gave way to freshwater reedswamps of *Typha* (reedmace) and open-water communities of *Nymphaea* (white water-lily). As the sea-level fell telmatic conditions gave way to drier terrestrial conditions. Tree and shrub taxa, such as *Salix* (willow), *Alnus* (alder), *Euonymus* (spindle), *Frangula* (alder buckthorn) and *Quercus* (oak) appeared in succession. This pattern of succession occurred not only in south-west Lancashire and the Fylde, but also in north Wales, in the valleys around Morecambe Bay and throughout the tidal flat palaeoenvironments of the Solway Lowlands. In the Lytham area, the altitude of the regression surface of Lytham VI is +3.03 ± 0.51m. O.D.: in south-west Lancashire, the altitude is +3.37 ±0.29m. Further south, in north Wales, altitudes of +2.4m. O.D. are recorded. Even to the north, near the southern coast of Morecambe Bay, altitudes of +2.9m. O.D. are common. The marine transgression surfaces are thus nearly horizontal over an extensive area. From Morecambe Bay northwards, however, altitudes increase and the cessation of marine conditions took place earlier, though often by only a few hundred years. On Ellerside Moss, east of the Leven estuary, for example, estuarine minerogenic sedimentation giving way to brackish-water and freshwater sedimentation is dated to 3,485 ± 105 bc (Hv-3844) at an altitude of +3.72m. O.D. In the Solway Lowlands (at Pelutho), however, estuarine sedimentation was maintained until 2,895 ± 100 bc (Hv-4418) at an altitude of +8.7m. O.D. An analysis of altitudes of the regressive surface of Lytham IV (Tooley 1978a) shows that there is an imperceptible gradient from Wales to the type area at Lytham. To the north, however, the gradient on the surface increases greatly. From Lytham to the Solway Lowlands the gradient is 4.8m./100km.

Lytham VI is also recorded in eastern and south-east England though at a lower altitude. This is explicable in terms of post-Lytham VI subsidence of the areas within the southern North Sea basin. In Hartlepool Bay, Lytham VI, that had transgressed much of the lowlands flanking the Tees estuary, ended at 3,290 ± 70 bc (Hv-

3459) at −0.36m. O.D. In the Fenland, the end of Lytham VI is registered at St German's at an altitude of −5.2m. O.D. (Godwin and Godwin 1933).

In the Somerset Levels, although some of the evidence is ambiguous and needs clarification, there is evidence of a Late Flandrian II (i.e. late Atlantic; see Chapter 1) age transgression that is registered on Shapwick Heath (Godwin 1943; Coles *et al.* 1973) and on Tealham Moor. The end of marine conditions is registered at altitudes of +0.55m. O.D. at Glastonbury Lake Village and +0.53m. O.D. at Drake's Drove (Godwin 1955). The extent of the transgression in the Somerset Levels and the subsequent extensive removal of marine conditions, initiating new plant successions, is a characteristic of Lytham VI. The changes in water depth and quality, in ground water régime and vegetation succession associated with this transgression must have had a profound effect on the resource and settlement potential of these areas.

Lytham VIa (2,850-2,595 bc) is poorly registered in the type area, but is strongly registered in the Fenland and Somerset Levels. The reason for this difference is that the slight positive movement of sea-level recorded at the beginning of Flandrian III (post-Atlantic times) was exaggerated by downwarping in southern England – a characteristic of the whole region, and not confined to south-east England alone (Devoy 1977). The effects of this downwarping were to maintain the transgression for a longer period than Lytham VIa recorded in the type area and over extensive areas. In the Somerset Levels, the transgression is recorded from Kenn, Avonmouth and Portbury (Hawkins 1971). In the Fenland, this transgression is characterised by the deposition of Fen Clay that began shortly after 2,740 ± 120 bc (Q-31) and penetrated as far landward as Glass Moor, Ramsey, where pine cones in a woody detrital peat overlaid by Fen Clay yielded a date of 2,395 ± 120 bc (Q-474) (Willis 1961). In the perimarine zone along the margins of the Fenland, unaffected by sedimentation of the Fen Clay directly, but registering a rise in the freshwater table, dates of 2,245 ± 110 bc (Q-544) at Wood Fen, Ely, and 2,655 ± 110 bc (Q-130) at Adventurer's Fen, Wicken, have been recorded. At Spalding, marine sedimentation began shortly after 2,495 ± 100 bc (St-3817). Further north, in the valley of the River Witham, south-west of Woodhall Spa in the Lincolnshire Fens, Fen Clay sedimentation began at 2,212 ± 130 bc (HA-150) and 1,995 ± 100 bc (St-3831) (Valentine and Dalrymple 1975). Marine conditions ended throughout the Fenland towards the end of the first millennium of Flandrian chronozone III (early Sub-Boreal times): at Saddle Bow 1,965 ± 120 bc (Q-490); at Denver Sluice a little before 2,135 ± 110 bc (Q-264). In the Netherlands, the deposition of Calais IV sediments from 2,650-1,850 bc (Oele 1977; Hageman 1969, gives dates of 2,600-1,800 bc) are similar in age to the Fen Clay sediments.

Lytham VII (1,750-1,200 bc) is registered as thin sheets of clay with iron partings and is of limited geographical extent. In the Humber Lowlands and along the Lincolnshire coast, the transgression was recorded more extensively. There is some evidence of a fall or halt in sea-level on the north side of the Humber associated with the prehistoric boats at Ferriby. Here, biogenic deposits at −0.9m. O.D. are overlaid by grey marine clay. A date on *Alnus* wood beneath prehistoric boat 3, embedded in this clay, gave an age of 1,170 ± 105 bc (Q-175) (Wright and Wright 1947; Wright and Churchill 1965; McGrail and Switsur 1975): the beginning of marine conditions here is before this date by an unknown amount. However, at Stoneferry, north of Kingston upon Hull, a channel was filled with estuarine silt and sand that contained molluscs at altitudes of −3.8 to −3.4m. O.D.; assays on *Cerastoderma edule* (L.) and *Macoma balthica* (L.) yielded dates of 1,825 ± 100 bc (St-3803) and 1,485 ± 200 bc (St-3804) respectively, and bear witness to a marine transgression underway at this time (Gaunt and Tooley 1974). At Chapel Point, on the Lincolnshire coast, saltmarsh sedimentation was underway between 1,993 ± 100 bc (Q-685) and 1,390 ± 100 bc (Q-686) between −1.64 and 0.0m. O.D. The nature of the sedimentation is confirmed by a rich plant macrofossil assemblage in the saltmarsh clay of *Triglochin* (sea arrow-grass), *Limonium* (sea lavender), *Armeria* (thrift), *Suaeda maritimia* (herbaceous seablite) and *Salicornia* (glasswort) (Swinnerton 1931; Godwin and Godwin 1934; Smith 1958a, c). In the Thames estuary, Devoy (1977) has recorded a marine transgression (Thames III) underway between 1,900 and 2,900 bc, with altitudinal limits of −5.21 to −0.90m. O.D. In the Netherlands, Duinkerke 0 is registered during the latter half of Lytham VII (Hageman 1969; Oele 1977).

In upland Britain, lack of detailed dating prevents any meaningful correlation, but Lytham VI appears to be associated with Sissons' Postglacial Transgression 1 (P.G.1) and Lytham VII with P.G.4 (Tooley 1976, 1978a; Sissons 1967).

Relative sea-level movements on the coast of west Lancashire have recently been summarised (Tooley 1978a). During the Neolithic (*s.l.*) the following movements have occurred in this area:

1. Sea-level rose rapidly between 4,050 and 3,850 bc at a rate approaching 0.6 mm./year, and attained a maximum altitude of −2.2m. O.D.

2. Sea-level fell between 3,825 and 3,550 bc to a nadir of about −3.4m. O.D.

3. Between 3,550 and 3,050 bc sea-level rose at a rate of 0.5 mm./year.

4. The opening of Flandrian chronozone III from 3,050 to 2,950 bc is marked by a rapid fall in sea-level from −1.1 to −1.9m. O.D. resulting in a very extensive removal of marine conditions throughout north-west England, and elsewhere in north-west Europe.

5. Sea-level rose to a maximum altitude of −1.0m. O.D. at about 2,550 bc and subsequently fell to a level for which there is as yet no index point.

6. A rise of sea-level was underway by 1,750 bc and at about 1,450 bc probably rose slightly above present Ordnance Datum.

7. Sea-level fell subsequently to −0.7m. O.D. about 1,150 bc.

8. Sea-level rose, transgressing biogenic sediments dated to 1,140 bc, at an altitude of −0.5m. O.D., and continued to rise, exceeding present mean tide level to an estimated altitude of +1.0m. O.D.

9. Sea-level fell to a minimum value close to present Ordnance Datum at 320 bc.

During these periods of oscillating sea-level, coastal depositional features, such as sand dunes, shingle banks and sand banks formed and unconsolidated cliffs were undercut as sea-level rose above its present levels. Sand dunes were active and unstable during periods of relatively low sea-level when sand could be winnowed from a much dilated foreshore (Jelgersma *et al.* 1970). On the Lancashire coast, sand dunes began to accumulate after 2,140 bc (Tooley 1978a) and this coincides with the oldest period of dune building in the Netherlands which was completed by 2,150 bc (Jelgersma *et al.* 1970).

The effect of an oscillating sea-level on low-lying coastal areas was to bring about periods of extensive marine transgressions and regressions, and to initiate new plant successions and vegetation structures as water quality and depth changed, as did the ground water régime. As a habitat for man, such changes would produce a changing and varied set of resources and microenvironmental conditions that were open for exploitation.

## Climate

The evidence for climatic change in the Neolithic period cannot be discussed in isolation. It is inextricably entwined with the evidence of the impact on the environment of Neolithic man himself. There is, therefore, no simple story to be told and the current state of ideas can be best understood by tracing their development. The story is most easily begun at that point where climatic interpretations received the first major challenge.

### *The Atlantic/Sub-Boreal transition: the hand of man or the effects of climatic change?*

Any understanding of the relationship of Neolithic man to his environment in Britain must be based on Iversen's classic work in Denmark published over thirty-five years ago. Iversen's new conclusion was both brilliant and dramatic. It was that he could see in his pollen diagrams evidence of forest clearance, farming and forest regeneration which could be attributed to the Neolithic period. A more detailed treatment of this work is given later (see pp. 153-6).

In his paper 'Landnam i Danmarks Stenalder' (Land occupation in Denmark's Stone Age) Iversen (1941) set out to examine critically the transition between the Atlantic and Sub-Boreal periods. He used a new high standard of pollen analysis which has subsequently only rarely been equalled. Iversen defined the transition as the point at which the ash curve rose at the same time as a decline in the curves of elm and ivy. In the Danish notation, these criteria are said to divide pollen Zone VII from pollen Zone VIII. (This definition is a slight modification of Jessen's earlier scheme. The British parallel, following Godwin's (1940a) scheme is the elm decline of Zone VIIa/VIIb). Iversen considered that these features were due to climatic factors and he later produced further detailed evidence that supported this view (Iversen 1944). From the effect of the abnormally hard winters of 1939-42 he demonstrated that winter temperature is critical for ivy, and indeed mistletoe and holly, at the present day in Denmark. By defining what he called the 'thermosphere' for these plants, and by comparison with the fossil pollen occurrences, he was able to graph the temperature changes at the Atlantic/Sub-Boreal transition. His conclusion agreed basically with the classical view, derived from bog-stratigraphic studies in Scandinavia, that there was an increase of continentality at the Atlantic/Sub-Boreal transition. This conclusion came to be disputed by Troels-Smith (1960a), however, who argued that elm, ivy and mistletoe either were, or may have been used as fodder plants. He regarded the vegetational changes at the time of the elm decline as being anthropogenic. What initially appeared to be the strongest and most critically-documented evidence for a climatic change in Europe at the end of the Atlantic period was thus called in question.

The evidence of the effects of Neolithic man on forest cover which Iversen's researches unveiled in most cases came later than the Danish Zone VII-VIII transition; that is to say, later than the beginning of the elm decline. Thus Iversen had little difficulty in distinguishing between climatic and anthropogenic effects. The separation of the Danish Neolithic clearance phases from the elm decline was not so large, however, as to prevent strong counter-argument to Iversen's interpretation by Nilsson (1948). Despite the current general acceptance of Iversen's views, Nilsson's paper is something which no serious student of the subject should neglect to read, together with Iversen's reply (1949).

In Britain the most marked effects of Neolithic man were subsequently found to coincide with the elm decline. Thus there is much greater difficulty than in Denmark in distinguishing between anthropogenic and climatic effects.

*Elm decline and climatic change: new evidence from absolute pollen diagrams*

The nature of the elm decline and the question of climatic change has generated an extensive literature (e.g. Smith 1961, 1970a; Tauber 1965; Seddon 1967; Frenzel 1966; Ten Hove 1968; Godwin 1975 – in which many further references may be traced). The idea that disease might have been responsible has again been raised by the recent outbreak of Dutch elm disease in England. This possibility has been mentioned by a number of workers (Troels-Smith 1960a; Smith 1961; Watts 1961; Heybroek 1963) and a variety of views expressed. Critical discussion of the disease problem is prevented, however, by the total absence of any relevant data. Other ideas, involving deliberate human activity, are discussed later (see p.152).

The fascination of the elm decline has undoubtedly been the difficulty presented by its apparently selective nature. Was man selective? Were animals selective? Was disease selective? Or was climate selective? We may seek still to answer these problems. They begin to diminish, however, when we see that a careful consideration, even of relative pollen diagrams, leads to the conclusion that it was not elm alone that was affected (cf. Smith 1970a, p.91). Elm was perhaps affected to a greater degree than other tree species but it is becoming clear from new types of pollen diagrams that other trees were certainly involved.

The difficulties presented by relative pollen diagrams, i.e. that if the percentage of one taxon decreases then the percentage of others must increase, is now being overcome by the availability of pollen diagrams calculated on absolute and concentration bases. In the latter the curves are independent but may vary with deposition rate. In the former the curves are a measure of pollen influx in terms of pollen grains falling on a unit surface area per year; the curves are thus independent in themselves, and independent of variations of deposition rate. In making it possible to measure deposition rates, radiocarbon dates have provided the basis for the construction of 'absolute' diagrams. These diagrams must be treated with due caution, however, because of the limitations of sampling, and of the radiocarbon method itself. The methodological limitations leave open the question of undetectable short-term variations in the deposition rate. In some instances there is stratigraphic evidence of such an occurrence.

Absolute pollen diagrams from two sites in the Lake District suggest that trees other than elm were affected at the time of the elm decline; these include oak at a lowland site (Barfield Tarn) and pine and birch at an upland site (Blea Tarn) (Pennington 1975b). This work is discussed in more detail later. Two pollen concentration diagrams are available from East Anglia (Sims 1973). Because of the uniformity of deposition rate suggested by radiocarbon dates, one of these (Hockham Mere) may be regarded as an absolute diagram. This demonstrates that there was an actual reduction of the pollen influx of other tree species, particularly of oak, at the elm decline. General forest reduction is perhaps most dramatically demonstrated, however, in an absolute pollen diagram from Abbot's

Way, a Neolithic trackway in the Somerset Levels (Beckett and Hibbert 1976; Hibbert, in press) which is reproduced here as Fig. 4.2. Here the curves for all taxa save perhaps birch show a marked decline. In addition, Beckett and Hibbert show that the decline of elm in absolute terms occurs slightly before it does in the relative pollen diagram. In view of these findings any argument about climatic change (or disease) that rests on the reduction of a single species, such as elm, must, of course, be considerably weakened, if not entirely abandoned.

*Recent views of the classical concept*

The view that there was an increase of continentality at the opening of Sub-Boreal times derives in essence from early work on bog stratification in Scandinavia resulting in the so-called Blytt-Sernander Scheme (see Godwin 1975, p.27; Fries 1965; von Post 1946 for summaries). As the pollen analytical zones became established so the names of the Blytt-Sernander periods (see Table 1.1, p.20) became transferred to them, together with the climatic implications. It has been pointed out on numerous occasions over the last twenty years, however, that the newer evidence does not always support the Blytt-Sernander scheme, and their periods should be used solely as names without climatic implication. The best evidence supporting the idea of an increase of continentality at the beginning of the Sub-Boreal period was that published by Iversen in 1944 relating to the effects of cold winters especially on ivy, mistletoe and holly. Despite the fact that his interpretation has been questioned by Troels-Smith, Iversen continued to believe that such a climatic change probably occurred (e.g. Iversen 1973). The possibility, though not the fact, clearly also remains in Troels-Smith's mind (Troels-Smith 1960a, p.29).

In the British Isles evidence of climatic change at the beginning of the Sub-Boreal period is scanty. The situation is perhaps best described by saying that what we understand of this period does not demand an explanation in climatic terms. The fact, for instance, that trees other than elm were affected at the Atlantic/Sub-Boreal transition makes it the more difficult to conceive of a climatic influence since some aspect of climate would have to be involved that affected a number of species with different tolerances in the same way. That the reduction of elm was brought about by colder winters or an increase of spring frosts is regarded as very unlikely by Oldfield (1963) who points out that in the pollen diagrams from the

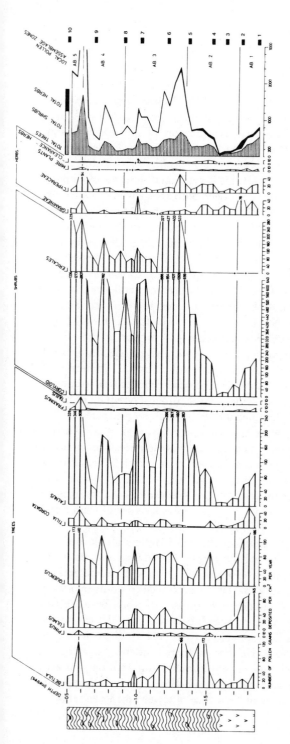

Figure 4.2. Absolute pollen diagram from Abbot's Way in the Somerset Levels. (From Beckett and Hibbert 1976.) In this diagram the curves for individual species are independent of each other. The feature of importance is that across the zone boundary AB 1/AB 2 dated to 2,824 ± 50 bc (SRR-542) there is a decline not only of the elm curve but of all the other tree species (save perhaps birch). Evidence of this kind affects our view of the significance of the 'elm-decline' which coincides with the major environmental impact of Neolithic man in Britain. It makes an explanation of the 'elm-decline' in terms of climatic change or disease less probable than has sometimes been maintained (see text). The following radiocarbon dates were obtained: 1. SRR-543, 4803 ± 50, 2. SRR-542, 4774 ± 50, 3. SRR-541, 4657 ± 55, 4. SRR-540, 4506 ± 45, 5. SRR-539, 4313 ± 55, 6. SRR-538, 4230 ± 45, 7. SRR-537, 4097 ± 50, 8. SRR-536, 3913 ± 45, 9. SRR-535, 3604 ± 45, 10. SRR-534, 3421 ± 45.

south-east Lake District, pollen of ivy, holly and lime, which are perhaps our most susceptible species, continues to be present through the period of the (primary) elm decline. The much more detailed analysis of the frequency of ivy pollen made by Walker (1966) for his pollen diagrams from the north Cumbrian lowland, does however show that a marked reduction occurred in his Cumbrian Zone C16 which covers the decline of the elm curve. Walker is of the opinion that if this is explained in terms of climatic change then 'its effects must have been both short-lived (about 1,000 years) and reversible' and inclines to the view that strong evidence of human interference during this phase probably negates any climatic interpretation. Godwin (1975), while speaking of a thermal maximum in the Atlantic period, finds it difficult to interpret the vegetational evidence of the Atlantic/Sub-Boreal transition in terms of any considerable fall of mean temperature, particularly in view of the fact that lime, our most thermophilous tree, holds its ground into the Sub-Boreal period. Neither does the work of H.H. Birks (1975) on pine stumps in Scottish blanket peats lend support to the idea of large scale climatic change at the beginning of the Sub-Boreal period. She states that 'any simple explanation ... in terms of climatic change cannot be upheld'. The occurrence of tree stumps in peat is precisely the type of evidence (the 'upper Forestian' of Lewis 1905, 1906, 1907, 1911; Samuelsson, 1910) that, by comparison with the Blytt-Sernander scheme had been previously taken as evidence of climatic change. While such studies will doubtless continue, it may be added to Birks's conclusion that in collecting large numbers of bog oaks for dendrochronological studies – many of which have been C-14 dated – members of the Palaeoecology Laboratory in Belfast have discovered a more or less continuous series from 5,500 bc onwards (Smith *et al.* 1972). This work perhaps shows a slight concentration of tree remains in the third millenium bc but can hardly be taken as confirming the greater abundance of wood in the Sub-Boreal period noted by Jessen (1949). It should also be pointed out that the analysis made by Jessen over a large number of sites could be misleading. A change in frequency of wood between two long periods (e.g. the Atlantic and Sub-Boreal periods) cannot be regarded as necessarily coinciding with the pollen analytical boundary between them. Neither is there evidence, as Godwin points out, from any change of peat humification, that bog surfaces became drier at the beginning of the Sub-Boreal period. Nor, so far, has there been any convincing evidence of lower lake levels, though it should be mentioned that Sims (1973) considers that he has evidence of temporary low water at Hockham Mere in East Anglia somewhat before the elm decline. On this basis he returns to the idea of climatic determination for the movement across Europe of agricultural populations culminating in a settling of previously nomadic peoples which is connected with the elm decline. In this conclusion, Sims follows the argument of Frenzel (1966) from high-altitude vegetational changes in the Alps that there was a cooler period from about 3,400 to 3,000 bc.

Work on the climatic implications of insects preserved in Flandrian deposits is still in its infancy. Osborne (1976) points out, however, that certain of the beetles from a deposit at Shustoke, Warwickshire, radiocarbon dated to 2,880 ± 100 bc (NPL-39) nowadays have a more northerly distribution. This he takes as being most readily explained in terms of 'a deterioration of the thermal environment'. Other species present at the site now have a more southerly distribution, but Osborne suggests that this may be due to lack of a suitable habitat in the Midlands today. Much further work is obviously required before it is possible to be certain that the insect evidence does, in fact, support the classical view.

### *Evidence of climatic change independent of biological considerations*

It is probably true to say that while the possibility of climatic change at the end of the Atlantic period is admitted by most British palaeo-ecologists, perhaps the majority would incline to the view that the vegetational changes are entirely explicable in terms of human activity. The solution to this problem may only come from evidence independent of biological argument. The rapid fall in sea-level from 3,050-2,950 bc mentioned by Tooley (1978a, and this volume, p.132) may well, for instance, have climatic implications. Before embarking on further discussion of the biological pointers to climatic changes, let us examine briefly some of the independent evidence.

Measurements of the $^{16}O/^{18}O$ ratios through the Greenland ice cap at Camp Century (Dansgaard *et al.* 1969, 1970; Johnsen *et al.* 1972) which reflect temperature conditions, show some fluctuations around the period with which we are concerned. Dansgaard and his colleagues point only to the broad conclusion, however, that the oxygen isotope curve illustrates the postglacial climatic optimum, and that this ended around 4,500 bp. Recalculation of the time scale

(Dansgaard, personal communication) shows that the end of the climatic optimum is in fact somewhat younger than this, and in any event, by comparison with 'calibrated' C-14 dates it is closer to the end of the Neolithic than the beginning. There is, however, a distinct drop in the oxygen isotope curve, indicating lower temperatures in Greenland, at 5,600-5,700 bp on the re-calculated timescale. Unfortunately, in addition to the dating problems we have to bear in mind that temperature fluctuations in Greenland may be out of phase with those in Europe (Dansgaard *et al.* 1975). For the moment, then, it is impossible to say whether this fall in the oxygen isotope curve, which coincides with the beginning of the Neolithic in Britain, has any significance for the climate of Western Europe.

The advance and retreat of glaciers is another line of independent evidence that may be examined. Denton and Karlén (1973) maintain that there was an interval of glacier expansion between 4,900-5,800 calendar years bp. These extremes of this range are taken from radiocarbon dates for peat on a moraine in Patagonia (I-3510, 3,110 ± 110 bc) and wood from a tree overrun by South Cascade Glacier, Washington (UW-99, 3,010 ± 90 bc). This work might be taken as suggesting a cooling during the period under discussion, but the relationship between glacier advance and retreat in the Americas to climatic change at the Atlantic/Sub-Boreal transition in Britain is, to say the least, likely to be complex.

Another possibly-independent measure of palaeoclimates is the chemical composition of lake sediments. It was suggested by Mackereth (1965, 1966) that the increased halogen concentrations in sediments may have been produced by an additional input of halogens from the sea through the intermediary of precipitation. He pointed out, however, that other explanations are possible. Mackereth's results from Angle Tarn in particular show an increasing iodine/carbon ratio during the Sub-Boreal period. Tutin (1969) was inclined to accept this as an indication of an increase of the precipitation/evaporation ratio just before 5,000 bp. Later work (Pennington and Lishman 1971) showed, however, that increasing iodine content of sediments was much more likely to be related to the inwash of soils.

*Stratigraphic and other evidence of climate change*

On the basis of changes of peat stratigraphy and pollen frequency at their Elan Valley site in mid-Wales, Moore and Chater (1969) suggest that there was a climatic change around the time of the elm decline, involving an increase of the precipitation/evaporation ratio. This idea, that conditions on the ground may have become wetter rather than drier, appears to be gathering some momentum. We may note, for instance, that Evans (1972), in reviewing the implications of his extensive studies on land mollusca states: 'A climatic shift to drier conditions at the beginning of, or at any time within the Sub-Boreal has not been detected ...' Warm summers there probably were, but the problem of whether or not a dry climate prevailed cannot be resolved on the available evidence. Further, Pennington *et al.* (1972) also see evidence pointing in the direction of increased wetness in their studies of blanket peat in north-west Scotland (their Region 1, around Loch Sionascaig). While the dates of peat growth perhaps need further confirmation by C-14 dating, at some sites its initiation was apparently due to waterlogging. They regard this as connected with a general rise of water tables around 4,400 bc. More widespread formation of blanket peat occurred around 3,000 bc. There are few signs of human influence in the area which could be related to the peat initiation (see also below). They conclude therefore, that where soil degradation had already reached a point where a thick layer of *mor* humus was forming, some climatic fluctuation may have crossed a threshold leading to swamping and peat formation.

These recent suggestions of increasing wetness in Neolithic times tend to add weight to the tentative conclusions of Conway (1954) in discussing her early work on blanket peats in the Pennines. She pointed out that there was often a stratigraphic change near the elm decline from a highly humified amorphous peat to a peat rich in *Sphagnum* (bog moss) leaves. If this change was not a natural development, then, Conway pointed out, it may have been a response to a climatic shift towards wetter conditions. As usual, however, we must face the difficulty of distinguishing between climatic and anthropogenic effects. As will be discussed later, (p.150) there may have been a raising of soil water tables as a result of deforestation.

The lack of good evidence for human influence at the elm decline in some areas of Scotland has been noted by Donner (1957, 1962) in the southern Grampians, and at Loch Kinord (Aberdeenshire) by Vasari and Vasari (1968). The elm decline in these areas therefore still stands out as requiring explanation. If this explanation is not in terms of a climatic effect, then it may be along the lines advanced by

Birks (1972a) in the case of her pollen diagram from Loch Maree (Ross & Cromarty). The slight elm decline dated to 3,200 ± 65 bc (Q-1006) with the presence of only a small amount of *Plantago lanceolata* is regarded as a reflection of a real elm decline further south so that the long-distance transport element of the pollen influx became reduced. Birks considers that the forests around Loch Maree were undisturbed until about 2,260 bc when over a period of *c.* 450 radiocarbon years they were replaced by bog and dwarf shrub communities. This process, particularly the reduction of pine, she sees as possibly having a climatic cause. While not ruling out effects of human activity she is inclined to the view that an increase of oceanicity most closely fits the available evidence.

In discussing the decline of pine in Scotland both from the evidence of pine stumps and of pollen diagrams, Birks (1975), remarks that the remarkable synchroneity of the decline of pine around 2,000 bc may have resulted from a regional increase of climatic wetness. Again, this is a situation where human involvement cannot be ruled out, but a climatic deterioration around this time is further supported by the increase of hydrophytes at Loch Park (Aberdeenshire) noted by Vasari and Vasari (1968) at the end of the Sub-Boreal period. While not closely dated, this increase is attributed to a rising water level associated with a change of climate to a more humid type. Evidence from the north of Ireland is beginning to point in a similar direction (cf. Smith 1975; Smith and Pilcher 1973) where the pine decline that may define the opening of the Sub-Atlantic period of Jessen (1949) falls around 2,000 bc. Jessen (1949) regarded this as a more oceanic period than the preceding Sub-Boreal. Dates for the stratigraphic division in Irish raised bogs between these periods are still very few. To the date previously quoted from Fallahogy, Co. Londonderry of around 2,500 bc (Smith 1958d, 1970b) – much older than supposed by Jessen – we may, however, now add a date for a clear stratigraphical change to a less-humified peat at Lackan, Co. Down investigated by the late Dr S.M. Holland of 2,155 ± 50 bc (UB-797) (Pearson and Pilcher 1975). (It should be noted, however, that these horizons cannot be the strict equivalent of Jessen's RS C (the recurrence surface 'C') since all his archaeological correlations showed Middle Bronze Age implements below that horizon). Thus evidence seems to be accumulating that in the northern and western parts of the British Isles the climatic deterioration normally associated with the Sub-Atlantic period may already have been under way at the end of the Neolithic period. While it is perhaps premature to argue this case with total conviction, it would be logical to think of critical thresholds being crossed earlier in those northern and western areas already generally wetter because of their geographical position and topography (cf. Smith 1965). In the same way, it should be no bar to acceptance that evidence for wetter conditions at the beginning of the Neolithic period comes almost entirely from the Highland Zone.

It appears then that the recent ideas on climatic change in the Neolithic point to a concept close to the original views of Andersson (1909). As pointed out by von Post (1946), Andersson opposed the ideas of Sernander (see p.136) and considered that there was a gradual deterioration of climate after an optimum. The existence of this optimum was to be amply confirmed by von Post's own world-embracing study of pollen diagrams. He distinguished only a period of increasing warmth, a period of maximum warmth, and a period of decreasing warmth.

In recalling the development of ideas of climatic history, Fries (1965) concludes, on the basis of the Scandinavian evidence, that there was not a single abrupt change, but that the change to a cooler and moister climate happened in stages, probably starting as early as 3,000 bc. On the other hand, Wright (1976) concludes that, with reference to North America, the climatic optimum (hypsithermal interval) must be regarded as having time-transgressive boundaries, ending in different regions at times between 7,000 and 3,000 years ago. Evidence for cyclic fluctuations of climate, however, is now very considerable, as illustrated for instance by the oxygen isotope work (e.g. Dansgaard *et al.* 1975). Certain aspects of cyclical variations are reviewed by Seddon (1967). More recently, Aaby (1976) has suggested that there were several fluctuations during the Neolithic period. His conclusions are based on the variation of peat humification and studies of rhizopods in Danish bogs. Aaby suggests that there was a basic periodicity of 260 or 520 years though, unfortunately, the analysis does not extend back to the beginning of the Neolithic period. We should bear in mind, therefore, that even if climate was deteriorating during Neolithic times, there would have been periods of relatively favourable conditions. The point has come when the simplistic concepts of the Blytt-Sernander scheme must surely be banished for ever. (Notwithstanding this conclusion, it should be pointed out that some schools of thought maintain that climatic changes were both relatively rapid and synchronous world-wide, and can be described by a developed Blytt-Sernander scheme (e.g. Bryson *et al.* 1970; Wendland and Bryson 1974. Cyclical climatic changes might, of course, affect organisms in a step-wise manner because of threshold and time-lag effects.)

## Soils

### Soil conditions at the end of the Mesolithic

The relationship between human activity, soil degradation and climatic change is evidently complex, and under active discussion by numerous workers (cf. Dimbleby 1976). As is pointed out in Chapter 3 (see pp. 106-9) Mesolithic man's activities appear to have induced permanent changes in already poor soils, and may have contributed to the initiation of peat growth in certain upland situations. It has also been argued by Mackereth (1965), from the results of chemical analyses in the Lake District, that the Mesolithic period was one of rapid soil-leaching. Mackereth regarded many of the non-limestone soils of north-west England as approaching the limit for regeneration of elm at the end of the Atlantic period. A similar argument based on ecological grounds has been advanced by Walker (1966). He sees the gradual decline of elm in the Atlantic period (in inland northern Cumbria) as being due to progressive soil depauperation, allowing its replacement by oak.

### Pedogenic processes and evidence from mollusca

The effects of human activity on soil will of course depend on the original soil structure and fertility. Despite the fact that primitive forms of agriculture and forest clearance itself are likely to lead to soil degradation, direct evidence that this occurred in the Neolithic period is rather sparse. Reconstruction of pedogenic processes presents a number of problems, however, since (if truly fossil) these soils represent a particular point in time and not a series of neat stages over a prolonged period. Moreover, it is not certain that in soils beneath prehistoric monuments pedogenic processes necessarily stopped once they were covered.

Soil conditions and development in the Neolithic, insofar as they can be understood, have been reviewed by J.G. Evans (1971, 1972) and in a more speculative way by Limbrey (1975), which makes lengthy discussion here inappropriate. Nevertheless, attention may be drawn to a number of important points. Evidence may be quoted showing that soils in Neolithic times were different from the present-day soils. As an example we may cite the non-calcareous brown earth beneath the Kilham barrow on the Yorkshire Wolds (Manby 1971). This stands in contrast to the present-day calcareous rendzina thought to have resulted from modern agricultural methods (Evans 1972). It is of interest here that had it not been for contrary indications from the spore-content of the buried soil it might have been interpreted as derived by decalcification from the chalk either as a result of leaching through the Atlantic period or the more immediate effects of human occupation. The soil does, however, show evidence of lessivation. That is, in broad terms, the washing down of the clay fraction from the upper to the lower layers of the soil. At Kilham, Evans suggests that this process followed as a direct result of forest-clearance and agriculture. A similar sequence is envisaged in the case of the soil buried beneath the henge bank at Marden (Wilts). Limbrey (1975) postulates that in certain cases the process of lessivation may have been initiated by Mesolithic disturbances and intensified in Neolithic times. This process she sees as culminating in the loss of the superficial eluviated horizon due to hill-wash and deflation as a result of cultivation. As she rightly states, such a process of soil degradation would be affected by a number of factors including intensity of cultivation, regrowth of woodland and manuring. Dimbleby (1976) points out that buried rendzina soils on the southern chalk have the appearance of truncation, which is corroborated at Windmill Hill by the biological evidence. He regards the reason for truncation as uncertain: it could be artificial though equally it could be due to erosion. The demonstration of Neolithic forest clearance on calcareous soils by means of snail analysis now seems to be well established, though considerable difficulties are introduced by the possibility of soil disturbances and cultivation (Evans 1972). Certain conflicts arise between the snail and pollen evidence, however, which may find explanation in differential times of preservation (Dimbleby and Evans 1974). Limbrey (1975) on the other hand, has argued that there may be a lacuna in certain snail profiles during a period of base depletion. The superficial mollusca would then reflect a stage of re-clearance when truncation of the profile exposed the base-rich lower horizons allowing renewed preservation of snail shells.

Examples of forest clearance may be given from apparently uncultivated soils at Ashcott under Wychwood (Oxon.) (Fig. 4.3) and Beckhampton Road (Wilts) where the mollusca from the turf

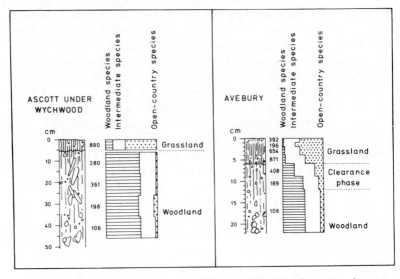

Figure 4.3. Summary diagrams showing the results of molluscan analyses at two sites on the southern calcareous uplands. The analysis from Ascott under Wychwood (Oxon.) is from the apparently uncultivated soil beneath the Long Barrow. (Conclusions from the soil pollen content are somewhat at variance with the conclusions from the molluscan evidence.) The results from Avebury (Wilts.) are from the soil beneath the henge. The apparently progressive forest clearance may be due to soil disturbance. (After Evans 1972.)

line are dominated by open-country species, as compared with woodland species immediately below (Evans 1972). At the former site the sketchy pollen evidence apparently conflicts with this implication. At the latter site, however, reasonable agreement was found between the snail and pollen evidence (Dimbleby and Evans 1974). The summary diagram of Evans's molluscan analyses of the Avebury soil, also given in Fig. 4.3, apparently illustrates a progressive deforestation. This could, however, be due to the soil disturbances which are thought to have taken place. Evans (1972, p.362) lists seven sites in which evidence of Neolithic clearance has been found and at which the process is best regarded as connected directly or indirectly with human activity. In soils where the molluscan fauna is indicative of open conditions Evans assumes that forest clearance had already taken place and this is often supported by the palaeobotanical evidence. Little evidence of woodland regeneration is found in the molluscan evidence, but contrarily the pollen evidence occasionally does indicate this probably to be the case, as for instance at Horslip Long Barrow (Wilts.). At the sites studied Evans generally finds evidence that, before burial, the soils beneath Neolithic earthworks supported stable short-turfed grassland with no cultivation taking place. He concludes that woodland regeneration was likely to have been prevented by grazing, which at three sites apparently continued for many centuries. The dating of such periods by means of C-14 measurements is, however, extremely difficult for various reasons including the conditions of preservation of the mollusca and the interpretation of the C-14 evidence which is only indirectly relevant to the problem.

*Soil erosion*

The question of soil erosion on the southern chalklands is dealt with by Evans (1972). He points to numerous instances of hillwash, but despite clearance early in the Neolithic (which he maintains was probably total and permanent), soil erosion does not appear to have begun on any scale until Iron Age and later times. We have seen, however, (p.145) that Limbrey (1975) places more emphasis on soil erosion as a result of cultivation. The difference of views is perhaps, as much as anything, a matter of scale. Whatever the scale of erosion was on the chalklands, it does stand in marked contra-distinction to what happened in the Highland Zone, of which the best investigated upland region, the English Lake District, may be taken as an example. Here the impact of the earliest clearances on soil stability was apparently much more immediate. The evidence for this, presented by Pennington (1970, 1975b; Tutin 1969), takes the form of stratigraphic changes in lake sediments and variations of chemical composition. At Barfield Tarn in the West Cumbrian coastal plain (Fig. 4.4), for instance, a change from an organic mud to a pink clay coincides with the elm decline. This, and other features, indicate clearance (probably involving the use of fire) of oak or oak-elm woodland for pasture and cereal cultivation. The pink clay deposition is interpreted as either a direct consequence of soil erosion resulting from cultivation on boulder clay around the tarn or, at least, an acceleration of a natural process by agricultural practices.

At Angle Tarn in the Central Mountains of the Lake District (Pennington 1970, 1975b) chemical analyses of the sediments have provided evidence of the inwash of acid soil horizons. Evidence of a

# BARFIELD TARN, SW CUMBERLAND 1965    ELM DECLINE

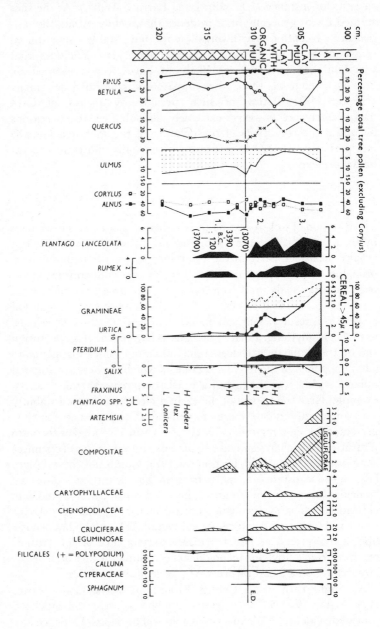

similar nature has also been produced from north-west Scotland (Pennington *et al.* 1972). At Loch Tarff, for instance, increases in the amounts of sodium, potassium, magnesium, and iron are correlated with pollen evidence of episodes of deforestation following the elm decline. The chemical evidence is taken as indicating accelerated erosion of mineral soils following clearance of forest on hill slopes. To this may be added the stratigraphic evidence of erosion found by Vasari and Vasari (1968) in the sediments of Loch Cuither (Skye) and Loch Park (Aberdeenshire), respectively at the beginning of, and during, the Sub-Boreal period.

Evidence of soil erosion on a quite local scale has been found at Ballynagilly, Co. Tyrone (Pilcher 1975; Pilcher and Smith 1979) where a charcoal layer, mainly of hazel, dated to 5,295 ± 90 bc (UB-18) was found deep in the mineral soil and 10 cm. below an iron pan on the downslope side of a Neolithic site. The sandy soil above the charcoal could only have been derived by hillwash.

*Peat initiation*

From studies at two sites on the Langdale Fells (Red Tarn Moss and Thunacar Knott) Pennington (1975b) shows that after destruction of the forest cover, blanket peat began to form on forest *mor* and on mineral soil. She does not see man alone as bringing about the initiation of peat growth but rather as tipping the balance towards peat growth under soil conditions which had already become more acid and subject to water-logging. The possibility of human activity having tipped the scales towards change, under conditions of stress, is discussed with reference to both Mesolithic and Neolithic times in Smith (1970a). That this may have been the case with the initiation of blanket peats, with which Pennington's Lake District studies agree, was put forward by Moore (1973) with respect to the uplands of mid-Wales. Here attention was drawn to the broad coincidence of human activity at the time of the elm

---

Figure 4.4. Relative pollen diagram from Barfield Tarn in the Cumbrian Lowland. (From Pennington 1970.) The stratigraphic change from an organic mud through to a pink clay at the elm-decline horizon (E.D.) is thought probably to be caused by soil erosion resulting from cultivation on the boulder clays around the tarn. Indications of human activity e.g. *Plantago* and *Rumex* pollen are present before the E.D. Horizon. The radiocarbon dates are in years bc.

decline with blanket peat initiation. Subsequently evidence from Exmoor was seen to conform to the same pattern (Merryfield and Moore 1974). Recently, Moore (1975) has summarised more widespread evidence and adopted a more general standpoint. He puts particular stress on the effects of deforestation on the soil water table, listing the experimental results of various authors showing that, following clearance, stream discharge from watersheds may increase by anything up to 40%. Moore is of the opinion, however, that a figure around 10% would be more realistic for Neolithic Britain. He cites other evidence showing that the water table rises as a result of clearance and thinning. In general, Moore concludes that both Mesolithic and Neolithic man could have influenced upland peat initiation, but points particularly to the circumstantial evidence of Neolithic activity broadly contemporaneous with the beginning of peat formation. A list of the relevant data (Moore 1975, Table 1) shows that the elm decline in most cases comes above the base of the peat. This is not taken by Moore as evidence that peat initiation necessarily began before the Neolithic since several Neolithic C-14 dates older than 5,000 bc can be quoted (cf. Smith 1974). Even if a pre-Neolithic date for blanket peat initiation is admitted, Moore is still inclined to regard its formation as connected with the effects of Mesolithic man. Moore's argument (most clearly stated in Merryfield and Moore 1974) that 'stock grazing in a woodland under climatic and soil nutrient stress (caused by deteriorating climate) could reduce regeneration and thereby tip the ecological balance in the favour of peat formation' cannot be denied. Moreover, he has elegantly demonstrated at Carneddau Hengwm progressive effects of human pressures of this and other kinds since Neolithic times. Nevertheless, there is no getting away from the fact that upland peat initiation often did start before the Neolithic, particularly in the Pennines (Conway 1947, 1954; Tallis and Switsur 1973; Tallis 1964a and 1964b; Hicks 1971; Durno 1958, 1959) even if this peat was in some cases supporting woodland rather than the herbaceous species characteristic of blanket peat. There is good evidence of upland peats being initiated in the Bronze Age, particularly in Northern Ireland (cf. Smith 1975). Thus it would be incorrect to think of general upland peat initiation in the Neolithic. Even in those cases cited by Moore, late-Atlantic paludification as suggested by Pennington might have been important. Indeed Moore and Chater (1969) earlier concluded that there was evidence from their work in mid-Wales of a climatic change involving an increase

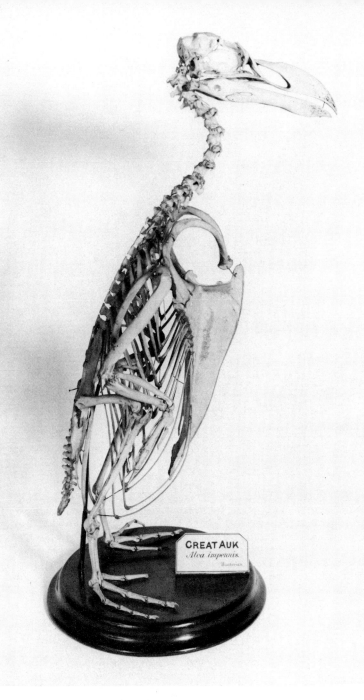

Plate 1 The Great Auk (*Pinguinus (=Alca) impennis*) became extinct in the last century – this skeleton may have been procured by Sir Joseph Banks in Iceland in the eighteenth century. The frequency of the bones of this flightless, colonial bird in shell middens in Scotland shows that it must have been an important element in the Mesolithic economy (Lacaille 1954; photography by kind permission of the trustees of the Hunterian Museum of the Royal College of Surgeons of England).

Plate 2 One of the many red deer frontlets found at the Mesolithic site of
Star Carr. Like most of the frontlets this had perforations through the
parietal bone, protuberances were smoothed away, and the weight was
reduced either by shortening the beam and tines or by hollowing them
out or both. It seems likely that the frontlets were used for stalking, ritual
or magic and emphasizes that it was not only as food that animals were
of interest to man. (Photography reproduced by permission of the
Trustees of the British Museum (Natural History).)

Plate 3 *facing page* The Star Carr dog. This very fragmentary skull was
originally identified as wolf, but close research by Professor Degerbøl of
Copenhagen (1961) on the size and crowding of the tooth sockets showed
that it came from a domestic dog. Since then further Mesolithic, and
even Palaeolithic, dog remains have been found in various parts of the
world. Plate 3A shows a side view of the skull and Plate 3B shows the
maxilla. (Photograph by kind permission of the Trustees of the British
Museum (Natural History).)

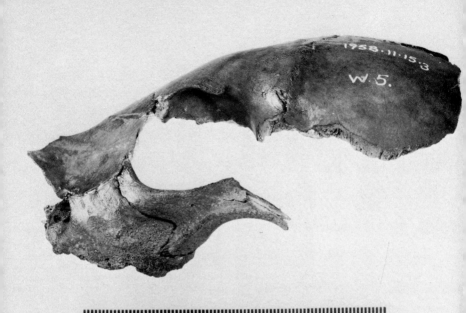

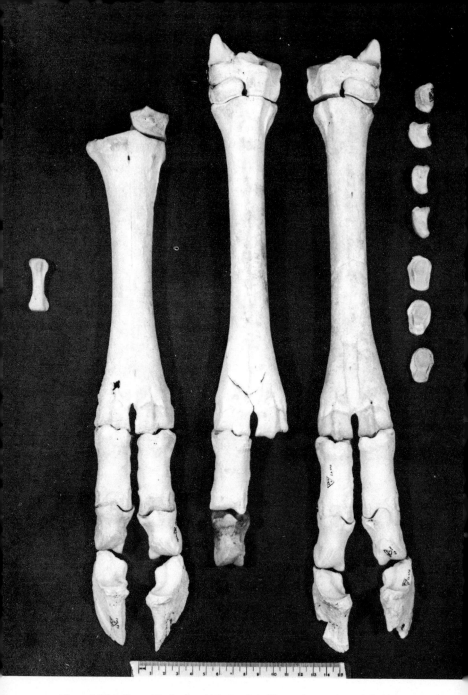

Plate 4 The Fussell's Lodge hide burial. These domestic cow bones were found on the top of the flint cairn in the earthen barrow of Fussell's Lodge; when articulated they clearly represent the remains of at least three of the feet and part of the tail of the same animal. Probably this is all that survived of an ox hide burial – certainly such finds emphasize the ritual importance of cattle in early Neolithic England (see Grigson 1966).

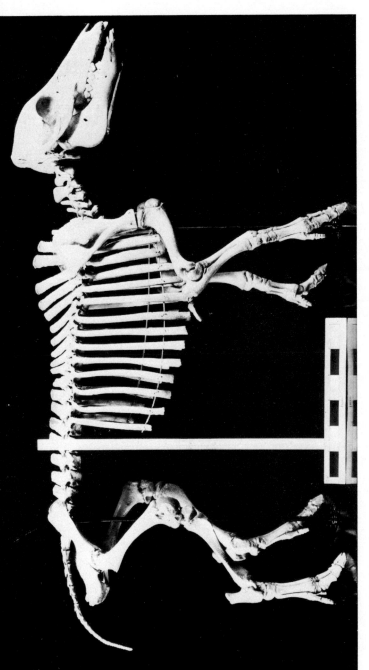

Plate 5 Windmill Hill pig. The excavations by Alexander Keiller in the primary levels of the ditches of the early Neolithic causewayed camp of Windmill Hill produced a series of complete skeletons of domestic animals and many broken ox skulls and horncores. This young pig's skeleton shows clearly the relatively long snout of primitive pigs (Jope and Grigson 1965; photograph by permission of the Alexander Keiller Museum).

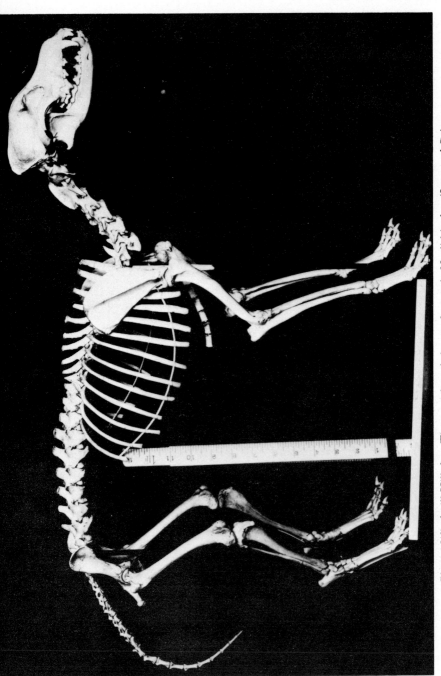

Plate 6 Windmill Hill dog. The complete skeleton of an early Neolithic dog (Jope and Grigson 1965; photograph by permission of the Alexander Keiller Museum)

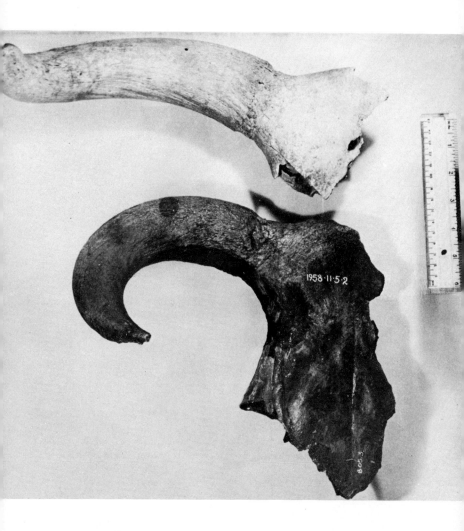

Plate 7 Maiden Castle ox. Part of the skull of one of the cattle from Maiden Castle causewayed camp (above). This was thought to represent a special domestic longhorn, but comparison with a skull from Mesolithic Star Carr (below) shows that it came from a wild cow *Bos primigenius*. Fairly large domestic cattle were also found (Photograph by Caroline Grigson by kind permission of the Trustees of the British Museum (Natural History)).

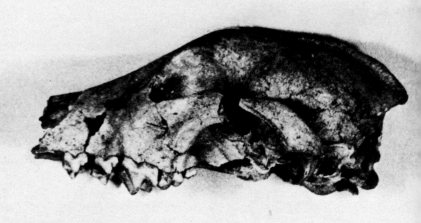

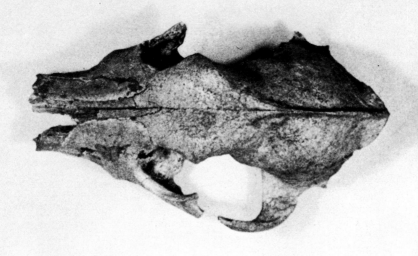

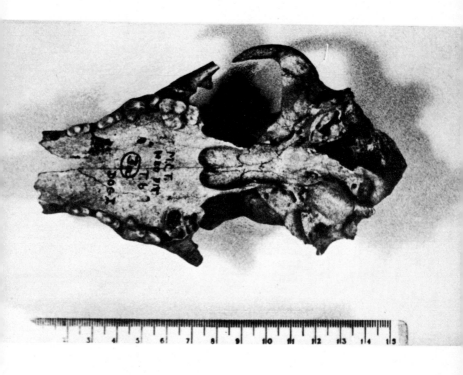

Plate 8 Maiden Castle dog. The remains of the skull of another early Neolithic dog from the causewayed camp of Maiden Castle; compare with the skeleton from Windmill Hill (Plate 6) (Photograph by Caroline Grigson with the kind permission of the Trustees of the British Museum (Natural History)).

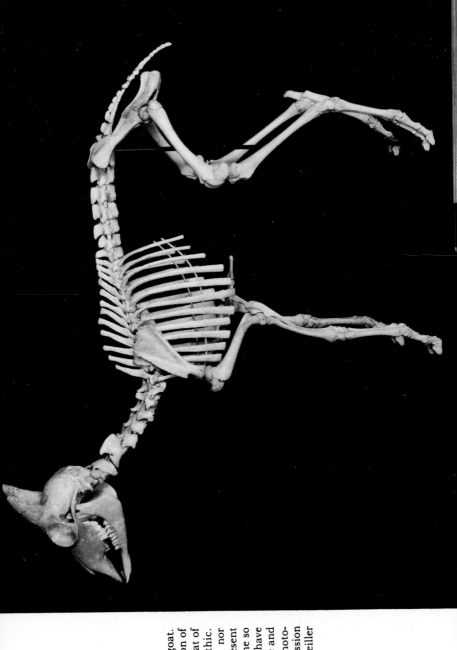

Plate 9 Windmill Hill goat. The complete skeleton of a young domestic goat of the early Neolithic. Neither wild goats nor wild sheep were present in Britain at that time so these animals must have been imported (Jope and Grigson 1965; photograph by permission of the Alexander Keiller Museum).

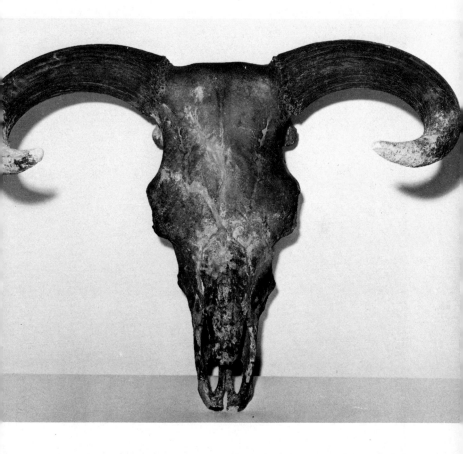

Plate 10 This fine skull of a large bull aurochs *Bos primigenius* from Lowes
Farm, near Littleport, was dated by stratigraphy to the early Bronze
Age. This date has now been confirmed by a radiocarbon date (BM-
1469; c.1400 bc) and so this is one of the latest finds known in Britain.
The aurochs may have died out soon after this (Shawcross and Higgs
1961; photograph reproduced by permission of the Faculty of
Archaeology and Anthropology, University of Cambridge).

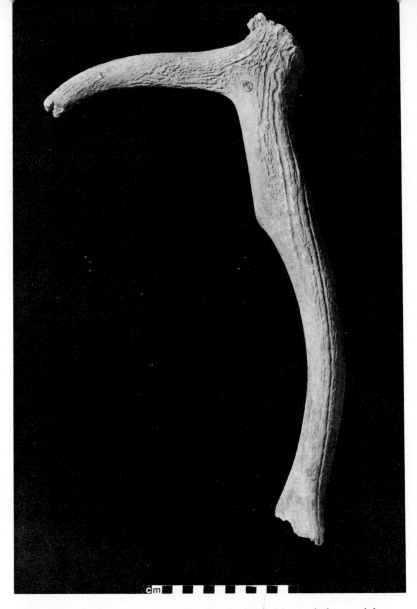

Plate 11 Late Neolithic antler pick. Hundreds of picks made from red deer antler were found in the late Neolithic flint mines of Grimes Graves and are common throughout the Neolithic in the waste material from constructional and mining work. The picks were made both from shed antler and from antler removed from deer that had been hunted. This shows that the economic use of animals was by no means restricted to being eaten. The picks were one of man's most important tools in ditch digging and mining in the early and late Neolithic. In this example, the beam (which forms the handle) has been shortened and all the tines are missing except the brow tine, which was the lever end and which shows signs of wear. (Photograph reproduced by permission of the Trustees of the British Museum (Natural History)).

in the precipitation/evaporation ratio at the time of the elm decline. The conclusion was based particularly on peat stratigraphy and pollen frequency index at their Elan Valley site. Presumably this is the 'climatic stress' to which Moore later alludes.

The processes culminating in blanket peat initiation at a site known to have been utilised by Neolithic man are perhaps best understood at Goodland, Co. Antrim (Case *et al.* 1969). The occupation material has a C-14 date of 2,625 ± 135 bc (UB-320 E) and the sequence of events, according to Dimbleby (1976) was as follows:

- (i)   clearance of forest associated with a brown podsolic soil
- (ii)  cultivation of a soil in which earthworms are active
- (iii) conversion to pasture, the soil progressively acidifying
- (iv)  the disappearance of the earthworms and the development of a leached soil with a thin iron pan
- (v)   the development of surface wetness, probably due to deterioration of soil structure
- (vi)  the onset of peat formation still within the Neolithic.

Dating of the basal peat by C-14 is still somewhat unsatisfactory (a summary is given in Smith *et al.* 1971) but the whole process appears to have taken no longer than a few centuries and may have been quite rapid. It must be said, however, that Mitchell (1972) takes the evidence as indicating a period of 500 years between the Neolithic occupation and the establishment of blanket bog. He sees soil exhaustion leading to podsolisation, the thin iron pan leading to waterlogging and colonisation by rushes. The slow decay of these rushes he suggests produced an impermeable 'precursor peat' sealing off the inorganic nutrients still in the soil and allowing invasion of the blanket bog species. Other Irish examples may be cited in which there appears to have been a considerable lapse of time between Neolithic occupation and subsequent peat formation. At both Beaghmore (Pilcher 1969) and Ballynagilly (Co. Tyrone) (ApSimon 1969; Pilcher and Smith 1979) the sites were subsequently occupied by Bronze Age peoples before peat began to form. At the former site the oldest date obtained for peat formation was 775 ± 55 bc (UB-63). At the latter site the base of the peat on the Neolithic occupation area has been dated to 575 ± 45 bc (UB-171). As noted above, the very poor sandy soil of this site was subject to erosion after the initial clearance but it is clear that peat formation was not an immediate consequence.

## Land-use

*The elm decline: general considerations*

Evidence from mollusca of forest clearance and the establishment of pasture on the southern chalklands has been mentioned in the section on soils. Elsewhere in Britain evidence of Neolithic land-use comes mainly from pollen analysis and much of our discussion must revolve around the 'elm decline' with which the Sub-Boreal period (pollen Zone VIIa or Flandrian chronozone III) begins.

We have seen already (p.135) that it was not necessarily elm alone that was reduced at the opening of the Sub-Boreal period and that this has weakened the arguments for a climatic effect. Insofar as elm was selectively reduced, however, it may be that a number of other factors could have been involved. These include the use of leafy shoots for animal fodder, an idea supported strongly by the work of Troels-Smith which is described below (p.156). The use of bark as human or animal food (Nordhagen 1954) and the stripping of bark by cattle (Smith 1975) are yet further possibilities. Elm appears to be a particularly nutritious species, though according to Nordhagen other species such as pine have been used as human food, particularly in periods of famine. The inner bark stripped from young twigs can be used either alone, or in combination with cereals, to make a flat bread. Regular stripping of young branches either for this purpose, or their use as cattle fodder would seriously affect the capacity of elm to provide pollen. The shoots require 7-8 years of growth before they come into flower.

Elm bark is particularly stringy and can be readily torn from the trunk by cattle, coming away in long strips up to a considerable height. A stand of elm in the Vale of Glamorgan known to the author was badly damaged by cattle in 1973. When revisited in 1978 numerous trees were dead and fallen and yet the majority, though generally damaged, had survived. They appeared not to have been further stripped by the cattle since the original attack. Further information on the propensity of cattle to strip elm bark would clearly be useful.

Much emphasis has come to be placed on the elm decline in the British Neolithic clearance phases. It is important to remember, however, that a decline of elm was not the major plank of the argument advanced by Iversen, who, working in Denmark – as we have seen – first discovered that clearance due to Neolithic man could be discerned in pollen diagrams. Iversen based his argument on the general decline of pollen of 'the elements of the high forest: oak, lime, ash and elm'. He spoke, for instance, of the 'sudden and unprecedented decline of pollen of all kinds of trees'. Two other features are of major importance in Iversen's argument. Firstly, the relative increase of herb pollen in his pollen density curves, which he took as an indication of the actual forest clearance. Secondly, the presence of the highest quantity of charcoal at that level. This charcoal, particularly at Ordrup Mose, near Copenhagen, Iversen attributed to the use of fire in forest clearance.

So much of our understanding of the effects of Neolithic man on his environment in Britain depends on the development of Iversen's ideas that these must now be rehearsed in more detail.

*Iversen's landnam phase*

The type of clearance discovered by Iversen has become known (after the Danish for 'land taking') as a landnam phase. Iversen divided his landnam phase into three stages. These can be seen in the generalised pollen diagram given in Fig. 4.5. Phase 1 included a relative increase of grass and other herb pollen together with a decline of the pollen of dominant trees. This he regarded as the phase of actual clearance. Phase 2 included pollen of cereals, *Plantago lanceolata* and various weed species. This, Iversen regarded as a farming phase, but from the evidence of rising curves for birch, sometimes alder and later hazel, he deduced that forest regeneration was already under way. He envisaged a 'grassy scrub and farming'. Phase 3 was defined on the basis of the relative decline of birch and recovery of the pollen curves for the high forest trees and, finally, the decline of hazel. These features, Iversen concluded, expressed the regeneration of the major forest elements, though in some instances pollen indicating agricultural activities continued to occur in small quantities. In the third phase Iversen envisaged the gradual regeneration of the forest cover almost to its pre-landnam constitution though in some instances containing more ash.

While the sequence of clearance, farming and regeneration was apparently the norm, Iversen drew attention to areas of poor soils where the forests were apparently open enough not to require clearance by fire. In the Jutland Heath region, for instance, he found minimal evidence of Neolithic clearance as such. Nevertheless, it was clear from the pollen diagrams that there was progressive deforestation from the Neolithic period onwards. Evidence of forest

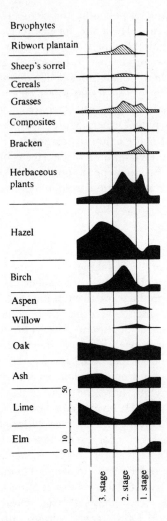

Figure 4.5. Generalised (relative) pollen diagram through the Danish landnam phase. (After Iversen 1973.) Iversen interpreted this sequence as: stage 1 – clearance; stage 2 – a short period of farming, and stage 3 – a period of forest regeneration. Iversen concluded that the farming episode lasted no more than 50-100 years and was carried out by a Neolithic population using a system of shifting agriculture. These ideas, published in 1941, form the fundamental basis of the interpretation of pollen evidence for Neolithic clearance and agricultural practices but their application to the British Isles is being modified as a result of recent work (see text).

regeneration is lacking in this area and, indeed, Iversen was of the opinion that there must have been many variations in the individual history of Neolithic clearances, particularly in respect of grazing intensity and duration (personal communication).

Notwithstanding his recognition of the many possible variations of clearance history, Iversen (1949) regarded the well-marked landnam phases as reflecting the succession after local occupation of short duration, and implied that they may have been conditioned by a single occupation fire. The resulting 'rapidly shooting trees, bushes and herbs' he supposed would have provided ideal food for free-ranging cattle. But with further regeneration, Iversen supposed that Neolithic man would have found it easier to move to a new spot and begin clearance anew. He was inclined to the view that the landnam phases may have been connected with settlements which had been suggested on archaeological grounds, to have lasted for a hundred years or so. The possibility of occupations lasting even shorter periods was clearly in his mind, however, and he mentions as little as 50 years (Iversen 1956). The idea of very short occupations received support from the results of experiments at Draved Forest in Jutland (Iversen 1956; Steensberg 1957) which showed that primitive agricultural techniques could not sustain a useful yield of cereals for more than a few years.

It is clear from his 1949 paper that Iversen did not regard the landnam phases as synchronous in different areas. The C-14 dates so far obtained show that the Danish landnam phases began around 2,600-2,500 bc and appear to correspond in time with the Middle Neolithic Funnel Beaker culture (Tauber 1972). But no C-14 measurements have so far been made that allow the durations of the landnam phases to be estimated. Neither has it yet been shown that they are different ages in different areas, which Iversen's theories would require.

Because of Iversen's untimely death in 1971, we shall never have the benefit of his mature view of the landnam phases in the light of the new evidence he was accumulating. It may be useful, therefore, to place on record the views he expressed in a letter to the author dated November 1970:

I have deliberately avoided using the term 'shifting agriculture' because I thought that agriculture might be understood as 'arable farming type'. It is the pastoral aspect which in my opinion characterizes the landnam phase in Danish diagrams, though pollen grains of cereals indicate some arable farming too. I regard it as essential that much more was burnt than necessary for cereal growing ... I have no objections to your reference to my interpretation – which does not mean that my view has not developed since 1956. Indeed, while maintaining the abruptness of the initial clearing and burning I think that solely based on ecological reasoning, I would put a minimum duration of at least 100 years for stage 2 in our diagrams.

## Modifications of Iversen's views

While Iversen apparently continued to think of the landnam phase in terms of a single clearance followed by a variable history of land-use, Troels-Smith (1954, p.52) came to the view that Iversen's landnam phase represents a series of forest clearances. This idea is receiving some support from work on the close parallels to the Danish landnam phase in Ireland (see p.167). For the moment, however, let us examine further the other modifications of Iversen's ideas made by Troels-Smith. These modifications resulted from extremely careful and detailed pollen analytical studies in the great Danish bog Aamosen and in association with excavations of the Swiss pile dwellings (Troels-Smith 1955a, 1956). At Aamosen, Troels-Smith noted that there were small but consistent traces of farming practices precisely at the elm decline of the Atlantic/Sub-Boreal transition (Danish pollen Zones VII-VIII; British Zones VIIa-VIIb) at a lower level than the landnam phase. These signs were: 1. the presence of cereal pollen, 2. the presence of plantain pollen, chiefly *Plantago major* (broad-leaved plantain), rather than *Plantago lanceolata* (ribwort plantain) which characterises the landnam phase, and 3. a few pollen grains of other species, but particularly of ramsons (or the wild garlic, *Allium* cf. *ursinum*). The pollen analytical data contained no evidence of pasture. Indeed the presence of ramsons, a delicate plant that would have been injured by trampling, is taken as an indication of the absence of pasture.

In explanation of this, Troels-Smith develops the ideas of Nordhagen (1954) and Faegri (1940) that the features are to be explained by the use of elm, particularly the leaves, as cattle fodder. The cattle are presumed not to have been allowed to range freely. Evidence of leafy branches preserved in what were apparently cattle stalls in the Swiss lake dwellings, much literary reference, and a little current use of leaf fodder, is adduced as support for his idea.

Troels-Smith (1960a) later extended his arguments to include also the use of ivy and several other species in the same way. So far as elm is concerned, Troels-Smith envisages the pollarding of trees at regular intervals of 2 or 3 years, thus preventing the shoots from flowering.

*The elm decline and the Neolithic in Britain*

Following Iversen's work in Denmark many British workers began to connect the appearance of weed type pollen, and particularly *Plantago lanceolata* (ribwort plantain), at the time of the elm decline with Neolithic agriculture. Godwin and Tallantire (1951), for instance, immediately recognised the importance of Neolithic activity in the history of the East Anglian Breckland as recorded in their pollen diagrams from Hockham Mere. Numerous similar instances have been provided also by the extensive work of Mitchell in Ireland (Mitchell 1956, 1976). There are, however, still relatively few instances of a clear stratigraphic correlation between Neolithic material and the elm decline. The classical example must be Shippea Hill, Cambridgeshire (Clark *et al.* 1935; Godwin and Clifford 1938; Godwin 1940b; Clark and Godwin 1962). The pollen diagram for this site showing the level of the Neolithic artifacts is reproduced here as Fig. 4.6. To this may be added the C-14 dated Neolithic trackways of the Somerset Levels some of which coincide fairly closely with the elm decline, as for instance the Chilton track (Coles *et al.* 1970). There are less satisfactory examples from Ireland at Dunshaughlin, Co. Meath (Mitchell 1940, 1951), and Newferry, Co. Antrim (Smith and Collins 1971).

The general temporal connection between Neolithic activity and the elm decline can be made, however, through the intermediary of C-14 dating. With the few earlier exceptions mainly in Northern Ireland, the radiocarbon results set out by I.F. Smith (1974, Figs. 13 and 18) and by Godwin (1970, Fig.1) show the Neolithic beginning after *c.* 3,400 bc. Despite the difficulties of definition, the C-14 dates for the elm decline surveyed by Smith and Pilcher (1973, Fig.2) start at broadly the same time. The oldest dates of this series for the beginning of the elm decline are Barfield Tarn (Cumberland) (Pennington 1970): 3,390 ± 120 bc (K-1097), Fallahogy (Co. Londonderry) (Smith and Willis 1962): 3,385 ± 120 bc (Q-555), Shippea Hill (Cambridgeshire) (Clark and Godwin 1962): 3,380 ± 120 bc (Q-585). The youngest dates, for the end of the elm decline,

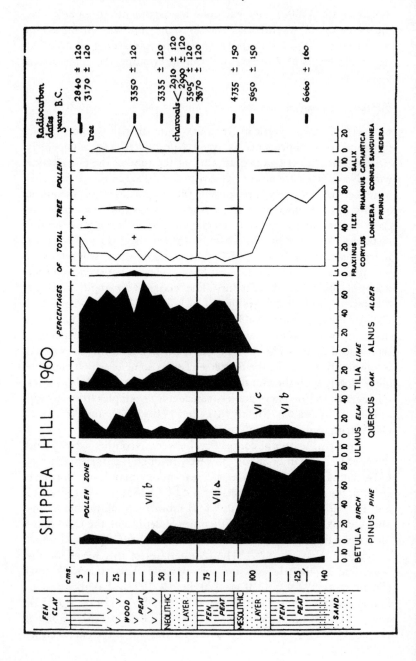

include Ballyscullion (Co. Antrim) (in Pilcher *et al*. 1971; Smith and Crowder, unpublished): 2,890 ± 60 bc (UB-113) and Flanders Moss (Perthshire) (Turner 1965): 2,620 ±120 bc (Q-577). The bulk of the dates, however, fall in the few hundred years before 3,000 bc and the dates which relate to the beginning of the elm decline have their mean values between 3,300 and 3,100 bc. As pointed out by Smith and Pilcher these results do not oppose the idea that the elm decline is synchronous within the limits of the methods. The limits are imposed by the uncertainties attached to the C-14 measurements themselves, the difficulties of definition and any errors due to sampling or contamination. It should be understood, however, that the dates do not *prove* that the elm decline was strictly synchronous, and they certainly allow a diachroneity of a century or two.

In spite of the range covered by the elm decline, its relative synchroneity, which has been suspected for many years, has led some authors to doubt whether Neolithic populations could have been responsible. The relative synchroneity may also be taken as an argument that the shifting agriculture envisaged by Iversen may not be a satisfactory explanation. As we have seen, Iversen makes a particular point of his expectation that the landnam phases would not have been synchronous. These problems begin to assume less importance, however, when we look at two recent developments. Firstly, there is mounting evidence of clearance before and during the elm decline (cf. Smith 1970a, p.90). Whether this can be attributed to Neolithic peoples is not yet always clear. In at least one instance, however, the presence of Neolithic man before the elm-decline is well attested. Secondly, certain clearances which began at the elm decline are being shown to be quite substantial, lasting some hundreds of years. Thus, while they may have involved slash-and-burn techniques, they may be presumed, in some cases at least, to

---

Figure 4.6. Relative pollen diagram from the deposits at Shippea Hill in the East Anglian Fenland. For references, see text. This is the classic example of the association of a Neolithic 'culture layer' with the 'elm-decline'. The diagram results from an analysis made in order to establish the radiocarbon chronology. It will be noted, however, that there is a discrepancy between the charcoal dates and the date for the Neolithic layer itself, presumably due to incorporation of older material into the layer. Using the current convention the C-14 dates are in years bc. (From Clark and Godwin 1962.)

represent more than one such episode. Let us examine these two features in more detail.

*Clearances before and during the elm decline*

At several Lake-District sites (Blea Tarn – see Fig. 4.12, Barfield Tarn – see Fig. 4.4 and Williamson's Moss) Pennington (1975b) has recorded traces of small forest clearance before the elm decline. At the two former sites, she dates these to between 3,700 and 3,100 bc and attributes them to Mesolithic peoples. While this idea is perhaps not out of line with our present understanding of the age of the Neolithic, it will be of considerable interest to see whether Neolithic material of pre-elm decline age is discovered in this area as it has been in Northern Ireland. It is worthy of passing note here that, in comparing these early clearings with Walker's evidence from the north Cumbrian lowland (Walker 1966), Pennington refers again to clearance in the Mesolithic. It is true that Walker places certain early clearances in his Cumbrian Zone C.16 at the end of pollen Zone VIIa (the Atlantic period), which he tentatively dates as beginning around 4,000 bc. This zone (C.16) is, however, the period in which the elm curve falls and could equally well be regarded as falling within the Sub-Boreal period. It is unfortunate that Walker's monumental work was carried out before ready access to C-14 dating facilities was available. The 4,000 bc date is derived by interpolation and comparison with the C-14 series from Scaleby Moss (Godwin *et al.* 1957) where the mean of three C-14 dates for the end of the elm decline is 3,014 bc. At Ehenside Tarn (see Fig. 4.7) and Bowness Common, Walker discovered a clearance in his Zone C.16 which involves both elm and oak and starts where the elm curve is still high. Both species recover in the subsequent Zones C.17 and 18. At these sites hazel pollen becomes abundant during the clearances. Hazel is extremely resistant to all kinds of damage (cf. Smith and Willis 1962; Godwin 1975) and its pollen often increases during clearance phases. Walker envisages the possibility of its becoming so abundant as artificially to depress the curves for other trees in his relative (i.e. percentage) pollen diagrams. He concludes that an elm decline may have thus been artificially produced in areas where there is no substantial evidence of local Neolithic clearance. This, he suggests, was the case at his sites at Oulton Moss and Scaleby Moss. Walker regards his evidence as showing early clearances on the Cumbrian coast (and this has been confirmed by

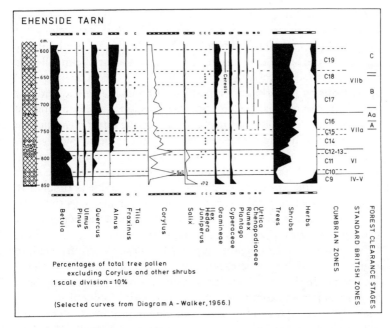

Figure 4.7. Selected curves from a relative pollen diagram from the Cumbrian coastal lowland at Ehenside Tarn. (Redrawn from data in Walker 1966.) The clearance phase (best exemplified by the rising total herb pollen curve) starts in Walker's Cumbrian Zone C16 while the elm curve is still high. Walker suggests that this zone began at about 4000 bc and Pennington (1975) takes the clearance as being Mesolithic. The Zone VIIa-VIIb boundary is drawn at a rather high level in comparison with the *Ulmus* curve, however, and the estimate of age is based on comparison with other sites. Clearance A may thus be Neolithic in age. Stage Aa, with lower values for the total herb pollen curve is thought to represent a period of regeneration and stages B and C further episodes of clearance. It was found to be impossible to correlate the well-known Neolithic artifact from the Tarn deposits unequivocally with the pollen sequence, though they may belong to the end of Zone C16. The diagram provides an example of clearance effects detectable during the 'elm-decline'.

Pennington) but with the peoples or techniques not spreading to the northern Eden Valley for perhaps a thousand years.

In the south-east of the Lake District, around the Head of Morecambe Bay, Oldfield (1963) distinguished a primary elm decline, followed by a landnam phase. It is to be regretted that the sampling interval in the diagrams available to him was rather wide and it would be of interest to see whether his conclusions are sustained by more detailed analysis. Nevertheless, we are bound to agree that the broad conclusion of a gradual decline of elm followed by a steeper fall is probably correct. Despite the lack of distinct weed species during the primary elm decline, Oldfield takes the evidence of a slight rise of grass pollen and bracken spores, as exemplified at Thrang Moss (Fig. 4.8), as probably signifying forest clearance for pasture. This, he suggests, may have eventually been colonised by alder and probably by hazel and ash. Elm may have recovered at some sites and Oldfield supposes that forest regeneration ensued before a second elm decline. This second elm decline is thought to represent a more typical clearance phase (landnam) with relatively abundant *Plantago lanceolata*, grasses and bracken increasing, and the presence of several weed species such as sorrels and mugwort. Hazel (and possibly alder) again appears to have been involved in regeneration of the woodland, with elm (and lime) eventually recovering. In the restored woodland cover ash appears to have been a more important component than previously. Oldfield describes some local differences of detail in the landnam phases. They were followed, however, by a series of further clearances, the first apparently pastoral and the second with evidence of cereal cultivation. Dating of these phases is difficult in the absence of C-14 dates, but Oldfield suggests they may relate to Beaker and middle Bronze Age activities respectively.

In neither of the two cases described, Walker's Cumberland Lowland work and Oldfield's synthesis for the south-east Lake District, is there any precise evidence of the date of the initiation of clearance or its duration. Some minor environmental modifications are suggested by the difficult evidence at Storrs Moss, in the southern Lake District (Powell *et al.* 1971) at the end of pollen Zone VIIa, however, immediately prior to Oldfield's primary elm decline. By comparison with C-14 dates from Foulshaw Moss, Oldfield suggests that these disturbances can be dated as early as *c.* 3,400-

Figure 4.8. Relative pollen diagram from Thrang Moss in the S.E. Lake District. (From Oldfield 1963.) The slight rise of grass pollen (*Gramineae*) and bracken spores (*Pteridium*) at the 'primary elm decline' is taken as probably indicating forest clearance for pasture. This took place before the marked elm decline which Oldfield associates with a Landnam phase with more abundant plantain (*Plantago*) pollen.

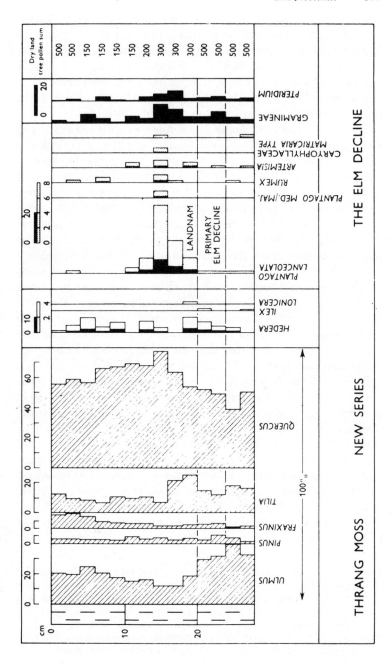

3,500 bc. Unfortunately also, at the classical site of Ehenside Tarn it was impossible for Walker to make clear correlation with the Neolithic cultural material. It seems unlikely, though, that this was connected with the earliest of the clearances (see Fig. 4.7). These stories, insofar as it has been possible within a short compass to relate them, illustrate the fact that the vegetational changes at the time of the elm decline are both complex and difficult to understand. Certainly we must not assume that a single event is recorded. The elm decline itself may disguise a number of different activities or types of land-use. This may be further illustrated by another reference to Sims's work at Hockham Mere and Seamere in East Anglia. Here, during a gradual fall of the elm curve immediately before its decline (but above a level dated to 3,260 ± 120 bc (Q-1049) at Hockham Mere) there are temporary declines of the tree pollen influx. The presence of *Plantago lanceolata* pollen and peaks of the grass pollen curve (and other features) are taken to indicate temporary opening(s) of the forest. The use of elm, ash and ivy as fodder is envisaged, together with felling or ringing to produce small localised clearings. While it would be possible to argue about the details of Sims's interpretation, and certain of his speculations, there is little doubt that some form of interference was going on before the marked elm decline and that this was in the Neolithic rather than the Mesolithic period.

Evidence from Newferry, Co. Antrim, where a series of occupation layers of Mesolithic and Neolithic age are stratified in diatomite deposits, was previously thought to point in a similar direction (Smith and Collins 1971; Smith 1975) though it now appears from more recent work (Smith, in press) that the evidence of early clearance can be more firmly attributed to Mesolithic man. There is, however, good radiocarbon-dated evidence of woodland clearance from the nearby Ballyscullion site (Fig. 4.9) at *c.* 3,700 bc bracketed by 3,865 ± 90 bc (UB-296) and 3,580 ± 60 bc (UB-116) (Smith 1975, Figs. 2, 3). The evidence takes the form of a decline of

---

Figure 4.9. Relative pollen diagram from a level below the classical 'elm decline' at Ballyscullion, Co. Antrim (see also Figure 4.10). (From Smith 1975.) A clearance phase with pollen of plantains (*Plantago*), bracken (*Pteridium*), cf. bistort (*Polygonum* cf. *bistorta*), nettle (*Urtica*) and goosefoot (*Chenopodiaceae*) occurs in the closely analysed section in the middle of the diagram. On the basis of the C-14 dates the clearance appears to have taken place at about 3,700 bc and to have lasted about 100 years.

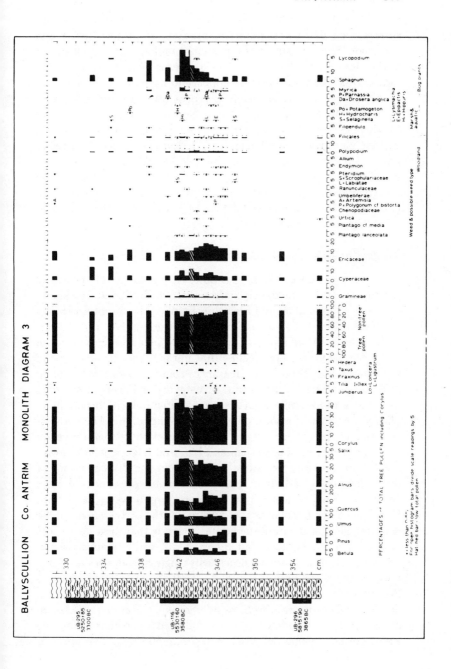

BALLYSCULLION   Co. ANTRIM   MONOLITH   DIAGRAM 3

tree pollen (first pine, then oak) together with the presence of weedy species such as ribwort plantain, bracken, cf. bistort, nettle and goosefoot. The clearance is less pronounced than the later clearance at the elm decline (Pilcher *et al.* 1971, see also Fig. 4.10). From the radiocarbon dates, however, it appears to have lasted perhaps 100 years and can hardly be taken as representing a single slash-and-burn episode. As is demonstrated by Smith (1975, Fig. 3) the dates for this clearance coincide with the four radiocarbon dates for the earliest Neolithic at Ballynagilly, Co. Tyrone. It could therefore have been carried out by Neolithic peoples though we cannot be certain that this was the case. Evidence from the settlement site at Ballynagilly for forest disturbance of this age is rather scanty (Pilcher 1975; Smith and Pilcher 1979; see also Figs 4.14 and 4.15) though not totally lacking.

### The duration of the early Neolithic clearances

We have seen above that there is quite clear evidence of opening of the forest cover immediately before the elm decline at Hockham, Seamere, Ballyscullion and Ehenside Tarn. At the three former sites the C-14 evidence shows that these clearances are Neolithic in age. At Thrang Moss and several other nearby sites we see evidence of clearance before the elm decline that initiates the classical type of landnam phase. These early clearances could be regarded as falling into the 'small temporary clearance' category of Turner (1965) who used the term to signify what Iversen had in mind with his landnam phases, i.e. short episodes followed by regeneration. (The classical evidence of forest regeneration – the rise of the pollen curves of colonising trees or shrubs such as birch and hazel – is not always present in the cases described though from the disappearance of the pollen of open-habitat plants it can be presumed to have occurred.) The evidence from Ballyscullion, however, and from Hockham Mere (insofar as the duration of the early phases can be determined from the published data) suggests that these clearances lasted not a few decades, but many. Thus, while relatively short, even these clearances are not necessarily single episodes of slash-and-burn. Perhaps the best example of a very short clearance phase in Britain is that discovered at Tregaron bog by Turner (1965). Here a detailed pollen diagram from rapidly-growing peat enabled her to distinguish a temporary clearance followed by regeneration, the whole episode lasting not much more than 50 years. This episode, however, dates not from the Neolithic, but some time between *c.* 700 and 400 bc. Short clearance phases of Neolithic age may, however, have been detected by Moore (in press) in his work at Llyn Mire in the Wye Valley (cf. Moore and Beckett 1971). Here, Moore appears to have identified at least two phases of clearance for cultivation of cereals followed by soil exhaustion within a period which he estimates as being as short as 20 years. These clearances come from a time probably not long after the elm-decline. By comparison, they serve to emphasise the great duration of the landnam phases distinguished in many areas of Britain, and particularly in Ireland, which have now been shown to last not for decades but for centuries. The Llyn Mire clearances may well, in fact, be a component within a longer clearance which might have been regarded as of landnam type.

*The duration of the landnam-type clearances*

While examples could be multiplied from unpublished work the three cases described by Pilcher *et al.* (1971) will illustrate the results of the application of radiocarbon dating to the study of the duration of Neolithic clearance phases. In Fig.4.10 three radiocarbon dated pollen diagrams covering the elm decline are presented. These all show the major features of a landnam phase, albeit rather variably. The details illustrate some points of interest and will be described later. Let us look first at the broad divisions, A, B and C. Stage A begins with a fall of forest tree pollen, usually elm and pine and is characterised by increased amounts of grass and occasional ribwort plantain pollen. This stage appears to have lasted 100-400 years (see Fig. 4.11) and at two of the sites cereal-type pollen is present. It may then represent a phase of clearance for arable farming. Since soil fertility drops off rapidly without sophisticated agricultural techniques, as illustrated in the experiments at Draved forest in Denmark (Iversen 1956; Steensberg 1957) arable agriculture carried out over such a long period may well have demanded the continual opening of new ground. At two of the sites (Ballynagilly and Beaghmore, see Pilcher 1975; Pilcher and Smith, 1979, and Pilcher 1969) the initial clearance was obviously rapid, since the pollen changes take place between adjacent samples. At the third site (Ballyscullion) there is a more typical slow decline of *Ulmus* which could reflect the process of clearance over a longer period (see also Smith 1958d, 1975; Smith and Willis 1962) and has

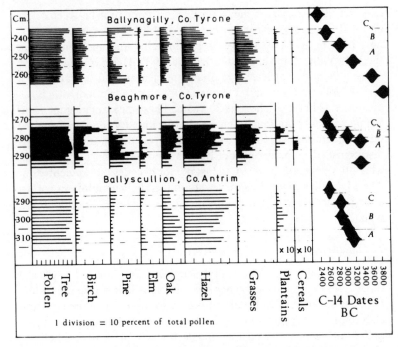

Figure 4.10. Radiocarbon dated pollen diagrams from three sites in Northern Ireland at the time of the 'elm-decline'. In each diagram a clearance of landnam-type is distinguished, and divided into three stages. (After Pilcher *et al.* 1971.) See also Figure 4.11. Using the current convention, the dates are in years bc.

some features in common with the 'primary elm decline' of Oldfield. Stage B, which appears to have lasted 150-200 years, has increased plantain values, but cereal pollen is absent. This, at least at two of the sites, appears to represent a change of farming methods, possibly a change to a pastoral emphasis. Hazel becomes more abundant in stage B and this may be taken as a beginning of forest regeneration. It is notable that cattle find the leaves of hazel unpalatable (cf. Smith and Willis 1962). Stage C, which is relatively short, lasting some 50-100 years, embraces the resurgence of tree pollen which betokens the recovery of the forests, in which birch seems to have been particularly involved at Beaghmore. In these three examples then, clearance phases started around 3,100-3,200 bc and appear to have ended in the period around 2,600-2,700 bc.

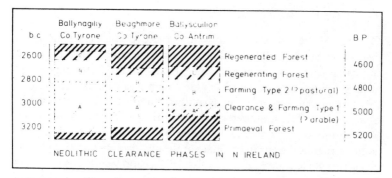

Figure 4.11. Summary diagram of the landnam-type Neolithic clearances at three sites in N. Ireland (see also Figure 4.10). The durations of the various phases are derived by interpolation on the C-14 dated deposition rate curves. In each case the whole episode lasted several centuries and cannot reflect a single episode of slash-and-burn. (From Smith 1975; modified after Pilcher *et al.* 1971.)

The evidence for long episodes of clearance in the Neolithic is not restricted to Ireland. From relative and absolute pollen diagrams from Abbot Moss (Beckett and Hibbert 1976; Hibbert, in press), it has been shown that clearance continued for about 200 years after *c.* 2,800 bc with forest regeneration proper not occurring until about 2,200 bc. Another example may be taken from Hockham Mere (Sims 1973) where the tree pollen minimum appears to have lasted about 200 years. And Pennington (1975b) shows that at Blea Tarn (Fig. 4.12) period A, the decline of tree pollen, lasted 200-300 years. At this site there is no evidence of forest regeneration. At Ennerdale, however, a regeneration phase (C) lasted about 100 years, with the periods A and B lasting some 150 and 200 years respectively. It is of interest to see that here a phase of reduced oak pollen deposition is over by just after 2,800 bc. To this we may add that the initial effects of the clearance starting at the elm decline at Hockham Mere, Norfolk, (Sims 1973) were over by level dated by Q-1046 to 2,800 ± 115 bc. Considering the possible errors involved these dates may not be very different from the end of the Irish clearance phases mentioned above. The evidence available begins to point therefore in some ways to the end of an era around the end of the first quarter of the third millenium bc. Firm connections with any cultural or economic changes at this time are as yet impossible, though further discussion is given later (p.205).

*The types of Neolithic clearances*

Our review so far then brings us to the point of seeing small clearances before the elm decline, several as yet not accurately dated but going back as early as *c*.3,700 bc. (Ballyscullion) and in progress around 3,200 bc (Hockham). These clearances may thus belong to the sort of pioneer phase of Neolithic colonists envisaged by I.F. Smith (1974). The supposed late Mesolithic clearances distinguished by Pennington could also be regarded in the same light. The conjecture that the landnam phase at the elm decline may be only one of a series of clearances (A.G. Smith 1970a) apparently now receives further support. The clearances at the time of the elm decline now shown to be substantial are seen to fall readily into line with I.F. Smith's (1974) idea that they may be connected with well established and expanding communities which 'started to transform the landscape by extensive forest clearances and by building the first monuments of earth and stone'.

*The consequences of the Neolithic clearances*

While we have pointed to instances of regeneration after the elm-decline clearances, these appear to have been most marked and most dramatic in Ireland, the Lake District and Somerset, possibly because elm appears to have been favoured there (see the isopollen map in Fig. 4.1) and it is the resurgence of this curve which often illustrates the woodland regeneration. We have, however, already instanced the Blea Tarn story where evidence of immediate regeneration is lacking. Pennington points out that the clearance taking place at *c*. 3,100 bc was in birch-pine woods, not oakwoods, and that it was maintained until at least *c*. 2,500 bc. As may be seen from Fig. 4.12, during this period there was a progressive decrease in

---

Figure 4.12. Combined relative and absolute pollen diagram from Blea Tarn, Langdale, Cumbria. (From Pennington 1975b.) The histogram bars represent percentages and the line graphs the annual deposition rate or pollen influx. The C-14 dates (SRR-16, 17 and 18) are quoted in years bp. The lower two delimit Pennington's Stage A clearance lasting 200-300 years (period of declining elm). The upper two C-14 dates delimit Pennington's Stage B (period of continuous *Plantago lanceolata*), lasting even longer. At the level marked *c*. 5,660 bp (*c*. 3,700 bc) Pennington detects a temporary episode of clearance with a minor elm decline and increase of grasses.

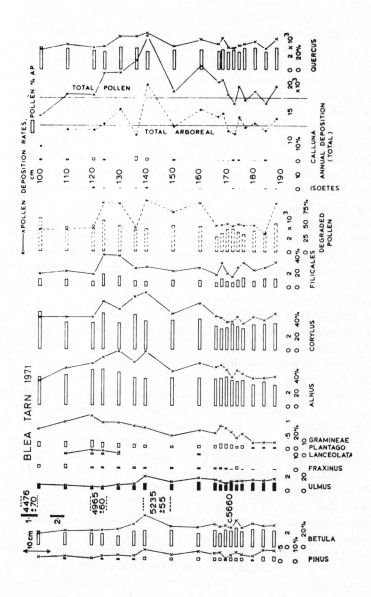

BLEA TARN 1971

the amount of tree pollen (in absolute terms) reaching the sediment, which could indicate continuing deforestation, and this appears to have been intensified at the time of the occupation of the axe-factory chipping floors at Thunacar Knot. These are on the opposite side of Great Langdale from Blea Tarn and have yielded C-14 dates of 2,730 ± 135 bc (BM-281) and 2,524 ± 52 bc (BM-676). As we have already seen, the activity in that area appears to have culminated in the formation of blanket peat (Pennington 1975a). The culmination of Neolithic clearances in open conditions has already been alluded to in the case of chalklands of southern England. The conclusions, as we have seen, are drawn from the biological evidence preserved beneath monuments. Unfortunately, deposits which might illuminate this process further have so far not been located in the south of England. We therefore lack the sort of pollen evidence for the longer history that is available in other regions. A pollen diagram from Wingham, Kent, however, (Godwin 1962a, 1975) illustrates that the Downs must have been quite deforested by the early or middle Bronze Age. Dimbleby (1976) regards the pollen and molluscan evidence from the sites on the chalk as showing that clearance was progressive. Evidence relating to woodland regeneration he regards as inconclusive.

Progressive deforestation is perhaps best illustrated by reference to the site at Hockham Mere (Godwin and Tallantire 1951) in the East Anglian Breckland, whose sandy soils today support wide expanses of grassland and heath. It was here that evidence for Neolithic forest clearance was first brought to light in Britain (Godwin 1944). Despite the modification of the story as a result of Sims's more recent work which shows a certain amount of forest regeneration after the earliest clearances (see p.164), the general drift subsequent to these is clearly towards increasingly open conditions. This is evidenced by the progressively larger proportion of non-tree pollen falling into the lake basin. The beginning of this increase may be presumed to have been in the Neolithic, though according to Sims's work not as an immediate consequence of the initial impacts. This progressive deforestation stands in dramatic contrast to the very slight signs of Neolithic influence at Old Buckenham Mere (Godwin 1967, 1968) just over 15km. to the east. This site is in an area of more fertile soils on glacial drifts where it is apparent that substantial clearance did not take place until the late Bronze Age. This contrast might be taken as illustrating the classical view of the attraction of early farmers to the lighter soils which, by their nature, would have been perhaps less densely wooded and more easily cultivated. It is known that the Breckland was sheep-walk in the Middle Ages and it has been argued that the area has not been recolonised by woodland because of heavy grazing by sheep, and more recently by rabbits. Perhaps we can envisage here the creation of pasture in Neolithic times and its maintenance by grazing pressure down to the present. We have implied earlier that such a history may also be true of the chalk uplands of southern England. Our concept of the Neolithic landscape of southern England should not be dominated, however, by the picture that is emerging of deforested chalklands. Palynological research in progress by K.E. Barber and L.E. Haskens in the Hampshire-Dorset Tertiary basin points to the possibility of a more or less persistent forest cover in the central part of the New Forest, where there is no evidence of Neolithic occupation. This stands in contrast to the Poole basin where there is an elm decline at a number of sites and where there are also indications that the woodland cover was relatively open prior to the limited Neolithic occupation (Barber 1975 and personal communication).

### Localisation of Neolithic clearings

By contrast with the southern chalklands the local nature of many Neolithic clearances may be instanced. Turner (1965) has pointed for example to the lack of evidence of Neolithic clearances even of her 'small-temporary' character following the marked elm decline at Flanders Moss in the Forth Valley. She is of the opinion that it is unlikely that there were no such clearances, but that they were simply too small to affect the pollen rain, the sampling site being over a mile from the nearest source of pollen. Despite the marked elm decline, Turner takes this as evidence contributing to the idea that the areas cleared were indeed quite small in extent.

The localisation of Neolithic clearance activity has been much more amply demonstrated by Hibbert (Coles *et al.* 1970) in the Somerset Levels. He points to the marked difference in the abundance of clearance indicators in the Chilton Moor deposits, near the emerging island of the Burtle Sands, as compared with the central parts of the Levels (Coles and Hibbert 1968). A point of interest that may be added is that the marked clearance here, as exemplified by Hibbert's pollen diagram 'Chilton Track 1' reproduced as Fig. 4.13, shows a high proportion of pollen of plants

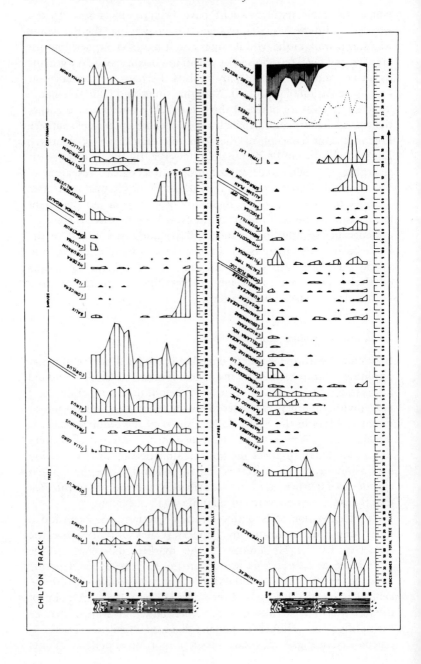

characteristic of broken ground. Despite the absence of cereal pollen Hibbert regards this as supporting the idea that the agriculture was mainly arable while not denying that the large amounts of plantain pollen indicate areas of grassland.

The three-dimensional approach to his Somerset results adopted by Hibbert provides a beautiful example of the way in which Neolithic clearances were in some instances quite localised. Hibbert's transects across the Somerset Levels are illustrated in Fig. 4.14 (Coles *et al.* 1973, Fig. 6). The lower transect shown in the figure runs north-south between the Wedmore ridge and the Polden Hills. The elm decline (hatched curve) is seen in all the diagrams but the abundance of shade-intolerant herbs (black curve) is clearly greatest on the southern side of the transect closest to the Polden Hills. The upper transect in the figure runs east-west from the Westhay 'island' towards the Burtle 'island'. The former is a low knoll of limestone emerging above the present organic deposits of the Levels; the latter is a similar emergence of sandy material. It is clear that the maximum impact of Neolithic man was at the western end of the transect where the basal sands emerge from the Levels (at Burtle and near the Honeygore site). The light soils of these beds appear then to have been the favoured sites for early clearance whereas the Westhay area may have remained uncleared. It is worthy of note that wood from species which could have grown only on the dry ground, as well as wood of possible fen trees was used in the construction of the Neolithic Somerset trackways. In the case of the Sweet trackway, for instance (Coles *et al.* 1973), Hibbert points out that of the fen trees only alder was used in the construction of the trackway, but that ash, elm, holly, lime and hazel used in construction or associated with the trackway, could only have been growing on the adjacent dry ground. These identified timbers do, of course, provide quite concrete evidence that the trees mentioned

---

Figure 4.13. Relative pollen diagram embracing the Neolithic trackway in The Somerset Levels known as Chilton Track 1. (From Hibbert, in press.) The trackway coincides in level with the end of the elm-decline at a level where weed pollen becomes particularly abundant. The high proportion of species characteristic of broken ground is taken by Hibbert as suggesting that the agriculture was mainly arable. The pollen types below 65cm. indicate open water and fen which developed after the end of a marine transgression. Above 65cm. wood fragments appear in the peat and the pollen curves indicate the development of fen wood.

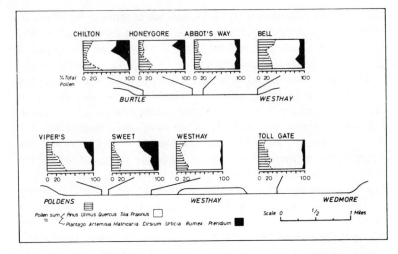

Figure 4.14. Composite relative pollen diagrams from transects across the
Somerset Levels. (From Coles *et al.* 1973.) The elm curve is hatched and
shade-intolerant herbs in black. The transects show localisation of the
Neolithic clearances (for explanation see text).

were felled by Neolithic man. The analysis of timbers also shows
that there was deliberate selection of suitable woods for specific
functions. The hazel rods which are abundant in certain of the
trackways, as Godwin (1960, 1975) has pointed out, would only
have grown as coppice shoots. It is inferred from the pollen diagrams
that considerable stretches of hazel coppice must have existed. This
may have involved a conscious form of woodland management,
though Rackham (in Coles *et al.* 1973) feels that in the case of Sweet
Track material the evidence is not conclusive enough to be confident
of artificial coppicing. The environmental implications of the
extensive and detailed work in association with the Neolithic trackways in the Somerset Levels have only been touched upon in this
short account and for further information the reader is referred to
the excellent Somerset Levels Papers (Coles *et al.* 1975a, 1976, 1977,
1978).

### Differentiation of land-use

We have now arrived at the point where we have seen evidence of the
impact of Neolithic man at various levels and with various results.
These range from quite local clearances of various durations to more

widespread clearances leading to increasingly open conditions. In some cases, however, the impact of Neolithic man appears to have been slight. We have already alluded to some areas of the Scottish highlands though even there new unpublished work appears to be pointing in the direction of a more widespread impact. We may further instance the Speyside pollen diagrams of O'Sullivan (1974). These amply demonstrate that the forests of Mesolithic and Neolithic times were mixed pine-birch in which the deciduous forest dominants oak, elm and alder were unimportant. Even these forests which must have been more readily susceptible to burning appear to have been relatively little affected until the late Neolithic or early Bronze Age.

In the southern Pennines, the work of Tallis (Tallis and Switsur 1973; Tallis 1964a, 1964b) has shown relatively little impact of Neolithic man. In the case of his Featherbed Moss site on the Snake Pass, for instance, Tallis points out that the area was probably remote from Neolithic settlement. From her studies on the Millstone Grits of the Derbyshire Pennine area around Sheffield, Hicks (1971) envisages a minor intrusion of Neolithic herdsmen around 3,000 bc, perhaps growing a little grain in temporary clearings. She suggests an intensification of clearance, though still on a small scale, in the middle/late Neolithic, perhaps connected with the local appearance of polished stone axes. Similarly, only slight evidence of Neolithic clearance was found by Tinsley (1975) at her sites on the Millstone Grit of the Nidderdale Moors north of Pateley Bridge, Yorkshire. She takes a small increase of grass and sorrel-type pollen as suggestive of use of the area for summer pasture in the later part of the Neolithic. Again, at Rishworth Moor, south-west of Halifax, Yorkshire, Bartley (1975) finds little evidence of Neolithic interference with the woodlands. It is of interest, however, to note that the relative abundance of grass pollen throughout the late Atlantic and early Sub-Boreal part of the diagram, suggests that the woodland at the site, which is at an altitude of 410m., was quite open, or even that woodland was restricted to lower slopes during the Neolithic period. A comparable instance of lightly wooded conditions may be instanced from Slieve Gallion, Co. Tyrone, (Pilcher 1973). Likewise, Simmons (1969b) and Simmons and Cundill (1974a) see the North York Moors as only lightly exploited in Neolithic times. Much the same kind of story is seen in the work of Bartley *et al.* (1976) in the lowland to the south and east of Durham. Here there was apparently only small scale and temporary clearance from about 3,200 bc, though possibly larger clearings were established around 2,600 bc at one of their sites. As in Central Rossendale (Lancs.) (Tallis and McGuire 1972) much of north Yorkshire appears then to have remained quite forested, with only small clearings, perhaps largely for pasture, until the Bronze Age.

Despite this wide agreement that Neolithic man had little impact on a large area in the Pennines, it may be that these uplands were used rather more extensively than the pollen evidence suggests. Neolithic utilisation of areas that were relatively open either naturally or as a result of management during the Mesolithic period may not have resulted in particularly strong pollen evidence. Damp moorland could have been grazed without a great floruit of ribwort plantain, for instance, which is often used as the key indicator of Neolithic pastoralism. Certainly Bartley's evidence from Rishworth Moor would bear such an interpretation. Tallis (1975) points out that the southern Pennine uplands which may have been opened up in the Mesolithic period could have continued in use as seasonal hunting grounds into the Neolithic. Use of such areas for grazing should perhaps also be considered as a possibility.

By contrast, as we have already seen (p.147), Neolithic man probably contributed to the marked environmental changes taking place in the Lake District with deforestation of the higher slopes and soil degradation. According to Moore (see p.149), the uplands of mid-Wales and Exmoor must also have suffered to a greater degree at the hands of Neolithic man than the uplands of north-east England. On Dartmoor also the effects of late Neolithic/early Bronze Age clearance may have been to induce local soil deterioration and blanket peat formation. (Simmons 1969a). Before this, however, towards the end of his Mesolithic/Neolithic continuum, Simmons finds evidence of only minor forest clearances generally followed by regeneration. Any of these clearances that remained open, he suggests may have so exposed the soils to leaching that would allow the development of blanket peat such as did indeed form at several sites at the end of pollen Zone VIIa and in early Zone VIIb.

Just as we have seen both local and regional differentiation of the effects of Neolithic practices, so there is evidence of certain possible altitudinal differences of land-use. In mid-Wales, for instance, Moore (in press) points out that the only evidence of cereal growing in the Neolithic is from the Wye Valley site at Llyn Mire, whereas the upland sites show evidence only of pastoral activity. He poses the question whether transhumance was practised, or whether separate cultures were involved.

That the uplands were differentially exploited in some areas is clear from Pennington's work in the Lake District which is dealt with below. It is an old idea that the southern chalk uplands were among the first areas to be cleared (e.g. see Childe 1940). What is surprising, perhaps, is to see mounting evidence even in the north of Ireland that it was in the uplands that cereals may have been grown. In Fig. 4.11 the two sites where cereal pollen is present in the Neolithic clearance phase (Beaghmore & Ballynagilly) are both upland sites. By contrast cereal pollen is sparse, if not entirely lacking, at lowland sites. The probability of cereal growing by Neolithic peoples at high altitude is brought out in the work of the late Dr S.M. Holland (Kirk 1974). She discovered numerous large grass pollen grains of cereal type in blanket peat dated to 2,735 ± 85 bc (UB-833) at *c.* 450m. on Slieve Croob, Co. Down, well above the present cultivation limit. Pennington (1975b), however, shows that in Cumbria clearance for agriculture involving cereal growing was in the lowland coastal plain, rather than the uplands. In the forests of the Lakeland valleys it is the elm alone which appears to have suffered and this, Pennington suggests, was possibly due to leaf-collecting for fodder in the manner proposed by Troels-Smith (1960a). While this possibility has been mooted by a number of authors for British sites the case made by Pennington, despite her caution, is perhaps the most reasoned and substantial for the British Isles. Both here and in other instances, however, the ability of the cattle to bark elms (Smith 1975) would provide an alternative explanation, particularly if they were turned into the forests in the autumn and winter. It is worthy of passing note that the use of leaf fodder does not necessarily carry the implication of stall-feeding. As may be observed today in the Himalayas, hobbled cattle can be managed under forest conditions by lopping branches daily for fodder. Other than the provision of this fodder the cattle appear to require little attention and need not be enclosed. In these regions leaves are also used as green manure, a practice which could have been used in Neolithic Britain. The only positive suggestion of manuring in the Neolithic so far has been the possible use of bracken fronds brought to light by Dimbleby (Dimbleby and Evans 1974).

*The use of fire in the Neolithic*

Primitive communities may have used fire in quite sophisticated ways to enhance the productivity of the environment, particularly in attracting and localising game animals. Numerous ethnographical parallels have been set out in an excellent essay by Mellars (1976) and the association of charcoal layers with vegetational changes is exemplified by Smith (1970a). Jacobi *et al.* (1976) conclude on the basis of several lines of evidence that Mesolithic populations may have used recurrent burning to suppress tree cover in the southern Pennine uplands. Such a practice, starting when the early postglacial forests were still light, seems a realistic possibility. It has sometimes been questioned, however, whether in the Neolithic period fire could have been used for clearance when the mature, damp, deciduous forest would have been extremely difficult to burn off. In the Draved experiment, for instance, in which the supposed methods of Neolithic agriculture were re-enacted, the cut-over forest could not be fired in the first season. In the second year, however, once the felled trees had dried burning was possible, but only by using long poles to turn continuously and advance the burning brushwood (Iversen 1956).

Despite the possible difficulty of firing deciduous forest, many organic deposits are found to contain charcoal in the Neolithic period. As an example we may cite Walker's record of charcoal just above the elm decline in the lake deposits of Langdale Combe (Walker 1965). Walker suggested that fire was indeed used as an agency of clearance in this area. Apart from those in the Pennine Mesolithic peats (Jacobi *et al.* 1976; Tallis 1975), perhaps the most abundant charcoal layers so far encountered are those described by Durno and McVean (1959) from the pine forest region of Ben Eighe (Wester Ross). These extend from the Boreal period to the present and the authors see fires not only as the dominant factor in the development of the vegetation, but as also responsible for extreme soil degradation. Durno and McVean do not discuss any possible involvement of man, however, and his importance in these processes must remain imponderable in that region. Stewart and Durno (1969) however, regard indiscriminate burning by early settlers, combined with a relatively dry climate, as responsible for the high charcoal content of peat at Moss of Cruden (Aberdeenshire). Here a continuous record of charcoal fragments was found. The authors regard both climatic and anthropogenic factors as being involved in a reduction of forest and extension of heath. This process apparently began in the Neolithic period since the base of the peat is dated to 3,070 ± 95 bc (NPL-94).

There is no unequivocal evidence for the use of fire alone as a clearance method in the Neolithic period. The presence of charcoal in peat and other deposits is, however, at least in some instances likely to be a reflection of more than accidental burning. Indeed, the short durations of some Neolithic effects on the forest cover demand an explanation in terms of the use of active physical methods rather than the prevention of regeneration by grazing animals. The best examples of the apparently deliberate use of fire in clearance, not surprisingly, come from the uplands. We have already mentioned Walker's suggestion for Langdale. The use of fire in the clearance of light pine-birch woodlands in this area has been further exemplified by Pennington (1975b). While the presence of pine in the forest is perhaps not a prerequisite for the use of fire it would certainly have facilitated its use. This appears to have been the case at Ballynagilly, Co. Tyrone, an upland site on poor sandy soils (Pilcher and Smith 1979). Here the evidence for burning in the form of C-14 dated charcoal of various species, is particularly clear. Again it must be emphasised, however, that there is no evidence that fire alone was employed in forest clearance. This section will be drawn to a close by recounting briefly the Neolithic history of the Ballynagilly site.

A pollen diagram for the mid-postglacial at Ballynagilly is given in Fig. 4.15. This diagram comes from a valley bog in close proximity to the archaeological site excavated by ApSimon (1969, 1976). The excavation revealed the foundations of a rectangular house with the remains of split-oak planking which was dated to 3,215 ± 50 bc (UB-201). Pine charcoal was found stratified into the valley bog deposits at a level where the pine and elm curves fall. This is the point at which the clearance phase (Stage A, Figs. 4.11, 4.16) begins. The date for this level, 3,195 ± 70 bc (UB-253) is indistinguishable from that for the house. Other areas of the site yielded charcoal of oak and hazel for which the C-14 dates were again found to be indistinguishable from that for the Neolithic house (UB-15 (oak charcoal) 3,245 ± 60 bc; UB-18 (hazel charcoal) 3,345 ± 90 bc). Pine, oak and hazel were thus all burnt. The clearance of the forest of which these trees were a component took place around 3,270 bc. It appears from the pollen diagram to have been a very rapid process, taking place in a period certainly less than 20 years, but possibly in as little as a single year. There then followed the

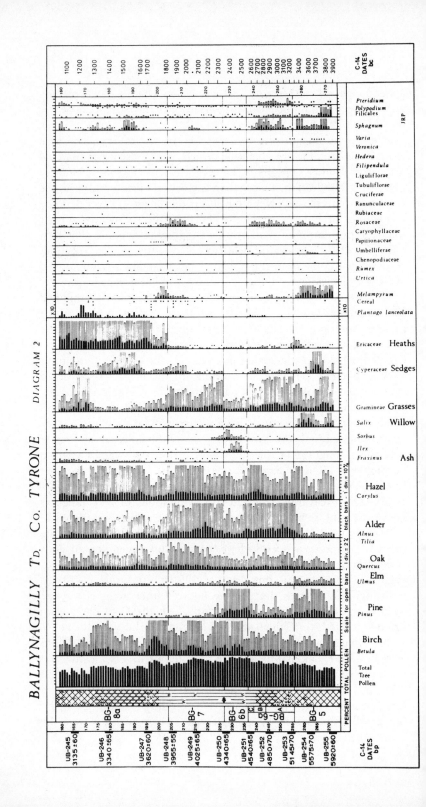

BALLYNAGILLY Td. Co. TYRONE    DIAGRAM 2

series of farming phases referred to on p.167 ending with a regeneration of the forest between *c.* 2,650 and 2,550 bc. Fig. 4.16 draws attention to the main features of the pollen diagram and includes a summary of the environmental changes inferred. It will be noticed from this diagram that the secondary forest which arose around 2,600 bc was itself attacked in Beaker times. Further clearances in the early Bronze Age, again with evidence of burning, appear to be connected with degeneration to heath.

## Crop husbandry: evidence from macroscopic remains (G.H.)

Despite the wealth of often indirect evidence of Neolithic farming from pollen studies, direct evidence from the crops themselves (other than cereal pollen) is remarkably sparse. Several decades of excavation of Neolithic and Bronze Age sites have produced only the most rudimentary assemblage of macroscopic remains, and the means of subsistence of the inhabitants of the excavated settlements remains a matter largely for speculation.

However, from the conspicuously more prolific finds of Neolithic crop remains in other parts of northern and central Europe it is clear that British sites can be expected eventually to yield substantially more information on early agriculture once the appropriate excavation techniques are adopted. Indeed, a growing interest in investigating the economic base of Britain's prehistoric populations has already led excavators of sites in many parts of Britain to use flotation machines for the mass recovery of macroscopic plant remains on a scale approaching that hitherto witnessed only on excavations of early agricultural sites in the Near East (see Williams 1973, 1976; Cherry 1978). Excavations on which flotation recovery has been used on a large scale already include several with Neolithic phases. Among these sites are Carn Brea in Cornwall, Hambledon Hill in Dorset where huge volumes were processed, Great Wilbraham Causewayed Camp in Devon, Alfriston, Offham Hill and Bishopstone in East Sussex, Grimes Graves in Norfolk, Fengate

---

Figure 4.15. Relative pollen diagram from organic deposits close to Neolithic and Bronze Age settlements at Ballynagilly, Co. Tyrone. A time-scale derived from C-14 measurements is given to the right. Pollen Zone BG 6a covers a clearance phase of landnam-type. (See also Figures 4.10 and 4.11.) A summary explanation is given in Figure 4.16. (From Pilcher and Smith 1979.)

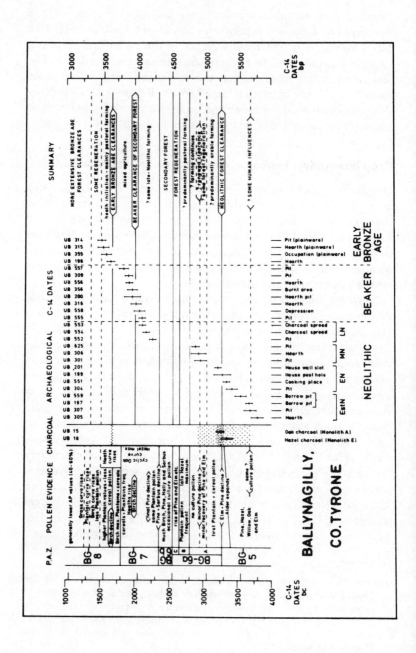

in Lincolnshire, Unstone in Derbyshire, Bog Head in Moray and Skara Brae in the Orkneys (Pryor 1974; Drewett *et al.* 1975, 1977; Bell 1977; Legge, forthcoming; Maclean and Rowley-Conway, in press; Mercer, in press). More sites such as Gwernvale in Powys (Britnell 1979) and Scord of Brouster in the Shetlands (Whittle 1979) are on the way. So far the full results from only three of these sites have been published. But with publication of all the other sites planned for the next few years, it can confidently be expected that the next decade will see substantial advances in our understanding of the subsistence patterns of Neolithic Britain.

*Nature of the evidence*

Remains of macroscopic structures such as seeds and fruits can survive in a number of different forms. From waterlogged deposits plant tissues are often recovered in relatively unaltered form. However, most archaeological deposits are (or were originally) aerobic, and in such environments plant tissues will generally survive only if they have been charred. These carbonised remains therefore represent the most universally available of all classes of macroscopic remains of plants. Impressions left by plant structures in pottery and daub make up a third source of evidence, and as an extra bonus, epidermal silica skeletons of cereal or grasses can sometimes be found adhering to the imprints. Lastly, wet-sieving of biologically active contexts such as latrines commonly reveals the presence of fossils of plant structures that have been largely decomposed and replaced by relatively insoluble salts. This last category of remains may yet turn up in deposits substantially earlier than the mediaeval contexts so far sampled for plant fossils of this sort.

In studies of early subsistence patterns, carbonised remains are generally the most useful of the various classes of evidence in that they are not only present on the majority of occupation sites but also, by virtue of their mode of preservation, stand a good chance of

Figure 4.16. Ballynagilly, Co. Tyrone: correlation of palaeo-environmental evidence (Figure 4.15) with C-14 dates from Neolithic-Bronze Age contexts. The division of the Neolithic follows ApSimon (1976). The pollen diagram on which this scheme is based is given in full in Figure 4.15, and in abstract in Figure 4.10. (After Pilcher and Smith 1979, where a fuller version may be found.)

reflecting activities involved in either the procuring of food or its preparation. Thus, the charring of the remains will generally have occurred on domestic fires, and, apart from wood charcoals, the carbonised remains will commonly include the following: first, foods charred in the course of cooking, secondly, harvested crops charred during drying, parching or malting and thirdly, charred residues from the burning of chaff and other burnable waste from the processing of grain or other food-plants. The charred remains of chaff are especially useful in that they provide not only the most precise means of identifying the crops that were under cultivation (Hillman, forthcoming a,b), but can also yield information on the sort of techniques used in their cultivation and processing (see Hillman, in press).

*Source of the finds to date*

In Britain, so far, carbonised remains of crop plants sufficiently well-preserved for identification to generic level have been published for a total of only four Neolithic sites, though more are on the way (see above). These four sites are Bishopstone in Sussex (Arthur 1977) Aston-on-Trent in Derbyshire (Reaney 1968), Nes Gruting in the Shetlands (Calder 1955) and Hembury in Devon (Helbaek 1952), though the Neolithic date of the Hembury grain has been contested. Most of the samples are small, and Hembury and Nes Gruting produced only single samples, though it should be added that the Nes Gruting sample was enormous, comprising over 12kg. of carbonised barley grain.

All the remaining evidence for our current picture of Neolithic crop husbandry in Britain is based on a grand total of less than 200 imprints of cereal grains found in sherds from about half that number of vessels (see Dennell 1976) which were excavated from a total of 18 sites concentrated largely in the southern half of England. Of the *c.* 200 impressions, 127 originate from the excavations at Windmill Hill in Wiltshire. Most of the work was completed three decades ago (Jessen and Helbaek 1944; Helbaek 1952), though smaller assemblages of Neolithic impressions have subsequently been examined by Helbaek (see Childe and Smith, 1954; Clark *et al.* 1960), Evans and Davies (1972) and Murphy (1978). Other Neolithic material has probably been published but was unknown to the author at the time of preparing this resumé.

*The major cereals*

Based on such scant evidence, generalisations are clearly hazardous. However, with the exception of the small sample of charred grain from Hembury, the finds have invariably been identified as one of three cereal types, namely emmer wheat (*Triticum dicoccum*), naked six-row barley (*Hordeum vulgare* var. *nudum*) or hulled six-row barley (*Hordeum vulgare*). Only the last named is cultivated in Britain today. It seems reasonable to assume that these three cereals were among the major crops of the Neolithic agriculturalists in at least some parts of southern Britain, a position they held throughout most of northern and central Europe at this time (see Willerding 1970). Then, as now, different soils and terrains doubtless favoured the cultivation of a different range of crops in different areas, though the only persuasive evidence published so far comes from Dennell's reassessment of Helbaek's results from Windmill Hill. This reassessment suggests that, as expected, the Neolithic farmers were well aware that the clay soils of the Frome-Bath area favoured wheat over barley, whereas the lighter soils overlying the chalk around Windmill Hill were rather better suited to the cultivation of barley (Dennell 1976).

The single sample of spelt wheat (*Triticum spelta*) recovered from one or more storage pits at Hembury causewayed enclosure was (and still is) such an anomaly that Helbaek (1952) insisted that it must be intrusive from nearby deposits of Iron Age date. However, the excavators are confident that the find is of indisputable Neolithic date on the basis of persuasive stratigraphic evidence (Smith *et al.* 1964, and personal communication). It is also worth remembering that, while there is no evidence as yet for spelt having established itself as a major crop anywhere in Britain or continental Europe before the Iron Age, small numbers of grains and spikelets of spelt have been found in Bandkeramic levels at a site on the Upper Vistula in Poland (Klikowska 1959, 1975) and also in slightly later Neolithic levels, first at a nearby site in Poland, secondly at two sites in the Upper Danube near Ulm, Germany (Bertsch 1949, 1955; Hopf 1968) and thirdly at a Michelsberg site near Tübingen (Schlichtherle 1977). Indeed, Hjelmqvist (1975) has now reported an imprint of a spikelet closely resembling that of spelt wheat on a sherd from an early Neolithic site as far north as Langeland in Sweden. These European finds clearly make a Neolithic date for the Hembury spelt rather more credible. On the other hand, the identification of some of these finds of early European spelt is not entirely convincing; at least some of the identifications appear to be based on a single feature of rachis-fracture supposedly unique to spelt but which I have also found in some present-day populations of emmer and other tetraploid glume-wheats. The match-box full of Hembury grain that apparently survives would perhaps suffice for a C-14 date and finally resolve the matter.

*Other crops*

Isolated Neolithic finds exist for three other introduced (Near-Eastern) domesticates. These are einkorn wheat (*Triticum monococcum*), domestic flax or linseed (*Linum usitatissimum*) and a free-threshing wheat tentatively identified at two (or perhaps three) sites as either bread wheat (*Triticum aestivum*) or club wheat (*T. aestivo-compactum*) (Helbaek 1952; Childe and Smith 1954; and some very dubious grains reported by Arthur 1977). Isolated finds from such a small number of small samples cannot possibly be assessed in terms of the likely agricultural role of the plants concerned. However, ample evidence exists for the widespread cultivation in northern and central Europe of all three crops (see Willerding 1970) and it is quite possible that bread-wheat and flax, at least, were grown in Britain as crops in their own right. On the other hand, it is equally possible that in Neolithic Britain they were never more than minor contaminants in the stands of emmer or barley. If flax was indeed cultivated at Windmill Hill, it could have been harvested either for the oil-rich seeds (linseed) or for the bast fibres (for making linen) or both. Early continental precedents exist in either case.

No pulse crops have yet been recovered from Neolithic sites in Britain, despite their widespread cultivation in northern Europe at this time (cf. Willerding 1970; Hopf and Zohary 1973; Knörzer 1974). Recently, the author has identified an impression of Celtic Bean (*Vicia faba* var. *minor*) in a Late Neolithic sherd from Ogmore on the coast of West Glamorgan. That cold climate was not the limiting factor is evident from the fact that pulse cultivation has been demonstrated for even the Vrå culture of Sweden, a culture which represents the northernmost advance of any form of crop husbandry in Neolithic Europe (Florin *et al.* 1958). So far, the earliest appearance of pulse crops in Britain is in the form of the domestic pea (*Pisum sativum s.l.*) recovered, first in Bronze Age levels on Jersey Pinnacle (Godfray and Burdo 1950) and, secondly, by flotation from 'a well-stratified midden deposit' in middle Bronze Age levels at Grimes

Graves in Norfolk (Legge, forthcoming, and personal communication). A single pea was also recovered by flotation from Iron Age levels at Bishopstone in Sussex (Arthur 1977) and another pulse crop – the 'Celtic Bean' (*Vicia faba* var. *minor*) was found in early Iron Age levels at Glastonbury, Meare and Whorlebury in Somerset (Percival 1934). Now it is clear that the Neolithic colonisers of Britain are unlikely to have abandoned their continental seed stocks or forgotten the expertise necessary for the cultivation of such valuable foods and it is quite probable that pulses like peas and field beans formed part of the basic Neolithic crop complement of the agricultural populations settled in many parts of Britain suited to the cultivation of these highly nutritious and agriculturally desirable legume crops.

It is less certain that the same argument can be extended to crops such as lentil (another pulse crop) or the northern millet (*Panicum mileaceum*), both of which currently make their British debut in Roman times in contexts that indicate direct import rather than local cultivation (Helbaek 1964; Willcox 1977). However, both plants were widely cultivated in Neolithic and Bronze Age Europe and may well have been able to produce adequate yields in the climate of southern Britain. Experiments to test this last possibility are currently under way at Little Butser Iron Age Farm using seed of primitive races of lentil, bitter vetch and cow pea collected in their original homeland in southern Anatolia.

### Gathered foods

Available evidence already indicates widespread utilisation during Neolithic times of wild plant foods such as acorns, blackberries, barberries, sloes, crab-apples, haws and hazel nuts, (see Godwin 1975; Legge, forthcoming; Murphy 1978). But relative to cereals and pulses, most wild food plants will be under-represented in the archaeological record in that they are inherently less likely to be charred (and thereby preserved) and most edible greens would leave no identifiable trace in any case. If only on the basis of ethnographic parallels, it might be safest to assume for the moment that most of the early agricultural communities continued to be substantially dependent on a wide range of wild food resources.

### Dating

The earliest available date for crop remains in Britain comes from Hembury where charcoals ostensibly contemporaneous with the contentious finds of spelt are dated to somewhere within the range

3,330-3,150 ± 150 bc (BM-130 and BM-138) (Smith 1974). A date of 2,510 ± 70 bc (Har-1662) has been published for charcoals from the feature from which the Bishopstone grain was floated (Bell, forthcoming) and some, at least, of the Windmill Hill remains fall into the same time bracket with a date of 2,580 ± 150 bc (BM-74) for charcoal from a ditch fill (Smith 1974).

*Other evidence for cultivation*

Most ard-marks, lynchets and field boundaries in Britain appear to be of post-Neolithic date, and the functions of many of the assemblages of Neolithic stone tools likely to have had an agricultural role remain equivocal in the ultimate analysis. However, recent work on field systems in County Mayo, Ireland, suggests that well-organised, large-scale division of land probably dates back to the Neolithic in many areas (Herity 1971; Caulfield 1978). It will probably be the results from work on this front that will ultimately demand the most dramatic changes to our views of Neolithic subsistence. As for Neolithic technology, carbon from the soil surface overlying the marks left by a ploughing implement beneath South Street Barrow in Wiltshire, has yielded a date of 2,810 ± 130 bc (BM-356) (Fowler and Evans 1967; J.G. Evans 1971), and it is an interesting measure of the widespread determination to represent the clearly competent Neolithic farmers as inexperienced experimenters that this same early date appears to have brought the mode of origin of the marks into some dispute.

With respect to this issue, it is perhaps not irrelevant to recall that near-eastern crop husbandry based on wheat, barley, peas and 'celtic' beans was already in a well advanced state by the end of the eighth millenium bc and that indirect but persuasive evidence is now accumulating for the adoption of some form of ard cultivation in that area before the end of the sixth millenium bc (A. Moore and T. Davidson, personal communication). It is not unreasonable to expect, therefore, that by the time temperate-adapted derivatives of this same agricultural tradition reached Britain, the techniques were reasonably sophisticated. The full range of adapted north European expertise and equipment (including some sort of ploughing device, in suitable areas) would presumably have been called into use as soon as the state of forest clearances and soil conditions allowed. The recovery of a 6,000-year-old ploughing implement resembling a rope-traction ard from Satrup Moor in Schleswig-Holstein reinforces this argument (see Steensberg 1973).

*Summary*

In conclusion, it must be stressed that the major questions concerning the beginnings of crop husbandry in Britain remain unanswered. We know very little of the relative importance of the different cereals, pulses and other crops in the overall food-economy of individual settlements or different areas of Britain and even less about the relative contribution of plant foods as against foods of animal origin. The continuing importance within the agricultural populations of foods gathered from the wild is still a matter for speculation, as is the likely nature of interaction between groups with different subsistence bases. The pattern of regional variation in subsistence-base as related to differences in topography, soils, vegetation cover and cultural traditions is yet another aspect that awaits attention. Eventually, further surveys of ancient field systems and large-scale recovery of plant remains from large numbers of early sites will provide more of the required data.

**Fauna** (C.G.)

This section deals only with the period of the earlier Neolithic as defined by Dr Isobel Smith (1974): beginning in the late fourth millenium and ending at about 2,100 bc, from this date onwards the late Neolithic overlaps in time with the early Bronze Age, and its fauna is discussed in Chapter 5. Thus we are concerned with the vertebrate fauna when the late Atlantic period gave way to the early Sub-Boreal. Almost all the faunal evidence comes from archaeological sites, either incorporated accidentally or left there by man. There is no independent method of assessment except for correlation with the preceeding and succeeding periods. Gaps in the record occur in areas with acid soil, where no bone is preserved, in areas sparsely occupied by man, and on sites from which the fauna has been inadequately reported.

*The wild fauna*

Virtually all the vertebrates present in Britain in the Mesolithic (see Table 3.5) survived through the Neolithic and into the Bronze Age. The only probable exception being the elk which was already absent in the late Boreal. The other ungulates, the aurochs, red deer and roe deer (*Capreolus capreolus* L.) are present on very many Neolithic sites. The aurochs seems not to be recorded for Scotland though this may only emphasise our partial knowledge of the Scottish Neolithic fauna. It may be that the aurochs (*Bos primigenius* Boj.) is not always distinguished from domestic cattle. Red deer (*Cervus elaphus* L.) is almost universal on Neolithic sites, including those on Orkney and the Outer Hebrides.

It has already been shown that a wild horse (*Equus* sp.) was probably present in small numbers in Britain (though not in Ireland) in the Mesolithic and this also seems to be true of the Neolithic; if so it must have been adapted to a woodland environment. The sites on which it has been found have been listed by Grigson (1966), and are scattered over England, Wales and Scotland; they are usually those in which many other wild species are recorded.

Wild boar (*Sus scrofa* L.) has been identified from only a few sites, but it is possible that, because it can be distinguished from domestic pigs solely by its larger size, and the size ranges overlap, it may sometimes have been missed.

Among the carnivores the wild cat (*Felis sylvestris* L.), which is now confined to the Highlands of Scotland, badger (*Meles meles* L.) and fox (*Vulpes vulpes* L.) were found in the primary levels of Windmill Hill (Jope 1965; Grigson 1965). The first postglacial record of the polecat (*Putorius putorius* L.) is from West Kennet long barrow in Wiltshire (Clarke 1962). The pine marten (*Martes martes* L.) was identified in Nutbane earthen barrow in Hampshire (Bunting *et al.* 1959). All these animals were also present in Dowel Cave (Bramwell 1959) among the Neolithic burials, but here the dating is not at all precise. Seal (probably the Atlantic seal *Halichoerus grypus* Fab.) is known from Northton on the Isle of Harris (Simpson, personal communication).

Red squirrel (*Sciurus vulgaris* L.) was also found in Dowel Cave and may predate the Embo find noted on p.218. The beaver (*Castor fiber* L.) is fairly common and of course its presence indicates running water in the vicinity. It is known from Wiltshire (West Kennet long barrow: Clarke 1962), from Norfolk (Grimes Graves: Clarke 1922; Andrews 1915), from Buckinghamshire (Whiteleaf long barrow: Childe and Smith 1954) and in Duggleby Howe in Yorkshire (Mortimer 1905). Hare is listed as *Lepus timidus* from Windmill Hill primary levels (Jope 1965), but it seems more likely that it would have been the brown hare (*L. capensis* L.) which inhabits deciduous woodland as well as open country. Hare (species not yet specified) has also been identified from the Neolithic at Northton on Harris (Simpson, personal communication).

Bat bones are rare on archaeological sites, but have been found in the flint mines of Grimes Graves (Clarke 1922; Andrews 1915) and in Dowel Cave (Bramwell 1959). A wide range of radiocarbon dates has been obtained from new excavations at Grimes Graves, but it is not at all clear how these relate to the animal remains which were discovered many years earlier and reported on only briefly; probably the fauna, like the dates, span the period of change from the earlier to the late Neolithic. All the four species found inhabit woodland and often winter in caves or mines; they were Bechstein's bat (*Selysius bechsteinii* Leisler), Daubenton's bat (*Leuconoë daubentonii* Leisler), found near water, Natterer's bat (*S. nattereri* Kuhl), and the whiskered bat (*S. mystacinus* Leisler). Bechstein's bat is now the rarest bat in Britain with a very restricted distribution in the south of England and its presence in Dowel Cave in Derbyshire suggests a warmer, wooded environment in the Midlands at the time of the Neolithic occupation of the cave.

Grimes Graves also had many rodent species: the field vole (*Microtus agrestis* L.), which was also found in flint mines at Stoke Down, Sussex, (Wade 1928), at Notgrove (Bate 1936a), at Maiden Castle (Jackson 1943) and, well-dated, in the pre-enclosure levels at Windmill Hill (Jope 1965); the bank vole (*Clethrionomys glareolus* Schreber), also found at Notgrove; and the wood mouse (*Apodemus sylvaticus* L.), also at Notgrove and Dowel Cave. The yellow-necked mouse (*Apodemus flavicollis* Melchior) was found at Dowel Cave and this seems to be the earliest dated record (but see p.115). *Arvicola terrestris* (the ground vole or water vole) was found in the tombs of Notgrove and St Nicholas, Glamorgan (Dawkins 1916), but not identified to subspecies level.

Grimes Graves is also the source of the identifications of Neolithic insectivores: the common shrew (*Sorex araneus* L.) and the mole (*Talpa europaea* L.), which was found at Notgrove as well.

The grass snake and the common toad were present at Grimes Graves, and frogs were found at Windmill Hill (Jope 1965) and at Maiden Castle (Jackson 1943).

Few bird bones are found on early Neolithic sites and very few have been identified to species, though blackbird (*Turdus merula*) and jackdaw (*Corvus monedula*) were found at West Kennet (Clarke 1962), and some sea birds have been identified from Northton

(Simpson, personal communication). Fish remains are even more scanty, though spines of the thornback ray (*Raia clavata*) are known at Dyserth Castle in an undated Neolithic level (Jackson 1915).

As already discussed in the chapter on the Mesolithic the wild fauna of Ireland in the postglacial is quite a separate entity from that of Britain, due to the formation of the Irish sea at an early date. The Irish mammalian fauna is very restricted (Wijngaarden-Bakker 1974); aurochs and roe deer (*Capreolus capreolus*) are never found there, although red deer is fairly common on Neolithic sites and might have been introduced in the Mesolithic. Wild pig seems to be rare, but as already mentioned there are difficulties over its identification. Horse has been found in Ireland in one or two Neolithic sites that predate its supposed introduction in Beaker times. The best dated find is from Circle L, Knockadoon, Lough Gur (2,460 ± 240 bc, D-40), but it is difficult to judge how reliably this dates the actual horse bones. Brown bear (*Ursus arctos*) is known from several Irish Neolithic sites and fox, badger, wild cat and the blue hare (*Lepus timidus* L.) also occur.

## Animals and man in Neolithic Britain

There are many aspects of the impact of the introduction of domesticated animals into Britain and Ireland both on the human economy and on the natural environment that should be discussed, but, as there is very little accurate work on the fauna of the earlier Neolithic, particularly on the relative numbers of animals, little can be said that is not largely speculation.

*The introduction of domestic animals.* It is clear that Neolithic man imported at least some of his domesticated animals into Britain. It is true that the wild forms of *Bos* and *Sus* were already present in Britain, but a preliminary analysis of cattle bone size (Grigson, forthcoming) suggests that there were no cattle here of intermediate size between wild and domestic cattle, as have been postulated for parts of the continent (Grigson 1969). There would have been no great trouble taking small cattle, even in small boats, across the channel, provided they were trussed up. Of course they must have been taken to Ireland by boat as there was no *Bos primigenius* there anyway. Sheep and goats had no wild forms in Britain and without any doubt at all must have been imported. The earliest sites so far published in which animal bones were both preserved and reported

on are the earthen barrows of Lambourn (Wymer 1965) 3,415 ±
180 bc (GX-1178) and Fussell's Lodge (Grigson 1966) 3,230 ±
150 bc (BM-134). Both sites contained bones of cattle and sheep or
goat.

The situation with pigs is complicated as they were probably
allowed to forage in woodland and there must always have been
accidental or deliberate outcrossing with the wild population. This
would have led to a very wide range of variation. Nevertheless small
pigs were absent from Britain in the Mesolithic and were present on
most Neolithic sites. However domestic pigs were not recorded from
the very earliest sites and are not identified with any certainty until
2,960 ± 150 bc (BM-73) in the pre-enclosure occupation at
Windmill Hill (Jope 1965; Grigson 1965; Plate 5). Whether this
absence is fortuitous or not will be established as further radiocarbon dating is done and further bone assemblages are studied.

Dogs were of course already in Britain in the Mesolithic and were
of some importance in the Neolithic (Plates 3, 6 and 8). The
relationship between man and dog, whether the dog is used for
hunting or for herding, is so intimate that one must imagine that
they too were brought to Britain.

*The effect of domestic animals on the environment.* One of the best known
effects on the environment of Neolithic man is forest clearance. Both
botanical and molluscan evidence shows that in many areas
woodland was replaced by grassland; presumably the wood was
cleared to allow pasturage for sheep, as well as for arable
agriculture, but the domestic animals as well as man would
themselves have affected the environment. As cattle are both
browsers and grazers it would not have been necessary to clear
woodland to provide them with pasture, but cattle can do an
immense amount of damage to woodland, particularly when many
animals are confined together, by stripping all browse within reach
and by trampling undergrowth and all smaller plants and seedings
into the earth. Goats are particularly destructive and are thought to
have contributed greatly to the deforestation around the
Mediterranean: perhaps the same process happened here. Sheep do
require pasture and once in it their close-cropping feeding habits
tend to discourage any possible regeneration of woodland. However
the presence of the full range of wild woodland mammals and of
domestic pigs confirms the botanical evidence for the survival of very
large tracts of rich deciduous woodland.

*The relative importance of wild and domestic animals in the economy.* As already mentioned the red deer, or at least its antler, is almost ubiquitous on Neolithic sites. There is little that a red deer can provide that could not be more easily procured from domestic animals with the vital exception of its antlers. Antler picks seem to have been one of the more important tools of Neolithic man, particularly in flint mining and in the construction of ditches (see Plate 11). Shed antler could be collected at certain times of the year; at other times the animals would have had to be hunted.

About 36 early Neolithic sites (excluding flint mines) have had their fauna reported in a way that allows one to establish the relative numbers of wild and domestic animal *species* present. Of these about 16 had no wild animal bones at all (except for some deer antler). The average number of wild species that might have been of use to man was just under two, contrasting with about four species in late Neolithic sites (see Chapter 5). Clearly wild animals were relatively unimportant in the economy, but it is interesting that most of those present apart from deer are fur-bearing.

As in later periods it is the coastal sites like Northton on Harris (Simpson, personal communication) that have the most wild animal species, but there are also quite a number in the chambered tombs and a surprisingly large number at the causewayed camp of Windmill Hill (Jope 1965; Grigson 1965). Here there were aurochs, fox, red deer, cat, horse, badger, hare and possibly wild pig. Windmill Hill is also the only Neolithic site from which large numbers of bones of wild and domestic animals were found and reported on in such a way that comparisons between the numbers of bones of the various species can be made. In the pre-enclosure occupation, out of 231 bones and teeth of large mammals only five red deer antler fragments and one red deer tooth were of wild animals; in the sample from the primary levels of the camp ditch, out of 1,300 bones and teeth 87 (or 6.7%) were of wild animals but this included 55 bones of cat, which seems disproportionately frequent (figures recalculated from Jope 1965).

*The domestic economy.* In the south of England at such sites as Waulud's Bank (Dyer 1964), Whitehawk Camp (Jackson 1934) the Trundle (Watson 1929) and Maiden Castle (Jackson 1943) it is clear that cattle were the main domestic animals with moderate numbers of sheep and goat and only a few pigs, but it is only at the causewayed camps of Windmill Hill, Robin Hood's Ball (Howard

1964), Abingdon (Case 1956) and Knap Hill (Connah 1965) and at the earthen Wor barrow (excavated by Pitt Rivers before 1898) that this can be established on bone counts. The relative numbers of domestic ungulates on most of these sites are summarised in Table 4.1. The importance of cattle for early Neolithic people is stressed by the fact that in the ditches of causewayed camps and earthen barrows (Maiden Castle: Jackson 1943; Whitesheet Hill: Jackson 1952; Beckhampton Road: Smith and Evans 1968; Fussell's Lodge: Grigson 1966) complete skulls or large parts of articulated skeletons have been found, and in earthen barrows what seem to be the remains of hide burials are quite frequent above the flint cairns (these are listed and discussed by Ashbee 1970; Piggott 1962 and Grigson 1966). Plate 4 shows the bones from Fussell's Lodge that are thought to represent a hide burial. Nevertheless in some barrows (West Kennet: Clark 1962; Whiteleaf Hill: Childe and Smith 1954; Nympsfield: Bate 1938) the number of pigs was said to equal that of cattle, though in each case rather few bones were found so this may not be significant.

It is not at all certain what was happening in the north of England at this time. Perhaps pig predominated here, but there is such a paucity of sites with bones that have been well-studied that it is impossible to be sure. In the earthen barrow of Willerby Wold in East Yorkshire only six bones of domestic animals were found – all cattle (Bramwell 1963), and cattle predominated at Kilham (Bramwell 1976), but at Hanging Grimstone (Mortimer 1905) the jaws of at least twenty pigs were associated with human burials, though the bones of other animals that presumably were present are not mentioned.

At Northton on Harris (Simpson, personal communication) sheep were as important as cattle in the Neolithic and there were no pigs. This seems to be a common pattern on island sites and presumably reflects the absence of woodland (J.G. Evans 1971): 'no pannage, no pigs', as Anthony Dent (1977) has recently written.

These domestic ungulates were undoubtedly eaten and the cattle probably provided milk, but the many other uses to which animals may be put should not be forgotten. One wonders whether cattle pulled the ploughs that marked the land surface under the South Street long barrow (Fowler and Evans 1967; J.G. Evans 1971); there is no way yet of knowing to what multifarious uses their skins were put, not to mention all the other inedible parts. Dogs were probably not eaten as they are often found as complete skeletons; there are

**Table 4.1 Percentages of domestic ungulates at Early Neolithic sites, showing how cattle appear to be the predominant domestic ungulates of the Early Neolithic in southern England. (Compare with Table 5.3.)**

| Sites | Date bc uncalib. | Pottery | Type of site | Percentages of domestic ungulates | Based on | Other species identified | No. bones identified | References |
|---|---|---|---|---|---|---|---|---|
| Robin Hood's Ball, Wilts. | — | Hembury | Causeway camp | pig 8, ox 76, sh/gt 16 | nos. | red deer (antler) | 81 | Howard 1964 |
| Windmill Hill, Wilts. | BM.73 2960±150 | Hembury | Occupation | pig 18, ox 66, sh/gt 16 | nos. | dog, red deer, field vole, frog | 182 | Jope 1965 |
| Windmill Hill, Wilts. | BM.74 2580±150 | Hembury | Causeway camp | pig 16, ox 60, sh/gt 24 | nos. | dog, horse, red deer, roe deer, aurochs, fox, badger, cat, hare, wild pig (?) | 961+ | Jope 1965 |
| Abingdon, Berks. | BM.351 3110±130 BM.354 2500±145 | Abingdon | Causeway camp | pig 0, ox 80, sh/gt 20 | nos. | — | 35 | Case 1956 |
| Knap Hill, Wilts. Ditch layers 5–8 | BM.205 2760±115 | Hembury | Causeway Camp | pig 5, ox 88, sh/gt 7 | nos. | red deer (antler) | 73 | Connah 1965 |

nos. = total numbers of bones.

fine examples from Windmill Hill (Grigson 1965) and at Maiden Castle (see Plates 6 and 8).

*The 'breeds' of domestic animals.* Many attempts have been made to classify early domestic animals into breeds and even into sub-species. This is of very doubtful value as it is difficult to define a breed in any way that is meaningful in a prehistoric context, and even modern skeletal postcranial material is almost impossible to assign to any particular breed. Probably the best that can be done is to arrange the animals in size groups.

The domestic cattle of the early Neolithic were small compared with the wild aurochs and with the larger modern breeds, but they were much bigger than those of the succeeding Bronze Age. It used to be thought that some of the larger cattle skulls found in the ditch at Maiden Castle represented a special breed of domestic long horn cattle (Jackson 1943). As suspected by Jewell (1962) on further examination of what remains of these skulls Grigson (forthcoming) was able to show that they came from *aurochs cows* (Plate 7). Most of the remainder of the Maiden Castle cattle bones were of ordinary domestic size.

The Neolithic sheep were very small and slender limbed, roughly equivalent in size and conformation to the modern Soay.

Goats are difficult to distinguish from sheep unless skulls or horn cores are present, but a complete skeleton of a young goat was found in the primary levels at Windmill Hill, and goats have been identified from some other sites. As with sheep a small animal is indicated. A photograph of a mounted skeleton of a young Neolithic goat is given in Plate 9.

Pigs too were small and, as one would expect, differ from most modern breeds, in having an elongated snout like that of the wild boar. A photograph of a mounted skeleton is given in Plate 5.

Dogs were relatively unspecialised and uniform in size and configuration (Harcourt 1974). A photograph of a complete skeleton is given in Plate 6.

## The Neolithic landscape

Despite the wealth of environmental evidence for the Neolithic period which has been touched upon in this chapter it is still in many ways deficient. The full range of analytical methods available has yet to be applied to a single site of archaeological or even purely environmental interest. It is thus still very difficult to make an informed environmental reconstruction for any particular locality. It is even more difficult to give a general view of the landscape of Neolithic Britain and to describe the changes that took place in time and space. The review that follows must, therefore, be extremely sketchy and to a great extent speculative. It may serve, however, to illustrate some of the limitations of our methods and gaps in our knowledge.

The extent of forest cover is, of course, one of the key elements in an environmental reconstruction. But when it comes to detail, both the range and nature of the evidence fail us. We still lack any substantial continuous pollen diagrams, for instance, that illustrate the history of the southern chalklands. By its very nature pollen evidence does not tell us the precise degree of forest cover because of the vicissitudes of pollen production, dispersal and deposition. We work largely in ignorance of the so-called 'pollen source area', so that the actual extent of Neolithic clearings still largely eludes us. The increased use of three-dimensional pollen diagrams adumbrated by Turner (e.g. Turner 1975) may eventually begin to resolve some of these difficulties. For the Neolithic these have so far been most successfully used by Hibbert (Coles *et al.* 1970; see Fig. 4.14). The preparation of three-dimensional pollen diagrams is, however, so time-consuming that they can never be used on a very wide scale.

Comparison of the fossil pollen spectra in the pollen diagrams with pollen spectra derived from present vegetation provides the principal means of assessing the degree of forest cover. For Britain this kind of information is woefully inadequate. Indeed, the present state of our vegetation largely prevents its acquisition. Turner (1964b) has suggested, on the basis of modern pollen samples, however, that very small clearings might not be detectable by pollen analyses unless they were created on the edge of the forest within a few hundred metres of the sampling site. She points out that if the sampling site in a bog is more than 500m. from the margin then the pollen rain will not include a large local component. Any clearance detected in such a sampling site may, therefore, involve a large pollen source area – say up to 10km. away – and cannot be the effect of one small clearance at the edge of the bog. Turner regards many of the clearances recorded in the palynological literature as falling into this wider category and thus as reflecting periods in which there was considerable human occupation of the region. Turner's conclusions as to the dispersal of pollen from woodland margins have been amply confirmed by the work of Tinsley and Smith (1974).

One way in which we can try to assess the degree of forest cover is by considering the proportion of tree pollen in the total. Even this statistic needs careful use, however, and requires an understanding of the contribution of non-tree pollen by local plant communities. Studies of modern pollen rain on the continent (e.g. Jonassen 1950; Heim 1962) have shown that only in an open landscape does the proportion of tree pollen fall below 50%. Heim shows that within the woodlands of the Ardennes tree pollen can vary between 64-92% of the total, with a mean of 72%. Now most pollen diagrams covering the British Neolithic have total tree pollen values in the upper end of this range, and the Neolithic clearances involve variations of only a few per cent. We can hardly doubt, therefore, that the countryside remained in general quite densely forested. As noted by Grigson in this chapter, the abundance of wild game found in some Neolithic sites confirms this deduction from the botanical evidence.

Despite the continuing general forest cover it is clear that the forests were not of uniform constitution over the whole of the British Isles. Insofar as we ever had what is sometimes known as climax forest in Britain, then this must surely have developed in the Atlantic period. The climax forest of Britain is often regarded as oakwood. But the pollen record, as exemplified in the isopollen maps of Birks *et al.* (1975; see Fig. 4.1) show, for instance, that alder must have been an important constituent of the lowland forest by the time the Neolithic began. The maps further demonstrate that large areas of Scotland must have been dominated by pine and birch. These tend to form rather light and open woodlands, particularly on poor soils, and we can envisage that patches of such woodland may also have existed on the poorer soils, particularly in the uplands, elsewhere in the British Isles.

In attempting to reconstruct the landscape of Neolithic Britain it is of considerable importance to know the height of the tree line. Unfortunately, this is still unknown with any reliability over the British Isles as a whole. Various estimates, based largely on considerations of lapse-rates, have been made by Taylor and his co-workers. A general altitudinal limit of 550m. (1,800ft) has been suggested for forest growth in prehistoric times in Wales (Walker and Taylor 1976). Taylor (1965) regards the tree line in Wales as having fallen from its highest level of *c.* 670m. (*c.* 2,200ft) in Atlantic times to between 305 and 365m. (1,000-1,200ft) in Sub-Atlantic times. Elsewhere, he states that in the Highland Zone tree lines did not reach their maximum until the Sub-Boreal period (Taylor 1975).

A better knowledge of the Neolithic tree lines will have to await the production of further high-altitude pollen diagrams and a critical analysis of the existing palaeobotanical data. A number of pointers come to mind from the available literature. From pollen analysis of a site at 430m. (1,400ft), the summit of Slieve Gallion, Co. Tyrone seems to have been relatively open throughout the postglacial (Pilcher 1973) and slightly lower – at 410m. (*c.* 1,350ft) – Bartley's site at Rishworth Moor, Yorkshire, appears to have been at about the tree line, or just above it, from late-Atlantic time onwards (Bartley 1975). Not all the high altitude Scottish sites listed by Durno and Romans (1969) appear to have been fully published. One site suggests, however, that woodland may have reached as high as *c.* 610m. (2,000ft) in the Atlantic period with a reduction after the elm decline. The site is on Muckle Cairn at the Head of Glen Esk in the Grampians (Durno 1959). Tree pollen values of around 70% suggest the presence of at least open woodland in the Atlantic period. After the elm decline the tree pollen values fall to 40-50% with much grass and, later, heath pollen. Tree pollen values of around 70% are also taken by Turner *et al.* (1973) as suggesting that open woodland existed in Upper Teesdale, at altitudes around 500m. (1,650ft) in Atlantic times. These authors suggest that after 3,000 bc the soils in Upper Teesdale became too wet for trees to regenerate and that there was a transition to blanket bog. A tree line at the altitude suggested by these figures would leave very considerable areas of the Highland Zone covered by grass and dwarf shrub communities or bogland.

Certain uplands would already have been supporting bog communities by the beginning of the Neolithic, not only in Scotland and the north of England, but as far south as Dartmoor. This open aspect of the landscape may in some areas have resulted from the depredations of Mesolithic population, particularly through continuous burning. The question has been raised as to whether Neolithic populations could have continued to exploit such areas, particularly by grazing, with very little sign of their activities being left in the pollen record. Certainly the importance of the upper woodland margin as a resource in the Mesolithic which has been emphasised in recent work (see p.105) leaves us to ask the question as to whether the Neolithic tree line would have been conditioned by climate and physiography alone.

The lowland landscape would have been similarly interrupted by mires of various descriptions. In certain coastal areas such as Somerset, inland East Anglia, the Lancashire coast and possibly in Humberside, fens and bogs would have covered considerable areas. Work in the latter area is still in progress. While the lowland bogs resulted from natural conditions of topography and relative sea-level changes, it is held by some workers that the initiation of upland peats was connected with Neolithic human activities – either by the effects of clearance on soil water tables or indirectly via stock grazing. The area of upland bog may well have increased during the Neolithic since there are indications of some peats beginning to form at about this time. The extent of such changes in terms of the area of land affected is, however, impossible to assess with any accuracy. It is perhaps of interest in setting this general scene to note that in reviewing some of the earlier work on blanket peats Durno and Romans (1969) showed that there had been a lowering of the altitude at which blanket peat formed throughout the Atlantic period. They further suggested that during the Sub-Boreal period (which includes the Neolithic) there was an increase of altitude at which blanket peat formed.

The connection between human activity, upland peat formation, and the deterioration of soils, is still somewhat imponderable. This is not only because of the nature of the evidence available but because climatic changes were probably also taking place. We may note, for instance, that it has been considered that by the end of the Atlantic period soil depauperation may already have occurred in some areas as a result of leaching over a long period of time (cf. Mackereth 1965; Walker 1966). We have seen also evidence of paludification in late Atlantic times. Indeed, insofar as the evidence regarding climate can be unravelled, there seems to be much more in favour of increasing wetness immediately before, and during, the Neolithic period than there is to support the classical view of increased continentality. In general terms the evidence seems to conform to the early ideas of a gradual deterioration after an optimum in the earlier half of the postglacial period. Cyclical variations seem to have occurred, however, and these may have affected the landscape both directly and indirectly by their influence on the intensity of human pressures. Any clear evidence of such processes in the Neolithic in Britain is at present lacking though further detailed bog-stratigraphic studies may well illuminate the position.

We have already alluded to the existence of lowland and coastal mires in the Neolithic period. The coastal areas would have been quite unstable, however, as a result of changes of relative sea-level. Vegetational changes from maritime, through fen, to fen-wood, and in the reverse direction would have been taking place in different areas at different times. Such areas would have been difficult of access and of passage but would have provided rich resources of wildlife. So far, it is only in the Somerset Levels that we see that the fens and fen-woods that became established after the end of a marine transgression were in any way brought under control by Neolithic man. And even there, the trackways were perhaps as much connected with communication as with the exploitation of the resource. The discovery and scientific excavation of settlement sites would undoubtedly much amplify our knowledge of the relationship between Neolithic man and his local environment in this kind of potentially rich coastal area.

The major impact of Neolithic man on the forest cover of Britain is seen just before 3,000 bc at the time of the elm decline. There is, however, considerable and widespread evidence of forest clearance before this, going back as early as *c.* 3,700 bc. Some of these clearances have been attributed by the original authors to late Mesolithic populations or left uncertain (cf. Spratt and Simmons 1976). It appears most probable, however, that they can be attributed to Neolithic pioneers. The pollen evidence for these clearances is very much in a minor key, involving sporadic occurrences of so-called 'culture' pollen and small shifts of the pollen curves. Insofar as their durations can be estimated, however, they appear to have lasted for considerable periods and to be more than single episodes of slash-and-burn. This is not to say that such techniques were not involved. Following Turner's considerations on pollen dispersal which are discussed above, only if these clearances took place very close to the sampling points can we regard them in any way as having been small. What we mean by small is still debatable. Turner speaks of pushing back the forest margin by a hundred metres or so: perhaps we should think in terms of a few hectares. At least some of the sites with these early signs of clearance have been selected as being in areas of known archaeological interest. Bearing in mind Turner's considerations, then, since the sampling points may have been close to occupation areas, we should not necessarily assume that the clearances involved 'large' areas such as might be the case for those which came later (p.207).

The clearances which began around the time of the elm decline were widespread, though less prominent in northern Scotland and some parts of northern England. There is good evidence from several localities that they were quite long-lived. They lasted for centuries rather than decades, and cannot represent single episodes of slash-and-burn. They must imply settled communities, but there is no denying that these communities may have used a forest-fallow system of agriculture. Unless manuring was effectively employed, the great length of these periods implies that new ground, either of virgin or secondary forest, must have been continuously opened. If the former, then the centres of land-use would have drifted imperceptibly across the landscape with the course of time. The effects of these clearances and the subsequent history of the cleared areas were variable. They sometimes resulted in soil erosion and sometimes apparently remained as open areas (see below). In other localities forest regeneration took place.

Forest regeneration appears to have been going on in a number of geographically distinct regions at roughly the same time, around 2,600-2,700 bc. This phenomenon has recently been discussed, and further exemplified by Whittle (1978) in an interesting paper which appeared just as this volume was going to press. Whittle discusses not only the regeneration of woodland in the middle of the third millenium bc, but takes certain of the molluscan evidence from the southern chalklands as indicating the cessation of cultivation. He envisages the creation of 'uncultivated grassland'. Such grassland would almost certainly not have persisted, however, in the absence of grazing. If the evidence bears his interpretation, then stock raising at least may be presumed to have continued. Whittle develops the argument that the population size and scale of resource exploitation may have been greater in the earlier Neolithic than for some time thereafter in many parts of the British Isles. He concludes that the evidence for woodland regeneration implies that the population outran its resources, further depleting them, and falling into decline. The depletion and decline he sees as occurring on the more marginal soils, settlement being forced back into those (lowland) areas where the soils were most durable. He takes the evidence of damage and lessivation of former forest soil under the Henge at Stanton Harcourt, Oxon. (Limbrey 1975) as indicating that not even the lowland soils were endlessly durable. The durability of soils would have depended to some extent on the effectiveness of any manuring practices that were carried out, and this is something on which we have virtually no evidence. Leaves could have been used as green manure, however, and it has been suggested that bracken may have been used in this way at one site (Dimbleby and Evans 1974).

One of Whittle's ideas is that the frequency of forest fallow periods would have been reduced as a result of pressure on resources. In order to be convinced of this we would have to be sure that some more stable and sophisticated system of agriculture was not in use; we should also have to be convinced that all the available land that could be profitably exploited by the available techniques was in fact so exploited. The pollen evidence of still extensive forest suggests that this is unlikely to have been the case. Clearly a survey of the relationship of Neolithic settlement to soil types – if it could be achieved with sufficient precision – might cast some light on this problem. While in no way dismissing Whittle's thesis, perhaps we should also examine more closely other possible factors in bringing about the forest regeneration, while remembering that it was not ubiquitous. Could there have been a climatic effect, for instance? A reversal of a climatic cycle might have influenced the productivity of the Neolithic farming techniques. It may not be without significance that the first of the dry/wet cycles distinguished by Aaby (1976) begins at *c.* 2,700 bc.

Our view of the Neolithic landscape and the systems of agriculture in use will be much affected by the evidence of field systems, particularly those emerging from beneath the blanket peat of the west of Ireland (Herity 1971; Caulfield 1978). Walls enclosing fields averaging three to four acres have been discovered, together with straight walls up to a mile in length. One of the walls abuts against the Court Cairn at Behy, Co. Mayo, and C-14 dates close to the base of the blanket peat near the Cairn are in the range 1,900-2,000 bc (Smith *et al.* 1973). Other radiocarbon evidence from the County Mayo sites tends to confirm the supposed Neolithic age of the field walls.

The existence of field systems in the Neolithic would presumably have the implication of a much more stable, semi-permanent system of agriculture than the slash-and-burn or forest-fallow systems that have dominated our minds for so long. Despite the evidence for generally persistent forest cover, such semi-permanent agriculture would not be out of line with recent palaeobotanical evidence. Long pollen diagrams using modern standards of analysis in the areas in which the enclosures are being found would undoubtedly throw much light on the question as to whether these areas were opened up on a scale much wider than we are accustomed to think of elsewhere. Further palaeoenvironmental evidence will, therefore, be awaited with much interest.

It is perhaps worthy of passing note that in coastal areas the use of seaweeds as manure would have been a distinct possibility. It is an intriguing thought that the present-day use of seaweeds in this way could have had so long a history. Nevertheless, some field walls possibly of Neolithic age are, of course, known from areas well inland (cf. Proudfoot 1958b).

The size of the clearings that were created at the time of the elm decline is again a matter of debate. Clearance can be detected over a wide area and clearings are therefore likely to have been abundant. Since the majority of sites at which they can be detected were not selected for any particular relevance to Neolithic occupations it seems likely that in only a small proportion of the sites would there have been clearings within a few hundred metres or so. That is to say we are unlikely to be seeing the effect of single small local clearances. It is much more likely that we are looking at a reflection of either a large number of small clearings dotted over the countryside or a smaller number of large clearings some distance from the pollen sampling sites. What is to be understood by 'large' in this context is even more debatable than the meaning of 'small'. We may note, however, that Sims (1973) – albeit by a rather tenuous argument – estimates that in the vicinity of Hockham Mere clearing was in the range of 35-80 sq.km. If we think of 'small' as being a few hectares perhaps we should think of 'large' as being several, or even tens of square kilometres. It would be virtually impossible, however, to distinguish pollen analytically between a large clearing and a number of small clearings of equal area without using closely-spaced detailed pollen diagrams. Moreover, if the forest-fallow system were extensively used it is perhaps likely that even large cleared areas would have been a mosaic of arable, pasture, scrub and regenerating forest. The idea of the Neolithic landscape as a mosaic, first put forward by Mitchell (1956, p.242), is indeed an attractive image. The mosaic of the intensively utilised areas would have formed a still larger mosaic with the more untouched forest, fens and bogs. The uncleared forest would not only have provided the resources of its wildlife, but could well have been used for cattle rearing without the need for clearance. As Grigson points out (p.195), it is only for sheep that extensive pasture is required. Sheep seem to have assumed importance at Northton on Harris and it should not go unnoticed that there is pollen evidence that the Outer Isles may have been virtually treeless even at the beginning of the Neolithic (cf. Blackburn 1946; Davidson *et al.* 1976).

Clearings would, of course, have been used for arable agriculture, possibly even at altitudes which might nowadays be surprising. So far as the evidence goes, it appears that emmer wheat and barley were the main cereals grown. The evidence of plant macro-remains suggests also that gathered plant foods would have been important. The species listed by Hillman (p.189) are generally fruits of shrubby plants. Forest margins and disturbed areas may thus have been valuable resources. It is known from pollen diagrams that hazel was often encouraged by the clearance practices, and if it were managed for pole production, as seems virtually certain, it could equally well have been managed for nut production. Whether habitats suitable for say, blackberry or crab apple were deliberately created is impossible to determine, but it would be surprising if they were not.

The more intimate aspects of the Neolithic landscape – the immediate human environment – would undoubtedly have been much influenced by farming and woodland management techniques. The deliberate coppicing of hazel appears well established from the Somerset Levels, and we have discussed the possible use of leaf fodder. Continuous lopping of forest trees, either for this purpose, or for use as green manure, would have produced an intimate landscape that would be quite strange in Britain today, but which would be quite unremarkable in, say, the foothills of the Himalayas.

We have seen that in some areas forest regeneration took place around the end of the first quarter of the third millenium bc. In other places evidence of regeneration is lacking and permanently open conditions appear to have been created. Perhaps the best examples are the East Anglian Breckland (Godwin and Tallantire 1951) and the Langdale sites in the Lake District uplands described by Pennington (1975b). We have seen also that permanent grassland appears to have been created on the southern chalk uplands. We have, however, no real knowledge of its extent or the degree of its persistence. The Neolithic activities on these uplands seem to have caused very little soil erosion, except perhaps by windblow (cf. Limbrey 1975) whereas in the Lake District, on the other hand, there was apparently widespread downwash of soils into the lake basins.

The environmental history of the later part of the Neolithic is perhaps least well known. This is largely because so much interest has revolved around the major initial impact. A detailed knowledge of this period will be forthcoming now that pollen diagrams closely dated by radiocarbon are becoming available. Renewed clearance after forest regeneration is apparent, particularly at some Irish sites and in north-west England but these clearances are so far undated. They tend perhaps to be somewhat over-emphasised in comparison with other areas because, once again, they involve a decline of elm which is always an obvious feature of pollen diagrams.

By the second millennium bc field systems may have been relatively common (cf. Fowler 1978). In the north-east of Ireland large areas of upland scrub and rough grazing were going over to blanket peat (cf. Smith 1975). Goddard (1971) connects this process with increased run-off due to deforestation. It has been pointed out in this chapter, however, that by about 2,000 bc climatic deterioration may already have been making itself felt in the more marginal situations in the Highland Zone.

A.G. Smith wishes to thank Mrs C.A. Green for assistance in preparing this chapter, particularly with the redrawn figures. He also wishes gratefully to acknowledge the contributions on specific topics or personal communications by those named in the text. Caroline Grigson thanks Dr D.D.A. Simpson for kindly allowing her to see the preliminary analysis of the bones from Northton, Harris. G. Hillman wishes to thank Dr M. Bell, Dr T. Legge and Mr P. Murphy for generously making available unpublished data (see text and bibliography) and Dr I.F. Smith for advice regarding the spelt from Hembury.

# 5. *The Bronze Age*

## HEATHER M. TINSLEY (with CAROLINE GRIGSON)

From about 2,500 bc the established Neolithic economies of the British Isles were gradually changed by the infiltration of folk from continental Europe. The first of these migrant groups to cross the channel were the Beaker people who had their homeland in the Rhine basin (Burgess 1974). They spread throughout the British Isles, mixing with the indigenous Neolithic inhabitants but having little impact on their lifestyle. They were, however, the precursors of the more highly organised Celtic groups of Urn Folk and Food Vessel people who came over to Britain in the first half of the second millenium bc. It was these groups who brought the knowledge of copper metallurgy to the British Isles, and in addition new forms of pottery and new systems of social organisation.

## Climate

The period of these migrations falls in the Sub-Boreal (Zone VIIb of Godwin's pollen assemblage zones) which has traditionally been regarded as more continental, and in particular more xerothermic, than the preceding Atlantic period which included the climatic optimum of the Flandrian Stage. At the start of this century, Sernander (1908) recorded well-humified peat layers in Swedish bogs which he interpreted as having formed in dry conditions. Later work established that the Sub-Boreal was associated with the decline or disappearance from Scandinavia of the saw sedge (*Cladium mariscus*) and the ivy (*Hedera helix*), both of which require warm winters (Iversen 1944).

As far as the British Isles are concerned there is not much evidence to support the theory of a continental Sub-Boreal period, and in particular the decline in *Cladium* and *Hedera* is much less marked than in Scandinavia. However, the implications from the study of the coleopteran fauna from a Bronze Age site on Thorne Moor, Yorkshire (Buckland and Kenward 1973) provide some evidence apparently to the contrary. A trackway in the peat has a radiocarbon date of 1,140 bc (3,090 ± 90 bp, B-336), placing it in the second half of the Sub-Boreal, and an insect fauna typical of oak woodland was found associated with it. Five of the species recovered are now restricted to a central European distribution, where dry continental conditions prevail, though in terms of total numbers recovered this non-British element is small (H. Kenward, personal communication). On the whole, though, recent evidence favours the view that in Britain the Sub-Boreal, together with the Atlantic period, formed part of one postglacial warm episode with oscillations in the degree of wetness. Bands of highly humified peat are found widely in British raised bogs indicating short periods of slower peat growth in drier conditions, and radiocarbon dating has established that these occur throughout the Sub-Boreal, though the majority are concentrated towards its end. In addition fills from a number of Bronze Age pits and ditches, including one of the Y-holes at Stonehenge, have been found to have a high proportion of particles in the silt grade which indicate sorting and transportation by the wind. Cornwall (1953) suggests that in order for wind to have been an agency in providing the fill at these sites, the climate must have been at least seasonally dry at some times in the Bronze Age.

During the postglacial warm period temperatures were significantly higher than in either the Boreal or the present. Estimates of the magnitude of the difference vary: Lamb (1963) suggests that summer temperatures were 2-3°C higher than present, but that the difference between winter temperatures was less than this. Taylor (1975) estimates that on average the difference between Sub-Boreal and present day temperatures was 1.0-1.5°C, resulting in a potential treeline some 200-300m. higher than that of today. Associated with the higher treeline there must have been a greater potential for upland settlement and agriculture.

*Climatic deterioration*

Although the exact nature of moisture conditions in the Sub-Boreal is open to question, there is no doubt that towards the end of this period cyclical climatic deterioration began to occur involving declining temperatures and increased wetness. This culminated in a markedly wet and cool period which denotes the opening of the Sub-Atlantic period between 800 and 500 bc and it was accompanied by quite widespread inundation around the British coast (Godwin

1975). The deterioration in climate was observed all over Europe, though the date of the first downturn from better climatic conditions varies. In continental Europe it may have begun as early as 3,000 bc, though warmer and drier periods interrupted this general decline, particularly around 1,200-1,000 bc (Lamb 1963). Possibly these disturbed climatic conditions and associated poor harvests provided a motive for the waves of Celtic migrants who were moving westwards from central Europe to the British Isles at this period. Lamb (1963) estimates that the decline in average temperature in the 500 years from 1,000 bc was of the order of 2°C.

### The evidence from peat stratigraphy

Peat bogs clearly reveal evidence for Sub-Boreal climatic deterioration in the form of recurrence surfaces. These appear as bands of dark, highly humified peat overlain by lighter-coloured fresh peat, the recurrence surface being the contact between the two peat types. These horizons represent a period of slow peat growth when the surface of the bog dried out, followed by a period of faster peat accumulation in wetter conditions. In some cases the highly humified horizon is oxidised and there may be a gap in the stratigraphy at this level due to erosion during the standstill phase. In other cases heath plants and birches spread onto the bog during the dry period, and macro-remains of these species are often found in the peat immediately below the recurrence surface. With the advent of moister conditions, pools began to form on the peat surface as water levels rose. These pools became colonised with plants of a regeneration complex, for example aquatic species of *Sphagnum* moss such as *S. cuspidatum* and *S. imbricatum* often associated with vascular plants like *Andromeda* and *Scheuchzeria*. The remains of these plants form the 'precursor peat'; the pale unhumified *Sphagnum* peat which lies above it is the product of rapid peat growth under wetter climatic conditions.

The significance of these changes in peat humification was first recognised by Weber (1900) who identified recurrence surfaces in a number of north European bogs. He believed that there was one synchronous horizon formed by the drying out of bog surfaces in Sub-Boreal time followed by rapid peat accumulation in the Sub-Atlantic. Weber termed this the *Grenzhorizont* and he assumed it to date from around 500 bc. However, further work by Granlund (1932) established that more than one recurrence surface could occur in the same bog. The dates of five recurrence surfaces identified by Granlund in a southern Swedish bog are given in Table 5.1; RY III is equivalent to Weber's *Grenzhorizont*. Nilsson (1935)

**Table 5.1. Granlund's Recurrence Surfaces**

| | |
|---|---|
| 1200 AD | RY I |
| 400 AD | RY II |
| 600 BC | RY III |
| 1200 BC | RY IV |
| 2300 BC | RY V |

later detected up to nine recurrence surfaces, the first being about 1,000 years older than Granlund's RY V. Recurrence surfaces have been identified at numerous raised bogs in the British Isles. Turner (1964) has recognised two at Tregaron Bog, Dyfed, the lower and more pronounced example being equivalent to the *Grenzhorizont*. Highly humified *Sphagnum imbricatum* peat from immediately below this horizon has a radiocarbon date of 1,004 bc (2,954 ± 70 bp, Q-389), and moderately humified *S. imbricatum* peat immediately above the horizon is dated to 696 bc (2,646 ± 70 bp, Q-388); the marked difference between these two dates suggests a standstill in peat growth, or even some erosion in the period before peat regeneration. The upper recurrence surface is bracketed by the dates 473 ad (1,477 ± 90 bp, Q-391) and 1,182 ad (768 ± 90 bp, Q-390) and could be equivalent to Granlund's RY I or RY II. In the peat of the Somerset Levels (Godwin 1960b), and at Chat Moss, Lancashire (Birks 1963-4), prominent recurrence surfaces have been identified and equated with the *Grenzhorizont*; in the latter case the horizon is dated to 695 bc (2,645 ± 100 bp, Q-683) (Godwin and Willis 1966). In Ireland, Jessen (1949) identified a prominent recurrence surface in many bogs which he equated with the *Grenzhorizont*, but Mitchell (1956) doubted this correlation both on palynological grounds and on the basis of the relationship of the horizon to Bronze Age implements embedded in the peat. It is now thought that there is no synchronous *Grenzhorizont* in Irish bogs, but that the feature identified by Jessen is, in many bogs, much more ancient than he believed. For instance at Fallahogy, Co. Derry, where the same stratigraphic horizon has been identified (Smith 1958d) the radiocarbon date for the fresh *Sphagnum* peat immediately above the recurrence surface is 2,531 bc (4,481 ± 120 bp, Q-558) (Godwin and Willis 1962).

The main recurrence surface of the Somerset Levels is closely associated with numerous wooden trackways which have been attributed to the late Bronze Age (Godwin 1960a) and a number of late Bronze Age artifacts have been found in the peat adjacent to the trackways (Dewar and Godwin 1963). Often the trackways show little sign of wear which suggests that they were very rapidly engulfed by the regenerating peat. The peat on which they were laid is highly humified and contains abundant macro-remains of *Calluna* indicative of fairly dry conditions before the deterioration. This is supported by evidence of erosion at two sites; at Meare Heath the peat below the trackway is some 400 years older than the timbers, and at Shapwick Heath there is a difference of 840 years.

The trackways vary in construction, some consist of timbers of varying sizes laid either longitudinally or transversely and fastened into place on the peat by short stakes, they were then often covered by layers of brushwood or heather. In some cases the timbers show mortice holes, and many display cuts from thick-bladed axes with strongly curved cutting edges which are characteristic of the late Bronze Age. Other tracks are much less substantial features, merely consisting of brushwood bundles laid side by side, and one recently excavated example of mid-Bronze Age date, the Eclipse track, is formed from woven brushwood hurdles laid on the surface of the peat (Coles *et al.* 1975b). The brushwood poles are predominantly hazel and it appears that in the Somerset Levels' area hazel was extensively coppiced in the Bronze Age. The trackways appear to have been constructed to facilitate communications between Bronze Age ridge-top settlements which were above the general level of the peat.

In recent years some earlier Bronze Age trackways have been discovered lower in the peat stratigraphy and the analysis of macro-remains and pollen from associated monoliths suggest that they too were built in response to wetter conditions, probably due to local fluctuations in the water table of the Levels (Coles *et al.* 1975c). There is now quite a range of Bronze Age radiocarbon dates available for trackways in the Somerset Levels (Table 5.2).

A number of trackways from other bogs in the British Isles have also been dated to the Bronze Age (Table 5.2). It appears that at several wetland sites similar solutions were adopted to solve the problem of communications that accompanied the deteriorating climatic conditions of the Sub-Boreal/Sub-Atlantic transition.

**Table 5.2 Radiocarbon dates for Bronze Age wooden trackways in British bogs.**

|  | Years bc | Years bp | Lab. no. |
|---|---|---|---|
| *Somerset Levels* |  |  |  |
| Eclipse Track | 1310 | 3460 ± 60 | HAR.680 |
| Meare Lake Track | 1340 | 3290 ± 70 | HAR.683 |
| Tinney's Tracks | 1090 | 3040 ± 70 | HAR.681 |
|  | 1070 | 3020 ± 70 | HAR.684 |
| Meare Heath Track | 890 | 2840 ± 110 | Q.52 |
|  | 900 | 2850 ± 110 | Q.52 |
| Westhay Track | 850 | 2800 ± 110 | Q.308 |
| Toll Gate House Track | 650 | 2600 ± 110 | Q.306 |
| Viper's Track | 680 | 2630 ± 110 | Q.312 |
|  | 570 | 2520 ± 110 | Q.7 |
| Nidon's Track | 635 | 2585 ± 100 | Q.313 |
| Shapwick Heath Track | 520 | 2470 ± 110 | Q.39 |
| *Pilling Moss, Lancashire* |  |  |  |
| Kate's Pad | 750 | 2760 ± 120 | Q.68 |
| *Brigg, Lincolnshire* | 602 | 2552 ± 120 | Q.77 |
| *Fordy, Cambridgeshire* | 610 | 2560 ± 110 | Q.310 |
| *Thorne Moor, South Yorkshire* | 1040 | 3090 ± 90 | B.336 |
| *Corlona Leitrim, Ireland* | 1345 | 3395 ± 170 | Gro. 272 |

*Other evidence for climatic deterioration*

The evidence for climatic worsening in the form of trackways and recurrence surfaces comes primarily from the lowlands. However, studies in south-west Cumbria suggest that this lowland change was also accompanied by worsening upland conditions (Pennington 1970). Pollen analyses of sediments from Devoke Water, Seathwaite Tarn and Burnmoor Tarn show clearance episodes apparently related to the pastoral use of these uplands and dated at Seathwaite Tarn to 1,090 bc (3,040 ± 140 bp, NPL-124). Bronze Age cairns and urn burials are widespread in this region, but towards the end of the Bronze Age the occupation appears to have ceased. At Burnmoor Tarn, between 1,200 and 500 bc, there is a fall in *Alnus* pollen followed by a rise in pollen of grasses and *Myrica* (bog myrtle) after 500 bc. In Pennington's view this could be interpreted as a replacement of upland alder woods by *Molinia-Myrica* swamp due to increasing wetness at a period which coincides with the building of the trackways in the mosses of lowland Britain.

At other sites in the uplands blanket peat began to extend during the Sub-Boreal period, in part a response to an increasing precipitation/evaporation ratio. Certainly this is the case in the Welsh uplands, where Moore (1973) found that the extension of blanket peat took place during the period of Bronze Age occupation.

However, at many sites it is clear that anthropogenic factors were also involved in the spread of upland peat. In the case of the radio-carbon dates for the inception of blanket peat growth, the range is far wider than the range of dates for the trackways and recurrence surfaces. For example, Pennine blanket peat began to form as early as the Boreal/Atlantic transition (5,500 bc) at some sites (Conway 1954; Hicks 1971), at various times in the Atlantic, at the Atlantic/Sub-Boreal transition and later in other physiographic situations (Tallis 1964a). From Ireland, studies in the Sperrin Mountains and in north-east Antrim (Smith 1975) show that blanket peat spread widely from the start of the Bronze Age, probably as a result of climatic deterioration allied with man's intervention (for further discussion of this see p.246).

There is evidence for relatively early climatic deterioration at some sites in the extreme north-west of Scotland. In a pollen diagram from Loch Maree, Ross and Cromarty (Birks 1972b), pollen of *Pinus* and *Quercus* decreases markedly at a level radio-carbon dated to 2,256 bc (4,206 ± 55 bp, Q-1005) to be replaced by pollen of plants from dwarf shrub and bog communities. Birks interprets this as a decline in local woodland and its replacement by bog and heath due to an increase in the oceanicity of the climate; human factors are considered unlikely to have been contributory as there is little archaeological evidence for contemporary occupation. Horizons of pine stumps in coastal peat beds further north have been radiocarbon dated to 2,470 bc (4,420 ± 102 bp, NPL-13) and 2,270 bc (4,220 ± 105 bp, NPL-14), and Lamb (1964) has attributed the decline of this forest to climatic deterioration.

## Regional contrasts

All the evidence discussed above seems to support the view that in Britain there was a gradual decline from the climatic optimum during the Sub-Boreal, probably beginning as early as about 2,400 bc, but with periods of better conditions intervening. The deterioration then became very rapid in the early part of the first millenium bc. Decline from the climatic optimum seems to have started first in the extreme west, judging by the early dates for the Irish recurrence surfaces and the evidence from north-west Scotland. The change towards more oceanic conditions then gradually began to affect Wales and the western part of England; it seems clear that the precipitation/evaporation ratio critical for peat growth was crossed at different times in varying topographical situations and this accounts for the spread of radiocarbon dates for recurrence surfaces and blanket peat initiation. It is possible that on the eastern side of the British Isles thresholds for renewed peat growth were not generally crossed as there is little stratigraphic evidence to support Sub-Boreal climatic deterioration from sites on the North Yorkshire Moors (Simmons and Cundill 1974a), or the east central Pennines (Tinsley 1973).

## Sea-levels

There is some limited evidence from the south coast of Britain for a marine transgression around the opening of the Bronze Age. At Wingham near Canterbury (a site discussed on p.232), Godwin (1962) observed that macro-remains in the peaty mud deposits indicated that the site became much wetter around 1,700 bc, possibly due to a rising water table associated with a marine transgression. This is supported by evidence from north-west England, where a marine transgression (Lytham VII) was underway between 1,750 and 1,200 bc (Tooley 1978a). Generally, though, during the Bronze Age, sea-levels around the British Isles appear to have been lower than at present. There is strong evidence for coastal emergence in both the Fenland region and the Somerset Levels. In the Fens peat dated to the Bronze Age has been recovered from 3m. below the existing sea-level (Godwin 1968), suggesting a eustatic fall of at least this magnitude. This coastal emergence, in conjunction with the somewhat drier conditions of the lowland mosses, resulted in widespread Bronze Age settlement of areas such as the Fenland and the Somerset Levels which had previously been subject to inundation. This expansion of lowland settlement limits was brought to an end by the widespread floodings of 500-800 bc which accompanied the climatic worsening at the opening of the Iron Age.

## Fauna

As in other prehistoric periods from the Mesolithic onwards almost all the evidence for the vertebrate fauna comes from archaeological sites. Most of it has therefore been subject to a cultural sieve, and since Bronze Age people were very largely dependent on domesticated flocks and herds, the remains of wild animals are sparse. Nevertheless, the finds fit in well between what is known of the Mesolithic fauna (see Table 3.5) and of the fauna in historical times. A few isolated finds of entire skeletons from organic deposits are also known. This account leans heavily on the published reassessments of the dating of Neolithic and Bronze Age sites by Smith (1974) and Burgess (1974), which show that the late Neolithic overlaps in time with the Beaker and early Bronze periods, so fauna from late Neolithic sites is included here.

*The wild fauna*

The full forest fauna that was present in Britain in the Mesolithic survived, with one exception, well into the Bronze Age. Only the elk, already absent in the late Boreal, is missing (Table 3.5). The first certain record of the red squirrel is from Embo chambered tomb in Sutherland (Clarke 1962-3). Our knowledge of small mammals in the Bronze Age is owed almost entirely to the finds of pellets probably produced by birds and found in post holes related to two of the round barrows in the early Bronze Age cemetery of Snail Down in Wiltshire (Clutton-Brock and Jewell, forthcoming). These contained the water vole (*Arvicola terrestris* subspecies *amphibius*), the common shrew (*Sorex araneus*), the pygmy shrew (*Sorex minutus*), the mole (*Talpa europea*), the wood mouse (*Apodemus sylvaticus*) and the field vole (*Microtus agrestis*), as well as bones of the slow worm and a lizard. *Arvicola terrestris* has been identified from a number of other Bronze Age sites, and the *reta* subspecies in particular has been recorded from a fissure cave in Hartledale, Derbyshire (Turk 1964a) which is south of its present range. The only record of the blue hare (*Lepus timidus* L.) in early postglacial Britain (excluding Ireland) is also from Hartledale, and remains of the brown hare (*L. capensis* L.) were found there as well (Turk 1964a). The house mouse (*Mus musculus*) is notably absent from Snail Down and probably had not been introduced at this date. Another site which is interesting for its small mammal fauna is Nornour in the Isles of Scilly. This is a mixed Bronze Age/Iron Age site with, as the author of the main bone report writes, virtually no stratigraphy (Turk 1967), so the dating of the finds is unfortunately not at all clear. The small mammals (Pernetta and Handford 1970) comprised the lesser white-toothed (or Scilly) shrew (*Crocidura suaveolens*) which, though absent from the rest of the British Isles, is still present in the Scillies and is possibly a relict from pre-isolation times, though it is considered by the authors to be a postglacial introduction), the root vole (*Microtus oeconomicus*), generally associated with arctic faunas and perhaps a chance introduction at that time, and *Apodemus sylvaticus*. *Mus musculus* has been identified at Nornour, but doubt has been shed on the identification by Pernetta and Handford. One very interesting find is that of the Common or Orkney vole *Microtus arvalis* at Midhowe, a chamber tomb that is almost certainly contemporary with the very late Neolithic Grooved Ware sites (Platt 1934). This vole, which is common in Europe, is absent from the rest of the British Isles (except Guernsey). Berry and Rose (1975) found that on genetical grounds the Orkney form is closest to that found today in Yugoslavia and suggested that it had been introduced into Orkney at about 2,000 bc.

The only known change during the course of the Bronze Age is the apparent extinction of the aurochs. This is quite commonly found in late Neolithic sites and is known from mixed Beaker and early Bronze Age contexts at Snail Down (Thomas, personal communication; Clutton-Brock and Jewell, forthcoming). A nearly complete bull's skeleton and a pair of large horncores were found in early Bronze Age peat at Lowes Farm near Littleport, Cambridgeshire (Plate 10), and County Farm, Mildenhall Fen, Suffolk (Shawcross and Higgs 1961). Both animals were clearly very large and so there is no reason to think that the aurochs diminished in size between Mesolithic and Bronze Age times. Another complete skeleton has recently been found at Charterhouse Warren Farm in Somerset in a cave swallet apparently associated with human and domestic animal remains (Everton 1975). It too, has now been dated to the early Bronze Age (1,295 ± 37 bc, BM-731) (Burleigh and Clutton-Brock, forthcoming). There seem to be no finds of aurochs anywhere in the British Isles after the early Bronze Age. It is interesting that all these late finds have been made in England and it could well be that far from surviving later in Scotland as so often claimed, the aurochs died out earlier in the north than in the south. While the extinction of the aurochs may have been encouraged by the climatic deterioration during the Bronze Age, particularly in the north, over-hunting by man must have been the main cause. It is sometimes claimed that there were two 'size forms' of the aurochs (e.g. by Bramwell 1974), but Degerbøl (1970) and numerous continental workers before him have shown that sexual dimorphism was very marked in the aurochs and the two size forms were merely bulls and cows.

The brown bear continued to be widely distributed: many finds are known from Ireland and Scotland (where a femur has been dated to 723 bc (2,673 ± 54 bp, BM-724), and a well preserved scapula was found at Ratfyn in Wiltshire (Jackson 1935a). The bear claws identified at Sant-y-Nyll, Glamorgan (Irvine 1959-60) are pig's teeth (King, personal communication). Although the wolf was clearly a pest throughout the Bronze Age and into mediaeval times, its remains on archaeological sites are remarkably rare.

A few walrus (*Odobenus rosmarus* L.) bones and teeth have been found at Jarlshof, Shetland (Platt 1932-3), and at Northton on the Isle of Harris in the Hebrides (Simpson, personal communication); presumably good use was made of occasional southerly forays such as the walrus has been known to make in this century. As would be expected, beavers were present in the Fens, but also in the West Country at Durrington Walls, in Wiltshire (Harcourt 1971a). Frogs, toads, lizards and slow worms are known from the British Bronze Age and frogs are commonly found on Irish sites of the same period. In Ireland generally all the late glacial relicts and animals introduced in the early postglacial (see Table 3.5) are present in the Bronze Age sites.

The Bronze Age bird fauna was richer than that of today and included several species that are now either extinct or only rarely found in the British Isles, such as the great auk, the white tailed or sea eagle (*Haliaetus albicella*), the goshawk (*Accipenser gentilis* L.) from the Beaker site at Newgrange in Ireland (Wijngaarden-Bakker 1974); the white stork (*Ciconia ciconia*), the crane (*Megalornis grus*), and the kite (*Milvus milvus*) from the late Neolithic of Durrington Walls, Wiltshire (Harcourt 1971a).

Fish remains are not common on Bronze Age sites, but it seems likely that salmonids and eels would have been plentiful, and perhaps the primary fresh-water fish (pike, perch and many others) had by the Bronze Age been spread into other rivers (deliberately or accidentally, by man) away from the south- and east-draining river systems. The chub (*Leuciscus cephalus*) was identified from grooved ware pits at Woodlands, Wiltshire (Jackson 1948) and pike at Plantation Farm, Cambridge (mixed late Neolithic and Beaker: Jackson 1933).

Reference has already been made in passing to molluscan and coleopteran faunas of Bronze Age date. Molluscan faunas in particular have yielded interesting information about environmental changes on the chalklands of the south of England, where the majority of studies has been carried out. The sites examined have mostly been soils buried beneath barrows, or ditch deposits, and results show that, throughout the Bronze Age, grassland and xerophile species of snails were favoured at the expense of woodland species; refuges for mesophile and shade-loving species persisted in the damp micro-environment of barrow ditches. A good example of the changes from shade-loving species, through intermediate types to open country species can be seen in Kerney's diagram from the Devil's Kneadingtrough (Fig. 5.1) which is discussed in detail below (page 232). In particular the expansion of *Vallonia* spp., which will tolerate open dry conditions, is very marked at this site. In passing, it may be noted that the normal coastal marine molluscs were present; one noteworthy find is that of the freshwater mussel in Ireland on the Island MacHugh, Co. Tyrone (Davies 1950).

Exotic elements have been recorded in coleopteran faunas dated to this period from the Wilsford shaft, Normanton Gorse, Wiltshire (Osborne 1969) and from the trackway site at Thorne Moor, Yorkshire, referred to earlier (Buckland and Kenward 1973), and from a bog oak found in the Cambridgeshire fens (Duffey 1968). The Thorne assemblage includes *Prostomis mandibularis, Rhysodes sulcatus, Zimioma grossa,* and *Mycetina cruciata,* all of which have continental distributions at the present day. Beetles with similar distributions recorded from the Wiltshire site are *Dermestes laniarius, Aphodius quadriguttatus* and *Onthophagus fracticornis,* and from Cambridgeshire *Cerambyx cerdo.* In addition certain species appear to have had their ranges restricted within the British Isles since the Bronze Age. A number of the species found at Thorne do not now live as far north as Yorkshire: these include *Colydium elongatum, Dryophthorus corticalis, Hypulus quercinus, Mesosa nebulosa, Microlomalus parallelopipedus* and *Platypus cylindricus.* In the case of *Melolontha hippocastani,* recorded from the Wilsford shaft, its range is now restricted to Scotland and northern England, though it is also found in northern and central Europe as far south as Italy. Buckland and Kenward (1973) suggest that the Thorne Moor fauna indicates that the climate has become more oceanic since the Bronze Age. However, Osborne (1969) feels that at Wilsford anthropogenic factors may well have influenced the ranges of some of the beetle species now absent from the British Isles, and he believes that had the Bronze Age climate of Wiltshire been much warmer and drier than the present a greater number of exotic elements than the 4 out of 138 species recorded at Wilsford would have been expected.

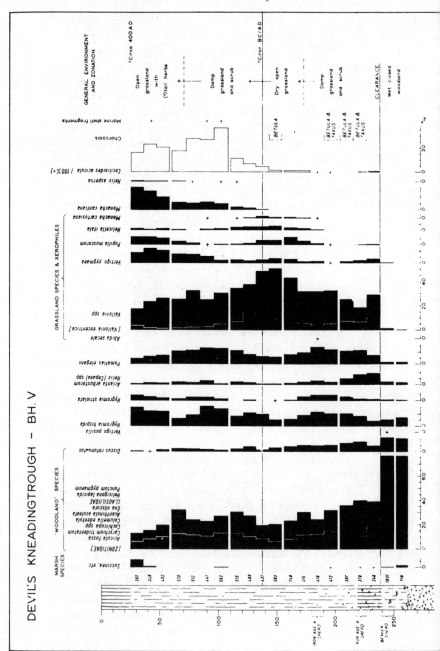

*Animals and man in Bronze Age Britain*

There are two aspects of the economy that can be discussed here. These are the relative importance of domesticated and wild animals, and the relative numbers of the domestic animals present. Unfortunately, animal bone reports are particularly sketchy for this period. Assessments of the numbers and relative numbers of animals present at a site are usually made in terms of total number of bones of each species or in terms of the minimum number of individuals (MNI), estimated in various ways from incompatible bones. The difficulty in using the estimates of minimum numbers is that authors tend to estimate them in different ways and often the method used is not stated. MNI estimates tend to favour the animals represented by only a few bones, and therefore on Bronze Age sites they are more useful for comparing numbers of pigs, cattle and sheep than for the less frequent wild animals. Even total numbers can be difficult – some authors exclude ribs, some exclude teeth, some use teeth only, others exclude antler and so on.

The general conclusion from the sum of the investigations made is that domestic animals are far more important than wild animals throughout the Bronze Age. One of the difficulties encountered in estimating the proportions of domestic and wild animals is that wild and domestic pigs and wild and domestic cattle overlap in size, and the size ranges are not fully established, although Degerbøl (1970) gives the range of variation for the aurochs and so to a limited degree does Grigson (1969); wild pig ranges have been partially established by Boessneck *et al.* (1963) and Clason (1967). There is now the suspicion that there were more wild boar and aurochs on the early sites than have been identified in the animal bone reports. It is not possible to make accurate estimates of relative numbers for these reasons and for those outlined previously. The proportion of wild animals identified in the faunal spectra from late Neolithic sites varies from 6.3 to 40.0% averaging 17.7% when based on the MNI, but when the proportion is calculated from total numbers (only available for six sites) the average percentage of wild animals is only 8.5%. For the middle and later Bronze Age there are only three sites from which estimates can be made (from total numbers of bones) and here the average is 3.5% wild animals. An outwardly less

---

Figure 5.1. Molluscan analyses from the Devil's Kneadingtrough, Kent, Borehole V. (From Kerney *et al.* 1964.)

accurate but more rewarding method of assessing the importance of wild animals is to count the numbers of wild species present at each site. On 16 late Neolithic sites the average number of wild species present is about four. At six Beaker sites, four mixed late Neolithic/Beaker/Bronze Age sites, and three early Bronze Age sites, the averages are all about three. This contrasts with seven middle and late Bronze Age sites where there is an average of 1.4 wild animal species.

Quite a different picture emerges from coastal sites, particularly in Scotland, which have much larger numbers of wild animals. At Embo, Sutherland, a later Neolithic tomb of the Orkney-Cromarty-Hebridean type dated to 1,920 bc (3,870 ± 100 bp, B-442), there were nine wild species in the lower level in the chamber and thirteen in the upper levels (Clarke 1962-3). In the Knowe of Ramsey on Orkney (a tomb of the same type: Henshall 1963) there were twelve wild species which included at least twelve individual red deer. At the Beaker site of Northton on Harris, the two middle layers yielded about thirteen wild species (Simpson, personal communication) and on Scilly, the late Bronze Age/Iron Age site of Nornour had about nine wild large vertebrate species· (Turk 1967; Pernetta and Handford 1970). At Jarlshof, a late Bronze Age site on Shetland, there were seals, walrus and whales, as well as 14 species of bird (Platt 1932-3 and 1933-4). Almost all these coastal sites have little, if any, pig, either wild or domesticated, and it may be that these wild animals provided something otherwise provided by pigs: possibly winter sustenance as pigs did not have to be culled in the autumn.

The apparent decrease in wild animals in the economy of the middle and the late Bronze Age is probably related to extensive forest clearance and the fact that the sites (at least those with animal bones) tend to be situated on the treeless tops of hills. In the earlier period the ungulates would have been hunted largely for food and the carnivores for fur. The decrease in wild animals may be related to the increasing numbers of sheep and perhaps to the increased farming efficiency which made hunted animals less necessary in the diet.

More accurate estimates of relative numbers of domestic pigs, cattle and sheep are possible, and the proportions of these animals, and of horses, are shown in Tables 5.3 and 5.4. It is quite clear that although all these animals are present in late Neolithic Grooved Ware sites the economy was in general dominated by pigs with moderate numbers of cattle (see Table 5.3). It would be interesting to compare the bones from these later Neolithic sites with those from the more or less contemporary sites of the Beaker and early Bronze Age cultures. However, it is not possible to talk about a typical English Beaker economy as most sites contain a mixture of late Neolithic or early Bronze Age pottery with the Beaker sherds.

There are no late Neolithic or predominately Beaker sites with animal bones that are definitely contemporary, which is what is needed to make cultural economic comparisons, but at Mount Pleasant (Harcourt, forthcoming) the mixed, but largely Beaker levels contained almost the same relative numbers as the preceding late Neolithic levels. The similarity is even greater if the figures are recalculated to include horse among the domestic animals (see Table 5.3). Other minor Beaker sites have proportionately more cattle, but each has so few bones that this may not be significant.

With the early Bronze Age (Table 5.4), there is a similar shortage of information and difficulty with dating, for example at the Snail Down cemetery on the Wiltshire Downs (Clutton-Brock and Jewell, forthcoming; Thomas, personal communication), it is not clear whether the bones are contemporary with the dated collared urn burial (1,540 bc, 3,490 ± 90 bp, NPL-141) or whether they came with refuse from an earlier Beaker settlement. However, they are probably later Bronze Age since in the cemetery as a whole pigs are reduced to 10% and sheep rise to 38%. The relative numbers of domestic animals are only properly recorded from one middle Bronze Age Deverel-Rimbury settlement: Shearplace Hill, Dorset (King 1962b), where only eighteen bones were identified; nevertheless pigs are greatly reduced in number. In the late Bronze Age Deverel-Rimbury settlement of Eldon's Seat (Phillipson 1968) pigs are down to 4% and sheep rise to 42%. The economy at the hillfort of Grimthorpe (dated 970 bc, 2,920 ± 130 bp, NPL-131) is fairly similar (Jarman *et al.* 1968). Perhaps the apparently increased farming efficiency in the middle Bronze Age made man less dependent on resources of the forest, particularly in winter; the increase in numbers of sheep probably allowed woollen garments and textiles to replace furs, and this seems to be attested by the presence of spinning and weaving equipment from Deverel-Rimbury settlements.

The generally accepted reduction in the size of domestic cattle between the Neolithic and the Bronze Age (Jewell 1963) has recently been made much more complicated by the realisation of the overlap in time between the late Neolithic, Beaker and early Bronze

Table 5.3. Percentages of domestic ungulates in Late Neolithic sites showing the relative importance of pigs in the domestic economy.

| | Date bc uncalib. | Pottery | Type of site | Percentages of domestic ungulates (pig / ox / sh/gt / horse) | Based on | Other species identified | No. bones identified | Reference |
|---|---|---|---|---|---|---|---|---|
| Durrington Walls, Wilts. 1966–8 | BM.398 1,977 ± 90 NPL.239 1,810 ± 140 | Grooved Ware | Henge | pig 68, ox 29, sh/gt 2, horse 1 | m.n.i. | dog, aurochs, red deer, roe deer, badger, pine marten, fox; birds | 8,500 | Harcourt 1971 |
| Durrington Walls, Wilts. 1952 | — | Grooved Ware | Post holes pre-henge | pig 61, ox 35, sh/gt 3.5, horse 0.3 | nos. and m.n.i. | none | 630 | Grahame 1954 |
| Durrington Walls, Wilts. 1970 | BM.703 1,523 ± 72 BM.702 1,647 ± 76 | Grooved Ware | pits | pig 67, ox 33, sh/gt 1, horse 0 | nos. | aurochs?, wild pig, roe deer, vole | 309 | Westley 1971 |
| Marden, Wilts. | BM.557 1,988 ± 48 | Grooved Ware | Henge ditch | pig 42, ox 42, sh/gt 11, horse 5 | m.n.i. | aurochs, wild pig?, red deer | 320 | Harcourt 1971a |
| Mount Pleasant, Dorset | BM.792 2,108 ± 71 BM.646 1,778 ± 59 | Grooved Ware | Henge ditch | pig 55, ox 26, sh/gt 16, horse 3 | m.n.i. | dog, goat?, aurochs, wild pig, red deer, fox; birds, incl. crane | 630* | Harcourt, forthcoming |
| Puddlehill, Beds. Pits 1, 2 & 3 | — | Grooved Ware | Pits | pig 60, ox 23, sh/gt 17, horse 0 | nos. | aurochs, red deer, roe deer, fox, bird | 183 | Ewbank 1964 |
| Puddlehill, Beds. Pit 6 | — | Grooved Ware | Pit | pig 67, ox 11, sh/gt 22, horse 0 | m.n.i. | aurochs, wild pig, red deer | 128 | Grigson 1976 |

| Sites | Date b.c. uncalib. | Pottery | Type of site | Percentages of domestic ungulates | Based on | Other species identified | No. bones identified | References |
|---|---|---|---|---|---|---|---|---|
| North Carnaby Temple, Boynton, Yorks. Sites 1, 2, 4,7,9,12,14 & 15 | — | Grooved Ware | Pits & occupation? | pig 60, ox 20, sh/gt 20, horse 0 | nos. | dog, aurochs, red deer | 38 | Bramwell 1974 |
| Low Caythorpe 1, Boynton, Yorks. | — | Grooved Ware | Pits & occupation? | pig 57, ox 32, sh/gt 11, horse 0 | nos. | dog, red deer | 29 | Bramwell 1974 |

nos. = total numbers of bones
m.n.i = minimum number of individuals
* Includes some bones from Woodhenge

**Table 5.4. Percentages of domestic ungulates in Bronze Age sites.**

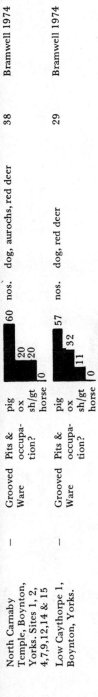

| Sites | Date b.c. uncalib. | Pottery | Type of site | Percentages of domestic ungulates | Based on | Other species identified | No. bones identified | References |
|---|---|---|---|---|---|---|---|---|
| MIXED LATE NEOLITHIC, BEAKER AND EARLY BRONZE AGE SITES | | | | | | | | |
| Windmill Hill, Wilts. Secondary silt of ditches | BM.75 1550 ± 150 | Grooved Ware/Beaker/Collared Urn | Occupation? | pig 21, ox 68, sh/gt 11, horse 0 | nos. | dog, aurochs, red deer, cat? | 87 | Jope and Grigson 1965 |
| Poors Heath, Risby, Suffolk | — | Beaker/Food Vessel | Barrow | pig 22, ox 43, sh/gt 26, horse 8 | nos. | dog, aurochs, wild pig?, red deer, roe deer, hare | 179 | Cornwall 1976 |

Table 5.4 continued

| Sites | Date b.c. uncalib. | Pottery | Type of site | Percentages of domestic ungulates | Based on | Other species identified | No. bones identified | References |
|---|---|---|---|---|---|---|---|---|
| Mount Pleasant, Dorset | BM.668 1680±60 BM.665 1695±43 BM.790 1669±55 | Grooved Ware/Beaker | Henge ditches secondary fill | pig 39, ox 36, sh/gt 25, horse 0 | m.n.i. | dog, aurochs, wild pig, red deer, roe deer, fox; song thrush, missel thrush, pintail, goose | 1,946 | Harcourt, forthcoming |
| Mount Pleasant, Dorset | BM.788 1556±55 BM.789 1509±53 | Grooved Ware/Beaker/Food Vessel/Collared Urn | Henge ditches, Bronze Age fill | pig 42, ox 25, sh/gt 33, horse 0 | m.n.i. | dog, goat, red deer, fox, badger | 454 | Harcourt forthcoming |
| **BEAKER SITES** | | | | | | | | |
| Newgrange, Co. Meath. A level Ireland | GrN 6344 2100±40 GrN 6342 1935±35 | Beaker | Settlement | pig 33, ox 60, sh/gt 6, horse 1 (nos.); pig 35, ox 44, sh/gt 14, horse 7 (m.n.i.) | nos. / m.n.i. | dog, red deer, cat, blue hare; goshawk, rail | 4,000 | Wijngaarden-Bakker 1974 |
| Hockwold-cum-Wilton, Norfolk | — | Beaker? | ? | pig 17, ox 77, sh/gt 5, horse 0 | nos. | dog, red deer, roe deer | 114 | Cram 1967 |
| **EARLY BRONZE AGE SITES** | | | | | | | | |
| Snail Down, Everleigh, Wilts. Sites I-IV,X,XI, XIII-XVII & XIX | NPL.141* 1540±90 | Collared Urn & other | Round barrows | pig 10, ox 47, sh/gt 38, horse 5 | nos. | dog, aurochs, red deer, roe deer. For rodents & insectivores see text | 480 | Clutton-Brock and Jewell, forthcoming Thomas, personal communication |

| Site | Date/Ref | Period | Context | pig / ox / sh/gt / horse | | Other species | Total | Reference |
|---|---|---|---|---|---|---|---|---|
| Gortnacargy, Co. Cavan, Ireland | — | Food Vessel | Cairn | pig 36, ox 38, sh/gt 26, horse 0 | nos. | blue hare | 47 | O'Riordain 1967 |

## MIDDLE AND LATE BRONZE AGE SITES

| Site | Date/Ref | Period | Context | pig / ox / sh/gt / horse | | Other species | Total | Reference |
|---|---|---|---|---|---|---|---|---|
| Shearplace Hill, Dorset | NPL.19 1180 ± 180 | Dev.–Rimbury | Settlement | pig 6, ox 72, sh/gt 22, horse 0 | nos. | none | 18 | King 1962 a and b |
| Ramshill, Oxon | HAR.229 1010 ± 80 – HAR.228 1070 ± 90 | ? | Enclosure Ditch | pig 5, ox 63, sh/gt 32, horse 0 | nos. | red deer (antler) | c.40 | Carter 1975 |
| Grimthorpe, Yorks. | NPL.137 970 ± 130 | 'Early Iron Age' | Hill-fort | pig 8, ox 58, sh/gt 26, horse 8 | nos. | dog, red deer, roe deer, fox | 735 | Jarman et al. 1968 |
| Eldon's Seat, Dorset | — | Dev.–Rimbury | Settlement | pig 4, ox 53, sh/gt 42, horse 1 | nos. | dog, red deer; bird | 1,003 | Phillipson 1968 |
| Ballinderry 11, Co. Offaly, Ireland | — | 'Late Bronze Age' | Settlement | pig c.15, ox c.80, sh/gt c.4, horse c.1. | nos. | red deer, badger, otter, cat, blue hare?, crane, wild duck | 630 lbs | Stelfox 1942 |

nos. = total number of bones
m.n.i. = minimum number of individuals
* Bones may antedate burial

In contrast to the Late Neolithic (Table 5.3) cattle once again predominate. On the mixed and Beaker sites the pattern is confused, but in England, in the Middle and Late Bronze Age, sheep begin to outnumber pigs.

Age cultures. However, it is still clear that the cattle of the late Neolithic sites were larger than those of the middle and late Bronze Age. Whether this was a gradual diminution or occurred suddenly (which would imply an introduction from elsewhere) is still open to question. On the whole, cattle from Beaker sites have been identified as *Bos longifrons* – that is an ox smaller than that of the Neolithic or 'Woodhenge' ox. Examples are Easton Down Beaker settlement (Jackson 1931a); Giants Hill, Skendleby: Beaker ditch level (Jackson 1935b); Gorsey Bigbury (Tetley 1938); and the Beaker levels at Stonehenge which Jackson (1935c) thought were Iron Age. At the Sanctuary, Overton Hill, Jackson (1931b) suggested that the cattle were larger than *B. longifrons*. A similar study of sheep sizes would be valuable – all that can be said is that Bronze Age sheep in Britain were small, slender limbed, and two-horned.

Horses are thought to have lived in Britain (but not in Ireland) as wild, probably forest, forms, in small numbers in the Mesolithic and Neolithic although the evidence is rather scanty. Horses are present, again in small numbers, on most of the earlier Bronze Age sites, including those of the late Neolithic. Their domesticated status has been rather uncertain, but now that horses have been clearly identified in the Beaker site at Newgrange (Wijngaarden-Bakker 1974) in Ireland, where they must have been deliberately introduced, their position as domesticates seems fairly clear. At Newgrange, horses seem to have been eaten for it is only in the Ewart Park metal-working phase of the later Bronze Age that harness and horse-drawn vehicle fittings are known (Burgess 1974), although it is possible that horses were ridden before this without the use of elaborate equipment. Horses continue to occur in small numbers in domestic refuse, but these finds probably do not reflect their true importance since they were unlikely to have been eaten at this time and at Eldon's Seat most of them died of old age (Phillipson 1968).

Dogs were present throughout the Bronze Age and do not seem to have been eaten, as complete skeletons are relatively common (Beaker Ash Pit C at Easton Down: Jackson 1935d; the ring ditch at Salmondsbury, Bourton-on-the-Water: Harding 1976; and at Jarlshof in the late Bronze Age midden: Platt 1933-4); dogs were important to the users of the Orkney-Cromarty-Hebridean tombs in Orkney for seven complete skeletons were found at Burray and twenty-four skulls on the chamber floor at Cuween Hill (Henshall 1963).

## The vegetation of Britain at the opening of the Bronze Age

At the start of the Bronze Age the British Isles were still largely forested, although the agricultural activities of successive Neolithic cultures had taken their toll and in some places the composition of the Atlantic forest had been permanently altered. On many areas of poorer soil *Ulmus* (elm) never regained its former status after its initial decline at the opening of the Neolithic period, and with the opening up of woodland *Fraxinus* (ash) expanded, becoming particularly widespread on calcareous soils such as the limestones of Derbyshire. *Tilia* (lime) probably occurred quite frequently in English woodlands at the start of the Bronze Age but was reduced throughout the period, and *Pinus* (pine) pollen shows a decline which is particularly marked in Ireland (see below).

In contrast to the national picture, a regional view shows that in some parts of the country the forest had been very much reduced by the start of the Bronze Age. On the sandy soils of Breckland a permanent change from forest to heath began in the Neolithic period (Godwin and Tallantire 1951); in a pollen diagram from the muds of Hockham Mere the curves for pollen of Gramineae (grasses) and Ericaceae (principally *Calluna*) rise shortly after the *Ulmus* decline to about 60% of total tree pollen, and continue to rise until modern times. Palynological investigations have also established that parts of the coastal plain of south-west Cumbria were more or less permanently deforested as a result of Neolithic activities (Walker 1966).

In almost all the upland areas of Britain, evidence from pollen diagrams suggests that high altitude woodland was already being thinned out by the start of the Bronze Age. It is still a matter of dispute whether the highest parts of Dartmoor, the Welsh uplands and the Pennines ever did carry forest. Certainly blanket peat was well established over north central Dartmoor in the Atlantic period (Simmons 1969a), at sites throughout the high Pennines (Conway 1954; Johnson and Dunham 1962) and on the Welsh uplands (Moore 1973). In the Lake District there is palynological evidence for the large scale destruction of upland forests before the Bronze Age and its replacement by grassy heath, particularly in the areas around the Neolithic axe factories at the head of Langdale (Pennington 1970).

As far as the Celtic immigrants were concerned, the status of the vegetation of the chalk downs of south-east England was of paramount importance, as this was the region most heavily settled and where their culture attained its highest development. Unfortunately the evidence from pollen analysis is fragmentary since there are few suitable deposits, but from the limited information available it appears that the downs were partially cleared by the beginning of the Bronze Age. Two pollen diagrams by Sir Harry Godwin from Frogholt, near Folkstone, and Wingham, near Canterbury, support this view. At Frogholt, fluviatile organic deposits began to accumulate after 1,030 bc (2,980 ± 130 bp, Q-354) and the pollen spectrum from the basal peat indicates a predominantly cleared environment by this date. Similarly at Wingham, pollen from the base of the deposit of peaty mud is typical of a largely deforested landscape and the radiocarbon date for the onset of accumulation is 1,155 bc (3,105 ± 110 bp, Q-110) (Godwin 1962a). Turner (1970) suggests that there was considerable variation in the amount of land cleared on the downs at different periods and in different localities; this hypothesis is supported by analyses of the molluscan fauna from sites in a coomb called the Devil's Kneadingtrough on the chalk escarpment near Brook in Kent (Kerney *et al.* 1964). Two sections were examined about 300m. apart, and at the Rifle Butts section in the upper part of the coomb there is evidence for two phases of local clearance, the second and more drastic being attributed to the Iron Age and the earlier one to the Bronze Age. The diagram from the second site (Borehole V) is illustrated in Fig. 5.1; the histograms suggest that complete clearance took place around this site much earlier than in the vicinity of the Rifle Butts section since woodland snail species decline markedly at 240cm. and just below this level a Beaker pottery fragment was recovered from the section. Above 240cm. the grassland species steadily increase, in particular *Vallonia* spp., and the woodland species never regain their former representation.

According to Evans (1972) molluscan faunas suggest that a number of sites on the chalk around Avebury and Stonehenge were open and dry in the first half of the second millenium bc. A soil profile from beneath the bank at Avebury illustrates this (Fig. 4.3): a fauna typical of a forest environment, dominated by shade-loving species such as *Carychium* and *Discus*, occurs in the lower part of the profile, to be replaced by a fauna typical of open country as the turf line is approached. Through the turf line there is a progressive impoverishment of the fauna, which becomes dominated by species of dry calcareous habitat including *Vallonia* spp., *Hygromia hispida*,

*Helicella itala* and *Cochlicopa*. Evans believes that all these changes in the Sub-Boreal molluscan fauna are attributable to man's exploitation of the environment, rather than to climatic change. Taken together with the diagrams from Brook, Wingham and Frogholt this suggests that partial clearance of the downs was carried out by Neolithic pastoralists, but that the intensity of the clearing activity was very variable. Some areas remained clear throughout the Bronze Age, whereas regeneration occurred elsewhere in periods of decreased population pressure. Certainly some areas of the now familiar plagioclimax grasslands of the chalk downs must have been in existence for about 5,000 years and these formed the chief grainlands during the Bronze Age. Jessen and Helbaek's (1944) detailed study of grain impressions on pottery and carbonised grains associated with archaeological sites has established that the principle crop at this period was barley (*Hordeum* spp.), but that emmer (*Triticum dicoccum*) and small spelt (*Triticum monococcum*) were also cultivated. The majority of cereal records of this type come from the south and east of the country although they are by no means confined to these areas.

## Woodland clearance: the highland/lowland division

Traditionally, Cyril Fox's highland/lowland division of the British Isles has been regarded as of great importance during the Bronze Age, dividing the prosperous and densely settled corn lands of the south and east from the scantily settled, largely wooded lands of the north and west where only pastoral agriculture was practised. Recently Burgess (1974) has stressed this division:

> ... thus from prehistoric times a predominantly pastoral highland zone has contrasted with a more arable lowland zone. The lower tracts of the highland zone are individually too small or scattered, their soil too often poor, to provide a basis for agricultural wealth and dense population, contrasting strongly with the broad arable expanses of the lowland zone so rich in the tractable soils sought by the prehistoric farmers.

Although this is true in general terms it conjures up an over-simplified picture of the Bronze Age environment. Evans (1972) has suggested that the concept of the highland/lowland division is only relevant to the Iron Age and later periods. Certainly there is abundant palynological evidence for quite extensive Bronze Age clearance and cultivation of cereals in the north and west of Britain, though in the early Bronze Age the cleared enclaves were small compared to those of the south and east.

*Clearance of lowland and valley sites*

Detailed work on the nature of Bronze Age clearances has been carried out by Turner (1965, 1970) at Tregaron Bog, Dyfed and Bloak Moss, Ayrshire. At these sites she identified small temporary clearances similar to the landnam episodes originally described by Iversen (1941) in Denmark. These clearances occurred at various times during the Bronze Age; at Bloak Moss three successive clearances have been identified dated 1,220 bc (3,170 ± 105 bp, Q-724), 1,100 bc (3,050 ± 105 bp, Q-725), and 1,270 bc (3,220 ± 105 bp, Q-726) (Godwin *et al.* 1965). Allowing for the standard deviations of these dates the three clearances cannot be separated, but they must all have taken place between 1,400 and 1,000 bc, and on the basis of calculated rates of peat accumulation Turner estimates that each episode lasted about 50 years.

A series of clearances has also been identified at Tregaron (Turner 1964a), the latest falling in the late Bronze Age and bracketed between the dates 696 bc (mean of 2,669 ± 110 bp and 2,624 ± 110 bp, Q-388) and 404 bc (2,354 ± 110 bp, Q-596). A detailed pollen diagram from this clearance is reproduced in Fig. 5.2. The total length of the phase is estimated at 50 years, and of this the actual deforestation took about 10 years with an occupation period of around 15 years. In the diagram tree pollen is seen to decline in the lower eight samples and pollen of *Corylus* (hazel) and the Gramineae increases, together with spores of *Pteridium* (bracken). As the clearing activity progressed it must have allowed increased pollen production by undershrubs and ground flora. In the occupation period between samples nine and eighteen, the frequencies of Gramineae pollen and *Pteridium* spores remain high and pollen of *Plantago lanceolata* (a species very widely associated with man's pastoral activities) increases. Above this there is a regeneration phase where the pollen of *Betula*, a pioneer species, increases, first at the expense of *Pteridium* and later at the expense of the Gramineae and *Plantago*, and this is followed by an increase in *Quercus* pollen as the high forest re-establishes itself. The forest composition is similar to that which preceded the clearance and no permanent changes appear to have occurred. The clearances at

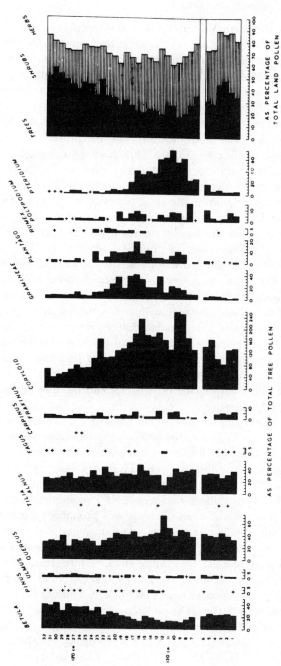

Figure 5.2. A 'small temporary clearance' in the pollen diagram from Tregaron Bog, Dyfed. (From Turner 1965.)

Bloak Moss are essentially similar in character, though in this case the pollen of *Fraxinus*, a light-demanding tree, appears for the first time at this level and persists as a member of the woodland canopy. Also at Bloak Moss grains of cereal pollen are associated with the occupation indicating that cultivation was carried out in addition to pastoral agriculture.

Turner has carried out further investigations at Bloak Moss to ascertain the likely size of the clearances by using three-dimensional pollen diagrams (Turner 1975). This involves correlating conventional pollen diagrams from different sites on the moss. The theory of pollen transfer proposed by Tauber (1965) led Turner to suggest that a core from a site near the edge of the bog (Site A) would reflect local vegetation up to a few hundred metres away, whereas a core from site K, 300 metres from the edge of the bog, would reflect changes over a much wider region. The dated clearances referred to above are from the site A core, and they reflect prehistoric man's use of a very small piece of forest up to a few hundred square metres around the site. In the pollen diagram from site K, which represents the regional picture, the pastoral indicators parallel those from site A, suggesting that the events at this site were typical of the region as a whole; it appears that throughout the Bronze Age successive groups were migrating into and out of the Bloak Moss region, making small clearances a few hundred metres in diameter and then moving on without causing any permanent disruption to the forest.

Small temporary clearances similar to those described by Turner have been identified at a number of low-lying sites in north and west Britain. From the Lake District there is evidence for a series of short term clearances in sediments from Thirlmere and Rydal Water (Pennington 1970). Pollen of barley (*Hordeum* spp.) has been found in association with these clearances, and Pennington infers that small scale pastoral and arable activity was probably typical of the woodlands surrounding the valley lakes during the Bronze Age. Similar clearances also occur at Holcroft and Lindow Mosses on the Triassic lowlands of south Lancashire and Cheshire (Birks 1965).

From Wales, in addition to Turner's sites, small temporary Bronze Age clearances have been described by Thomas (1965) from a bog at Llanllwch, Dyfed. The pollen diagram shows two clearance phases occurring between the *Ulmus* decline and a recurrence surface dated 1,254 bc (mean of 3,230 ± 100 bp, Q-458 and 3,178 ± 100 bp, Q-459). These are tentatively ascribed to the early and middle Bronze Age, and although the agricultural indicator species present are primarily pastoral, cereal pollen also occurs. A third clearance phase immediately above the radiocarbon-dated horizon is attributed to late Bronze Age activity in the area. Quite marked forest clearance seems to have begun in Speyside in the early Bronze Age (O'Sullivan 1974) at a horizon dated to 1,685 bc (3,635 ± 205 bp, UB-850); however in northern Scotland generally, evidence for pre-Iron age woodland clearance is strictly limited.

In two areas of the north-west of the British Isles, the Cumberland lowlands and Ireland, Bronze Age clearance seems to have been on a different scale from Turner's small temporary clearances. Walker's (1966) work on the Cumberland lowlands established that partial clearance took place in Neolithic times but became more extensive in the Bronze Age as it was 'given new impetus during the period from 1,750 bc-1,400 bc when a new economy, more sedentary and utilising cereals widely, became established'. It seems likely that this new impetus was a result of Beaker migrations into the area and it resulted in the permanent deforestation of much of this coastal strip. In Ireland too, the Bronze Age clearances of lowland areas appear to have been quite spectacular. At Littleton Bog, County Tipperary, Mitchell (1965) cites evidence for limited activity in the early Bronze Age, followed by much more extensive clearance with herbaceous pollen values rising to 14% of total pollen; Mitchell dates this to around 1,800 bc and suggests that it is associated with the arrival of technically more advanced middle Bronze Age folk. Rather similar evidence occurs in two pollen diagrams from northern Ireland; at Sluggan Bog, County Antrim, woodland declines gradually in Beaker and early Bronze Age times with two further extensive clearance episodes in the late Bronze Age (Smith 1975), and at Gortcorbies, County Londonderry, a marked clearance phase with a radiocarbon date of 2,025 bc (3,975 ± 75 bp, UB-382) is attributed to the Beaker folk whose artifacts are widespread in the area.

It is unfortunate that sites for which pollen diagrams are available are rarely related to archaeological sites from which animal remains have been recorded. However, two of Grigson's comments on the Bronze Age fauna can usefully be considered in the light of the evidence for increasing woodland clearance in the Bronze Age: the extinction of the aurochs and the decline in numbers of wild animals associated with cultural sites must undoubtedly have been related to this environmental change.

*The Sub-Boreal decline in* Tilia *and* Pinus

A permanent decline in pollen of *Tilia* (lime) is a feature of a number of pollen diagrams from lowland sites in the British Isles, and it is usually associated with Sub-Boreal clearance phases. It was once thought that this *Tilia* decline was a result of the worsening climatic conditions but it is now established that man's activities were responsible (Turner 1962). *Tilia* was selectively felled for its bast and nutritious leaves, and also possibly because of its tendency to grow on the better soils. The *Tilia* decline is particularly marked in pollen diagrams from the North Yorkshire Moors, an area where *Tilia* grew particularly abundantly prior to the Sub-Boreal (Simmons 1969b). The diagram from Moss Swang (Fig. 5.3), a channel mire at an altitude of 175m., shows a pronounced *Tilia* decline at 200cm. (the TF horizon). Above this the pollen of clearance indicators, which include *Plantago* spp., Compositae, *Rumex*, Chenopodiaceae, *Urtica, Pteridium, Spergula arvensis* and *Melampyrum*, increase markedly and the first cereal pollen occurs. The diagram is not radiocarbon dated, but the tentative chronology established by Simmons in relation to other diagrams from the area places the Moss Swang *Tilia* decline at the start of the middle Bronze Age, a period of fairly intensive exploitation of these uplands.

Widespread radiocarbon dating of the *Tilia* decline at other British sites has established that it is metachronous (Table 5.5), occurring in connection with the activities of different cultural groups in different areas depending on the intensity of environmental exploitation. At Whixall Moss, Holme Fen and Thorne Waste (first decline) the decline in *Tilia* took place in the middle to late Bronze Age, while at Shapwick Heath on the Somerset Levels it appears to have taken place during the Neolithic, and at Thorne Waste the second decline took place in the Iron Age.

**Table 5.5. Radiocarbon dates for the *Tilia* decline (after Turner 1962)**

|  | Years bc | Years bp | Lab. no. |
|---|---|---|---|
| Whixall Moss (Clwyd/Salop border) | 1277 | 3227 ± 115 | Q.467 |
| Shapwick Heath (Somerset) | 2015 | 3965 ± 115 | Q.644 |
| Holme Fen (East Anglia) | 1440 | 3390 ± 120 | Q.403 |
|  | 1445 | 3395 ± 120 | Q.404 |
| Thorne Waste (South Yorkshire) |  |  |  |
| 1st decline | 1210 | 3160 ± 115 | Q.481 |
|  | 971 | 2921 ± 115 | Q.482 |
| 2nd decline | 368 | 2318 ± 110 | Q.479 |

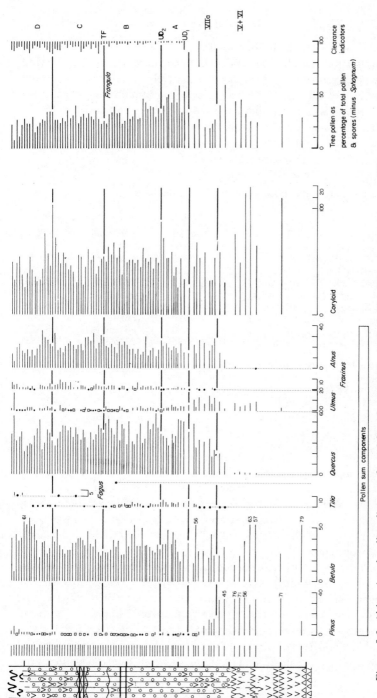

Figure 5.3. Abbreviated pollen diagram from Moss Swang, North Yorkshire Moors, showing tree pollen types and clearance indicators. (Reproduced from Simmons 1969b.)

At some sites in the British Isles *Pinus* shows a decline which is parallel to that of *Tilia*, and it is particularly marked in Ireland where pine seems to have been extensively exploited for fuel and timber. As with the *Tilia* decline it was originally thought to be a synchronous horizon and was used to define the Sub-Boreal/Sub-Atlantic transition in Ireland. However, Mitchell (1956) suggested that it was a metachronous feature and recent radiocarbon dates (Table 5.6) tend to confirm this view.

**Table 5.6. Irish radiocarbon dates for the *Pinus* decline.**

|  | Years bc | Years bp | Lab. no. |
|---|---|---|---|
| Ballynagilly (County Tyrone) | 2390 | 4340 ± 65 | UB.250 |
| Beaghmore ( .. .. ) between | 1930 | 3880 ± 65 | UB.91 |
| and | 2575 | 4525 ± 55 | UB.92 |
| Slieve Gallion ( .. .. ) | 2215 | 4165 ± 80 | UB.274 |
| Lough Lark ( .. .. ) * | 2005 | 3955 ± 75 | UB.380 |
| Ballyscullion (County Antrim) | 2250 | 3200 ± 85 | UB.111 |
| Breen Bog ( .. .. ) | 1820 | 3770 ± 95 | UB.370 |
| Ballypatrick ( .. .. )* | 1730 | 3680 ± 95 | UB.265 |
| Glen's Bridge ( .. .. )† | 1660 | 3610 ± 75 | UB.376F |
| Altnahinch ( .. .. ) | 795 | 2745 ± 70 | UB.333 |

\* Sample immediately below *Pinus* decline
† Sample immediately above *Pinus* decline
Source: A.G. Smith *et al*. 1971

*The clearance of upland woodland*

At valley and lowland sites Bronze Age clearance resulted in the creation of grassy enclaves, usually temporary, in a more or less continuous forest cover. However, at upland sites the impact of Bronze Age man on the environment was more profound; in a number of widely separated areas there is evidence for large scale clearance and the permanent replacement of woodland by heath and bog communities.

In the Pennines radiocarbon dating has been used extensively to establish the influence of successive Bronze Age groups on the vegetation. From North Yorkshire the extension of heath over the Pennine moors at the expense of mixed *Quercus-Betula-Alnus* woodland has been radiocarbon dated to 1,930 bc (3,880 ± 100 bp, GaK-2934) (Tinsley 1975). The nature of this change can be seen in the pollen diagram from Fountains Earth, a topogenous bog at a height of 365m. (Figs. 5.4 and 5.5). At the zone N-C/N-D boundary tree pollen begins a steady and marked decline and there is a sudden rise in pollen of Ericaceae. At the same horizon an expansion occurs in pollen of the Gramineae, *Plantago lanceolata, Rumex acetosella* and other agricultural weeds which strongly suggests that woodland clearance rather than climatic deterioration was responsible for the extension of heath. The radiocarbon date links this clearance with the Beaker occupation of the Vale of York to the east of the moors where a series of massive henge monuments was erected. The Beaker people probably used the uplands for pasture as the woodland must have been easier to clear than the dense forest of the clay vale. Tree pollen values decline steadily throughout zone N-D in the Fountains Earth pollen diagram and the failure of woodland to regenerate following the Beaker activities may well be a result of exposure on the high parts of the moors, as pollen diagrams from more sheltered sites at lower altitudes in this area show regeneration of trees after the initial clearances.

On the eastern edge of the Pennines in Derbyshire (the 'East Moor') the Bronze Age clearances were a little later and in all cases they were followed by regeneration (Hicks 1971). At Leash Fen the main clearance is dated to 1,500 bc (3,450 ± 110 bp, GaK-2287) and this agrees well with radiocarbon dates for Bronze Age artifacts from the East Moor (an unurned burial 3,480 ± 150 bp, BM-212; a collared urn 3,000 ± 150 bp, BM-177; food vessels 3,440 ± 150 bp, BM-178). As remains of collared urns are usually more widespread than food vessels, Hicks attributes this clearance to the Urn Folk. The palynological evidence suggests that they had an economy which was primarily pastoral, but cereal pollen grains occur at one site (Hipper Sick), suggesting some limited cultivation.

The third area of the Pennines where detailed studies of this type have been carried out is central Rossendale on the extreme western edge (Tallis and McGuire 1972). The pollen diagram from Deep Clough shows pronounced clearance phases in the middle and late Bronze Age which resulted in the creation of a largely open landscape of heath and bog. The earlier clearance is radiocarbon dated to 1,590 bc (3,540 ± 120 bp, B-147) and Tallis and McGuire suggest that it may be associated with several middle Bronze Age burial mounds which occur on the surrounding uplands. Palynological investigations at one of these barrows on Winter Hill give interesting complementary evidence of clearance. Counts were

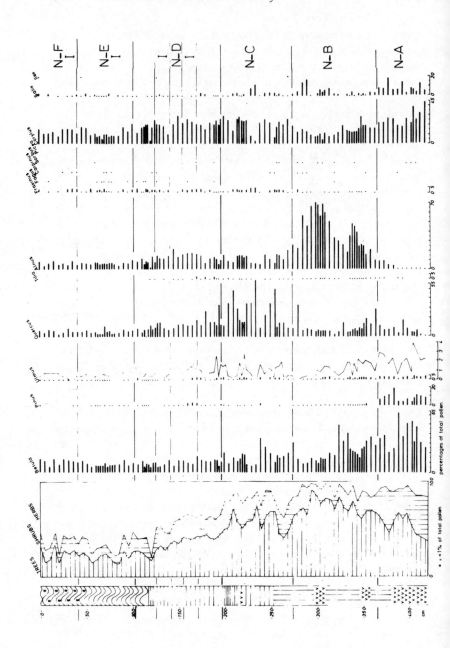

made in the buried soil and in the turves composing the mound itself (Dimbleby 1962) and the results are shown in Fig. 5.6. The pollen spectrum from the buried surface (T1) suggests a fairly open environment, with pollen of *Calluna* and Gramineae forming over 50% of the pollen sum, whereas tree pollen is much better represented in the spectra from the turves. Dimbleby interprets this as evidence that the barrow was built in a treeless clearing with turves brought from open woodland some distance away.

Fundamental changes in vegetation also occurred at upland sites in the Lake District during the Bronze Age (Pennington 1970). In particular the *Quercus* woodlands of south-west Cumbria which covered the hills between 210m. and 330m. were severely reduced. The middle Bronze Age settlement of this area was extensive and cairns with urn burials and stone circles are frequent. The decline in these upland woods is recorded in pollen diagrams from Devoke Water, Burnmoor Tarn and Seathwaite Tarn. At the latter site the decrease in *Quercus* pollen, which is accompanied by increases in pollen of Gramineae and herbs, has been dated to 1,080 bc (3,030 ± 140 bp, NPL-124) and Pennington interprets this as a phase of pastoral upland use by middle Bronze Age folk. At higher altitude sites in the Lake District blanket peat began to form in Neolithic times but there seems to have been a general acceleration in peat growth in the Bronze Age (Pennington 1970); Moore (1973) reached a similar conclusion regarding the uplands of central Wales.

There is evidence from Dartmoor of pre-Neolithic clearance of upland oak forest and the consequent extension of heath and bog communities (Simmons 1969a). However, it was again during the Bronze Age that extensive areas of oak woodland were cleared from the flanks of the moors. Hut circles, burials and ritual monuments testify to widespread settlement at this period, and in pollen diagrams from Postbridge and Taw Head Simmons attributes a series of undated clearances of progressively increasing magnitude to the Bronze Age settlers. During the early part of the Bronze Age, clearances appear to have been solely in connection with pastoralism, but cereal pollen occurs in the later clearances at Postbridge. Further evidence for grain production occurs at

---

Figure 5.4. Pollen diagram from Fountains Earth, North Yorkshire (part 1). (Reproduced by permission of the Institute of British Geographers from Tinsley 1976.)

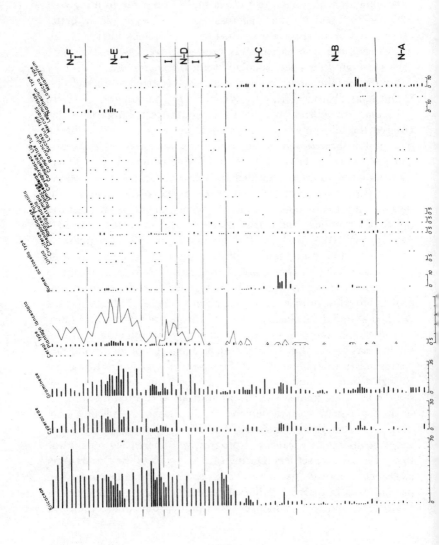

Cholwichtown on the southern edge of the moor where soil samples from beneath an early Bronze Age stone row yielded cereal pollen, and at Trowlesworthy Warren, lynchets in Bronze Age pounds also suggest that cultivation was taking place (Price and Tinsley 1976).

Environmental changes very similar to those described for Dartmoor took place on the North Yorkshire Moors during the Bronze Age, with upland oak-alder woodland being widely reduced (Simmons and Cundill 1974a). Again the clearances seem to have been largely pastoral, though cereal pollen occurs at one site, Yarsley Moss, and also in the buried soil beneath the middle Bronze Age barrow at Springwood (Dimbleby 1962). From palynological evidence Simmons (1969b) suggests that clearance activity on these moors was 'low-moderate' at the time of the Beaker and Food Vessel occupations, but more intensive later on. This is in keeping with the known distribution of early Bronze Age artifacts, which lie mainly to the south of the upland, whereas middle Bronze Age burials are widely scattered over the moors. Dimbleby's detailed palynological work on the soils associated with these burials suggests that as the forest was reduced during the Bronze Age, it was first replaced by hazel scrub and mixed grassland, and then later gave way to heathland communities. Fleming (1971) believes that prior to the extension of heath the cleared land was used for cereal cultivation, as he maintains that abundant animal forage would have been available in the lowland woods. However, Fleming's arguments are not supported by the palynological evidence and Professor Dimbleby's view is that the gradual replacement of forest by heath tallies with the influence of ranging, grazing animals on the high parts of the moor with cultivation mainly confined to lower altitudes. In this context it is interesting to note the change in emphasis in the domestic economy during the Bronze Age, from pigs to sheep and cattle, which has been described by Grigson (see above). Clearly though, there is abundant evidence for cereal cultivation in the upland zone of Britain during the Bronze Age from sites in the Pennines, the Lake District, Dartmoor and the North Yorkshire Moors.

The pattern of upland woodland clearance and extension of heath

Figure 5.5. Pollen diagram from Fountains Earth, North Yorkshire (part 2). (Reproduced by permission of the Institute of British Geographers from Tinsley 1976.)

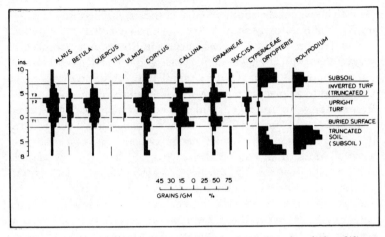

Figure 5.6. Soil pollen diagram through the buried surface below Winter Hill barrow, Lancashire. (Redrawn from Dimbleby 1962 by permission of the Oxford University Press.)

which has been described for England and Wales also occurred in Ireland where blanket peat extended during the Bronze Age. Smith (1975) has shown that Irish radiocarbon dates for the inception of blanket peat formation (i.e. basal peat samples) fall into two groups. The first comprises early Bronze Age dates around 1,700 bc which may even be referable to the Beaker period (Table 5.7). Pollen diagrams from these sites show sharp rises in heath pollen at the expense of trees at the radiocarbon-dated levels. The second group of dates are late Bronze Age and fall around 750 bc (Table 5.7). Smith has stressed the marked coincidence between the radiocarbon dates

Table 5.7. Radiocarbon dates for basal peat samples at upland sites in Northern Ireland.

|  | Years bc | Years bp | Lab. no. |
|---|---|---|---|
| *Early Bronze Age* |  |  |  |
| Ballypatrick Forest (County Antrim) | 1730 | 3684 ± 95 | UB.265 |
| Cushendall ( .. .. ) | 1755 | 3705 ± 65 | UB.346 |
| Glen's Bridge ( .. .. ) | 1660 | 3610 ± 75 | UB.376F |
| Lough Lark ( .. .. ) | 2005 | 3955 ± 75 | UB.380 |
| *Late Bronze Age* |  |  |  |
| Altnahinch ( .. .. ) | 775 | 2725 ± 85 | UB.332F |
| Beagh's Forest ( .. .. ) | 570 | 2520 ± 70 | UB.347 |
| Loughermore (County Londonderry) | 950 | 2900 ± 70 | UB.337F |

Source: A.G. Smith *et al.* 1971

for blanket peat initiation and the dates for the first metal-using culture in Ireland, but he points out that there is also a strong correlation between the lower altitudinal limit of blanket peat and the 1,250mm. isohyet, implying that Sub-Boreal climatic deterioration may also have influenced the spread of blanket peat.

This question of distinguishing between the effects of man and of climatic deterioration in pollen diagrams is important at all upland sites in the British Isles. Nevertheless, the majority of sites which have been discussed are well below the theoretical treeline and consequently man's activities seem more likely to have been the initiating factor in woodland decline. Once the protection of mature trees was removed the exposure factor would have militated against regeneration at exposed sites. A summary of information on Bronze Age clearance is contained in Table 5.8.

*Changes in soil fertility*

The question of declining soil fertility during the Bronze Age is inextricably linked with the climatic and anthropogenic factors which have already been discussed. In areas where rainfall was heavy, clearance was inevitably accompanied by soil deterioration due to the increased leaching which followed the destruction of the canopy. It is interesting to speculate on the degree to which man's activities actually created new pedological trends which would not have developed under undisturbed conditions. Ball (1975), in

**Table 5.8 Bronze Age forest clearance : a summary of available information.**

|  | *Upland sites* | *Lowland sites* |
|---|---|---|
| Clear of forest at the opening of the Bronze Age | North central Dartmoor. Summits of Welsh uplands, central Pennines, Scottish highlands. Summits of Lake District hills and fells at the head of Langdale. | Parts of the chalk downs. Parts of Breckland. Parts of the Cumbrian coastal plain. |
| Extensive clearance during the Bronze Age | East and west central Pennines. Lake District fells. North Yorks Moors. Irish and Welsh uplands. Dartmoor. | Cumbrian coastal plain. Chalk downs. Breckland. Parts of the Irish lowlands. Speyside. |
| Small temporary clearances during the Bronze Age | Southern Pennines. | Valley sites in central and south Wales, Ayrshire, Kirkcudbrightshire and the Lake District. Somerset Levels. |

discussing this problem, concludes that in the highlands processes have been moving in the direction of podsolisation, gleying and peat formation throughout postglacial time, and that man's intervention merely hastened these trends.

In the case of some of the British heathlands, Dimbleby (1962) has established that quite spectacular soil deterioration occurred during the Bronze Age. On the eastern edge of the North Yorkshire Moors, soils beneath Bronze Age barrows show some remarkable contrasts. There is a continuum from an unleached soil with only slight iron removal in the eluvial horizon beneath the Bickley Moor barrow, to a soil with fairly intensive leaching and traces of a thin iron pan beneath Reasty Top barrow. The soils outside the barrows, which are beneath heath vegetation, have strongly indurated iron pans. From this continuum Dimbleby infers that rapid soil development took place in this area during the Bronze Age, producing a thin iron pan podsol from what was originally an unbleached soil. Since the Bronze Age, the differentiation of horizons has been greatly intensified, producing the well developed modern podsols. Excavations of barrows of varying ages in the lowland heaths of the south and east did not, however, produce any conclusive evidence of a similar continuum; indeed one barrow at Portesham on Black Down covered a well developed podsol, although the palynological evidence suggested that the contemporary vegetation was deciduous forest. Dimbleby concludes that at certain sites the activities of man have greatly accelerated the natural climatic trends towards podsolisation, and that for the British heathlands the Bronze Age was particularly important in this respect.

In addition to this evidence for deterioration in the base-status of soils during the Bronze Age it is also clear that soil erosion was initiated at some sites. At Devoke Water in the Lake District there is a significant fall in the organic content of the sediments at the level of the middle Bronze Age clearances, indicating the inwashing of mineral material from the catchment (Pennington 1970). Stripes of inorganic material occurring in some of the bogs of the North Yorkshire Moors are also thought to be a result of soil erosion consequent upon man's activities (Simmons *et al*. 1975). The earliest of these stripes predates the *Ulmus* decline, but at two sites, St Helena 'A' and Ewe Crag Slack 'B', features of this type are attributed to the Bronze Age.

The decline in soil fertility and the accompanying erosion which took place during the Bronze Age was a direct consequence of the introduction of metal technology to the British Isles, since the bronze axe was a far more potent instrument of woodland destruction than its polished stone predecessor. Environmental deterioration was particularly marked in the marginal upland woodlands. Here exploitation by man probably reached a peak during the Bronze Age, owing to the favourable climate. As climate worsened towards the end of the Sub-Boreal, and upland settlement retreated, woodland failed to regenerate, and heath and bog communities spread over the former grazing lands. In contrast, much of the lowlands of Britain, apart from the chalklands of the south and east, were subject only to temporary clearance during the Bronze Age. The exploitation of the large areas of dense forest which covered the Midland plain, and the lowlands of Yorkshire and Lancashire was not accomplished until the development of more sophisticated iron tools.

H.M. Tinsley is grateful to Professor G.W. Dimbleby, Dr M.P. Kerney, Professor I.G. Simmons and Dr Judith Turner for permission to reproduce figures from their work.

Caroline Grigson is grateful to those who have allowed her to quote from unpublished work or who have answered tedious questions on dating, particularly Dr Isobel Smith, Dr Juliet Clutton-Brock (British Museum, Natural History), Dr D.D.A. Simpson (Leicester University); Nicholas Thomas (Bristol); Richard Burleigh (British Museum), G.J. Wainwright (Department of the Environment) and Dr Paul Ashbee of Norwich.

For permission to use unpublished work on Mount Pleasant, Dorset, carried out for the Ancient Monuments Laboratory, Caroline Grigson is grateful to the Chief Laboratory Officer, Ralph Harcourt, and Dr G.J. Wainwright.

# 6. *The Iron Age*

## JUDITH TURNER

### Introduction

The environment of Iron Age Britain differed from that of earlier periods in two important respects, in its climate and in its vegetation. The climate appears to have been much wetter, having deteriorated quite significantly since the middle of the Bronze Age, and the vegetation differed in that there was considerably less forest in many parts of the country.

There were of course other changes, minor ones in the sea-level, further soil deterioration, the introduction of new plant and animal species, changes in the relative importance of those already here and possibly some extinctions. But these changes were not of such magnitude, nor so far-reaching in their effects, as those in the climate and vegetation.

The evidence for climatic deterioration is complicated and difficult to interpret, but because the climate has such an important affect on subsistence, and through this on settlement patterns, the evidence is presented and discussed in detail. As far as the vegetation is concerned, much material has accumulated during the last two decades, and so it too is reviewed at greater length than the other aspects of the environment.

Traditionally the Iron Age is thought to begin in the sixth century before Christ with the coming of the Halstatt culture, although recently in outlining the nature of the period Cunliffe (1974b) traces its origin back into the Bronze Age, beginning his summary of it with a phase of conservatism which lasted from about 1,000-750 bc. In discussing the environment of the Iron Age I find myself in a similar position for some of the factors affecting it were operating in the Bronze Age. Just as today's environment is the result of at least ten thousand years of development under the influence of autogenic and varying climatic factors as well as the activities of successive prehistoric cultures, so too was the environment of the Iron Age. For this reason the treatment of certain topics has meant looking briefly at earlier periods too, and in the case of climate, considering the whole of the first millenium bc and not just the last six centuries of it.

Similar considerations apply to the end of the Iron Age. Many of the environmental changes that were occurring within the period continued after the Roman invasion and as it would make little sense to stop somewhat arbitarily at that point, the environmental changes in their entirety have been considered, even though this has occasionally meant discussing events that happened in the first few centuries ad.

## Climate

The most impressive evidence for climatic change between the Bronze and Iron Ages in Britain comes from the stratigraphy of peat bogs, the nature of which reflects past climates. The use of climatic indicator plants such as ivy (*Hedera helix*), holly (*Ilex aquifolium*) and mistletoe (*Viscum album*) as proposed by Iversen (1944), is unreliable for the Iron Age because of the difficulty of disentangling the climatic from the anthropogenic factors which have influenced them (Troels-Smith 1960a). Similarly data from oxygen isotope measurements of deep sea and continental ice cores are not necessarily directly relevant to Britain.

### Peat stratigraphy

The study of peat stratigraphy has a long history and it is necessary to consider it before looking at the British evidence. The work of Blytt and Sernander, which led to a division of the postglacial into the following five climatic periods is familiar to many:

| | | |
|---|---|---|
| Sub-Atlantic | cold and wet | – oceanic |
| Sub-Boreal | warm and dry | – continental |
| Atlantic | warm and wet | – oceanic |
| Boreal | warm and dry | – continental |
| Pre-Boreal | sub-arctic | |

They described the stratigraphy of Scandanavian peat deposits and recognised a succession of peat types each of which they suggested had formed under a different climate. A fen peat with remains of trees in it is overlain by a fen peat without wood, which in turn is overlain by an ombrogenous peat with wood in it and finally by ombrogenous peat without wood. The trees were thought to have grown on the peat when the climate was dry, during the periods they called Boreal and Sub-Boreal.

Very few British peat deposits show such stratigraphy, although the early work of Lewis on the wood layers in Scottish bogs has often been quoted as evidence that there have been two warm dry periods in Scotland too, Britain's equivalent of the Boreal and Sub-Boreal. Lewis (1905, 1906, 1907, 1911) showed that in the Scottish bogs there were sometimes one, sometimes two wood layers, the latter being referred to as the Upper and Lower Forest Beds. Recently, however, Hilary Birks (1975) has critically re-examined these wood layers with the aid of radiocarbon dating and shown that they are not synchronous. Those that occur in the north-west Highlands have been dated in a number of places to the time between 2,550 and 2,050 bc, whereas those occurring in the eastern Highlands and also those in Galloway in south-west Scotland are more heterogeneous in age, most of them being some 2,000 years older. Whilst the former, admittedly, are mid-Sub-Boreal in age, the latter are Atlantic and so, as she points out, the occurrence of the pine stumps in Scottish peat bogs cannot be taken as evidence that the Blytt and Sernander climatic periods apply to Scotland as well as to Sweden.

Despite this, the terms are widely used and whilst they have a useful chronological function, independent evidence is required for establishing the nature of their climates in Britain. Fortunately, for the two most recent periods, the Sub-Boreal and Sub-Atlantic, there is such evidence from studies on recurrence surfaces, work which was also pioneered in Scandanavia and in Germany.

Attention was first drawn to recurrence surfaces by Weber (1900) who described a two-fold division of raised bogs into a lower highly-humified, dark-coloured peat, which he called *Schwarztorf*, and an upper fresh-looking, weakly-humified, light-coloured peat, the *Weisstorf*. They were sometimes separated by a few centimetres of *Vorlaufstorf*, or precursor peat, a fresh peat which had formed on an extremely wet bog surface. The junction between the two peats is the recurrence surface and Weber called it the *Grenzhorizont* and dated it by association with archaeological artifacts to the period between 1,000 and 750 bc. This horizon is familiar to British peat stratigraphers, as it occurs in very many of our raised bogs, both large and small, and also in many of our upland blanket peats. It is, for example, well developed in the Pennines. As dark well-humified peat forms when bog surfaces are relatively dry and covered with tussocks of cotton grass (*Eriophorum vaginatum*) and heather (*Calluna vulgaris*) and fresh-looking, weakly-humified peat forms when bog surfaces are wet for extended periods and dominated by bog moss (*Sphagnum* spp., especially *S. imbricatum*), the *Grenzhorizont* was interpreted as representing a change from a relatively warm and dry climate to a cooler and wetter one.

Since Weber described the *Grenzhorizont* many other people have looked at the stratigraphy of raised bogs and shown that it is a good deal more complicated than was at first supposed. Granlund (1932) recognised five recurrence surfaces (Swedish *rekurrensytor*), the most pronounced of which is usually called the *Grenzhorizont* or S.W.K. (*Schwarz-Weisstorf Kontakt*). He dated them, again by reference to artifacts, to 2,300 bc (the lowest in the series, called RY V), 1,200 bc (RY IV), 500 bc (RY III), which falls within the Iron Age, ad 400 (RY II) and ad 1,200 (RY I). The situation became even more complicated when Nilsson (1935) described nine such horizons. These series of recurrence surfaces were interpreted either as meaning there had been a step-like deterioration of climate (Granlund 1932) or that there had been an oscillating climate (Godwin 1954).

*Recent work on recurrence surfaces*

With the development of radiocarbon dating in the 1950s came the possibility of testing one of the assumptions crucial to a climatic interpretation, namely that a particular recurrence surface is synchronous throughout a bog, and also of seeing whether or not recurrence surfaces in different bogs really formed at the same time, as Granlund and others had suggested. The evidence now available from the dates confirms the importance of climate but also indicates that local factors affect the formation of a recurrence surface as well. There is, however, a considerable measure of disagreement as to the importance of local factors.

Van Zeist (1954) suggested that local factors may have been more important than the early stratigraphers realised, when he found that a major recurrence surface was of several different ages in seven profiles of one bog. He dated the surface pollen-analytically by reference to the rise in *Fagus* pollen on the diagram and concluded that 'It is certain that besides climatological factors the local conditions had great influence on the transition from older to younger *Sphagnum* peat'.

A similar investigation was carried out by Lundqvist (1962) on the main recurrence surface of two Swedish bogs, Lidamossen near Eskilstuna and Högmossen, Gastrikland, and he obtained radiocarbon dates for the peat above and the peat just below the recurrence surface in a number of places on each bog (see Table 6.1). All pairs of dates showed a difference of a few hundred years,

**Table 6.1. Radiocarbon dates of the main recurrence surfaces on Lidamossen and Högmossen, Sweden.**

LIDAMOSSEN

| Sample site number | Sample depth in cm. | Laboratory code | Date | | |
|---|---|---|---|---|---|
| 4 | 120 | St.463 | 700 ± 85 | ad | 1260 |
| 4 | 130−135 | St.464 | 1020 ± 90 | ad | 940 |
| 7 | 70−80 | St.467 | 540 ± 85 | ad | 1420 |
| 7 | 80−85 | St.469 | 850 ± 85 | ad | 1110 |
| 2 | 40−50 | St.470 | 245 ± 80 | ad | 1715 |
| 2 | 60−70 | St.471 | 670 ± 105 | ad | 1290 |

HÖGMOSSEN

| Sample site number | Sample depth in cm. | Laboratory code | Date | | |
|---|---|---|---|---|---|
| 22 | 150 | St.655 | 1145 ± 60 | ad | 815 |
| 22 | 160 | St.656 | 1280 ± 90 | ad | 680 |
| 14 | 125 | .St.673 | 1135 ± 80 | ad | 805 |
| 14 | 160 | St.674 | 1485 ± 75 | ad | 475 |
| 26 | 110 | St.679 | 810 ± 90 | ad | 1150 |
| 26 | 130 | St.680 | 1090 ± 70 | ad | 870 |

425, 320 and 310 radiocarbon years in cores 2, 4 and 7 at Lidamossen, and 280, 135 and 350 at sites 26, 22, and 14 at Högmossen. Although this can be accounted for partly by the fact that, with the one exception of Lidamossen 7, the samples dated were not contiguous vertically, there being 10cm. and in one case as much as 35cm. of peat between them, it is nevertheless clear that on each bog the peat stopped forming at different times in different places. However it is also apparent that there was only one episode of drying out followed by one episode of regeneration in each case. For example at Lidamossen before the late thirteenth century, peat was either growing very slowly indeed or not at all and at various times after that, i.e. after ad 1260 peat growth was renewed, first in one part of the bog, then later in another. Similarly at Högmossen the peat either stopped accumulating or formed very slowly up until the middle of the ninth century ad and from then on grew more rapidly, again starting earlier in some parts of the bog than others. In assessing the significance of these dates Lundqvist concluded: 'Thus it is the local conditions which are most significant. Earlier particular emphasis was laid on the climate, but this is certainly only of secondary importance.'

The only British recurrence surface which has been studied in detail from this point of view is in Rusland bog in the southern part of the Lake District (National Grid Reference SD 334887) and Dickinson (1975) came to just the opposite conclusion, showing by pollen analysis and radiocarbon dating that it is synchronous across the entire bog. Pollen diagrams from four places on the bog indicate that the recurrence surface formed just above the end of a clearance phase (clearance phase B). The first few centimetres of peat above the surface have been dated at each place with the following results:

Radiocarbon years

| | | |
|---|---|---|
| Site E | SRR-120 | ad 439 ± 50 |
| Site F | SRR-121 | ad 415 ± 50 |
| Site G | SRR-123 | ad 398 ± 55 |
| Site H | SRR-125 | ad 589 ± 55 |

The surface is clearly synchronous at Sites E, F and G and Dickinson attributes the slightly anomalous result at H to the fact that the recurrence surface there was not as well defined as at the other three sites, because the upper peat was a pool and hummock complex peat which does not form such a sharp junction with the lower peat as the weakly humified *Sphagnum imbricatum* peat, which occurs elsewhere in the bog.

It is not easy to recognise the exact position of a recurrence surface at any given point, if by exact position one means the moment at which the inferred deterioration in climate caused renewed or more vigorous peat growth, and it is doubtful whether many of the peat samples actually dated in the earlier investigations were collected with such precision as those at Rusland. Instead of relying just on field characters Dickinson measured the rate of peat growth throughout the section at each site. This can be done by measuring the pollen concentration in successive samples of equal volume and assuming that it is low in peat which has formed rapidly and high in peat which has accumulated slowly. In this way it is possible to detect the beginning of rapid peat growth more accurately.

Synchroneity of recurrence surfaces between five different Danish bogs has been demonstrated recently by Aaby (1976). He has not only shown a large measure of synchroneity between the five sites but also that there appears to be a 260-year cycle in the climatic shifts. Although periodicity of climate is outside the scope of this chapter, Aaby's fine piece of work goes a long way towards validating the use of recurrence surfaces as climatic indicators. Whilst considerable caution is still required in interpreting the data, there is no doubt in my mind that the evidence for climatic change in the first millenium bc from this source is very strong indeed and cannot be explained simply in terms of local factors.

*The evidence for climatic deterioration from 1,200 to 600 bc*

First there is the well-substantiated evidence from the Somerset Levels, where, between the Polden and the Mendip Hills peat was forming from about 1,550 bc onwards (Godwin and Willis 1959) on the almost flat surface of the brackish water blue-grey clays which had been deposited in the valleys as a result of a marine transgression earlier in the postglacial. At first plants such as *Phragmites communis* and *Cladium mariscus* formed large areas of reed swamp and built up to two metres of coarse-textured peat. Hydroseral succession took place and fen woods replaced these swamps and eventually, as the peat surface was raised above the influence of the calcareous ground water draining off the surrounding limestone hills, large raised bogs began to form. This was happening by about 2,000 bc. The bog surfaces at that time were relatively dry and easily walked upon, and one would have expected them to have remained so under a stable climate. But at a number of sites the raised bog peat is interrupted by a layer of *Cladium* peat which represents flooding of the old bog surfaces with calcareous water from the hills. Moreover, at the junction of the raised bog peat and the *Cladium* peat a number of prehistoric wooden trackways has been found, trackways which had been laid across areas that were becoming increasingly wet so that the local inhabitants could continue to use their customary direct routes from one area of high ground to another. The tracks have been described and many have now been radiocarbon dated (Godwin 1960a; Coles *et al.* 1970, 1973, 1975, 1977). The dates given in Table 6.2 cover the period from 890 to

Table 6.2. Radiocarbon dates of the trackways which have been found below the major flooding horizon in the Somerset Levels.

|  | Laboratory code | Date in radiocarbon years |  |
|---|---|---|---|
| Meare Heath Track | Q.52 | 2840 ± 110 | 890 bc. |
|  |  | 2850 ± 110 | 900 bc. |
| Shapwick Heath Track | Q.39 | 2470 ± 110 | 520 bc. |
| Westhay Track | Q.308 | 2800 ± 110 | 850 bc. |
| Toll Gate House Track | Q.306 | 2600 ± 110 | 650 bc. |
| Viper's (Dewar's A) Track | Q.7 | 2520 ± 110 | 570 bc. |
|  | Q.312 | 2630 ± 110 | 680 bc. |
| Nidon's (Dewar's B) Track | Q.313 | 2585 ± 120 | 635 bc. |
| Viper's Platforms | Q.311 | 2410 ± 110 | 460 bc. |
|  |  | 2460 ± 110 | 510 bc. |

460 bc with a mean of 676 bc. The raised bog peat underlying the tracks has also been dated in several places and the peat from above them in three places. The former range from 1,360 to 532 bc and the latter from 678 to 247 bc. The surface of these bogs must have been dry before 850 bc and must have been getting wetter from about that time up to at least 450 bc and possibly even 250 bc.

In South Wales at Llanllwch bog, near Carmarthen, there is a clear recurrence surface about 120cm. from the surface of the deposit. A laminated pool peat overlies a highly humified *Sphagnum-Calluna-Eriophorium* peat (Thomas 1965). The top of the highly humified peat has been dated to 1,228 bc (Q-459)* and the pool peat above to 1,280 bc (Q-458). There is therefore no evidence that the bog actually stopped growing at any time and the pool peat appears to have been forming a little earlier than when the trackways were being built in Somerset.

There is a similar recurrence surface in each of three raised bogs in the Teifi valley, near Tregaron, Dyfed, in mid-Wales. Continuous 2cm. thick samples of peat from above and below this surface on the South-east Bog have been dated (Godwin and Willis 1960). The well humified *Sphagnum-Calluna* peat below gave a date of 1,004 bc (Q-389), the mean of two determinations, and the weakly humified peat just above, also the mean of two determinations, was 696 bc (Q-388). This means that the bog stopped growing for about 300 years from 1,000 bc onwards and only began again around 700 bc. This

---

* Radiocarbon dates mentioned in the text are listed in years bp with their standard errors in Table 6.3 on pp. 258-9.

**Table 6.3.** Radiocarbon dates of Iron Age trackways and recurrence surfaces in Britain mentioned in the text.

| Laboratory code | Date in radiocarbon years |
|---|---|
| D.   29 | $1620 \pm 130$ |
| GaK.2027 | $2570 \pm 80$ |
| 2028 | $3390 \pm 90$ |
| 2072 | $3660 \pm 80$ |
| 2288 | $2290 \pm 100$ |
| 2289 | $2090 \pm 100$ |
| 2291 | $1910 \pm 100$ |
| 2292 | $1530 \pm 90$ |
| 2913 | $3150 \pm 100$ |
| 3031 | $1730 \pm 100$ |
| 3033 | $2060 \pm 120$ |
| 3670 | $2200 \pm 80$ |
| 3713 | $1730 \pm 120$ |
| 3879 | $1570 \pm 90$ |
| LJ.  908 | $3380 \pm 150$ |
| NPL. 116 | $1560 \pm 130$ |
| 117 | $1750 \pm 130$ |
| 118 | $1370 \pm 190$ |
| Q.   68 | $2760 \pm 120$ |
| 83 | $1514 \pm 100$ |
| 106 | $2340 \pm 130$ |
| 110 | $3105 \pm 110$ |
| 348 | $2490 \pm 130$ |
| 349 | $2640 \pm 110$ |
| 354 | $2980 \pm 130$ |
| 383 | $2307 \pm 110$ |
| 388 | $2669 \pm 110$ and $2624 \pm 110$ |
| 389 | $3029 \pm 110$ and $2879 \pm 110$ |
| 458 | $3230 \pm 110$ |
| 459 | $3178 \pm 100$ |
| 479 | $2329 \pm 110$ |
| 541–3 | $2712 \pm 120$ |
| 570 | $1858 \pm 110$ |
| 575 | $1731 \pm 120$ |
| 596 | $2354 \pm 110$ |
| 682 | $3070 \pm 150$ |
| 683 | $2645 \pm 100$ |
| 721 | $1370 \pm 90$ |
| 722 | $1535 \pm 90$ |
| 723 | $2375 \pm 90$ |
| 724 | $3170 \pm 105$ |
| 726 | $3320 \pm 105$ |
| 852 | $1400 \pm 50$ |
| 854 | $2251 \pm 50$ |
| 855 | $2685 \pm 50$ |

**Table 6.3. (continued)**

| Laboratory code | Date in radiocarbon years |
|---|---|
| SRR.  88 | 2212 ± 55 |
| 89 | 2205 ± 45 |
| 100 | 2488 ± 75 |
| 404 | 2064 ± 60 |
| 405 | 852 ± 60 |
| 413 | 1355 ± 50 |
| 415 | 1954 ± 70 |
| 600 | 1842 ± 70 |
| T.1085 | 2280 ± 120 |
| 1086 | 2370 ± 130 |
| UB.  87 | 2090 ± 70 |
| 163 | 2725 ± 55 |
| 261D | 2275 ± 65 |
| 387 | 2055 ± 65 |
| 388 | 1385 ± 65 |

has very similar implications with regard to the prevailing climate as the evidence from the Somerset Levels.

Another bog with a comparable history is Chat Moss, on the Cheshire-Greater Manchester border, where Birks (1963-4) has described the recurrence surface. The top of the moderately humified *Sphagnum* peat has been dated to 1,120 bc (Q-682) (Godwin and Switsur 1966), a date similar to that from Tregaron, and the unhumified *Sphagnum cuspidatum* pool peat above to 695 bc (Q-683), a date inseparable from the one for renewed peat growth at Tregaron. From Pilling Moss, further north, there is the date for Kate's Pad, thought to be a trackway, of 810 bc (Q-68) (Godwin and Willis 1960) and Flander's Moss, in the Forth valley in Scotland, has a recurrence surface which can be traced across the whole of the extensive deposit. Only the peat 0-6cm. below the surface has been dated with a result, 762 bc (Q-541-3), which fits well with those from the sites already mentioned.

In addition to this evidence from raised bogs there is also evidence from upland peats. Like raised bogs, these so-called blanket peats are dependent for their water supply on precipitation and some of them also develop recurrence surfaces. There is a well-developed one in the Pennines, which has been described by a number of authors; Tallis (1964a) found it at five different sites in the southern Pennines and equated it with Weber's *Grenzhorizont*. This was later confirmed when it was dated at Featherbed Moss in Derbyshire (Tallis and

Switsur 1973) to 735 bc (Q-855), the very time when fresh peat was beginning to form on so many of the lowland raised bogs.

In the northern Pennines there is evidence from a few sites of renewed growth after an interval of well over a thousand years. This renewed growth has been dated at Red Sike Moss on Widdybank Fell in Upper Teesdale to 1,440 bc (GaK-2028), only marginally before the recurrence surface at Llanllwch, and on a neighbouring bog, Weelhead Moss, the peat just below the major recurrence surface has been dated to 1,200 bc (GaK-2913) (Turner *et al.* 1973).

To this evidence from recurrence surfaces may be added that from studies on the growth rates of some of the Pennine peats. At East Moor, Derbyshire, Hicks (1971) has obtained a series of radio-carbon dates in association with a pollen diagram and these can be used for calculating the rate of peat accumulation. The peat which had formed during the 1,000 years below the level dated to 340 bc (GaK-2288), had formed slowly at an average rate of 1cm. in 17 (22)* years, whilst that which had formed between 340 bc and ad 40 (GaK-2292) had done so much more quickly, at about 1cm. in 1.8 (2.3)* years.

Growth rates at lowland sites can also be cited. At Bloak Moss in Ayrshire, southern Scotland, the peat was growing rapidly between 1,370 bc and 1,220 bc (Q-726 and 724), 1cm. taking 3 (4.5)* years to form. This contrasts with earlier and later rates in the same bog of 1cm. in 28 (40)* and 1cm. in 40 (45)* years respectively, further evidence for climatic deterioration at a time only marginally earlier. than the recurrence surface at Llanllwch.

Allowing for the fact that as well as climatic change, local factors may have affected the water tables of the bogs discussed, it seems reasonable to conclude that the climate may have begun to deteriorate, if only slightly, as early as about 1,250 bc, causing recurrence surfaces to form, as at Llanllwch, and peat to grow faster, as at Bloak Moss, and then deteriorated more rapidly after about 850 bc, when people started building the trackways in Somerset, reaching its wettest by about 650 bc, by which time it had caused renewed peat growth on most of the dried out bog surfaces.

If one accepts this evidence for climatic deterioration it means that the Iron Age cultures in Britain developed in a climate less warm and dry than that of the Bronze Age and that in the early Iron

---

* Figures in brackets with asterices are based upon growth rates calculated from corrected dates (after McKerrell 1975).

Age people were living in a cooler and wetter Britain than that of their predecessors. This poses an interesting question for the archaeologist. Is there a causal link between the deteriorating climate of the first half of the first millenium before Christ and the development of the Iron Age culture in Britain?

*Evidence for a warm climate from 400 bc to ad 450*

All the evidence so far discussed is relevant to a climate change which culminated in the early Iron Age. But one also wishes to know about the later stages of the Iron Age and Roman times. The fact that vines were grown in Britain at that time has led to the suggestion that it was warmer then than now. There is some evidence from bog stratigraphy to support this view.

Very few recurrence surfaces have been dated to this period and most of those that have lie in bogs very close to the sea or large estuaries and for reasons which will be discussed later need not necessarily indicate climatic change. But there is a pine stump layer in Whixall Moss, Shropshire, which is thought to have formed when the bog surface was dry, and has been radiocarbon dated by Godwin and Willis (1960) to 357 bc (Q-383).

Further evidence that the climate was drier and warmer comes from the rates of peat growth on raised bogs which have been closely radiocarbon dated over this period. For example at Tregaron bog, the rate before 404 bc (Q-596) was 1cm. in 3 (4)* years and thereafter only 1cm. in 46 (52)* years. Similarly at Bloak Moss in Ayrshire there is a change in rate at 425 bc (Q-723) from 1cm. in 40 (45)* years to 1cm. in 84 (94)* years. In both cases the slower growth rate continued until at least ad 450.

The evidence to date indicates a deteriorating climate leading up to and during the first part of the Iron Age and a warmer drier climate after about 400 bc for the rest of the period.

## Sea-levels

There appears to have been comparatively little change in relative sea-level around the coast of Britain during the Iron Age, that is compared with the changes of earlier periods like the Mesolithic. The main eustatic rise following the last ice age had finished some few thousand years earlier and the main isostatic recovery of northern Britain had already taken place. Nevertheless there is evidence for slight relative movements, of the order of a couple of metres, in certain coastal areas and although these were slight compared with the main eustatic rise, they would certainly have affected the lives of the people living there.

In the Fenland of East Anglia there is evidence for a rise in sea-level which deposited silt over an extensive area around the Wash and also further inland along the main rivers. This silt was colonised in Roman times *c.* ad 80-90 (Salway 1970) and, with a break in the third century, remained so until the early fifth. The region does not appear to have been settled either earlier or later, and it is difficult to avoid the conclusion that the Roman occupation of the region was a direct consequence of the rise in sea-level which deposited the silt.

In Somerset too, marine clay containing artifacts of Romano-British age has been deposited along the coastal strip and in the estuaries of the Parrett and Axe, where it covered the pre-existing peat almost entirely (Willis 1961). There too, it made settlement and agriculture possible where previously there had been less productive peat land.

In northern England, in both the north-west and the north-east, there is evidence from radiocarbon-dated contacts between marine and freshwater deposits for two marine transgressions during the period with which we are concerned. For the north-west, in the area between the Solway and the Mersey, Tooley (1974) has demonstrated a transgression, called Lytham VIII, between about 1,000 and 500 bc. There is evidence for a slight regression shortly before 320 bc and a further transgression, Lytham IX, which reached its maximum just before ad 350. For the north-east coast Gaunt and Tooley (1974) have shown a rise at the same time as Lytham VIII, throughout the Humber lowlands and Lincolnshire, and Smith (1958c) has recorded a later one, which probably corresponds with Lytham IX, on the south side of the Humber estuary.

Wherever such changes in sea-level created new estuarine mud flats, there would have been additional habitats for a limited number of plants and animals and hence fresh opportunities for gathering shrimps and mussels and for catching fish and snaring wild fowl, and also for obtaining salt. Although Iron Age people would probably not have lived entirely off such resources, they would certainly have made good use of the new land which became available after periods of marine transgression.

Evans (1969) has demonstrated this rather nicely at Northton on the Isle of Harris where he has studied the changing molluscan fauna in a midden which was being used through Neolithic, Bronze and Iron Age times. In the Bronze Age levels of this midden, shells of the limpet (*Patella vulgaris*), which is common on rocky shores, were most abundant, whereas in successive Iron Age levels these shells decrease in quantity and shells of the common cockle (*Cardium edule*), an inhabitant of muddy estuarine flats, become more abundant. There can be little doubt that the diet of the local inhabitants was reflecting the availability of the molluscs and also of the types of habitat in the area.

The effect of marine transgressions would undoubtedly have been felt well inland too, in the perimarine zone. Higher sea-levels and the deposition of silt would have slowed down drainage in flat areas like the Humber estuary and the Somerset levels, and the bogs that previously had been dry would have become much wetter. This would affect lake villages such as those at Glastonbury and Meare and necessitated the building of trackways to keep the old routes across the bogs open.

The possibility that coastal bogs may become wetter with a rise in sea-level must be borne in mind when using the recurrence surfaces within them as indicators of climatic change. Some of the recurrence surfaces already discussed lie within the influence of changing sea-level, and it is possible that in addition to the climatic deterioration, rising sea-level was a factor in their formation. This by no means invalidates the evidence for climatic deterioration in the first millenium BC, which is well founded on recurrence surfaces in bogs hundreds of metres above sea-level, such as those at Tregaron and in the Pennines. But it does draw attention to the complex relationship between climate, sea-level and bog stratigraphy. If the rising sea-level between 1,000 and 500 bc, which has been demonstrated for the north-west and north-east of England, was widespread and eustatic in nature, it would pose a problem, for one expects a eustatic rise to occur when the climate is globally warmer and the ice in high latitudes melting faster than usual. And yet this is the very time that the climate was deteriorating. The later transgression, which deposited the silts that were occupied in the Roman period occurred at a time when there is evidence for a warmer climate and is therefore less problematic. It may be that some of the transgressions that have been demonstrated were not due to the eustatic rises in sea-level at all but to some local factor. A great deal more work will need to be done before these complex relationships between climate and sea-level can be understood.

## Vegetation

*Introduction*

Biological remains such as grain and bones, which are found on archaeological sites, are used by archaeologists, together with such artifacts as querns and spindle whorls, for reconstructing the economy of the culture they are studying. For the Iron Age a good account of the mixed farming that was practised in the south-east and the mixed or mainly pastoral economy of the north and west already exists (see Cunliffe 1974a). In this section palaeobiological data, mainly from non-archaeological sites, are presented with a view to reconstructing the nature of the environment (rather than the economy) in which man lived; an approach I hope will prove complementary to that of the archaeologist. The independent palaeobiological evidence is either from peat and lake-mud deposits with radiocarbon-dated sequences of sub-fossil pollen assemblages, which indicate the nature of the vegetation that produced the pollen, or from the sub-fossil mollusc assemblages which are formed in calcareous environments.

It is only since the development of radiocarbon dating in the 1950s and its wider use in the 1960s that such data have accumulated, and it is now possible to recognise regional contrasts within Britain both at the beginning and during the Iron Age. I should like to stress, however, that in drawing attention to the contrasts that appear to exist, I am using the data available today and that further research will undoubtedly modify the picture as new sites are studied.

The pattern that emerges is as follows. At the beginning of the Iron Age there was a marked contrast between areas in the south-east of England with light calcareous soils, which were already settled and being farmed and which retained only a fraction of their original forest cover, and most of the rest of Britain, where the forest was more or less intact, except where open moorland already existed in the uplands.

During the Iron Age the forests were cleared nearly everywhere in Britain and the land was farmed, often for long periods. The time at which they were cleared, however, varies from one region to another and covers the period from about 400 bc to ad 400.

*The chalklands of the south-east and associated areas*

Evidence for the extensively cleared nature of the chalkland at the beginning of the Iron Age comes partly from a small number of radiocarbon-dated pollen diagrams and partly from series of fossil molluscan assemblages. In the drier calcareous regions of Britain, which were not glaciated during the last glaciation, there are fewer places with deposits suitable for pollen analysis than in other parts of the country and consequently there is not an over-abundance of such evidence. Godwin (1962a) took advantage of the chance discovery of two reasonably thick organic beds, one at Frogholt near Folkestone and one at Wingham in Kent, to study the vegetational history of the region. The deposit at Frogholt consisted of a fluviatile organic mud which was forming between 1,030 (Q-354) and 540 bc (Q-348), a period of some five hundred years spanning the Late Bronze Age and Early Iron Age. He showed that a considerable amount of disforestation had already taken place by the beginning of the period, the pollen of weed species being a mixture of arable and pastoral types, and also that at 690 bc (Q-349) there was a 'late phase of greatly accelerated disforestation' which he suggested might indicate 'the influence of a powerful new culture entering the region ... the first Iron Age settlement'.

The peaty organic muds at Wingham had formed during an extended period embracing most of the Bronze Age, the pre-Roman Iron Age, and part at least of the Roman occupation. The 248cm. of deposit includes within it organic material from 90-100cm. which has been dated to 390 bc (Q-106) and some from 175-185cm. dated to 1,155 bc (Q-110). At this site, too, Godwin found evidence for early disforestation, as early as 1,600 bc, and again also for a phase of increased disforestation, between the two radiocarbon-dated levels, which he correlated with that of the Iron Age at Frogholt.

These diagrams from Frogholt and Wingham indicate what was happening on the chalk soils of the South Downs. Godwin (1968) has also published a diagram from a site in a region of glacial drift in East Anglia, Old Buckenham Mere. This mere contains a long sequence of uniform organic muds and the pollen diagram from it covers the whole of the postglacial as well as part of the late-glacial period. Although it was not possible to provide an absolute chronology by radiocarbon dating because of the calcareous nature of the sediments, Godwin suggested a time scale for the 950cm. of deposit by assuming a uniform rate of sedimentation and by accepting 3000 bc for the elm decline at the beginning of the Neolithic. Dated in this way the diagram indicates quite clearly the progressive disforestation of the region from the late Bronze Age onwards, with a rapid extension of open land in the pre-Roman and Roman Iron Age. The ratio of pasture and arable weeds changes during the later part of the Iron Age, there being more weeds of pasture in the early stages, more weeds of arable land in the later. The only crop pollen that has been found for the period is that of wheat (*Triticum*). Crops such as rye (*Secale*), flax (*Linum*) and hemp (*Cannabis*) do not appear to have been grown there in quantity until the Anglo-Saxon period.

The evidence from sub-fossil molluscs differs from that from pollen in that the assemblages are not usually preserved in such uniformly deposited media. Series of mollusc assemblages have been found in buried soils in both the dry valleys of the chalk where they are sealed in by ploughwash and in soils beneath prehistoric mounds. Like pollen, these assemblages indicate the nature of the environment, woodland, open grassland etc., but their dating is often not so straightforward. Even so in many cases considerable precision has proved possible, either because artifacts have been found within the buried soil or overlying ploughwash, or because charcoal, which can be radiocarbon dated, is associated with the buried turf lines. An excellent account of the information that can be obtained by these methods is given by Evans (1972). In discussing the habitat changes that have taken place in calcareous regions in Britain, he demonstrates the development of a woodland fauna in the postglacial which gives way, mainly in the third millenium bc, to one of scrubland and eventually to one of open country. Many of the sites from which the data have been obtained are dated to the Neolithic and it is clear that just before the soil was buried there was open grassland in the region with no sign of ploughing. Similarly for the Bronze Age sites. (See Chapters 4 and 5 for further details concerning these two periods.) Evidence for widespread ploughing does not occur until the Iron Age at the majority of sites.

Evans describes a number of soils which were buried during the Iron Age and which contain molluscs of the period. The one at Pink Hill (Evans 1972) 2km. south east of Princes Risborough in Buckingham, is a good example. The buried soil, which is 20cm. thick, overlies a compact chalky loam and is itself overlain by 80cm. of ploughwash. It contains a mixture of shade-loving and open-country molluscs indicating a partially cleared landscape whereas the overlying ploughwash has an increasing number of open-country types. The ploughwash is thought to be Iron-Age because it contains pottery and flakes referable to the Iron Age and higher up two Romano-British sherds. The evidence from this site therefore, like that from the pollen sites, is that there was a great increase in the amount of open country in the area during the Iron Age. Evans (1966) has found evidence of a similar sequence at Pitstone in Buckinghamshire on the Icknield Way where a late Bronze Age soil containing a scrub and grassland fauna is overlain by Iron Age ploughwash.

So the biological evidence both mollusc and pollen from sites studied in south-eastern England all points to the fairly open landscape of the Bronze Age becoming even more open during the Iron Age and, associated with this decrease of woodland, a change in emphasis from pastures to cultivated fields. As many authors have pointed out, this is entirely consistent with the evidence from the field patterns, monuments, settlements and artifacts of the region.

The only other part of the country which is known to have been largely cleared by the beginning of the Iron Age is the Magnesian limestone outcrop in the east of County Durham where Bartley *et al.* (1976) have recently described an unusual intensity of clearance with the cultivation of cereals, dated at Bishop Middleham to 1,710 bc (GaK-2072).

*Clearance during the pre-Roman Iron Age*

There are several areas in the country where forest was first cleared extensively during the pre-Roman Iron Age. The blanket mires of Exmoor have recently been studied by Merryfield and Moore (1974) and their radiocarbon-dated pollen diagram from The Chains, the deepest area of peat on an upland plateau site, shows increased farming and woodland clearance between 350 bc and ad 400. A second diagram from the area, from a shallower peat deposit at Hoar Tor, also shows this increased human pressure on the area during the Iron Age and Roman periods and on this diagram cereal pollen is recorded for the period at values of up to 10% of the total tree pollen. Moore suggests that there was an increased amount of stock grazing in the woodlands and, because they were already under climatic and nutrient stress as the result of the deteriorating climate and prolonged leaching, this grazing pressure tipped the balance in favour of peat formation.

The blanket mïres of Dartmoor have also been studied and Simmons (1964, 1969a) noted an intensification of clearance at a level which he attributes to the pre-Roman Iron Age. This intensification occurs despite the fact that Iron Age settlement is concentrated on the margins of the Moor, and not, as it had been during the Bronze Age, on the Moor itself. Whether this was due to the Bronze Age folk continuing to live in the uplands during the Iron Age and keeping them open, or whether it was caused by the stock grazing associated with the new lower settlements, is not clear. As on Exmoor, peat was continuing to develop at this time, possibly for the same reasons, and there would have been less good grazing available.

Another area with extensive pre-Roman Iron Age clearance is mid-Wales. A pollen diagram from Tregaron Bog (Turner 1964a) at 170m. in the Teifi valley shows a rise in the grass pollen frequency from values of less than 20% to well over 100% of the total tree pollen at a level radiocarbon dated to 404 bc (Q-596). The pollen catchment of this bog is now grassland and rough grazing up to 350m. O.D. and it is interesting to note that only 7.5km. from the site is the hill of Pen-y-Bannau capped by a trivallate fort.

Two other diagrams from central Wales (Moore 1968) also show intensification of forest clearance in the Iron Age. One from Borth Bog on the coast lies very near sea-level, the other is from near the summit of Plynlimmon at 607m. O.D. Both show increased values for grasses and ribwort plantain (*Plantago lanceolata*) pollen in the pollen Zone C of the local sequence, which Moore attributes to the Iron Age. He has based this dating on the position of a Roman road ad 43-78, stratified into a peat deposit with a similar sequence of pollen zones at Blair yr Esgair, and on the position of a mediaeval track stratified into another bog at Llyn Gynon.

Similarly from Lancashire, Birks (1963-4) has shown that forest clearance was taking place in the pre-Roman Iron Age around Chat Moss. The grass and *Plantago lanceolata* pollen frequencies rise to quite high values at a level in the diagram which has been dated to 695 bc (Q-683). Across the other side of the Pennines at Thorne Waste near the Humber estuary in Yorkshire, a short pollen diagram shows that extensive forest clearance also took place in this region at a level radiocarbon dated to 379 bc (Q-479) (Turner 1962). Much of the Pennines were also cleared during this period. Hicks (1971) has shown that there was wholesale forest clearance at first associated predominantly with pasture on the East Moor of Derbyshire. This clearance was found on no less than six diagrams and is radiocarbon dated to the period from 340 bc (GaK-2288) to 140 bc (GaK-2289) at Leash Fen. Cereal pollen has been found in small quantities after this time and eventually above a level dated ad 40 (GaK-2291) a mixed economy was practised in the area until ad 420 (GaK-2292). During this period of mixed economy pollen of walnut (*Juglans*) and hemp or hops (*Cannabis/Humulus* type) as well as cereal pollen values of 1-2% total tree pollen, have been recorded.

There is further evidence from Featherbed Moss in Derbyshire, some 24km. to the north-west (Tallis and Switsur 1973), where a well-marked clearance on the diagram covering the period 301 bc (Q-854) to ad 550 (Q-852), is indicative of grassland, although a few cereal pollen grains were found attesting that cereals were also being grown in the area. The pollen assemblage zone of this clearance was originally described by Tallis (1964a) from a number of sites in the south Pennines as far apart as Wessenden Head Moor, east of Oldham, and Goyt Moss, west of Buxton, and including Kinder Scout, and although it has only been securely radiocarbon dated at Featherbed Moss it is in all probability synchronous across large parts of the southern Pennines.

The Nidderdale Moors in Yorkshire have been studied by Tinsley (1975) who, on the basis of pollen diagrams from seven sites, describes a further expansion of heath at the expense of woodland during the Iron Age. A certain amount of clearance had already taken place during the Bronze Age, but during the Iron Age tree pollen percentages dropped to near their modern values and the herbaceous pollen types indicate the predominance of pastoralism in the area, but with some arable. Cereal pollen was found. The beginning of this phase was dated at one site to 250 bc (GaK-3670) but Tinsley thinks it could have been slightly earlier.

Also of late pre-Roman Iron Age is the widespread clearance described by Bartley *et al.* (1976) for parts of the eastern lowlands of Co. Durham. Bartley's diagram from Thorpe Bulmer near Hartlepool shows a major clearance with arable farming. Hemp (*Cannabis*) appears to have been grown immediately next to the site from the time of the clearance, 114 bc (SRR-404) until late Saxon times ad 1098 (SRR-405), with a peak in cultivation at ad 220 (GaK-3713).

*Areas with pre-Roman and Roman clearance*

There are also upland regions in northern Britain where some extensive clearance took place early in the Iron Age, and some later, in the Romano-British period.

The North Yorkshire Moors is one such region and the current evidence has been reviewed by Spratt and Simmons (1976). The palaeobotanical evidence is not all based on a radiocarbon chronology, but in an area that has been so intensively studied dating by association is more reliable than in many. Atherden (1976) has described a zone of extensive forest clearance on three diagrams, Fen Bogs, May Moss and Simon How Moss, with a level just above its lower boundary dated at Fen Bogs to 330 bc (T-1085). It lasted until ad 420 (T-1086). She divides the period into three phases, the first when the emphasis was on pastoralism, the second, probably beginning in the first century before Christ, with more arable farming and the third with the emphasis again on pastoral farming. Jones (1971) has described similar widespread clearance and the associated spread of grass and heath on a number of diagrams from Cleveland to the north-east of the area and Cundill (1971) has described several from the central watershed. Only one of these, that from Wheeldale Gill (Simmons and Cundill 1974a) has a radiocarbon date for the level. It is late, ad 380 (GaK-3879). Reviewing all this evidence it is difficult to conclude other than that it supports the idea that forest clearance was taking place throughout the Iron Age on a scale greater than it had been during the Bronze Age, and that, as Spratt and Simmons point out, 'by the end of the Iron Age it appears that the essential lineaments of the present landscape were clear'.

The northern Pennines too show a variation in the time when extensive forest clearance took place. The area now occupied by the Cow Green Reservoir at 470m. O.D. appears to have been largely cleared by the end of the Bronze Age. Peat from the floor of the reservoir basin yielded a diagram which shows the replacement of oak and alder woods by open grassland and heather moor at a level dated to 1,200 bc (GaK-2913), and at Tinkler's Sike on Widdybank Fell beside the reservoir the same pollen frequency changes have been dated to 620 bc (GaK-2027) (Turner *et al.* 1973). Higher up the same valley Chambers (1974) has evidence from Valley Bog on the Moor House National Nature Reserve of clearance during the pre-Roman Iron Age. This bog is at 550m. O.D. and to the south and east the hills rise to peaks of over 750m. O.D., Cross Fell, the highest Pennine summit at 893m., being only just 7km. to the west. The diagram shows a spread of heather and grassland at the expense of trees at a level bracketed by two dates, 262 bc and 255 bc (SRR-88 and 89). Chambers also found evidence for grassland as early as 538 bc (SRR-100) in the Tees lowlands near Darlington on his diagram from Neasham Fen.

But there is also evidence that many other places within the region were forested in the pre-Roman Iron Age. Roberts *et al.* (1973) have shown that extensive clearance of the woods occurred in mid-Weardale at altitudes around 350m. O.D. in Romano-British times. A date of 110 bc (GaK-3033) was obtained at Stewart Shield Meadow, a small bog in the hills to the north of the Wear and one of ad 220 (GaK-3031) at Bollihope Bog in the hills to the south. The pollen diagrams from these sites give a picture of grassy vegetation in the environment of these bogs and there are hut circles, thought to be of Romano-British origin, not far from the one at Bollihope. In both cases the area appears to have remained cleared until late mediaeval times.

There is also evidence from Hallowell Moss near Durham City that the Wear lowlands too were first extensively cleared at that time (Donaldson and Turner 1977). A date of 4 bc (SRR-415) was obtained for the beginning of this period of open landscape which lasted only until ad 595 (SRR-413). The pollen diagram indicates that both arable and pastoral farming were practised.

For Hutton Henry in east Durham (Bartley *et al.* 1976) there is also evidence for a very large clearance at a level dated to Roman times, ad 108 (SRR-600).

*Areas cleared in Roman times*

Another area which appears to have been cleared extensively in Romano-British times is the Somerset Levels. This region has been intensively studied for many years and in the early pollen diagrams from the region Godwin (1948) recognised that there had been two main phases of agricultural activity which, without the aid of radio-carbon dates, he correlated with (a) the middle to late Bronze Age and (b) the middle and late Iron Age to Romano-British times. The types of pollen found indicated that cereals were being grown and that there was also pasture in the area. There is now an extremely large number of radiocarbon dates available from the region, most of which were determined on the wood of the numerous prehistoric trackways that have been found, or on peat associated with them. There is also a considerable number of new pollen diagrams. (See Coles *et al.* 1970, 1971, 1973, 1975, 1977.)

In 1963, Godwin briefly summarised the extant data (Dewar and Godwin 1963) and I quote from what he then wrote (p.47).

> In all our pollen diagrams the period covered by the Late Bronze Age sees a considerable expansion of the curves of agricultural indicators ... The implication of considerable arable cultivation cannot be avoided ... This phase of intensive agricultural activity ... is certainly succeeded by a decline, and then, in the period immediately preceding the second flooding episode (*c.* 0-ad 50), the curves for agricultural indicators reach far higher values than ever before. *Plantago* pollen is shown in the Decoy Pool Wood diagram as over 50 per cent of the total tree pollen and it is accompanied by very high frequencies of miscellaneous herb families and genera typical of both arable land and pasture. This activity occurs at the time of the Glastonbury and Meare lake villages, particularly the latter (which lies actually within our area) and the strong evidence of collected crops and of extensive spinning and weaving in the hut sites leave little doubt of the agricultural basis of the economy of these people.

Another place where the woods were extensively cleared during the Roman period is in the Forth Valley near Flanders Moss. A pollen diagram from the site (Turner 1965) shows a short-lived maximum in grass and plantain pollen somewhere between levels radiocarbon dated to ad 219 (Q-575) and ad 92 (Q-570).

## Post-Roman clearance

There remains now a number of regions to consider which were largely forested throughout the pre-Roman and Roman Iron Age, where clearance did not begin until well into the first millenium after Christ. These regions are in north-west England and south-west Scotland. The most intensively studied of these is the Lake District, from which Pennington (1970) has evidence from at least ten tarns of a phase of agriculture following disforestation which she attributes to the Brigantian period. At two of these sites it has been radiocarbon dated, at Burnmoor to ad 390 (NPL-116) and at

Devoke Water to the period from ad 200 (NPL-117) to ad 580 (NPL-118). Associated with these episodes of clearance she has found the pollen of cereals indicating that they were cultivated in the uplands at levels higher than either before or since. This Brigantian phase was not the first that had occurred in the Lake District. Pennington (1970) describes earlier clearances associated with the Great Langdale Axe Factory and with the Bronze Age cairns of south-west Cumberland between 215 and 277m. (see pp. 170-2, 231), but there is no doubt that the Brigantian forest clearance was widespread within the area.

Smith (1958b) has described a phase of intense agricultural activity in three pollen diagrams from south-western Westmorland, a phase which occurred at the same time as wetter conditions on the mires, and which was subsequently radiocarbon dated to ad 436 (Q-83) (Godwin and Willis 1960). This is the first clearance on the diagram; earlier periods, which include most of the Roman and pre-Roman Iron Ages, are characterised by low frequencies of pollen types indicative of clearance and agriculture.

Walker's (1966) diagrams from the Cumberland lowland show that the very early pattern of agriculture established in Neolithic times continued with very little change through the Bronze and early Iron Ages and that it was not until after the Romans had left that there was a real expansion in farming. His diagram from Ehenside Tarn indicates that clearance continued from then until about ad 800 and that both flax (*Linum*) and hemp (*Cannabis*) or hops (*Humulus*) were cultivated.

From further north in lowland Ayrshire, Turner (1965) has described extensive clearance of the local woodland in the neighbourhood of Bloak Moss. It has been dated to ad 415 (Q-722) and lasted only until ad 580 (Q-721) when the forest regenerated.

From the hills of Galloway, Birks (1972a) has attributed the first extensive forest clearance on her diagram from Snibe Bog to this period, correlating it with the clearances already described from Ayrshire, lowland Cumberland and the Lake District.

There is no evidence on the radiocarbon-dated pollen diagrams from further north in Scotland to suggest that comparable extensive clearance also occurred there at this time. Pennington *et al.* (1972) and Birks (1972b) have studied the north-west and both have shown that moorland and blanket bog had begun to spread in the region at the expense of forest well before the Iron Age. Birks is of the opinion that this was a natural process in the area around Loch Maree in Ross and Cromarty but Pennington *et al* have shown that it was at least partly anthropogenic at some of their sites. Unlike further south in Britain, once the trees had been replaced, for whatever reason, forest did not regenerate.

*Ireland*

In Ireland too there is plenty of evidence for widespread forest clearance during the Iron Age, although it is often later rather than earlier.

In 1956 Mitchell defined his VIII-IX pollen zone boundary on the basis of a final fall in the elm pollen which occurred on a large number of pollen diagrams from lowland raised bogs. Hazel spread at the same time and in view of the low values for the pollen of pasture indicators like *P. lanceolata* he interpreted the changes as meaning that woodland had been cleared for growing vegetables and cereals. He tentatively dated the horizon to the beginning of the Christian period about ad 500, a suggestion in keeping with the radiocarbon date of ad 330 (D-29) which had been obtained for a pine stump layer just below it in a bog at Clonsast. Subsequently the horizon was dated at several sites by McAulay and Watts (1961), who commented that it seemed well founded at about ad 300. It is a little difficult to tell from Mitchell's 1956 diagrams, for which not all herbaceous grains were identified, how extensive a clearance of woodland is represented by this boundary at his various sites, but he later produced clear evidence from Littleton Bog, Co. Tipperary (1965) for increased farming activity associated with it.

Pilcher (1969) has found evidence for extensive clearance a little earlier than this on a pollen diagram from Beaghmore, Co. Tyrone, where it is dated to 140 bc (UB-87). The clearance, in contrast to those described by Mitchell, was mainly for pasture.

From a bog at Gortcorbies, Co. Londonderry, Smith, Pilcher and Pearson (1971) have found two levels reflecting extensive clearance, the first, at which elm pollen falls to insignificant values, is dated to 105 bc (UB-387), the second, at which there is a tenfold increase in *P. lanceolata* pollen, a clearance for pasture, to ad 565 (UB-388).

More recently Singh and Smith (1973) have studied the area of Lecale in Co. Down where there is good evidence for forest clearance but problems about dating it. At Ballydugan there is a catastrophic fall in the tree pollen associated with a rise in *P. lanceolata* pollen and the inwash of silt from disturbed soils at 150cm. where the VIII-IX boundary is drawn. At Magheralagan Lake, less than 2km. away, the diagram shows the beginning of a gradual decline in the pollen at this level and at a third site, Woodgrange, there is a modest fall in the tree pollen well above the VIII-IX boundary. The fall at this latter site has been dated to 1,430 bc (LJ-908) which is much earlier than one would expect for a level above the VIII-IX boundary.

It should perhaps also be mentioned that besides the north of Scotland there are a limited number of sites, Llanllwch in South Wales, Whixall Moss in Shropshire, Cannons Lough in Ireland, where no large-scale clearance has been demonstrated, and which appear to have been surrounded by woodland for the whole of the Iron Age.

*Conclusions*

The data have been summarised in Fig. 6.1. They show that at the beginning of the Iron Age the light, often calcareous soils, mainly of the south and east, had been extensively cleared of forest, and that even small patches of light soils, such as the limited stretches of sugar limestone in upper Teesdale and some northern coastal strips were already being exploited. Elsewhere the forest, though by no means unaffected by man, was still recognisably forest, varying in both density and species composition with altitude, aspect and soil type as it had done earlier in the postglacial; thin upland woods interspersed with blanket bog and heath contrasting with dense valley and lowland forest. Within it animals were grazed as they had been since Neolithic times and there were small clearings, usually temporary in nature, associated with shifting agriculture. In formerly-cleared areas light-demanding trees and shrubs such as birch were locally dominant and of similar age, but to the untrained eye the forest would have differed little from those of the previous millenium. Then, between 400 bc and ad 100 large areas in the south-west of England, Wales, parts of Ireland, and central and north-eastern England were cleared and both uplands and lowlands subsequently used for settled agriculture or permanent grazing for the very first time. Mixed farming appears to have been practised in a surprisingly wide range of habitats. A little woodland remained, as indeed it does today, but by early Roman times the open nature of our modern landscape already existed in

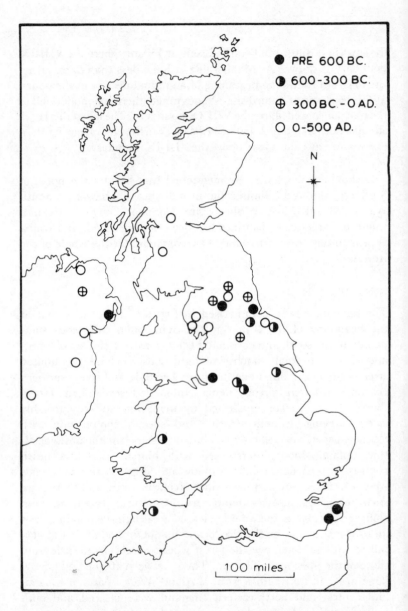

Figure 6.1. A map to show the location of sites mentioned in the text, at which the first extensive clearance of forest has been radiocarbon dated. Note the concentration of late dates, 0- ad 500 in Scotland, north-western England and Ireland, of early dates (before 300 bc) in southern England, Wales and north-eastern England, and of dates between 300 bc and 0 in north-eastern England.

these areas. Only to the north and west, north-west England and Scotland, did the essentially forested nature of the landscape remain, not to be cleared until some 300 years later.

This biological evidence often parallels the archaeological evidence but, as several authors have been at pains to point out, in some regions the two are at variance. There are however possible reasons. Where transhumance was practised, if the people concerned were living in the valleys or neighbouring lowlands and using the uplands for only part of the year, they may well have left few artifacts or settlements in the very places where they were having most impact on the vegetation.

## Flora and fauna

### The flora

The increase in open habitats which occurred during the Iron Age had its consequences for both the flora and fauna. Species which had been abundant towards the end of the glaciation, but severely restricted in distribution during the forest period, were able to spread into the new habitats, becoming the weeds of today, and some new species, both wild and cultivated, were introduced from the continental mainland. Godwin (1975) lists fifty-three weeds and ruderals which appeared for the first time in a Romano-British context, including such plants as opium poppy (*Papaver somniferum*), woad (*Isatis tinctoria*), corn marigold (*Chrysanthemum segetum*) and tufted vetch (*Vicia cracca*), alongside plants such as mugwort (*Artemisia vulgaris*) and sorrel (*Rumex* sp.) which were increasing in numbers with the new habitats. Certain woodland species, which are strongly dependent on light, also expanded at this time: ash (*Fraxinus excelsior*), elder (*Sambucus nigra*) and hawthorn (*Crataegus* sp.), for example, whilst others, maple (*Acer campestre*) and gorse (*Ulex europaeus*) appeared for the first time.

### The fauna

Changes in the fauna during the Iron Age, or indeed during any prehistoric period, are not as well documented as changes in the flora, and there is no one text equivalent to Godwin's *The History of The British Flora*, which contains Quaternary records of all plant species. Two groups that have been studied in detail and are well documented are the molluscs and the insects, but in the case of the insects, and also to some extent the molluscs, the most significant results of such studies concern earlier changes in climate and the environment than those of the Iron Age. The same is true of the vertebrates.

The fauna of the Iron Age was essentially similar to today's, but contained several species that have recently become extinct in Britain, for example the wolf (*Canis lupus*) and the beaver (*Castor fiber*), but the relative abundance of various species was quite different. Many wild animals are directly dependent upon the vegetation for their food and even carnivores rely indirectly upon plants, whatever their place in the food chain. And so with the decrease in woodland and increase in open land that took place in the Iron Age there were corresponding changes in the animal populations, and those species which thrive best in open habitats increased at the expense of the shade-tolerant ones. This has been demonstrated most clearly by Evans (1972) for snails, as for example at Pitstone and Pink Hill (see p.266). Unfortunately snails are preserved in calcareous areas and so this change from shade-loving to xero- and heliophiles cannot be demonstrated everywhere. Indeed in much of the chalkland it had occurred somewhat earlier, associated with Neolithic or Bronze Age occupation. Some of the larger mammals were affected too, deer for example became rarer in the south of Britain, judging by the number of bones found in archaeological sites.

The decrease in the amount of woodland was also a factor affecting domestic animals. Clark (1952) has pointed out that the relative abundance of the three major domestic animals changed in the Iron Age with sheep becoming more important relative to cattle and pigs. He attributes this to the increased amount of pasture suitable for sheep and the decreased amount of woodland available for the cattle and pigs, the wild ancestors of which were both woodland animals.

There were certain changes too within the species. For example white sheep with a finer fleece were introduced by the Romans (Ryder 1969), and Jewell (1962) has shown that cattle were small during the Iron Age. The average size of bones found at British sites is less than the average for earlier or later periods. For further details readers are referred to more specialised accounts such as those in Ucko and Dimbleby (1969).

## Soils

With the deterioration of climate during the first millenium before Christ and the large scale deforestation with associated agriculture and grazing one would have expected there to have been a substantial acceleration of soil deterioration and the formation of many more podsols.

This process had been going on throughout the postglacial and one of the most striking early examples is that investigated at Goodland Townland in Co. Antrim, where, during Neolithic times, the original oak forest was felled and during the period of occupation a thin iron pan developed on the soils which were being cultivated. Mitchell (1972) argues that this iron pan impeded drainage and allowed rushes (*Juncus* sp.) to invade the area and that their debris isolated the vegetation from the mineral soil and allowed bog plants to grow and eventually peat to form.

It is clear that this same process continued during the Bronze Age and into the Iron Age, for Smith, Pilcher and Pearson (1971) have described blanket peat from Beaghmore, Co. Tyrone, which overlies Bronze Age stone circles and alignments. The base of this blanket peat has been dated to 325 bc (UB-261D) and peat in a ditch of a cairn, which indicates an upper limit to the period of cairn construction, to 775 bc (UB-163).

Podsolisation did not always lead to blanket peat formation; often, and particularly in areas of lower rainfall, it led to heathland, as the work of Dimbleby (1962) has shown. He has studied over thirty sites in heathland areas in the north and south of England, from places as far apart as the North York Moors, the New Forest and Kent, many of them with close archaeological associations, and has recorded not only the physical characteristics of the soils but also their pollen. He concluded that the majority of the podsols were of secondary origin, having arisen as the result of man's activities in the area, particularly during the Bronze Age. This is well illustrated at Bickley Moor in Yorkshire, where the soil on the moor may be compared with the fossil Bronze Age soil buried beneath a barrow. The moor soil contained an indurated thin iron pan which continued over the top of the barrow, whereas the soil beneath the barrow was scarcely bleached and could not be regarded as a podsol. The iron pan could only have formed since the Bronze Age.

Tinsley (1975) has described the spread of heath on the Nidderdale Moors in Yorkshire, which took place during the Iron

Age. On a long pollen diagram it is radiocarbon dated to 250 bc (GaK-3670) onwards, although, as she stresses, it happened at other times in other parts of the Pennines. Certainly in the northern Pennines, where there is a great variation in altitude, and hence rainfall, from west to east, the soils deteriorated and peat started to form earlier in the areas with the higher rainfall, and there is quite a good correlation between onset of peat formation and present-day rainfall. High rainfall can cause podsolisation and it may well be that the climatic deterioration of the early Iron Age also contributed towards the spread of heath in some areas. Indeed most authors are agreed that both man and climate were factors; it is only the relevant importance of the two and of the role of geology and topography that is difficult to assess and about which it is impossible to generalise. One can only conclude that at the beginning of the Iron Age more of Britain was covered with more heath and bog than during the early Neolithic.

## Conclusions and speculations

The conclusion that vast tracts of the British countryside were cleared of trees and used for both grazing and growing crops is inescapable and this needs emphasis, for it happened largely in areas where preservation of artifacts is likely to be poor because of the acid nature of the soils, and the archaeological record therefore unlikely to reflect the full extent of it. It is perhaps fortunate that pollen preserves best in the very conditions most destructive to many other materials, and vice versa. The idea of widespread clearance makes sense in archaeological terms, however, for the development of an iron technology with the mass production of iron axes is an essential prerequisite for large-scale disforestation.

The importance of climate in the history of the Iron Age, although less well founded, cannot be over-emphasised as it gives rise to a number of questions. In what way did the climatic deterioration of the late Bronze Age affect the development of the British Iron Age? One can only speculate. Cunliffe (1974a) attributes the local movement of people off the moors of Devonshire into the valleys to the wetter weather but it would be surprising if such movements were not more numerous. Even in considering invasions from the continent (assuming this is still fashionable) one must take into account the possibility that the deteriorating climate on the continent was a factor promoting the early migrations.

And what effect would a warmer drier climate in the late Iron Age have had? Would perhaps the early Belgic invaders be partly responding to the pressures of overpopulation after a couple of centuries of productive farming in an equable climate? Would a warmer climate account for the increased number of massive underground silos that were constructed after the fourth or third centuries bc (Cunliffe 1974a). It may well only have been possible to store grain successfully in this way, once the climate had improved and the soils were drier. Such questions are not easy to answer, but are undoubtedly worth asking in the combined endeavours of archaeologists, geographers and biologists to understand the way in which our Iron Age predecessors lived.

# 7. *Culture and Environment*

## I.G. SIMMONS

One of the difficulties of providing an overview of man-environment relations during British prehistory is the uneven distribution of the evidence in both space and time. We must accept that certain types of environment are under-represented in the palaeoecological record. The chalklands of southern England, for example, have yielded few pollen diagrams, and even though much valuable evidence has been gained from studies of mollusca at and near archaeological sites, the regional ecological history of this type of terrain is not well known for the postglacial period. River terraces, too, are not the sort of environment to have accumulated the density of evidence which would enable us to investigate the magnitude of the impact of agriculturalists upon what appeared to the early people (and to us via air photography) as attractive places to settle. Similarly, the well-drained lowland areas of central and eastern England, which must have been the heartland of the mixed forest of Flandrian II, have yielded less evidence about its nature than some places where its equilibrium was likely to have been more easily disturbed. There is lacking also an even spread of long pollen diagrams from organic deposits which yield estimates of the relative impact of different cultures around the same site, which are possibly the most interesting types of diagram in this context; however, the increased application of C-14 dating has meant that shorter diagrams, particularly for post-Neolithic times, can make a full contribution to regional ecological history.

When we add to these problems the notorious difficulties of interpretation of palaeoecological evidence like the imperfect understanding of pollen catchment areas of bogs and lakes, or the hazards imposed by cultural selectivity upon the meaning of bone finds, to say nothing of the extrapolations needed to reconstruct climatic history, it becomes obvious that any picture must be provisional and that it is likely to vary with the viewpoint and reading of the author, as well as to be modified as new findings emerge. (What is perhaps surprising is the extent to which studies agree in their findings from place to place, although it must be admitted that correlations between artifactual data and pollen diagrams are always easier to make when the evidence is more general and more tenuous: 'Bronze Age clearance' covers a wide range of phenomena on some diagrams.) The accumulation of basic data for plants at any rate rests on a secure basis in the form of Sir Harry Godwin's *History of the British Flora* (1975); an equivalent for animals is badly needed; its analogue in terms of climatic history is Lamb's (1977) synthesis of much of the available evidence. Limbrey's (1975) book on soils, while not exactly the same kind of treatment, comes closest to providing a *vade mecum* on this important element of the human environment.

## Man's impact during non-forested phases

Although the great emphasis of investigations has been the effects of man upon the woodland environments of the Flandrian Stage of postglacial time, we ought not to dismiss entirely the periods of the remission of ice during the Pleistocene, the last fluctuations of arctic conditions during the Late Devensian Stage, and the early part of the Flandrian Stage, when mesocratic forest was either not yet established or was being rendered unviable by the deterioration of climate, but when human societies were present, albeit at low densities and at the hunter-gatherer level of technology.

The evidence for environmental manipulation by these Palaeolithic and early Mesolithic groups is sparse, but not totally absent. As far as plant communities are concerned, it centres around the presence of charcoal in deposits which yield other evidence of tundra, heath or low scrub vegetation. At Kildale Hall in Yorkshire, Jones (1976) has reported the skeleton of a *Bos primigenius* in a shallow mire with charcoal and pollen of a heathlike vegetation, dated 8,400 ± 200 bc (GaK-2707). In the Netherlands, the prevalence of a layer of charcoal from the burning of vegetation of Allerød age is sufficiently wide for the phenomenon to be known as the Usselo layer, from its find-site (van der Hammen 1957; Hijszeler 1957). By analogy with the contemporary Arctic, we know that tundra and contiguous vegetation types such as birch woodland and juniper-birch scrub will burn, especially the lichen-tundra which is important as winter feed for large mammal herbivores. We know also that burning of Boreal forests (i.e. those proximate to the tundra in time or space and generally dominated by conifers such as *Pinus* or *Picea*) enhances the representation of the deciduous and shrub elements of such forests (e.g. *Betula, Populus, Salix*) which in turn allow increases in the density of mammals such as the moose or elk (*Alces alces*). None of this provides proof of the manipulative efforts of early man in tundra, park-tundra and Boreal woodland environments but it suggests a framework in which the idea is not totally outrageous: the use of fire to stampede animals into traps, for example, or to encourage browse at a time of rapid habitat change towards closed forest does not seem to be outside the bounds of all likelihood. (Dr Carl Sauer once suggested to the author that the 'Pleistocene overkill' phenomenon in North America was enhanced by the use of fire as an aid in hunting which simultaneously reduced the winter forage for mammal herbivores. Is it over-imaginative to see a similar sequence interacting with climatic change and co-operative hunting to reduce greatly mammals which became extinct during the Late Devensian and Early Flandrian Stages in Britain?). However, the pollen diagrams from Star Carr reveal no widespread clearance effects in the birch forest. The regular use of fire during the last phases of tundra-like vegetation and on into the accumulating forests might strengthen Smith's (1970a) interpretation of the high frequency of *Corylus* pollen at that time and subsequently for most of the Mesolithic period. (It should be emphasised that the representation of hazel pollen in the present 'interglacial' is, stage for stage, much higher than in other interglacials.) The usefulness of this shrub for its adaptable wood, its nuts and its mammal-feeding browse is scarcely to be challenged, and a manipulative tool such as fire ensured that its representation in plant communities was not too much diminished by the normal shading processes of the succession which produced closed 'mature' forest. Acceptance of this idea carries the far-reaching implication that the mixed-oak forest of Flandrian II was not in fact a totally 'natural' community but had some of its successions deflected by human activity, although it is very difficult to imagine that the gross physiognomy of the formation was affected: an amplification of the representation of one set of the seral phases which were part of the mosaic of communities seems more likely.

## The differentiation of the forest matrix

The environmental impact of late Mesolithic, Neolithic, Bronze Age and Iron Age peoples is largely associated with their effects upon the mixed oak forest ecosystem which was established as the major community over much of Britain by 7,000 bp. But before giving these processes their rightful place, we should mention that the temporary recession of deciduous forest was not unknown in interglacial times, as Wymer points out on pp. 59-60. At Hoxne and at Mark's Tey, lake deposits of Hoxnian interglacial age yielded pollen analyses which showed a diminution in forest and the expansion of grass pollen. In the same layers at Hoxne, charcoal and Palaeolithic implements were found. Had such phenomena occurred in a Neolithic context, we would have no hesitation over their interpretation as man-made features. They were in any case soon erased by events of much greater magnitude, whereas the consequences of some of the Flandrian clearances are with us today.

The mixed oak forest of the mid-postglacial period provided a matrix out of which successive human societies hewed a set of cultural landscapes, changing the components of its ecology as they did so. But it is important not to think of the initial forest as comprising an unbroken blanket of tree-clad terrain all the way from the Dingle Peninsula to the Ural Mountains. Although the forest was in equilibrium in the sense that it was self-regenerating, and that there were no secular changes in the dominant species, we ought not to forget that in Britain there was a succession of sea-level changes, rising and falling, which produced spatial changes in coastal ecosystems; there is evidence for considerable meandering of rivers which would have created open habitats for herbaceous communities; the damming activities of beavers throw back aquatic succession to an early phase and, if the dams are broken, a new terrestrial set of seres then begins; known changes of lake levels during the Flandrian would have initiated new successions, and recurrence surfaces on bogs bear witness also to changing plant communities; high precipitation would probably have increased the number of landslips within the forests and added to the number of open patches inherent in the normal death and regeneration pattern of forests. Any of these open areas might have been held open or retarded in their seral advance by the activities of herbivorous mammals. The difficult question of the height of the tree-line must also be mentioned: although the evidence is often difficult to interpret, and the forest certainly reached high altitudes on the uplands, it seems likely that some summit and plateau areas in Britain south of the Scottish Highlands (e.g. the northern Pennines, north Wales, central Wales) were never forested in Flandrian times, thus adding another open area to the diversity of communities.

Within this setting, the pre-agricultural peoples of the late Mesolithic pursued their economy. Their effects on the ecosystems are mostly chronicled for the uplands and for the sandy lands of south and east England, and are generally small in extent, amounting often to no more than the transient appearance of a forest 'clearance phase' accompanied by a few ruderal pollen, in an area known to possess Mesolithic implements. Such an ephemeral token of their presence is to be expected: what are less likely are the indications that, on some of the lowland areas now heath, with sandy substrates, the soils appear to have broken down under Mesolithic occupance, and that at the upper edge of the forest burning produced hard scrub at the expense of forest, and that eventually the removal of the trees caused such an interference with the water relations of the soils that blanket peat was formed. Thus, in two environments, Mesolithic groups created quasi-permanent changes in ecology and landscape. We must not overstress the magnitude of these changes: they were small in aggregate area, even if widespread in occurrence.

The advent of Neolithic culture brought the agricultural economy which was to be the mainstay of all later prehistory, diversified no doubt by hunting and gathering where this was still profitable. Neolithic agriculture is associated with shifting agriculture in a forest setting, with temporary clearances being succeeded by forest regeneration. The phenomenon of the 'elm decline' which seems to herald the Neolithic in palaeobotanical terms, is also attributed to human activity and, in particular, to the use of elm branches and bark for cattle fodder. *Ulmus* bark may also have been used directly by man for food, since it contains starch, proteins, fats, oils and sugars; the bark of the branches not more than 2-3 years old is particularly nutritious in this way, and there is documentary evidence of the practice in Norway until 1895, and of 'chewbark', elm bark collected by children, in Northumberland in 1853. (Parenthetically, we might note that the Ainu of Hokkaido used the bark of *Ulmus* for making skirts, but this practice seems to be unknown in European folk-ways.) But even as the clearances filled up again with trees, the elms came back before later disappearing more permanently under the impact of a more long-lasting form of agriculture.

Within Neolithic Britain evidence is beginning to emerge that the small temporary clearance in forested land is not the whole picture. J.G. Evans (1975) suggests that on the Chalk and allied areas, on lighter and well-drained soils in the Breckland and on the coastal plain of Cumberland, and probably in parts of the middle and upper Thames, large permanent clearances occurred, and thus permanent fields become a possibility. Wiltshire henges, to press the point, have produced buried soils which can be interpreted to show the maintenance of grassland by grazing animals for as long as 500 years. So some regional differentiation of environmental impact seems to be emerging during the Neolithic period.

The higher archaeological visibility of the Bronze Age in terms of field systems and settlements is paralleled by palaeoecological evidence for the addition of pasturalism to cereal agriculture and hence for a renewed attack on the forests, including, as Turner (1962) has suggested, the selective felling of lime (*Tilia*) possibly because it was an indicator of good agricultural soils. Again, however, the Bronze Age seems to have been characterised by temporary clearances rather than large permanent forest recessions, although here and there the pollen analytical evidence can be read as meaning rather large clearances, even though there may be eventual recovery of the forest. The two major domesticated animals of the time were pig and cattle and if they were herded freely through the woods, they would not affect regeneration as badly as sheep, whose numbers were now rapidly increasing. In the uplands of north-east Yorkshire, Spratt and Simmons (1976) hazarded the suggestion that pastoralism was the dominant land use on higher ground, whereas cereal cultivation was prevalent on the slopes and between the inter-fluvial ridge and the dale bottoms at *c*. 245m., although, in this area at least, the pollen of *Calluna vulgaris* climbs to permanently high values during the Bronze Age, suggesting the acidification of soils and the establishment of heathland on a virtually permanent basis. If some of the grassland created by grazing, or the non-colonisation by trees of abandoned fields then became bog in upland areas, and if the mires had a lower carrying capacity for grazing domesticates than the preceding grassland, there would have been an incentive for Bronze Age folk (and their successors) to move downhill, clearing as they went and perhaps leaving behind them some apparently irreversible ecological changes, especially where field systems were created as on southern Dartmoor and on the North York Moors.

The Iron Age, it is assumed, brought an enhanced ability to alter

the environment: iron technology, the plough, and the high proportion of sheep (Godwin 1975) are all set within the context of a
climatic deterioration which did not favour the regeneration of forest
after clearances. The ability to manipulate the environment was
probably linked to the need to do so: most writers suggest that the
intensification of settlements must denote an increase in human
population. Forest disappearance on a large scale is therefore
characteristic of the Iron Age and some considerable regional
differentiation, with concentrations upon tillage on lower ground
and pastoralism in the uplands is generally accepted. We may
assume that, in many uplands, much of the forest had disappeared
by the middle of the Iron Age, and that peat growth and continued
pastoralism ensured that it did not return: on drier slopes, acid
grassland, heather and bracken took its place. Characteristically, in
upland areas the main centres of Iron Age economic activity are
lower in altitude than those of the Bronze Age. If we accept that in
some parts of Britain the occupied places were the precursors of
mediaeval villages, then the Iron Age was perhaps the first time that
the major lineaments of the patterns of our rural landscape were
established.

The outcome of the agricultural millenia includes gross
environmental changes as outlined above, and the secondary
changes that must have flowed therefrom: the changes in river
regime, for example, that would have followed the deforestation; the
additional particulate loads, especially from upland catchments,
that must have been deposited in estuaries, tidal flats and lagoonal
zones, or in the perimarine zones of low lying coasts; the continued
shift from brown forest soils to the podsolic type; the continued
inception of blanket bog in places where slope and precipitation
allowed it once the forest cover had been broken down.

On a more detailed scale, a whole new flora became important.
Cereals brought in from continental Europe were a staple food:
wheat and barley equally in the Neolithic but barley held pride of
place in the Bronze Age, with rye, oats and spelt introduced still
later. Other economic crops were also first recorded in the Neolithic
and Bronze Age: examples include flax, Good King Henry, crab
apple, dwarf cherry and wild plum. The increased frequency of
disturbed ground and other man-made habitats allowed the
expansion of numerous plants unable to tolerate shade or closed
communities, which had last flourished in the Late Devensian but
had hung on in seral habitats, above the tree line, or in unstable

places like river cliffs, shingle banks and coastal sand dunes. Godwin (1975) gives a list of 35 weeds and ruderals first recorded in the Neolithic and Bronze Ages, and this list omits the commonest plantains, sorrels and mugworts which colonised the new suite of waste places. Concomitantly, many shrubs of woodland successional stages either appeared for the first time or extended their representation: field maple, box, gorse and wild roses are all recorded for the first time in the Neolithic/Bronze Age period, and species such as ash, hazel, birch and elder all increased in quantity, some no doubt encouraged by man because of their usefulness. Godwin also points out that the last two tree species to immigrate to Britain in postglacial time appeared during the agricultural phase of prehistory, and both beech and hornbeam are noted for their swift response to the removal of competition from previously undisturbed deciduous forest.

It is inconceivable that parallel trends were not followed in animal communities. Evidence is much sparser than with plants, but we know that domesticates like sheep were introduced, and assume that the tamed versions of cattle and pig were brought in by immigrant cultures rather than bred out of the native strains. The dog is known to have been present at Star Carr and presumably thereafter. What must be mostly inferred rather than directly recorded is the effect of environmental change on animal populations. Good evidence from archaeological sites exists for groups such as mollusca and insects (J.G. Evans 1972, 1975) but for larger mammals supposition is necessary. Numbers of red deer probably decreased as total woodland and scrub areas declined, with adaptation (eventually at a cost of smaller beasts) to open moorland habitats; the increase in roe deer where secondary woodland and scrub increased in area; of the general diminution of predators when the productivity of mammals decreased; and the rise of species of 'edge' habitats, like the fox, able to subsist on a wide variety of foods. Where predators were a threat to a domesticated species, then, doubtless they were labelled pests and became the objects of man-led efforts at extermination: the wolf and birds of prey may well have suffered thus. We might expect something similar in attitudes to the bear, noticing in passing that although bear-cults are quite common in near-recent north-temperate and sub-arctic groups, the ceremonies usually end with the bear being dead.

Putting together the evidence from about 10,000 bp to 1,900 bp, it appears to be the current view that, for much of Britain, the Iron

Age represents the period of heaviest impact of prehistoric man upon the environment. In part, of course, the view stems almost inevitably from the cumulative impact of successive cultures, with perhaps a key theme being the spread of permanent agriculture in fixed fields. This was paralleled by continuing grazing of domesticates in the remaining forests and on grassland long since bereft of tree cover. Thus was the forest matrix of Mesolithic time differentiated into a diversity of cultural habitats, and, for the Iron Age, archaeologists have argued that territorial division and demarcation was complete in some areas: the land was all occupied, so further environmental impact would result from the processes of intensification of the manipulation of the biota and soils rather than the spatial extension of such practices.

The accumulation of more detailed evidence about all the phases of prehistory will enable further inferences to be drawn. Nothing, for example, has been said about relative population numbers at various times, yet presumably their growth is the driving force behind much of the environmental alteration discussed. It would be good to have data on the frequency and spread of Mesolithic burning of the forest edge, and to have more estimates of the area under agriculture and pastoralism at different times in the same place. We could then make a first approximation at testing Boserup's hypothesis for agricultural change as elaborated for the hunting-gathering to agriculture transition by Cohen (1976). The expected sequence, in its simplest form, would be:

Free hunting → manipulative hunting (i.e. hunting intensified spatially) → herding → agriculture → agriculture and pastoralism.

and there is enough similarity in this sequence to our knowledge of Britain's prehistory to impart interest. Yet without considering the complexity imparted by the role of immigrant groups, the activities of social sub-sets within communities (both of which might, for instance, inject pastoralism into the sequence before agriculture), the model is clearly too simplistic.

## Conclusion

We can end uncontroversially by requesting more knowledge of all the periods and all the processes discussed. Certain environments still lack good sequences covering more than one period, and most of them need more data about wild animals, especially the large herbivores. Equally, we need more examples of comprehensive examinations of environmental data right at archaeological sites rather than, as so often is necessarily the case, in their general vicinity. A Star Carr for every period, and at least for both lowland and upland, would be a good data set to begin with.

Although the sequence of environmental effects portrayed here is without doubt provisional in many ways, one finding seems generally acceptable: that prehistoric peoples in Britain were influential changers of their ecology and their landscapes in their time, and even afterwards where the later impress of man has not been so intensive. The major lineaments of the landscape of the uplands of today, in terms of their treelessness and much of their blanket bog, originated at the hands of prehistoric cultures, even if most government documents still refer to them as areas of 'natural' beauty. In the lowlands also, settlement patterns and field boundaries are in places still traceable to their prehistoric forebears. Even if environmental impact of prehistoric times has been dwarfed by more recent agricultural, urban and industrial processes, it is not to be overlooked in any serious account of the development of our landscape or the history of our ecology.

# Bibliography

Aaby, B. 1975 'Cykliske Klimavariationer de sidste 7500 åv påvist ved undersøgelser af hogmøser og marine transgressionsfaser', *Danm. Geol. Unders. Årbog* 1974, 91-104.

Aaby, B. 1976 'Cyclic climatic variations in climate over the past 5,500 yr. reflected in raised bogs', *Nature* (London) 263, 281-4.

Alabaster, C. and Straw, A. 1976 'The Pleistocene context of faunal remains and artifacts discovered at Welton-le-Wold, Lincolnshire', *Proc. Yorks. Geol. Soc.* 41 (1, no.8), 75-93.

Albrethsen, S.E. and Brinch Petersen, E. 1976 'Excavation of a Mesolithic cemetery at Vedbaek, Denmark', *Acta Archaeologica* Copenhagen 47, 1-28.

Andersen, S.T. 1961 'Interglacial plant successions in the light of environmental changes', *Sixth INQUA Congress*, Warsaw 1961, vol. II, 359-68.

Andersen, S.T. 1970 'The relative pollen productivity and pollen representation of north European trees, and correction factors of tree pollen spectra', *Danm. Geol. Unders.* 11 (96), 1-99.

Andersen, S.T. 1973 'The differential pollen productivity of trees and its significance for the interpretation of a pollen diagram from a forested area', in Birks, H.J.B. and West, R.G. (eds), *Quaternary Plant Ecology*. 14th Symposium of the British Ecological Society. Oxford, 109-15.

Anderson, S.S. 1972 'The ecology of Morecambe Bay. II. Intertidal invertebrates and factors affecting their distribution', *J. Appl. Ecol.* 9, 161-78.

Andersson, G. 1909 'The climate of Sweden in the Late-Quaternary period', *Sver. Geol. Unders. Afh. Ser. C. No. 218, 1-88.

Andrews, C.W. 1915 'Mammalian and other bones', in Clarke, W.G. *Report on the Excavations at Grimes Graves, Weeting, Norfolk, March-May 1914.* London, 218-19.

ApSimon, A.M. 1969 'An early Neolithic house in Co. Tyrone', *J.R. Soc. Antiq. Ireland* 99, 165-8.

ApSimon, A.M. 1976 'Ballynagilly and the beginning and end of the Irish Neolithic', *Dissertationes Archaeologicae Gandenses* 16, 15-30.

Arthur, J.R.B. 1977 'The plant remains', in Bell, M. 'Excavations at Bishopstone, Sussex', *Sussex Archaeol. Collections* 115.

Ashbee, P. 1970 *The Earthen Long Barrow in Britain.* London.

Atherden, M.A. 1976 'The impact of late prehistoric cultures on the vegetation of the North York Moors', *Trans. Inst. Br. Geogr.* 1(3), 284-300.

Ball, D.F. 1975 'Processes of soil degradation: a pedological point of view', in Evans, J.G. *et al.* (eds), *The Effect of Man on the Landscape: the Highland Zone.* C.B.A. Research Report No. 11, 20-7.

Barber, K.E. 1975 'Vegetational history of the New Forest: a preliminary note', *Proc. Hants. Field Club Archaeol. Soc.* 30, 5-8.

Barber, K.E. 1976 'History of vegetation', in Chapman, S.B. (ed), *Methods in Plant Ecology*. Oxford, 5-83.

Bartley, D.D. 1975 'Pollen analytical evidence for prehistoric forest clearance in the upland area west of Rishworth, W. Yorkshire', *New Phytol.* 74, 375-81.

Bartley, D.D. *et al.* 1976 'The vegetational history of parts of south and east Durham', *New Phytol.* 77, 437-68.

Bate, D.M.A. 1936a 'Animal remains', in Clifford, E.M. 'Notgrove long barrow, Gloucestershire', *Archaeologia* 86, 156-7.

Bate, D.M.A. 1938 'Animal remains from Nympsfield long barrow', in Clifford, E.M. 'The excavation of Nympsfield long barrow, Gloucestershire', *Proc. Prehist. Soc.* 4, 212-13.

Battarbee, R.W. 1973 'Preliminary studies of Lough Neagh sediments. II. Diatom analysis from the uppermost sediment', in Birks, H.J.B. and West, R.G. (eds), *Quaternary Plant Ecology*. 14th Symposium of the British Ecological Society. Oxford, 279-88.

Beckett, S.C. and Hibbert, F.A. 1976 'An absolute pollen diagram from the Abbot's Way', in Coles, J.M. *et al.* (eds), *Somerset Levels Papers* 2. Cambridge, 24-7.

Bell, M. 1977 'Excavations at Bishopstone, Sussex', *Sussex Archaeol. Collections* 115.

Bendell, J.F. 1974 'Effects of fire on birds and mammals', in Kozlowski, T.T. and Ahlgren, C.E. (eds) *Fire and Ecosystems*. London, 73-138.

Benzler, J.H. and Geyh, M.A. 1969 'Versuch einer zeitlichen Gliederung Von Dwog – horizonten mit auf die problematik der 14C – datierung von bodenproben' *Z. Deutsch. Geol. Ges.* 118, 361-7.

Berglund, B.E. 1971 'Littorina transgressions in Blekinge, South Sweden: a preliminary survey', *Geol. För. Stockh. Förh.* 93 (3:546), 625-52.

Berry, R.J. and Rose, F.E.N. 1975 'Islands and the evolution of *Microtus arvalis* (Microtinae)', *J. Zool. London* 177, 395-409.

Bertsch, K. and F. 1949 *Geschichte unserer Kulturpflanzen*. Stuttgart.

Bertsch, K. 1955 'Die Früchte und Samen', in Paret, O. *Das Steinzeitdorf Ehrenstein bei Ulm ( Donau)*, 60-4.

Birks, H.H. 1972a 'Studies in the vegetational history of Scotland. II. Two pollen diagrams from the Galloway Hills, Kirkcudbrightshire', *J. Ecol.* 60, 183-217.

Birks, H.H. 1972b 'Studies in the vegetational history of Scotland. III. A radiocarbon-dated pollen diagram from Loch Maree, Ross and Cromarty', *New Phytol.* 71, 731-54.

Birks, H.H. 1973 'Modern macrofossil assemblages in lake sediments in Minnesota', in Birks, H.J.B. and West, R.G. (eds) 1973, *Quaternary Plant Ecology*. 14th Symposium of the British Ecological Society. Oxford, 173-89.

Birks, H.H. 1975 'Studies in the vegetational history of Scotland. IV. Pine stumps in Scottish blanket peats', *Phil. Trans. R. Soc. Lond.* (B) 270, 181-226.

Birks, H.J.B. 1963-4 'Chat Moss, Lancashire', *Mem. Proc. Manchr. Lit. Phil. Soc.* 106, 22-45.

Birks, H.J.B. 1965 'Pollen analytical investigations at Holcroft Moss, Lancashire and Lindow Moss, Cheshire', *J. Ecol.* 53, 229-314.

Birks, H.J.B. 1973 'Modern pollen rain studies in some arctic and alpine environments', in Birks, H.J.B. and West, R.G. (eds), *Quaternary Plant Ecology*. 14th Symposium of the British Ecological Society. Oxford, 143-68.

Birks, H.J.B. 1974 'Numerical zonation of Flandrian pollen data', *New Phytol.* 73, 351-8.

Birks, H.J.B. 1977 'Recent woodland history in South Cumbria, as evidenced by pollen analysis of mor humus layers'. Paper given at the British Ecological Society Meeting. Lancaster.

Birks, H.J.B. *et al.* 1975 'Pollen maps for the British Isles 5000 years ago', *Proc. Roy. Soc. Lond.* (B) 189, 87-105.

Bishop, M.J. 1975 'Earliest record of man's presence in Britain', *Nature* (London) 253 95-7.

Blackburn, K.B. 1946 'On a peat from the island of Barra, Outer Hebrides', *New Phytol.* 45, 44-9.

Blackley, C.H. 1873 *On the Quantity of Pollen Found Floating in the Atmosphere During the Prevalance of Hay Fever, and its Relation to the Intensity of the Symptoms*. London.

Boessneck, J. *et al.* 1963 'Seeberg Burgaschisee-Sud. Die Tierreste', *Acta Bernensia*, II, pt. 3, 117-96.

Bramwell, D. 1959 'The excavation of Dowel Cave, Earl Sterndale 1958-9', *Derby. Arch. J.* 79, 97-109.

Bramwell, D. 1960 'Some research into bird distribution in Britain during the late glacial and post-glacial periods', *Bird Report 1959-60 of the Merseyside Naturalists Assoc.*, 51-8.

Bramwell, D. 1963 'Animal bones', in Manby, T.G. 'The excavation of the Willerby Wold long barrow, East Riding of Yorkshire', *Proc. Prehist. Soc.* 29, 204.

Bramwell, D. 1971 'Excavations at Fox Hole Cave, High Wheeldon, 1961-70', *Derby. Arch. J.* 91, 1-19.

Bramwell, D. 1974 'Animal remains from Rudston and Boynton grooved ware sites', in Manby, T.G. 'Grooved ware sites in the north of England', *Brit. Arch. Reps.* 9, 103-8.

Bramwell, D. 1976 'Animal bones', in Manby, T.G. 'Excavation of the Kilham long barrow, East Riding of Yorkshire', *Proc. Prehist. Soc.* 42, 157-8.

Brinch Petersen, E. 1973 'A survey of the late Pleistocene and Mesolithic of Denmark', in Kozlowski, S.K. (ed.) *The Mesolithic of Europe*. Warsaw, 77-127.

Brink, van den, F.H. 1973 *A Field Guide to the Mammals of Britain and Europe*. London.

Brinkhuizan, D.C. 1977 'The fish remains', in Woodman, P.C. 'Recent excavations at Newferry, Co. Antrim', *Proc. Prehist. Soc.* 43, 197.

Bristow, C.R. and Cox, F.C. 1973 'The Gipping Till: a re-appraisal of East Anglian glacial stratigraphy', *J. Geol. Soc., London* 129, 1-37.

British Standards Institution 1961 *Methods of Testing Soils for Civil Engineering Purposes*. British Standard 1377, 1-140.

Britnell, W. 1979 'Excavations at Gwernvale Chambered Tomb', *Antiquity*

Brothwell, D. and Higgs, E. 1969 *Science in Archaeology: a survey of progress and research*. London.

Bryson, R.A. *et al.* 1970 'The character of late-glacial and post-glacial climatic changes', in Dort, Jr, W. and Jones, Jr, J.K. (eds), *Pleistocene and Recent Environments of the Central Great Plains*. Dept. of Geology, Univ. Kansas, Special Publication 3, 53-74.

Buckland, P.C. and Kenward, H.K. 1973 'Thorne Moor: a palaeo-ecological study of a Bronze Age site', *Nature* (London) 241, 405-6.

Bunting, G.H. *et al.* 1959 'Report on the animal bones', in Morgan, F. de M. 'The excavation of a long barrow at Nutbane, Hants.', *Proc. Prehist. Soc.* 25, 47-9.

Burgess, C.B. 1974 'The Bronze Age', in Renfrew, C. (ed), *British Prehistory: a new outline*. London, 165-232.

Burleigh, R. and Clutton-Brock, J. 1977 'A radiocarbon date for *Bos primigenius* from Charterhouse Warren Farm, Mendip', *Proc. Univ. Bristol Spelaeol. Soc.* 14(3), 255-7.

Butzer, K.W. 1972 *Environment and Archaeology*. London.

Calder, C.S.T. 1955 'Report of the discovery of numerous stone-age house sites in Shetland', *Proc. Soc. Antiq. Scotland*. 89, 340-97.

Calkin, J.B. 1934 'Implements from the Higher Raised Beaches of Sussex', *Proc. Prehist. Soc. East Anglia* 7, 333-47.

Calkin, J.B. and Green, J.F.N. 1949 'Palaeoliths and Terraces near Bournemouth', *Proc. Prehist. Soc. London*. 15, 21-37.

Campbell, J.B. 1977 *The Upper Palaeolithic of Britain*. Oxford.

Campbell, J.B. and Sampson, C.G. 1971 'A new analysis of Kent's Cavern, Devonshire, England', *Univ. Oregon Anthropological Papers* 3, 1-40.

Carreck, J.N. 1976 'Pleistocene mammalia and molluscan remains from 'Taplow' Terrace deposits at West Thurrock, near Grays, Essex', *Proc. Geol. Ass.* 87(1), 83-91.

Carter, H.H. 1975, 'Animal bones' and 'Details of the stratified animal bones', in Bradley, R. and Ellison, A., 'Rams Hill', *Brit. Arch. Reps.* 19, 118-22, 229-37.

Case, H.J. 1956 'The Neolithic causewayed camp at Abingdon, Berks.', *Antiq. J.* 36, 16-18.

Case, H.J., *et al.* 1969 'Land use in Goodland Townland, Co. Antrim, from Neolithic times until today', *J.R. Soc. Antiq. Ireland* 99, 39-53.

Caulfield, S. 1978 'Neolithic fields; the Irish evidence', *Brit. Arch. Reps.* 48, 137-43.

Chambers, C. 1974 *The vegetational history of Teesdale*. Unpublished Ph.D. Thesis, University of Durham.

Cherry, J. 1978 'Questions of efficiency and interpretation in assemblage sampling', in Cherry, J. *et al.* 'Sampling in contemporary British archaeology', *Brit. Arch. Reps.* 50, 293-320.

Childe, V.G. 1940 *Prehistoric Communities of the British Isles*. London.

Childe, V.G. and Smith, I.F. 1954 'Excavation of a Neolithic barrow on

Whiteleaf Hill, Bucks', *Proc. Prehist. Soc.* 20, 219.

Churchill, D.M. 1965 'The kitchen midden site at Westward Ho!, Devon, England: ecology, age and relation to changes in land and sea level', *Proc. Prehist. Soc.* 31, 74-84.

Clark, J.G.D. 1938 'Microlithic industries from the tufa deposits at Prestatyn, Flintshire and Blashenwell, Dorset', *Proc. Prehist. Soc.* 4, 330-4.

Clark, J.G.D. 1947 'Whales as an economic factor in prehistoric Europe', *Antiquity*, 21, 84-104.

Clark, J.G.D. 1952 *Prehistoric Europe: the economic basis*. London.

Clark, J.G.D. (ed.) 1954 *Excavations at Star Carr*. Cambridge.

Clark, J.G.D. 1972 *Star Carr: a case study in bioarchaeology*. Addison-Wesley Modular Publications in Anthropology No. 10. Reading, Mass.

Clark, J.G.D. and Godwin, H. 1962 'The Neolithic in the Cambridgeshire Fens', *Antiquity* 36, 10-23.

Clark, J.G.D. *et al.* 1935 'Report on recent excavations at Peacock's Farm, Shippea Hill, Cambridgeshire', *Antiq. J.* 15, 284-319.

Clark, J.G.D. *et al.* 1960 'Excavations at the Neolithic site at Hurst Fen, Mildenhall, Suffolk', *Proc. Prehist. Soc.* 26, 202-45.

Clarke, A.S. 1962 'Animal bones', in Piggott, S. 'The West Kennet long barrow excavations 1955-6', *Ministry of Works Archaeological Report* 4, 53-5.

Clarke, A.S. 1962-3 'The animal bones', in Henshall, A.S. and Wallace, J.C., 'The excavation of a chambered cairn at Embo, Sutherland', *Proc. Soc. Antiq. Scot.* 96, 35-6.

Clarke, D. 1976 'Mesolithic Europe: the economic basis', in Sieveking, G. de G. *et al.* (eds), *Problems in Economic and Social Archaeology*. London, 449-82.

Clarke, W.G. 1922 'The Grimes Graves fauna', *Proc. Prehist. Soc. E. Anglia* 3, 431-3.

Clason, A.T. 1967 *Animals and Man in Holland's Past*. Groningen.

Cleve-Euler, A. 1951-3 'Die Diatomeen von Schweden und Finnland', *K. Svenska Vetensk-Akad. Handl. Fjarde.* 2(1), 1-163; 3(3), 1-153; 4(1), 1-158; 4(5), 1-255.

Clutton-Brock, J. and Jewell, P. (forthcoming) 'The remains of wild and domestic animals. The Bronze Age barrow cemetery at Snail Down, Everleigh, Wiltshire'.

Cohen, M.N. 1976 *The Food Crisis in Prehistory*. New Haven.

Coles, J.M. and Hibbert, F.A. 1968 'Prehistoric roads and tracks in Somerset, England: 1. Neolithic', *Proc. Prehist. Soc.* 34, 238-58.

Coles, J.M. *et al.* 1970 'Prehistoric roads and tracks in Somerset, England: 2. Neolithic', *Proc. Prehist. Soc.* 36, 125-51.

Coles, J.M. *et al.* 1971 'The early settlement of Scotland: excavations at Morton Fife', *Proc. Prehist. Soc.* 37, 284-366.

Coles, J.M. *et al.* 1973 'Prehistoric roads and tracks in Somerset, England. 3. Sweet Track', *Proc. Prehist. Soc.* 39, 256-93.

Coles, J.M. *et al.* 1975a *Somerset Levels Papers* 1. Cambridge.

Coles, J.M. *et al.* 1975b 'The Eclipse Track' in *Somerset Levels Papers* 1, 20-4.

Coles, J.M. *et al.* 1975c 'Tinney's Ground 1974' in *Somerset Levels Papers* 1, 43-52.

Coles, J.M. *et al.* 1976 *Somerset Levels Papers* 2. Cambridge.

Coles, J.M. *et al.* 1977 *Somerset Levels Papers* 3. Cambridge.

Coles, J.M. *et al.* 1978 *Somerset Levels Papers* 4. Cambridge.

Collins, D. and Collins, A. 1970 'Cultural evidence from Oldbury, Kent', *Univ. London Inst. Archaeol. Bull* 8-9 (1968-9), 151-76.

Connah, W.G. 1965 'Excavations at Knap Hill, Alton Priors, 1961', *Wilts. Archaeol. Nat. Hist. Mag.* 60, 17-18.

Conway, V.M. 1947 'Ringinglow bog, near Sheffield. Part 1, Historical', *J. Ecol.* 34, 149-81.

Conway, V.M. 1954 'Stratigraphy and pollen analysis of southern Pennine blanket peats', *J. Ecol.* 42, 117-47.

Coope, G.R. 1975 'Climatic fluctuations in north-west Europe since the last interglacial, indicated by fossil assemblages of Coleoptera', in Wright, A.E. and Moseley, F. (eds), *Ice Ages: ancient and modern*. Geological Journal Special Issue No. 6, 153-68.

Coope, G.R. 1977 'Quaternary Coleoptera as aids in the interpretation of environmental history', in Shotton, F.W. (ed), *British Quaternary Studies: recent advances*. Oxford, 55-68.

Coope, G.R. *et al.* 1961 'A late Pleistocene fauna and flora from Upton Warren, Worcestershire', *Phil. Trans. R. Soc. Lond.* (B) 244, 379-421.

Cornwall, I.W. 1953 'Soil science and archaeology with illustrations from some British Bronze Age monuments', *Proc. Prehist. Soc.* 19, 129-47.

Cornwall, I.W. 1976 'Report on the animal bones', in Vatcher, F. de M. and Vatcher, H.L. 'The excavation of a round barrow near Poor's Heath, Risby, Suffolk', *Proc. Prehist. Soc.* 42, 289-92.

Cram, L. 1967 'Report on the animal bones from Hockwold', *Proc. Camb. Antiq. Soc.* 60, 75-80.

Crompton, E. 1952 'Some morphological features associated with poor drainage' *J. Soil. Sci.* 3, 277-89.

Cundill, P. 1971 *Ecological history and the development of peat on the central watershed of the North Yorkshire Moors*. Unpublished Ph.D. Thesis, University of Durham.

Cunliffe, B. 1974a *Iron Age Communities in Britain*. London.

Cunliffe, B. 1974b 'The Iron Age', in Renfrew, C. (ed), *British Prehistory: a new outline*. London, 49-86.

Dadd, M.N. 1970 'Overlap of variation in British and European mammal populations', *Symp. Zool. Soc. Lond.* 26, 117-25.

Damon, P.E. *et al.* 1970 'Arizona dates for dendrochronologically dated samples', in Olsson, I.U. (ed.), *Radiocarbon Variations and Absolute Chronology*. Proceedings of the 12th Nobel Symposium, Stockholm, 615-18.

Damon, P.E. *et al.* 1973 'Dendrochronologic calibration of the carbon-14 time scale', in Rafter T.A. and Grant-Taylor, T. (eds.), *Proceedings of the Eighth International Conference on Radiocarbon Dating*. Wellington, New Zealand. A 28-A 43.

Dansgaard, W. *et al.* 1969 'One thousand centuries of climatic record from Cape Century on the Greenland ice sheet', *Science* (N.Y.) 166, 377-81.

Dansgaard, W. *et al.* 1970 'Ice cores and palaeoclimatology', in Olsson, I.U.

(ed.), *Radiocarbon Variations and Absolute Chronology*, Proc. 12th Nobel Symposium. Stockholm, 337-51.

Dansgaard, W. *et al.* 1975 'Climatic changes, Norsemen and modern men', *Nature*, (London) 255, 24-8.

Davidson, D.A. *et al.* 1976 'Palaeoenvironmental reconstruction and evaluation: a case study from Orkney', *Trans. Inst. Brit. Geog.* N.S. 1, 346-61.

Davies, O. 1950 *Excavations at Island MacHugh*. Natural History and Philosophy Society, Belfast.

Davis, M.B. 1963 'On the theory of pollen analysis', *Am. J. Sci.* 261, 897-912.

Davis, M.B. and Deevey, E.S. 1964 'Pollen accumulation rates: estimates from late-glacial sediment of Rogers Lake', *Science* (N.Y.) 145, 1293-5.

Dawkins, W.B. 1916 'The animal remains', in Ward, J. 'The St Nicholas chambered tumulus, Glamorgan', *Archaeologia Cambrensis* 71, 264-6.

Degerbøl, M. 1961 'On a find of a Preboreal domestic dog (*Canis familiaris* L.) from Star Carr, Yorkshire', *Proc. Prehist. Soc.* 27, 35-54.

Degerbøl, M. 1970 'The urus (*Bos primigenius* Bojanus) and Neolithic domesticated cattle (*Bos taurus domesticus* Linné) in Denmark', *Det Kong. Danske Videnskab. Selskb. Biologiske Skrifter*, 17 (1), 5-177.

Degerbøl, M. and Krog, H. 1951 'Den europaeiske Sumpskildpadde (*Emys orbicularis* L.) i Danmark', *Danm. Geol. Unders.* II series, no. 78, 1-130.

Dennell, R.W. 1976 'Prehistoric crop cultivation in southern England: a reconsideration', *Antiq. J.* 56, 11-23.

Dent, A. 1977 'Orkney pigs', *Ark, J. Rare Breeds Preservation Trust* 4(9), 304.

Denton, G.H. and Karlén, W. 1973 'Holocene climatic variations – their pattern and possible cause', *Quaternary Research* 3, 155-205.

Destombes, J.P. *et al.* 1975 'A buried valley system in the Strait of Dover', *Phil. Trans. R. Soc. Lond.* (A) 279, 243-56.

Devoy, R.J.N. 1977 *Flandrian sea-level changes and vegetational history of the Lower Thames Estuary*. Unpublished Ph.D. Thesis, University of Cambridge.

Dewar, H.S.L. and Godwin, H. 1963 'Archaeological discoveries in the raised bogs of the Somerset Levels, England', *Proc. Prehist. Soc.* 29, 17-49.

Dickinson, W. 1975 'Recurrence surfaces in Rusland Moss, Cumbria (formerly North Lancashire)', *J. Ecol.* 63(3), 913-35.

Dickson, C.A. 1970 'The study of plant macrofossils in British Quaternary deposits', in Walker, D. and West, R.G. (eds.), *Studies in the Vegetational History of the British Isles*. Cambridge, 233-54.

Digerfeldt, G. 1975 'A standard profile for Littorina transgressions in western Skåne, South Sweden', *Boreas* 4, 125-42.

Dimbleby, G.W. 1957 'Pollen analysis of terrestrial soils', *New Phytol.* 56, 12-28.

Dimbleby, G.W. 1962 *The Development of British Heathlands and their Soils*. Oxford Forestry Mem. 23.

Dimbleby, G.W. 1963 'Pollen analysis at a mesolithic site at Addington, Kent', *Grana Palynologica* 4, 140-8.

Dimbleby, G.W. 1965 'Post-glacial changes in soil profiles', *Proc. R. Soc. Lond.* (B) 161, 355-62.

Dimbleby, G.W. 1969 'Pollen Analysis', in Brothwell, D. and Higgs, E.S. (eds), *Science in Archaeology*, London (2nd ed.); 167-77.

Dimbleby, G.W. 1975 'Summary and conclusions' in Evans, J.G. *et al.* (eds), *The Effect of Man on the Landscape: the Highland Zone*, C.B.A. Research Report, No. 11, 127-9.

Dimbleby, G.W. 1976 'Climate, soil and man', *Phil. Trans. R. Soc. Lond.* (B) 275, 197-208.

Dimbleby, G.W. 1978 'Changes in ecosystems through forest clearance', in Hawkes, J.G. (ed.) *Conservation and Agriculture*. London, 3-16.

Dimbleby, G.W. and Bradley, R.J. 1975 'Evidence of pedogenesis from a neolithic site at Rackham, Sussex', *J. Archaeol. Sci.* 2, 179-86.

Dimbleby, G.W. and Evans, J.G. 1974 'Pollen and land-snail analysis of calcareous soils', *J. Archaeol. Sci.* 1, 117-33.

Donaldson, A.M. and Turner, J. 1977 'A pollen diagram from Hallowell Moss, near Durham City', *J. Biogeogr.* 4, 25-33.

Donner, J.J. 1957 'The geology and vegetation of the late-glacial retreat stages in Scotland', *Trans. Roy. Soc. Edinb.* 63, 221-64.

Donner, J.J. 1962 'On the post-glacial history of the Grampian Highlands of Scotland', *Commentat. Biol.* 24, 1-29.

Drake, R.E. *et al.* 1980 'KBS Tuff dating and geochronology of tuffaceous sediments in the Koobi flora and Shungura Formation, East Africa', *Nature* (London) 283, 368-72.

Drewett, P. *et al.* 1975 'The excavation of an oval burial mound of the third millenium bc at Alfriston, East Sussex, 1974', *Proc. Prehist. Soc.* 41, 119-52.

Drewett, P. *et al.* 1977 'The excavation of a Neolithic causewayed enclosure on Offham Hill, East Sussex 1976', *Proc. Prehist. Soc.* 43, 201-42.

Du Saar, A. 1978 'Diatom investigations of a sediment core. Downholland Moss – 15', in Tooley, M.J. 1978a, *Sea-level Changes in North-west England during the Flandrian Stage*. Oxford.

Duffey, E.A.J. 1968 'The status of *Cerambyx* L. (Col., Cerambycidae) in Britain', *Entomol. Gaz.* 19, 164-6.

Dunning, G.C. 1976 'Salmondsbury, Bourton-on-the-Water', in D.W. Harding (ed.), *Hillforts*. London.

Durno, S.E. 1958 'Pollen analysis of peat deposits in eastern Sutherland and Caithness', *Scott. Geog. Mag.* 74, 127-35.

Durno, S.E. 1959 'Pollen analysis of peat deposits in the eastern Grampians', *Scott. Geog. Mag.* 75, 102-11.

Durno, S.E. and McVean, D.N. 1959 'Forest history of the Beinn Eighe Nature Reserve', *New Phytol.* 58, 228-36.

Durno, S.E. and Romans, J.C.C. 1969 'Evidence for variations in the altitudinal zonation of climate in Scotland and northern England since the Boreal period', *Scott. Geog. Mag.* 85, 31-3.

Dyer, J.R. 1964 'A secondary Neolithic camp at Waulud's Bank, Leagrave', *Bedford Archaeol. J.* 2, 15.

Emiliani, C. 1964 'Palaeotemperature analysis of the Caribbean cores A254-BR-C and CP-28', *Bull. Geol. Soc. Am.* 75, 129-44.

Emiliani, C. 1968 'The Pleistocene epoch and the evolution of Man', *Current Anthropology* 9 (1), 27-30

Epstein, S. *et al.* 1970 'Antarctic ice sheet: stable isotope analyses of Byrd Station Cores and interhemispheric climatic implications', *Science* (N.Y.) 168, 1570-2.

Erdtman, G. 1924 'Studies in the Micropalaeontology of postglacial deposits in northern Scotland and the Scotch Isles, with especial reference to the history of the woodlands', *Proc. Linn. Soc.* 46, 449-504.

Erdtman, G. 1928 'Studies in the post-arctic history of the forests of North Western Europe. I. Investigations in the British Isles', *Geol. För. Stockh. Förh.* 50 (2.373), 123-92.

Eronen, M. 1974 'The history of the Litorina Sea and associated Holocene events', *Comm. Physico-Mathematicae* 44(4), 79-188.

Evans, A.M. and Davies, J.W. 1972 'Appendix II: Report on the examination of pottery sherds from Broome Heath, Ditchingham, Norfolk,' in Wainwright, G.J. 'The excavation of a Neolithic settlement on Broome Heath, Ditchingham, Norfolk', *Proc. Prehist. Soc.* 38, 1-97.

Evans, E.E. 1975 'Highland landscapes: habitat and heritage', in Evans, J.G. *et al.* (eds), *The Effect of Man on the Landscape: the Highland Zone.* CBA Research Report No. 11, 1-5.

Evans, J.G. 1966 'Late-glacial and post-glacial subaerial deposits at Pitstone, Buckinghamshire', *Proc. Geol. Ass.* 77, 347-64.

Evans, J.G. 1969 'The exploitation of molluscs', in Ucko, P.J. and Dimbleby, G.W. (eds), *The Domestication and Exploitation of Plants and Animals.* London, 477-84.

Evans, J.G. 1971 'Habitat changes on the calcareous soils of Britain: the impact of Neolithic man', in Simpson, D.D.A. (ed.), *Economy and Settlement in Neolithic and Early Bronze Age Britain and Europe.* Leicester, 27-73.

Evans, J.G. 1972 *Land Snails in Archaeology.* London.

Evans, J.G. 1975 *The Environment of Early Man in the British Isles.* London.

Evans, P. 1971 'The Phanerozoic time-scale. A supplement. Part 2. Towards a Pleistocene time-scale', *Special Publication* 5, Geol. Soc. London.

Everton, R.F. 1975 'A *Bos primigenius* from Charterhouse Warren Farm, Blagdon, Mendip', *Proc. Univ. Bristol Spelaeol. Soc.* 14 (1), 75-82.

Ewbank, J.M. 1964 'Animal bones', in Field, N.H. *et al.* 'New Neolithic sites in Dorset and Bedfordshire', *Proc. Prehist. Soc.* 30, 364-6.

Faegri, K. 1940 'Quatärgeologische untersuchungen im Westlichen Norwegen. II. Zur spätquatären geschichte Jaerens', *Bergens Mus. Arb. Naturvit. rekke* No. 7, 1-201.

Faegri, K. and Iversen, J. 1964 *Textbook of Pollen Analysis.* New York.

Fairbridge, R.W. and Hillaire-Marcel, C. 1977 'An 8000 yr palaeoclimatic record of the "Double-Hale" 45 yr solar cycle', *Nature* (London) 268, 413-16.

Fitch, F.J. and Miller, J.A. 1970 'Radioisotopic age determination of Lake Rudolf artifact site', *Nature* (London) 226, 226-8.

Fleming, A. 1971 'Bronze Age agriculture on the marginal lands of north-east Yorkshire', *Agric. Hist. Rev.* 19, 1-24.

Florin, S. *et al.* 1958 *Vråkulturen. Stenåldersboplatserna vid Mogetorp, Östra vrå och Brokvarn.* Stockholm: Kungl. Vitterhets Historie och Antikvitets Akademien.

Fowler, P.J. 1978 'Pre-Medieval fields in the Bristol region', *Brit. Arch. Reps.* 48, 29-47.

Fowler, P.J. and Evans, J.G. 1967 'Plough marks, lynchets and early fields', *Antiquity* 41, 289-91.

Francis, E.A. 1975 'Glacial sediments: a selective review', in Wright, A.E. and Moseley, F. (eds) *Ice Ages: ancient and modern.* Geological Journal Special Issue No. 6, 43-68.

Fraser, F.C. and King, J.E. 1954 'Faunal Remains', in Clark, J.G.D. (ed.), *Excavations at Star Carr.* Cambridge, 70-95.

Frenzel, B. 1966 'Climatic change in the Atlantic/Sub-Boreal transition on the Northern Hemisphere: botanical evidence', in Sawyer, J.S. *et al.* (eds), *World Climate from 8,000 to 0 BC.* London, 99-123.

Fries, M. 1965 'Outlines of the late-glacial and post-glacial vegetational and climatic history of Sweden, illustrated by three generalized pollen diagrams', in Wright Jr, H.E. and Frey, D.G. (eds), *International Studies on the Quaternary* (Special Paper No. 84), Boulder, Colorado: Geological Society of America Inc., 55-64.

Gaunt, G.D. and Tooley, M.J. 1974 'Evidence for Flandrian sea-level changes in the Humber Estuary and adjacent areas', *Bull. Inst. Geol. Sci.* 48, 25-41.

Geyh, M.A. 1969 'Versuch einer chronologischen Gliederüng des marinen Holozans an der Nordseekuste mit Hilfe der Statistischen Auswertung von ¹⁴C-Daten', *Z. Deutsch. Geol. Ges.* 118, 351-60.

Ghazzawi, F.M. 1933 'The littoral diatoms of the Liverpool and Port Erin shores', *J. Mar. Biol. Assoc.* N.S. 1, 165-76.

Gibbard, P.L. and Stuart, A.J. 1975 'Flora and vertebrate fauna of the Barrington Beds', *Geol. Mag.* 112 (5), 493-501.

Gladfelter, B.G. 1972 'Cold climate features in the vicinity of Clacton-on-Sea, Essex (England)', *Quaternaria* 16, 121-35.

Goddard, A. 1971 *Studies of the vegetational changes associated with initiation of blanket peat accumulation in north-east Ireland.* Unpublished Ph.D. Thesis, Queen's University, Belfast.

Godfray, A. and Burdo, C. 1949-50 'Excavations at the Pinnacle', *Bull. Soc. Jersiaise* 15-16 (in Helbaek, H. 1963).

Godwin, H. 1933 'British Maglemosian harpoon sites', *Antiquity* 7, 36-48.

Godwin, H. 1934a 'Pollen analysis. An outline of the problems and potentialities of the method. Part I. Technique and interpretation', *New Phytol.* 33, 278-305.

Godwin, H. 1934b 'Pollen analysis. An outline of the problems and potentialities of the method. Part II. General applications of pollen analysis', *New Phytol.* 35, 325-58.

Godwin, H. 1940a 'Pollen analysis and forest history of England and Wales', *New Phytol.* 39, 370-400.

Godwin, H. 1940b 'Studies in the post-glacial history of British vegetation.

III. Fenland pollen diagrams. IV. Post-glacial changes of relative land-and sea-level in the English Fenland', *Phil. Trans. R. Soc. Lond.* (B) 230, 239-303.

Godwin, H. 1943 'Coastal peat beds of the British Isles and North Sea', *J. Ecol.* 31, 199-247.

Godwin, H. 1944 'Age and origin of the "Breckland" heaths of East Anglia', *Nature* (London) 154, 6-10.

Godwin, H. 1948 'Studies in the post-glacial history of British vegetation. X. Correlations between climate, forest composition, prehistoric agriculture and peat stratigraphy in Sub-Boreal and Sub-Atlantic peats of the Somerset levels', *Phil. Trans. R. Soc. Lond.* (B) 233, 275-86.

Godwin, H. 1954 'Recurrence surfaces', *Danm. Geol. Unders.* RII (80), 22-30.

Godwin, H. 1955 'Studies in the post-glacial history of British vegetation. XII. The Meare Pool region of the Somerset Levels', *Phil. Trans. R. Soc. Lond.* (B) 239, 161-90.

Godwin, H. 1956 *The History of the British Flora: a factual basis for phytogeography.* Cambridge.

Godwin, H. 1960a 'Prehistoric wooden trackways of the Somerset Levels: their construction, age and relation to climatic change', *Proc. Prehist. Soc.* 26, 1-36.

Godwin, H. 1960b 'The Croonian Lecture. Radiocarbon dating and Quaternary history in Britain', *Proc. R. Soc. Lond.* (B) 153 (952), 287-320.

Godwin, H. 1962a 'Vegetational history of the Kentish chalk downs as seen at Wingham and Frogholt', *Veröff. Geobot. Inst.* Zurich 37, 83-99.

Godwin, H. 1962b 'Half-life of Radiocarbon', *Nature* (London) 195, 984.

Godwin, H. 1967 'The ancient cultivation of Hemp', *Antiquity* 41, 42-50, 137-8.

Godwin, H. 1968 'Studies in the post-glacial history of British vegetation. XV. Organic deposits of Old Buckenham Mere, Norfolk', *New Phytol.* 67, 95-107.

Godwin, H. 1970 'The contribution of radiocarbon dating to archaeology in Britain', *Phil. Trans. R. Soc. Lond.* (A), 269, 57-75.

Godwin, H. 1975 *The History of the British Flora.* Cambridge. (2nd ed.).

Godwin, H. and Clifford, M.H. 1938 'Studies in the post-glacial history of British vegetation. I. Origin and stratigraphy of Fenland deposits near Woodwalton, Hunts. II. Origin and stratigraphy of deposits in Southern Fenland', *Phil. Trans. R. Soc. Lond.* (B) 229, 323-406.

Godwin, H. and Godwin, M.E. 1933 'Pollen analysis of Fenland peats at St. German's, near King's Lynn. *Geol. Mag.* 70 (826), 168-80.

Godwin, H. and Godwin, M.E. 1934 'Pollen analysis of peats at Scolt Head Island, Norfolk', in Steers, J.A. (ed.) 1934, *Scolt Head Island: the story of its origin, the plant and animal life of the dunes and marshes.* Cambridge, 64-76.

Godwin, H. and Switsur, V.R. 1966 'Cambridge University natural radiocarbon measurements VIII', *Radiocarbon* 8, 390-400.

Godwin, H. and Tallantire, P.A. 1951 'Studies in the post-glacial history of British vegetation. XII. Hockham Mere, Norfolk', *J. Ecol.* 39, 285-307.

Godwin, H. and Willis, E.H. 1959 'Cambridge University natural radio-carbon measurements I', *Am. J. Sci. Radiocarbon Supplement* 1, 63-75.

Godwin, H. and Willis, E.H. 1960 'Cambridge University natural radiocarbon measurements II', *Radiocarbon* 2, 62-72.

Godwin, H. and Willis, E.H. 1962 'Cambridge University natural radiocarbon measurements V', *Radiocarbon* 4, 57-70.

Godwin, H. and Willis, E.H. 1966 'Cambridge University natural radiocarbon measurements VIII', *Radiocarbon* 8, 390-400.

Godwin, H. *et al.* 1957 'Radiocarbon dating and post-glacial vegetational history: Scaleby Moss', *Proc. R. Soc. Lond.* (B) 147, 352-66.

Godwin, H. *et al.* 1965 'Cambridge University natural radiocarbon measurements VII', *Radiocarbon* 7, 205-12.

Gordon, A.D. and Birks, H.J.B. 1972 'Numerical methods in Quaternary palaeoecology. I Zonation of pollen diagrams', *New Phytol.* 71, 961-79.

Gordon, A.D. and Birks, H.J.B. 1974 'Numerical methods in Quaternary palaeoecology. II. Comparison of pollen diagrams', *New Phytol.* 73, 221-49.

Grahame, T. 1954 'The animal bones from the Neolithic settlement site', in Stone, J.F.S. *et al.* 'Durrington Walls', *Wiltshire. Antiq. J.* 34, 175-7.

Granlund, E. 1932 'De Svenska hogmössarnas geologi', *Sver. Geol. Unders. Afh.* Ser C, 26, No. 373, 1-193.

Gray, J. 1965 'Extraction techniques. Pt. III. Techniques in palynology' in Kummel, B. and Raup, D. (eds), *Handbook of Paleontological Techniques.* London, 530-87.

Grigson, C. 1965 'Faunal remains: measurements of bones, horncores, antlers and teeth', in Smith, I.F. *Windmill Hill and Avebury: Excavations by Alexander Keiller 1925-39*, Oxford, 145-67, and plates IX, X and XI.

Grigson, C. 1966 'Animal remains from Fussell's Lodge long barrow, including a possible ox-hide burial, with discussion on the presence of the horse in Neolithic Britain', in Ashbee, P. 'The Fussell's Lodge long barrow excavations 1957', *Archaeologia* 100, 63-73, and plate XX.

Grigson, C. 1969 'The uses and limitations of differences in absolute size in the distinction between the bones of the aurochs (*Bos primigenius*) and domestic cattle (*Bos taurus*)', in Ucko, P.J. and Dimbleby, G.W. (eds), *The Domestication and Exploitation of Plants and Animals.* London, 277-94.

Grigson, C. 1976 'The animal bones from Neolithic pit 6 Puddlehill', in Matthews, C.L., 'Occupation sites on a Chiltern range. Part 1 Neolithic, Bronze Age, and Early Iron Age', *Brit. Arch. Rep.* 29, 11-18.

Grigson, C. 1978 'The late glacial and early Flandrian ungulates of England and Wales – an interim review', in Limbrey, S. and Evans, J.G. (eds), *The Effect of Man on the Landscape: the Lowland Zone.* C.B.A. Research Report No. 21, 46-56.

Grigson, C. (forthcoming) 'The domestic animals of the earlier Neolithic in Britain', in Nobis, G. (ed.), *Die Anfänge des Neolithikums vom Orient bis Nordeuropas.* Cologne.

Grootes, P.M. 1978 'Carbon-14 time scale extended: comparison of chronologies', *Science* (N.Y.) 200, 11-15.

Hageman, B.P. 1969 'Development of the western part of the Netherlands during the Holocene', *Geologie Mijnb.* 48 (4), 373-88.

Hallam, J.S. *et al.* 1973 'A Late Glacial elk with associated barbed points from High Furlong, Lancashire', *Proc. Prehist. Soc.* 39, 100-28.

Hammen, T. van der 1957 'The age of the Usselo culture', *Geol. Mijnb.* 19, 396-7.

Harcourt, R.A. 1971a 'Animal bones from Durrington Walls', in Wainwright, G.J. and Longworth, I. 'Durrington Walls 1966-8'. *Rep. Res. Comm. Soc. Antiq. London* 29, 338-50.

Harcourt, R.A. 1971b 'Animal bones from Marden', in Wainwright, G.J. *et al.* 'The excavation of a late Neolithic enclosure at Marden, Wiltshire', *Antiq. J.* 51, 234-5.

Harcourt, R.A. 1974 'The dog in prehistoric and early historic Britain', *J. Archaeol. Sci.* 1, 151-75.

Harcourt, R.A. (forthcoming) 'The animal bones', in Wainwright, G.J. 'Mount Pleasant Excavations 1970-71', *Research Rep. Soc. Antiquaries.*

Harding, D.W. 1976 *Hillforts.* London.

Havinga, A.J. 1963 'A palynological investigation of soil profiles developed in cover sand', *Meded. Landboogesch, Wageningen* 63, 1-92.

Haworth, E.Y. 1969 'The diatoms of a sediment core from Blea Tarn, Langdale'. *J. Ecol* 57(2), 429-39.

Hawkins, A.B. 1971 'The Late Weichselian and Flandrian transgressions of south-west Britain', *Quaternaria* 14, 115-30.

Haworth, E.Y. 1976 'The changes in the composition of the diatom assemblages found in the surface sediments of Blelham Tarn in the English Lake District during 1973', *Ann. Bot.* 40, 1195-205.

Heim, J. 1962 'Recherches sur les relations entre la végétation actuelle et le spectre pollinique récent dans les Ardennes Belges', *Bull. Soc. Roy. Bot. Belgique* 96, 5-92.

Helbaek, H. 1952 'Early crops in southern England', *Proc. Prehist. Soc.* 18, 194-233.

Helbaek, H. 1963 'Late Cypriote vegetable diet at Apliki', *Skrifter Utgivna av Svenska Institutet i Athen* 4, 8, 171-86.

Helbaek, H. 1964 'The Isca grain, a Roman plant introduction in Britain', *New Phytol.* 63, 158-64.

Hendey, N.I. 1964 *An Introductory Account of the Smaller Algae of British Coastal Waters. Part V. Bacillariophyceae (Diatoms).* London.

Henshall, A.S. 1963 *The Chambered Tombs of Scotland,* vol. 1. Edinburgh.

Herity, M. 1971 'Prehistoric fields in Ireland', *Irish Univ. Rev.* 1, 258-65.

Heybroek, H.M. 1963 'Diseases and lopping for fodder as possible causes of a prehistoric decline of *Ulmus*', *Acta Bot. Neerl.* 12, 1-11.

Hibbert, F.A. (in press) 'The use of absolute pollen analysis in determining the activities of prehistoric man in the Somerset Levels (England)', *Proc. IVth Int. Palyn. Conf.*

Hibbert, F.A. and Switsur, V.R. 1976 'Radiocarbon dating of Flandrian pollen zones in Wales and northern England', *New Phytol.* 77, 793-807.

Hibbert, F.A. *et al.* 1971 'Radiocarbon dating of Flandrian pollen zones at Red Moss, Lancs', *Proc. R. Soc. Lond.* (B) 177, 161-76.

Hicks, S.P. 1971 'Pollen-analytical evidence for the effect of prehistoric agriculture on the vegetation of North Derbyshire', *New Phytol.* 70, 647-68.

Hijszeler, C.C.W.J. 1957 'Late-glacial human cultures in the Netherlands', *Geol. Mijnb.* 19, 288-302.

Hillman, G.C. (in press) 'Grain processing at 3rd Century Wilderspool', in Hinchliffe, J. and Williams, J.H. (eds), *Excavations at Wilderspool*, H.M.S.O. Monograph.

Hillman, G.C. (forthcoming, a) 'Alternative criteria in chaff identifications: an example from the Mycenae remains', *J. Arch. Sci.*

Hillman, G.C. (forthcoming, b) 'Rachis remains and the identification of free-threshing wheats', *J. Arch. Sci.*

Hjelmqvist, H. 1975 'Getreidearten und andere Nutzpflanzen aus der frühneolitisch Zeit von Langeland', in Skaarup, J. *Stengade: Ein langeländischer Wohnplatz mit Hausresten aus der frühneolitischen Zeit*, Rudkøbing: Meddelelser fra Langelands Museum.

Hofmann, E. 1908 *The Young Beetle-Collector's Handbook*. London.

Hollin, J.T. 1977 'Thames interglacial sites, Ipswichian sea levels and Antarctic ice surges', *Boreas* 6, 33-52.

Hopf, M. 1968 'Früchte und Samen', in Zürn, H. 'Das jungsteinzeitliche Dorf Ehrenstein (Kreis Ulm)', *Veroff. Staatl. Amt f. Denkmalpflege Stuttgart*, Reihe A. (H), 10, 7-77.

Hopf, M. and Zohary, D. 1973 'Domestication of pulses in the Old World', *Science* (N.Y.) 182, 887-94.

Howard, M.M. 1964 'Animal bones', in Thomas, N. 'The Neolithic causewayed camp at Robin Hood's Ball, Shrewton', *Wilts. Archaeol. Nat. Hist. Mag.* 59, 20-2.

Huckerby, E. and Oldfield, F. 1976 'The Quaternary vegetational history of the French Pays Basque', *New Phytol.* 77, 499-526.

Huddart, D. *et al.* 1977 'The coasts of north-west England', in, Kidson, C. and Tooley, M.J. (eds), *The Quaternary History of the Irish Sea*. Geological Journal Special Issue No. 7. Liverpool, 119-54.

Hustedt. F. 1927-62 *Die Kieselalgen. Deutschlands, Österreichs und der Schweiz unter Berücksichtigung der übrigen Länder Europas sowie der angrenzenden Meeresgebiete*. Akademische Verlagsgesellschaft. Leipzig.

Hustedt, F. and Aleem, A.A. 1951 'Littoral diatoms from the Salstone, near Plymouth, *J. Mar. Biol. Assoc.* 30, 177-96.

Hyde, H.A. 1950a 'Studies in atmospheric pollen. IV. Pollen deposition in Great Britain in 1943. Part I. The influence of situation and weather'. *New Phytol.* 49, 398-406.

Hyde, H.A. 1950b 'Studies in atmospheric pollen. IV. Pollen deposition in Great Britain, 1943. Part II. The composition of the pollen catch', *New Phytol.* 49, 407-20.

Hyde, H.A. 1951 'Studies in atmospheric pollen. V. A daily census of pollens at Cardiff for the six years 1943-8', *New Phytol.* 51, 281-93.

Hyde, H.A. 1955 'A census of atmospheric pollen and its possible applications', *Proc. Linn. Soc.* 165(2), 107-12.

Hyde, H.A. 1963 'Pollen-fall as a means of seed prediction in certain trees', *Grana Palynologica* 4 (2), 217-30.

Hyde, H.A. and Williams, D.A. 1944 'Studies in Atmospheric Pollen. I. A daily census of pollens at Cardiff', *New Phytol.* 43, 49-61.

Hyde, H.A. and Williams, D.A. 1945 'Studies in atmospheric pollen. II. Diurnal variations in the incidence of grass pollen', *New Phytol.* 44, 83-94.

Irvine, G. 1959-60 'Report on bones and teeth found at Sant-y-nyll Site'. *Trans. Cardiff. Nat. Soc.* 89, 26-9.

Iversen, J. 1937 'Undersögelser over Litorinatrangressione i Danmark', *Medr. Dansk. Geol. Forenen.* 9, 223-32.

Iversen, J. 1941 'Landnam i Danmarks Stenalder', *Danm. Geol. Unders.* Ser. 4, 66, 20-68.

Iversen, J. 1944 '*Viscum, Hedera* and *Ilex* as climate indicators', *Geol. För. Stockh. Förh.* 66, 463-83.

Iversen, J. 1949 'The influence of prehistoric man on vegetation', *Danm. Geol. Unders.* Ser. 4, 3(6), 1-25.

Iversen, J. 1956 'Forest clearance in the Stone Age', *Scient. Am.* 194, 36-41.

Iversen, J. 1958 'The bearing of glacial and interglacial epochs on the formation and extinction of plant taxa', in Hedberg, O. (ed.) 1958, *Systematics of Today* Uppsala Univ. Arsskr. 158 (6), 210-15.

Iversen, J. 1969 'Retrogressive development of a forest ecosystem demonstrated by pollen diagrams from a fossil mor', *Oikos Suppl.* 12, 35-49.

Iversen, J. 1973 'The development of Denmark's nature since the last Glacial', *Danm. Geol. Unders.* Ser. 5, No. 7-C, 1-126.

Jackson, J.W. 1915 'Note on the vertebrate and molluscan remains from Dyserth Castle', *Archaeologia Cambrensis* 70, 77-82.

Jackson, J.W. 1931a 'Animal bones', in Stone, J.F.S. 'A settlement of the Beaker period on Easton Down, Winterslow, S. Wilts', *Wilts. Archaeol. Nat. Hist. Mag.* 45, 368-9.

Jackson, J.W. 1931b 'Report on the animal remains from the Sanctuary. *Wilts. Archaeol. Nat. Hist. Mag.* 45, 330-2.

Jackson, J.W. 1933 'Animal remains', in Clark, G. 'Report on an early Bronze Age site in the south-eastern fens', *Antiq. J.* 13, 278.

Jackson, J.W. 1934 'Report on the animal remains', in Curwen, E.C. 'Excavations in Whitehawk Neolithic camp, Brighton 1932-3', *Antiq. J.* 14, 127-9.

Jackson, J.W. 1935a 'Report on the animal remains from Pit 5', in Stone, J.F.S., 'Some discoveries at Ratfyn, Amesbury', *Wilts. Archaeol. Nat. Hist. Mag.* 47, 66-7.

Jackson, J.W. 1935b 'Report on the skeleton of a small ox of Beaker age from Giants Hills', *Archaeologia* 85, 96-8.

Jackson, J.W. 1935c 'The animal remains from the Stonehenge excavations of 1920-26', *Antiq. J.* 15, 430-40.

Jackson, J.W. 1935d 'Report on the skeleton of the dog from Ash Pit C', in Stone, J.F.S., 'Excavations at Easton Down, Winterslow', *Wilts. Archaeol. Nat. Hist. Mag.* 47, 76-8.

Jackson, J.W. 1943 'Animal bones', in Wheeler, R.E.M., *Maiden Castle, Dorset.* London, Society of Antiquaries, 360-7.

Jackson, J.W. 1948 'Report on animal bones', in Stone, J.F.S. and Young,

W.E.V. 'Two pits of grooved ware date near Woodhenge', *Wilts. Archaeol. Nat. Hist. Mag.* 52, 300-1.

Jackson, J.W. 1952 'Report on skull of Ox', in Piggott, S. 'The Neolithic camp on Whitesheet Hill, Kilmington Parish', *Wilts. Archaeol. Nat. Hist. Mag.* 54, 409-10.

Jacobi, R.M. 1973 'Aspects of the "Mesolithic Age" in Great Britain', in Kozlowski, S.K. (ed.), *The Mesolithic in Europe.* Warsaw, 237-65.

Jacobi, R.M. 1976 'Britain inside and outside Mesolithic Europe', *Proc. Prehist. Soc.* 42, 67-84.

Jacobi, R.M. *et al.* 1976 'The southern Pennine Mesolithic and the ecological record', *J. Archaeol. Sci.* 3, 307-20.

Jarman, M.R. 1972 'European deer economies and the advent of the Neolithic', in, Higgs, E.S. (ed.) *Papers in Economic Prehistory.* Cambridge, 125-47.

Jarman, M.R. *et al.* 1968 'Animal remains', in Stead, I.M. 'An Iron Age Hill Fort at Grimthorpe, Yorkshire, England', *Proc. Prehist. Soc.* 34, 182-9.

Jelgersma, S. 1961 'Holocene sea-level changes in the Netherlands', *Med. van de Geologishe Stichting* C6, 7. 1-100.

Jelgersma, S. 1966 'Sea level changes during the last 10,000 years', in Sawyer, J.S. *et al.* (eds), *World Climate from 8,000-0 BC.* London, 54-71.

Jelgersma, S. *et al.* 1970 'The coastal dunes of the western Netherlands: geology, vegetational history and archaeology', *Meded. Rijks Geol. Dienst.* NS. 21, 93-167.

Jenny, H. 1941 *Factors of Soil Formation.* New York.

Jessen, K. 1949 'Studies in late Quaternary deposits and flora history of Ireland', *Proc. Roy. Irish Acad.* 52B, 85-290.

Jessen, K. and Helbaek, H. 1944 'Cereals in Great Britain and Ireland in prehistoric and early historic time', *Kong. Danske Vidensk. Selsk.* 3 (2) 1-68.

Jessen, K. and Milthers, V. 1928 'Stratigraphical and palaeonotological studies of interglacial fresh-water deposits in Jutland and north-west Germany', *Danm. Geol. Unders.* II. 48, 1-379.

Jewell, P.A. 1962 'Changes in size and type of cattle from prehistoric to mediaeval times in Britain', *Z. Tierzücht. Zücht Biol.* 77 (2), 159-67.

Jewell, P.A. 1963 'Cattle from British archaeological sites', in Mourant, A.E. and Zeuner, F.E. (eds), *Man and Cattle.* Royal Anthropological Institute, London, 80-100.

Jochim, M. 1976 *Hunter-Gatherer Subsistence and Settlement, a Predictive Model,* London.

Johnsen, S.J. *et al.* 1972 'Oxygen isotope profiles through the Antarctic and Greenland ice sheets', *Nature* (London) 235, 429-34.

Johnson, G.A.L. and Dunham, K.C. 1962 *The Geology of Moor House.* Monographs of the Nature Conservancy, No. 2, H.M.S.O.

Jonassen, H. 1950 'Recent pollen sedimentation and Jutland Heath diagrams', *Dansk Botanisk Arkiv.* 13(7), 1-51.

Jones, R.L. 1971 *A contribution to the late Quaternary ecological history of Cleveland, north-east Yorkshire.* Unpublished Ph.D. Thesis, University of Durham.

Jones, R.L. 1976 'The activities of Mesolithic man: further palaeobotanical evidence for north-east Yorkshire', in Davidson, D.A. and Shackley, M.L. (eds), *Geo-archaeology: earth science and the past*. London, 355-67.

Jope, M. 1965 'Faunal remains: frequencies of ages and species', in Smith, I.F. (ed.), *Windmill Hill and Avebury: Excavations by Alexander Keiller 1925-39*. Oxford, 142-5.

Jope, M. and Grigson, C. 1965 'Faunal remains', in Smith, I.F. (ed.), *Windmill Hill and Avebury: Excavations by Alexander Keiller 1925-39*. Oxford, 141-67.

Jørgensen, S. 1963 'Early Postglacial in Aamosen: geological and pollen-analytical investigations of Maglemosian settlements in the West Zealand Bog Aamosen', *Danm. Geol. Unders*. II. 87, 1-79.

Jowsey, P.C. 1966 'An improved peat sampler', *New Phytol*. 65, 245-8.

Kellaway, G.A. *et al*. 1975 'The Quaternary history of the English Channel', *Phil. Trans. R. Soc. Lond*. (A) 279, 189-218.

Kennard, A.S. 1944 'The Crayford Brickearths', *Proc. Geol. Ass*. 55, 121-69.

Kerney, M.P. 1963 'Late-glacial deposits on the Chalk of south-east England', *Phil. Trans. R. Soc. Lond*. (B) 246, 203-54.

Kerney, M.P. 1968 'Britain's fauna of land mollusca and its relation to the post-glacial thermal optimum', *Symp. Zool. Soc. London*. 22, 273-91.

Kerney, M.P. 1971 'Interglacial deposits in Barnfield Pit, Swanscombe, and their molluscan fauna', *J. Geol. Soc. London* 127, 69-93.

Kerney, M.P. 1977 'British Quaternary non-marine Mollusca: a brief review', in Shotton, F.W. (ed.), *British Quaternary Studies: recent advances*. Oxford, 31-42.

Kerney, M.P. *et al*. 1964 'The late-glacial and post-glacial history of the chalk escarpment near Brook, Kent', *Phil. Trans. R. Soc. Lond*. (B) 248, 135-204.

King, J.E. 1962a 'Report on animal bones', in Wymer, J.J., 'Excavations at the Maglemosian sites at Thatcham, Berkshire, England', *Proc. Prehist. Soc*. 28, 329-61.

King, J.E. 1962b 'Report on animal bones', in Rahtz, P. 'Excavations at Shearplace Hill, Sydling St Nicholas, Dorset, England', *Proc. Prehist. Soc*. 28, 325.

Kirk, S.M. 1974 'High altitude cereal growing in County Down, Northern Ireland? A note', *Ulster J. Archaeol*. 36-37, 99-100.

Klikowska, M. 1959 'Odciski ziarn zbóz i innych gatunków traw na ulamkach naczyń z neolitycznego stanowiska kultury cerceraniki wstegowej w Strzelcach w pow. Mogileńskim', *Fontes Archaeologici Posnaniensis* 10, 101-5.

Klikowska, M. 1975 'Najstarsze zboza z wykopalisk polskich', *Archeologia Polski* 20, 83-143.

Knörzer, K.H. 1974 'Bandkeramischer Planzenfunde von Bedburg-Garsdorf, Kreis Bergheim/Erft', *Rheinische Ausgrabungen* 15, 173-92.

Kolp, O. 1976 'Submarine Uferterrasen der südlichen Ost- und Nordsee als Marken des Holozänen Meeransteigs und der Uberflutungsphasen der Ostsee', *Peterm. Geogr. Mitt*. 120, 1-23.

Kukla, G.J. 1977 'Pleistocene land-sea correlations. I. Europe', *Earth Sci. Rev*. 13, 307-74.

Kummel, B. and Raup, D. (eds) 1965 *Handbook of Paleontological Techniques*. London.

Lacaille, A.D. 1954 *The Stone Age in Scotland*. Oxford.

Lamb, H.H. 1963 'On the nature of certain climatic epochs which differed from the modern (1900-39) normal, *Proc. of the WMO/UNESCO Rome 1961 Symposium on Changes of Climate*. Paris, 125-50.

Lamb, H.H. 1964 'Trees and climatic history in Scotland', *Q. Jl. R. Met. Soc.* 90, 382-90.

Lamb, H.H. 1966 'Britain's climate in the past', in *The Changing Climate*, London, 170-95.

Lamb, H.H. 1977 *Climates: present, past and future*, vol. 2, London.

Lamb, H.H. *et al.* 1966 'Atmospheric circulation and the main climatic variables between 8,000 and 0BC: meteorological evidence', in Sawyer, J.S. *et al.* (eds) *World Climate from 8,000 to 0BC*. London, 174-217.

Laughlin, W.S. 1968 'An integrating biobehaviour system', in Lee, R.H. and De Vore, I. (eds), *Man the Hunter*. Chicago, 304-20.

Layard, N.F. 1903 'A recent discovery of Palaeolithic implements in Ipswich', *J. Roy. Anthrop. Inst.* 33, 41-3.

Layard, N.F. 1904 'Further excavations on a Palaeolithic site at Ipswich', *J. Roy. Anthrop. Inst.* 34, 306-10.

Layard, N.F. 1906 'A winter's work on the Ipswich Palaeolithic site', *J. Roy. Anthrop. Inst.* 36, 233-6.

Layard, N.F. 1920 'The Stoke Bone-bed, Ipswich', *Proc. Prehist. Soc. East Anglia*, 3 (2), 210-19.

Legge, A. (forthcoming) 'Grimes Graves; the agricultural economy', in Mercer, R.J., *The Excavation of a Flint Mine Shaft at Grimes Graves, Norfolk, England*. Society of Antiquaries, London.

Lewis, F.J. 1905 'The plant remains in the Scottish peat mosses. Part I. The Scottish Southern Uplands', *Trans. Roy. Soc. Edinb.* 41, 699-723.

Lewis, F.J. 1906 'The plant remains in the Scottish peat mosses. Part II. The Scottish Highlands', *Trans. Roy. Soc. Edinb.* 45, 335-60.

Lewis, F.J. 1907 'The plant remains in the Scottish peat mosses. Part III. The Scottish Highlands and the Shetland Islands', *Trans. Roy. Soc. Edinb.* 46, 33-70.

Lewis, F.J. 1911 'The plant remains in the Scottish peat mosses. Part IV. The Scottish Highlands and Shetland, with an appendix on the Icelandic peat deposits', *Trans. Roy. Soc. Edinb.* 47, 793-833.

Limbrey, S. 1975 *Soil Science and Archaeology*. London.

Lundqvist, G. 1962 'Geological radio-carbon datings from the Stockholm station', *Sveriges Geol. Undersok. Arsbok.* 56, Ser. C, No. 589, 8-12.

McAulay, I.R. and Watts, W.A. 1961 'Dublin Radiocarbon Dates 1', *Radiocarbon* 3, 26-38.

McBurney, C.B.M. 1965 'The Old Stone Age in Wales', in Foster, I. Ll. and Daniel, I.G. (eds), *Prehistoric and Early Wales*. London.

Mace, A. 1959 'An Upper Palaeolithic open-site at Hengistbury Head, Christchurch, Hants', *Proc. Prehist. Soc.* 25, 233-59.

McGrail, S. and Switsur, V.R. 1975 'Early British boats and their chronology', *Int. J. Nautical Archaeology and Underwater Exploration* 4, 191-200.

Mackereth, F.J.H. 1965 'Chemical investigation of lake sediments and their interpretation', *Proc. R. Soc. Lond.* (B) 161, 295-309.

Mackereth, F.J.H. 1966 'Some chemical observations on post-glacial lake sediments', *Phil. Trans. R. Soc. Lond.* (B) 250, 165-213.

McKerrell, H. 1975 'Correction procedures for C-14 dates', in Watkins, T. (ed.), *Radiocarbon Calibration and Prehistory.* Edinburgh, 47-100.

Maclean, K. and Rowley-Conway, P. (in press) 'Carbonised material from Bog Head, Focharbers'.

Manby, T.G. 1971 'The Kilham long barrow excavations 1965 to 1969', *Antiquity* 45, 50-3.

Mangerud, J. *et al.* 1974 'Quaternary stratigraphy of Norden, a proposal for terminology and classification', *Boreas* 3, 109-28.

Matthews, J. 1969 'The assessment of a method for the determination of absolute pollen frequencies', *New Phytol.* 68, 161-6.

Mellars, P.A. 1974 'The Palaeolithic and Mesolithic', in Renfrew, C. (ed.), *British Prehistory, a new outline.* London, 41-99.

Mellars, P.A. 1975 'Ungulate populations, economic patterns and the Mesolithic landscape', in Evans, J.G. *et al.* (eds), *The Effect of Man on the Landscape: the Highland Zone.* CBA Research Report, No. 11, 49-56.

Mellars, P.A. 1976 'Fire ecology, animal populations and man: a study of some ecological relationships in prehistory', *Proc. Prehist. Soc.* 42, 15-45.

Mellars, P.A. 1978 'Excavation and economic analysis of Mesolithic shell middens on the island of Oronsay (Inner Hebrides)', in Mellars, P.A. (ed.) *The Early Postglacial Settlement of Northern Europe.* London, 371-96.

Mercer, R.J. (in press) 'Excavations at the Neolithic settlement of Carn Brea, Redruth, Cornwall', *Cornish Archaeology.*

Merkt, J. and Streif, H. 1970 'Stechrohr-Bohrgeräte für limnische und marine Lockersedimente', *Geol. Jb.* 88, 137-48.

Merryfield, D.L. and Moore, P.D. 1974 'Prehistoric human activity and blanket peat initiation on Exmoor', *Nature* (London) 250, 439-41.

Michael, H.N. and Ralph, E.K. 1971 *Dating Techniques for the Archaeologist.* London.

Michels, J.W. 1973 *Dating Methods in Archaeology.* New York.

Miller, U. 1964 'Diatom floras in the Quaternary of the Göta river valley (western Sweden)', *Sver. Geol. Unders. Afh.* Ca. 44, 1-67.

Mitchell, G.F. 1940 'Studies in Irish Quaternary deposits: some lacustrine deposits near Dunshaughlin, County Meath', *Proc. R. Ir. Acad.* 46B, 13-37.

Mitchell, G.F. 1951 'Studies in Irish Quaternary deposits: No. 7', *Proc. R. Ir. Acad.* 53B, 111-206.

Mitchell, G.F. 1956 'Post-Boreal pollen diagrams from Irish raised bogs', *Proc. R. Ir. Acad.* 57B, 185-251.

Mitchell, G.F. 1965 'Littleton Bog, Tipperary: an Irish agricultural record', *J.R. Soc. Antiq. Ir.* 95, 121-32.

Mitchell, G.F. 1972 'Soil deterioration associated with prehistoric agriculture in Ireland', *24th Int. Geol. Cong. Symposium* 1. *Earth Sciences and the Quality of Life,* 59-68.

Mitchell, G.F. 1976 *The Irish Landscape*. London.
Mitchell, G.F. *et al.* 1973 'A correlation of Quaternary deposits in the British Isles', *Geol. Soc. London Special Report No. 4.*
Moir, J. Reid 1927 *The Antiquity of Man in East Anglia.* Cambridge.
Moir, J. Reid 1930 'Ancient Man in the Gipping-Orwell Valley, Suffolk', *Proc. Prehist. Soc. East Anglia* 6, 182-221.
Moir, J. Reid and Hopwood, A.T. 1939 'Excavations at Brundon, Suffolk (1935-7)', *Proc. Prehist. Soc. London* 5, 1-32.
Molleson, T. and Burleigh, R. 1978 'A new date for Goat's Hole Cave', *Antiquity.* 52 (205), 143-5.
Moore, P.D. 1968 'Human influence upon vegetational history in north Cardiganshire', *Nature* (London) 217, 1006-9.
Moore, P.D. 1973 'The influence of Prehistoric cultures upon the initiation and spread of blanket bog in upland Wales', *Nature* (London) 241, 350-3.
Moore, P.D. 1974 'Prehistoric human activity and blanket peat initiation on Exmoor', *Nature* (London) 250, 439-41.
Moore, P.D. 1975 'Origin of blanket mires', *Nature* (London) 256, 267-269.
Moore, P.D. (in press) 'Neolithic land use in mid-Wales', *Proc. IVth Int. Palyn. Conf.*
Moore, P.D. and Beckett, P.J. 1971 'Vegetation and development of Llyn, a Welsh mire', *Nature* (London) 231, 363-5.
Moore, P.D. and Chater, E.H. 1969 'Studies in the vegetational history of mid-Wales. I. The post-glacial period in Cardiganshire', *New Phytol.* 68, 183-96.
Morgan, A.V. 1973 'The Pleistocene geology and the area north and west of Wolverhampton, Staffordshire, England', *Phil. Trans. R. Soc. Lond.* (B) 265, 233-97.
Mörner, N.-A. 1969 'The Late Quaternary history of the Kattegatt Sea and the Swedish west coast', *Sver. Geol. Unders. Afh.* C. 640, 1-487.
Mörner, N.-A. 1976 'Eustatic changes during the last 8,000 years in view of radiocarbon calibration and new information from the Kattegatt region and other northwestern European coastal areas', *Palaeogr., Palaeoclimatol., Palaeoecol.* 19, 63-85.
Morrison, I.A. 1976 'Comparative stratigraphy and radiocarbon chronology of Holocene marine changes on the western seaboard of Europe', in Davidson, D.A. and Shackley, M.L. (eds), *Geoarchaeology: earth science and the past.* London, 159-73.
Morrison, M.E.S. 1959 'Evidence and interpretation of "Landnam" in the north-east of Ireland', *Botaniska Notiser* 112, 185-204.
Mortimer, J.R. 1905 *Forty Years' Researches in British and Saxon Burial Mounds of East Yorkshire.* London.
Murphy, P. 1978 'Some impressions of plant remains on prehistoric pottery from the Oxford region', in Whittle, A. (forthcoming monograph).
Murphy, P. (undated) 'Report on Neolithic plant remains identified from Spong Hill, North Elmham, Norfolk', to be published in *East Anglian Archaeology.*

Nilsson, T. 1935 'Die pollenanalytische Zonengliederung der spät- und post-glazialen Bildungen Schonens', *Geol. For. Stockh. Förh.* 57, 385-562.

Nilsson, T. 1948 'On the application of the Scanian post-glacial zone system to Danish pollen diagrams', *K. Danske Vidensk. Selsk. Biol. Skr.* 5(5), 1-53.

Nilsson, T. 1952 *Kompendium i kvartärpaleontologi och kvartäpaleontologiska Undersökningsmetoder.* Lunds Universitet.

Nilsson, T. 1964 'Standardpollendiagramme und C$^{14}$-Datierungen aus dem Ageröds Mosse im mittleren Schonen', *Lunds Univ. Årsskr.* NF 2, Bd. 59, Nr. 7, 1, 1-52.

Nordhagen, R. 1954 'Ethnobotanical studies on barkbread and the employment of wych-elm under natural husbandry'. *Danm. Geol. Unders.* Ser. 2, 80, 262-308.

Oakley, K.P. 1947 'Early Man in Hertfordshire', *Trans. Herts. Nat. Hist. Soc.* 22 (5), 247-56.

Oakley, K.P. 1968 'The date of the "Red Lady" of Paviland', *Antiquity* 42 (168), 306-7.

Oakley, K.P. 1971 'Radiocarbon Dating of Proto-Solutrean in Wales', *Nature* (London) 231, 112.

Oele, E. 1977 'The Holocene of the western Netherlands', in Paepe, R. (ed.), *Southern Shores of the North Sea,* X INQUA Congress, Guidebook for Excursion C17, 50-6. Norwich.

Oldfield, F. 1963 'Pollen analysis and man's role in the ecological history of the southeast Lake District', *Geogr. Annlr.* 54, 23-40.

Olsson, I.U. (ed.) 1970 *Radiocarbon Variations and Absolute Chronology.* Proc. 12th Nobel Symposium. Stockholm.

O'Riordain, A.B. 1967 'A prehistoric burial site at Gortnacargy, Co. Cavan.', *J. Soc. Antiq. Ireland* 97, 61-73.

Osborne, P.J. 1969 'An insect fauna of late Bronze Age date from Wilsford, Wiltshire', *J. Animal Ecol.* 38, 555-6.

Osborne, P.J. 1976 'Evidence from the insects of climatic variations during the Flandrian period: a preliminary note', *World Archaeology* 8, 150-8.

O'Sullivan, P.E. 1974 'Two Flandrian pollen diagrams from the east-central Highlands of Scotland', *Pollen Spores* 16, 33-57.

Paterson, T.T. and Tebbutt, C.F. 1947 'Studies in the Palaeolithic succession in England, No. III: palaeoliths from St Neots, Huntingdonshire', *Proc. Prehist. Soc.* 13, 1-36.

Pears, N.V. 1968 'Post-glacial tree-lines of the Cairngorm Mountains, Scotland', *Trans. Bot. Soc. Edinb.* 40, 361-94.

Pearson, G.W. and Pilcher, J.R. 1975 'Belfast radiocarbon dates VIII', *Radiocarbon* 17, 226-38.

Pearson, G.W. *et al.* 1977 'Absolute radiocarbon dating using a low altitude European tree-ring calibration', *Nature* (London) 270, 25-8.

Peck, R.M. 1973 'Pollen budget studies in a small Yorkshire catchment', in Birks, H.J.B. and West, R.G. (eds), *Quaternary Plant Ecology.* 14th Symposium of the British Ecological Society. Oxford, 43-60.

Pennington, W. 1943 'Lake sediments: the bottom deposits of the north basin of Windermere, with special reference to the diatom succession', *New Phytol.* 42 (1), 1-27.

Pennington, W. 1970 'Vegetation history in the north-west of England: a regional synthesis', in Walker, D. and West, R.G. (eds), *Studies in the Vegetational History of the British Isles: essays in honour of Harry Godwin.* Cambridge, 41-79.

Pennington, W. 1973a 'Absolute pollen frequencies in the sediments of lakes of different morphometry' in, Birks, H.J.B. and West, R.G. (eds), *Quaternary Plant Ecology.* 14th Symposium of the British Ecological Society. Oxford, 79-104.

Pennington, W. 1973b 'The recent sediments of Windermere', *Freshwat. Biol.* 3, 363-82.

Pennington, W. 1975a 'A chronostratigraphic comparison of Late-Weichselian and Late-Devensian subdivision, illustrated by two radiocarbon-dated profiles from western Britain', *Boreas* 4, 157-71.

Pennington, W. 1975b 'The effect of Neolithic man on the environment in north-west England: the use of absolute pollen diagrams', in Evans, J.G. *et al.* (eds), *The Effect of Man on the Landscape: the Highland Zone.* CBA Research Report No. 11, 74-86.

Pennington, W. and Lishman, J.P. 1971 'Iodine in lake sediments in northern England and Scotland', *Biol. Rev.* 46, 279-313.

Pennington, W. *et al.* 1972 'Lake sediments in northern Scotland', *Phil. Trans. R. Soc.* (B) 264, 191-294.

Percival, J. 1934 *Wheat in Great Britain.* Reading.

Pernetta, J.C. and Handford, P.T. 1970 'Mammalian and avian remains from possible Bronze Age deposits on Nornour, Isles of Scilly', *J. Zool. Lond.* 162, 534-40.

Phillipson, D.W. 1968 'Excavations at Eldon's Seat, Encombe, Dorset. Part III: Animal bones', *Proc. Prehist. Soc.* 34, 226-9.

Piggott, S. 1962 'Heads and hoofs', *Antiquity* 36, 110-8.

Pilcher, J.R. 1969 'Archaeology, palaeoecology and $^{14}$C dating of the Beaghmore stone circle site', *Ulster J. Archaeol.* 32, 73-91.

Pilcher, J.R. 1973 'Pollen analysis and radiocarbon dating of a peat on Slieve Gallion, Co. Tyrone, N. Ireland', *New Phytol.* 72, 681-9.

Pilcher, J.R. 1975 'Speculations on Neolithic land clearance', *Irish Archaeological Research Forum* 11(1), 1-6.

Pilcher, J.R. and Smith, A.G. 1979 'Palaeoecological investigations at Ballynagilly, a Neolithic and Bronze Age settlement in Co. Tyrone, N. Ireland, *Phil. Trans. R. Soc.* (B) 286, 345-69.

Pilcher, J.R. *et al.* 1971 'Land clearance in the Irish neolithic: new evidence and interpretation' *Science,* (N.Y.) 172, 560-2.

Pitt-Rivers, A.H.L.-F. 1898 'List of animal remains from the ditch of Wor Barrow, Handley Down', in *Excavations at Cranborne Chase* 4, 123-35 plus measurement charts. Privately printed.

Platt, M.I. 1932-3 'Report on the animal remains from Jarlshof, Sumburgh, Shetland', *Proc. Soc. Antiq. Scot.* 67, 127-36.

Platt, M.I. 1933-4 'Report on the animal remains from Jarlshof, Sumburgh Shetland', *Proc. Soc. Antiq. Scot.* 68, 313-9.

Platt, M.I. 1934 'Report on the animal remains', in Callender, J.G. 'A long stalled chamber cairn or mausoleum near Midhowe, Rousay, Orkney', *Proc. Soc. Antiq. Scot.* 68, 348-50.

von Post, L. 1916 'Forest tree pollen in south Swedish peat bog deposits',

Lecture to the 16th Convention of Scandinavian naturalists in Kristiana (Oslo) 1916. Translated by Davis, M.B. and Faegri, K. 1967 *Pollen Spores* 9 (3), 375-401.

von Post, L. 1946 'The prospect for pollen analysis in the study of the earth's climatic history', *New Phytol.* 45, 193-217.

von Post, L. and Granlund, E. 1926 'Sodra Sveriges Torvillgångar I', *Sver. Geol. Unders. Afh.* Serie C. 19 (335), 1-127.

Powell, T.G.E. *et al.* 1971 'Excavations in Zone VII peat at Storrs Moss, Lancashire, England, 1965-7', *Proc. Prehist. Soc.* 37, 112-37.

Praeger, R.L. 1888 'The estuarine clays at the new Alexandra dock, Belfast, with a list of fossils', *Proc. Belfast Nat. Field Club* Appendix II, 2, 29-51.

Praeger, R.L. 1896 'Report upon the raised beaches of the north-east of Ireland with special reference to their fauna', *Proc. Roy. Irish Acad.* 4, 30-54.

Price, D.G. and Tinsley, H.M. 1976 'On the significance of soil profiles at Trowlesworthy Warren and Wigford Down', *Rep. Trans. Devonshire Ass. Advmt. Sci.* 108, 147-57.

Proudfoot, V.B. 1958a 'Problems of soil history. Podzol development at Goodland and Torr Townlands, Co. Antrim, Northern Ireland', *J. Soil Sci.* 9, 186-98.

Proudfoot, V.B. 1958b 'Ancient Irish field systems', *Advancement of Science* 14, 369-71.

Pryor, F. 1974 'Fengate', *Current Archaeology* 4, 332-9.

Radley, J. *et al.* 1974 'The excavation of three "narrow blade" mesolithic sites in the southern Pennines, England', *Proc. Prehist. Soc.* 40, 1-19.

Rafter, T.A. 1975 'Radiometric dating – achievements and prospects in the Quaternary', in Suggate, R.P. and Cresswell, M.M. (eds), *Quaternary Studies*. The Royal Society of New Zealand. Bulletin 13, 45-52.

Raistrick, A. and Blackburn, K.B. 1931 'The late-glacial and post-glacial periods in the North Pennines (West Yorkshire and Durham). Part I. The glacial maximum and retreat. Part II. Possible glacial survivals in our flora', *Trans. North Nat. Union* 1 (1), 16-36.

Raistrick, A. and Blackburn, K.B. 1932 'The late-glacial and post-glacial periods in the North Pennines. Part III. The post-glacial peats', *Trans. North. Nat. Union* 1 (2), 79-103.

Ralph, E.K. and Michael, H.N. 1970 'MASCA radiocarbon dates from *Sequoia* and bristlecone pine samples', in Olsson, I.U. (ed.), *Radiocarbon Variations and Absolute Chronology*. Proc. 12th Nobel Symposium. Stockholm, 619-23.

Rankine, W.F. *et al.* 1960 'Further excavations at a mesolithic site at Oakhanger, Selborne, Hants', *Proc. Prehist. Soc.* 26, 246-62.

Reaney, D. 1968 'Beaker burials in south Derbyshire', *Derbyshire Arch. J.* 88, 67-81.

Renfrew, C. (ed.) 1974 *British Prehistory: a New Outline*. London.

Reid, C. 1896 'An early kitchen midden at Blashenwell', *Proc. Dorset Nat. Hist. Ant. Field Club* 17, 67-75.

Reid, C. 1899 *The Origin of the British Flora*. London.

Ritchie, J. 1920 *The Influence of Man on Animal Life in Scotland*. Cambridge.

Roberts, B.K. *et al.* 1973 'Recent forest history and land use in Weardale, Northern England', in Birks, H.J.B. and West, R.G. (eds), *Quaternary Plant Ecology*. 14th Symposium of the British Ecological Society. Oxford, 207-21.

Roe, D.A. 1964 'The British Lower and Middle Palaeolithic: some problems, methods of study and preliminary results'. *Proc. Prehist. Soc.* 30, 245-67.

Roe, D.A. 1968 'A Gazetteer of British Lower and Middle Palaeolithic sites', *Research Rep: Council for British Archaeology* 8, 1-355.

Roe, D.A. 1975 'Some Hampshire and Dorset hand-axes and the question of Early Acheulian in Britain', *Proc. Prehist. Soc.* 41, 1-9.

Romans, J.C.C. and Robertson, L. 1975 'Soils and archaeology in Scotland', in Evans, J.G. *et al.* (eds), *The Effect of Man on the Landscape: the Highland Zone*. CBA Research Report No. 11, 37-9.

Round, F.E. 1965 *The Biology of the Algae*. London.

Roux, I. and Leroi-Gourhan, A. 1965 'Les defrichements de la periode atlantique', *Bull. Soc. Prehist Fr.* 61, 309-15.

Ryder, M.L. 1969 'Changes in the fleece of sheep following domestication (with a note on the coat of cattle)', in Ucko, P.J. and Dimbleby, G.W., (eds), *The Domestication and Exploitation of Plants and Animals*. London, 495-521.


Salway, P. 1970 'The Roman Fenland', in Phillips, C.W. (ed.), *The Fenland in Roman Times*. Royal Geographical Society Research Series 5, 1-21.

Samuelsson, G. 1910 'Scottish peat mosses: a contribution to the knowledge of the Late-Quaternary vegetation and climate of northwestern Europe', *Bull. Geol. Instn. Univ. Uppsala* 10, 197-260.

Sawyer, J. *et al.* (eds) 1966 *World Climate from 8,000 to 0 BC*. London.

Scharff, R.F. 1907 *European Animals, their Geological History and Geographical Distribution*. London.

Schlichtherle, H. 1977 'Abdrüke in Hüttenlehm aus michelsberger Gruben bei Ammerbuch – Reusten, Kreis Tübingen', *Fundberichte aus Baden-Wurttemberg*, Band 3, 107-14.

Schofield, J.C. 1970 'Correlation between sea level and volcanic periodicities of the last millenium', *J. Geol. Geophys.* 13 (3), 737-41.

Seddon, B. 1967 'Prehistoric climate and agriculture: a review of recent palaeoecological investigations', in Taylor, J.A. (ed.), *Weather and Agriculture*. Oxford, 173-85.

Sernander, R. 1908 'On the evidence of postglacial changes of climate furnished by the peat-mosses of Northern Europe', *Geol. För. Stockh. Förh.* 30, 465-78.

Shackleton, N.J. 1977 'Oxygen isotope stratigraphy of the Middle Pleistocene', in Shotton, F.W. (ed.), *British Quaternary Studies: recent advances*. Oxford, 1-16.

Shackleton, N.J. and Opdyke, N.D. 1973 'Oxygen isotope and palaeo-magnetic stratigraphy of Equatorial Pacific Core V28-238: oxygen isotope temperatures and ice volumes on a $10^5$ year and $10^6$ year scale', *Quaternary Res.* 3, 39-55.

Shackley, M.L. 1973 'A contextual study of the Mousterian industry from Great Pan Farm, Newport, Isle of Wight', *Proc. Isle of Wight Nat. Hist. and Archaeol. Soc.* 6 (8), 542-54.

Shawcross, F.W. and Higgs, E.S. 1961 'The excavation of a *Bos primigenius* at Lowe's Farm, Littleport', *Proc. Camb. Antiq. Soc.* 54, 3-16.

Shotton, F.W. 1967a 'Age of the Irish Sea glaciation in the Midlands', *Nature* (London) 215, 1366.

Shotton, F.W. 1967b 'The problems and contributions of methods of absolute dating within the Pleistocene Period', *Q.J. Geol. Soc. Lond.* 122, 357-83.

Shotton, F.W. 1972 'An example of hard-water error in radiocarbon dating of vegetable matter', *Nature* (London) 240, 460-1.

Shotton, F.W. and Osborne, P.J. 1965 'The fauna of the Hoxnian Interglacial deposit of Nechells, Birmingham', *Phil. Trans. R. Soc. Lond.* (B) 248, 353-78.

Simmons, I.G. 1964 'Pollen diagrams from Dartmoor' *New Phytol.* 63, 165-80.

Simmons, I.G. 1969a 'Environment and early man on Dartmoor, Devon, England', *Proc. Prehist. Soc.* 35, 203-19.

Simmons, I.G. 1969b 'Pollen diagrams from the North York Moors', *New Phytol.* 68, 807-27.

Simmons, I.G. 1969c 'Evidence for vegetation changes associated with Mesolithic man in Britain', in Ucko, P.J. and Dimbleby, G.W. (eds), *The Domestication and Exploitation of Plants and Animals*. London, 111-19.

Simmons, I.G. 1975a 'Towards an ecology of mesolithic man in the uplands of Great Britain', *J. Archaeol. Sci.* 2, 1-15.

Simmons, I.G. 1975b 'The ecological setting of mesolithic man in the highland zone', in Evans, J.G. *et al.* (eds), *The Effect of Man on the Landscape: the Highland Zone*. CBA Research Report No. 11, 57-63.

Simmons, I.G. and Cundill, P.R. 1974a 'Late Quaternary vegetational history of the North York Moors. 1. Pollen analyses of blanket peats', *J. Biogeogr.* 1, 159-69.

Simmons, I.G. and Cundill, P.R. 1974b 'Late Quaternary vegetational history of the North York Moors. II. Pollen analyses of landslip bogs', *J. Biogeogr.* 1, 253-61.

Simmons, I.G. and Dimbleby, G.W. 1974 'The possible role of ivy (*Hedera helix* L.) in the mesolithic economy of Western Europe', *J. Archaeol. Sci.* 1, 291-6.

Simmons, I.G. *et al.* 1975 'Inorganic layers in soligenous mires of the North Yorkshire Moors', *J. Biogeogr.* 2, 49-56.

Sims, R.E. 1973 'The anthropogenic factor in East Anglian vegetational history: an approach using A.P.F. techniques', in Birks, H.J.B. and West, R.G. (eds), *Quaternary Plant Ecology*. 14th Symposium of the British Ecological Society. Oxford, 223-36.

Singer, R. *et al.* 1973 'Excavation of the Clactonian Industry at the Golf Course, Clacton-on-Sea, Essex', *Proc. Prehist. Soc.* 39, 6-74.

Singh, G. and Smith, A.G. 1973 'Post-glacial vegetational history and relative land- and sea-level changes in Lecale, Co. Down'. *Proc. R. Ir. Acad.* 73 (B1), 1-51.

Sissons, J.B. 1967 *The Evolution of Scotland's Scenery.* Edinburgh.

Smith, A.G. 1958a 'The context of some Late Bronze Age and Early Iron Age remains from Lincolnshire', *Proc. Prehist. Soc.* 24, 78-84.

Smith, A.G. 1958b 'Two lacustrine deposits in the south of the English Lake District', *New Phytol.* 57, 363-86.

Smith, A.G. 1958c 'Post-glacial deposits in south Yorkshire and north Lincolnshire', *New Phytol.* 57, 19-49.

Smith, A.G. 1958d 'Pollen analytical investigations of the mire at Fallahogy Td., Co. Derry', *Proc. R. Ir. Acad.* 59B, 329-43.

Smith, A.G. 1961 'The Atlantic/Sub-Boreal transition', *Proc. Linn. Soc. Lond.* 172, 38-49.

Smith, A.G. 1965 'Problems of inertia and threshold related to post-glacial habitat changes', *Proc. R. Soc. Lond.* (B) 161, 331-42.

Smith, A.G. 1970a 'The influence of Mesolithic and Neolithic man on British vegetation: a discussion', in Walker, D. and West, R.G. (eds), *Studies in the Vegetational History of the British Isles: essays in honour of Harry Godwin.* Cambridge, 81-96.

Smith, A.G. 1970b 'Late-glacial and post-glacial vegetational and climatic history of Ireland: a review', in Stephens, N. and Glasscock, R.E. (eds), *Irish Geographical Studies.* Department of Geography, The Queen's University Belfast, 65-88.

Smith, A.G. 1975 'Neolithic and Bronze Age landscape changes in Northern Ireland', in Evans, J.G. *et al.* (eds), *The Effect of Man on the Landscape: the Highland Zone.* C.B.A. Research Report No. 11, 64-74.

Smith, A.G. (in press) 'Palynology of a Mesolithic-Neolithic site in Co. Antrim, N. Ireland', *Proc. IVth Int. Palyn. Conf.*

Smith, A.G. and Collins, A.E.P. 1971 'The stratigraphy, palynology and archaeology of diatomite deposits at Newferry, Co. Antrim, Northern Ireland', *Ulster J. Archaeol.* 34, 3-25.

Smith, A.G. and Pilcher, J.R. 1973 'Radiocarbon dates and vegetational history of the British Isles', *New Phytol.* 72, 903-14.

Smith, A.G. and Willis, E.H. 1962 'Radiocarbon dating of the Fallahogy Landnam phase', *Ulster J. Archaeol.* 24-5, 16-24.

Smith, A.G. *et al.* 1971 'Belfast radiocarbon dates III', *Radiocarbon* 13, 103-25.

Smith, A.G. *et al.* 1973 'Belfast radiocarbon dates V', *Radiocarbon* 15, 212-28.

Smith, A.G. *et al.* 1971 'New radiocarbon dates from Ireland', *Antiquity* 45, 97-102.

Smith, A.G. *et al.* 1972 'Dendrochronological work in progress in Belfast: the prospects for an Irish post-glacial tree-ring sequence'. *Proc. 8th Internat. Conf. on Radiocarbon Dating* 1, A92-6.

Smith, I.F. 1974 'The Neolithic', in Renfrew, C. (ed.), *British Prehistory: a new outline.* London, 100-36.

Smith, I.F. and Evans, J.G. 1968 'Excavation of two long barrows in North Wiltshire', *Antiquity* 42, 138-42.

Smith, I.F. *et al.* 1964 'New Neolithic sites in Dorset and Bedfordshire, with a note on the distribution of Neolithic storage pits in Britain', *Proc. Prehist. Soc.* 30, 352-82.

Smith, J.A. 1869 'Notice of remains of the reindeer *Cervus tarandus* found in Ross-shire, Sutherland, and Caithness', *Proc. Soc. Antiq. Scot.* 8, 186-222.

Smith, W.G. 1894 *Man the Primeval Savage.* London.

Smith, W.G. 1916 'Notes on the Palaeolithic floor near Caddington', *Archaeologia* 67, 49-74.

Soulsby, J.A. 1976 'Palaeoenvironmental interpretation of a buried soil at Achnacree, Argyll', *Trans. Inst. Brit. Geogr.* NS 1, 279-83.

Southern, H.N. 1964 *The Handbook of British Mammals.* Oxford.

Sparks, B.W. 1961 'The ecological interpretation of Quaternary non-marine molluscs', *Proc. Linn. Soc. London* 172, 71-80.

Sparks, B.W. and West, R.G. 1972 *The Ice Age in Britain.* London.

Spratt, D.A. and Simmons, I.G. 1976 'Prehistoric activity and environment on the North York Moors', *J. Archaeol. Sci.* 3, 193-210.

Starkel, L. 1966 'Post-glacial climate and the moulding of European relief', in Sawyer, J.S. *et al. World Climate from 8,000 to 0 BC.* London, 34-9.

Steensberg, A. 1957 'Some recent Danish experiments in Neolithic agriculture', *J. Agric. Hist. Rev.* 5, 66-73.

Steensberg, A. 1973 'A 6,000-year-old ploughing implement from Satrup Moor', *Tools and Tillage* 2, 105-18.

Stelfox, A.W. 1942 'Report on the animal remains from Ballinderry 2 crannog', *Proc. Roy. Irish. Acad.* 47C, 67-8.

Stewart, J.M. and Durno, S.E. 1969 'Structural variations in peat', *New Phytol.* 68, 167-82.

Stockmarr, J. 1971 'Tablets with spores used in absolute pollen analysis', *Pollen Spores* 13 (4), 615-21.

Straw, A. 1973 'The glacial geomorphology of central and north Norfolk', *East Midland Geographer* 5 (7), No. 39, 333-54.

Streif, H. 1972 'The results of stratigraphical and facial investigations in the coastal Holocene of Woltzeten/Ostfiesland, Germany', *Geol. För. Stockh. Förh.* 94 (2), 291-9.

Stuart, A.J. 1974 'Pleistocene history of the British vertebrate fauna', *Biol. Rev.* 49, 225-66.

Stuart, A.J. 1976 'The history of the mammal fauna during the Ipswichian/Last Interglacial in England', *Phil. Trans. R. Soc. Lond.* (B) 276 (945), 221-50.

Suess, H.E. 1970 'Bristlecone Pine calibration of the radiocarbon timescale 5,200 BC to the present', in Olsson, I.U. (ed.) 1970, *Radiocarbon Variations and Absolute Chronology.* Proc. 12th. Nobel Symposium. Stockholm, 303-12.

Sutcliffe, A. 1960 'Joint Mitnor Cave, Buckfastleigh. A report on excavations carried out during 1939-41 by the late A.H. Oglivie', *Trans. Torquay Nat. Hist. Soc.* 13 (1), 1-28.

Sutcliffe, A.J. and Kowalski, K. 1976 'Pleistocene rodents of the British Isles', *Bull. British Museum (Natural History)* 27 (2), 1-147.

Swinnerton, H.H. 1931 'The post-glacial deposits of the Lincolnshire coasts', *Q. Jl. Geol. Soc. London* 87, 360-75.

Szabo, B.J. and Collins, D. 1975 'Ages of fossil bones from British inter-glacial sites', *Nature* (London) 254, 680-2.

Tallis, J.H. 1964a 'Studies on southern Pennine peats. I. The general pollen record', *J. Ecol.* 52, 323-31.

Tallis, J.H. 1964b 'Studies on southern Pennine peats. II. The pattern of erosion', *J. Ecol.* 52, 332-44.

Tallis, J.H. 1975 'Tree remains in southern Pennine peats', *Nature*, (London) 256, 482-4.

Tallis, J.H. and McGuire, J. 1972 'Central Rossendale: the evolution of an upland vegetation. I. The clearance of woodland', *J. Ecol.* 60, 721-37.

Tallis, J.H. and Switsur, V.R. 1973 'Studies on southern Pennine peats. VI. A radiocarbon-dated pollen diagram from Featherbed Moss, Derbyshire', *J. Ecol.* 61, 743-51.

Tauber, H. 1965 'Differential pollen dispersion and the interpretation of pollen diagrams', *Danm. Geol. Unders.* Ser. 2, No. 89, 1-69.

Tauber, H. 1972 'Radiocarbon chronology of the Danish Mesolithic and Neolithic', *Antiquity* 46, 106-10.

Tauber, H. 1977 'Investigations of aerial pollen transport in a forested area', in Clayton, K. (ed), *X INQUA Congress, Birmingham 1977 Abstracts*, 461.

Taylor, H. 1927 'King Arthur's Cave, near Whitchurch, Ross-on-Wye', *Proc. Bristol Univ. Spel. Geol. Soc.* 3 (1), 59-83.

Taylor, J.A. 1965 'Climatic change as related to altitudinal thresholds and soil variables', in Johnston, C.G. and Smith, L.P. (eds), *The Biological Significance of Climatic Changes in Britain*. London, 37-50.

Taylor, J.A. 1975 'The role of climatic factors in environmental and cultural changes in prehistoric times', in Evans, J.G. *et al.* (eds), *The Effect of Man on the Landscape: the Highland Zone*. CBA Research Report No. 11, 6-19.

Ten Hove, H.A. 1968 'The *Ulmus* fall at the transition Atlanticum/Sub-Boreal in pollen diagrams', *Palaeogeogr., Palaeoclimatol., Palaeoecol.* 5, 359-69.

Ters, M. 1973 'Les variations du niveau marin depuis 10000 ans, le long du littoral Atlantique Français', *Le Quaternaire: géodynamique, stratigraphie et environnement*. Centre National de la Recherche Scientifique. Comité National Français de L'INQUA. 114-35.

Tetley, H. 1938 'Animal bones' in Jones, S.J. *et al.* 'The excavation of Gorsey Bigbury'. *Proc. Univ. Bristol Spelaeol. Soc.* 5, 53.

Thomas, G.S.P. 1977 'The Quaternary of the Isle of Man', in Kidson, C. and Tooley, M.J. (eds), *The Quaternary History of the Irish Sea*. Geological Journal Special Issue 7, 155-78.

Thomas, K.W. 1965 'The stratigraphy and pollen analysis of a raised bog at Llanllwch near Carmarthen', *New Phytol.* 64, 101-17.

Tinsley, H.M. 1973 *A Palynological Study of Changing Woodland Limits on the Nidderdale Moors*. Unpublished Ph.D. Thesis, University of Leeds.

Tinsley, H.M. 1975 'The former woodland of the Nidderdale Moors (Yorkshire) and the role of early man in its decline', *J. Ecol.* 63, 1-26.

Tinsley, H.M. 1976 'Cultural influences on Pennine vegetation with particular reference to North Yorkshire', *Trans. Inst. Br. Geog.* N.S 1, 310-22.

Tinsley, H.M. and Smith R.T. 1974 'Surface pollen studies across a woodland/heath transition and their application to the interpretation of pollen diagrams', *New Phytol.* 73, 547-65.

Tooley, M.J. 1970 'The peat beds of the south-west Lancashire coast', *Nature in Lancashire* 1, 19-26.

Tooley, M.J. 1974 'Sea-level changes during the last 9,000 years in north-west England', *Geog. J.* 140, 18-42.

Tooley, M.J. 1976 'Flandrian sea-level changes in west Lancashire and their implications for the 'Hillhouse Coastline', *Geol. J.* 11 (2), 37-52.

Tooley, M.J. (ed.) 1977 *The Isle of Man, Lancashire Coast and Lake District.* X INQUA Congress, Guidebook for Excursion A4. Norwich.

Tooley, M.J. 1978a *Sea-level Changes in North-West England during the Flandrian Stage.* Oxford.

Tooley, M.J. 1978b 'The history of Hartlepool Bay.' *Int. J. Nautical Archaeology and Underwater Exploration* 7(1), 71-5.

Tooley, M.J. 1978c 'Holocene sea-level changes: problems of interpretation', *Geol. För. Stockh. Förh.* 100(2), 203-12.

Tratman, E.K. *et al.* 1971 'The Hyaena Den (Wookey Hole), Mendip Hills, Somerset', *Proc. Univ. Bristol. Spelaeol. Soc.* 12 (3), 245-79.

Tratman, E.K. *et al.* (forthcoming) 'A new radiocarbon date for Gough's Cave, Somerset'.

Travis, C.B. 1926 'The peat and forest bed of the south-west Lancashire coast', *Proc. Lpool. Geol. Soc.* 14, 263-77.

Treacher, M.S. *et al.* 1948 'On the ancient channel between Caversham and Henley, Oxfordshire, and its contained flint implements', *Proc. Prehist. Soc.* 14, 126-54.

Troels-Smith, J. 1937 'Datering of Ertebøllebopladser ved hjaelp af Litorina – transgressioner og pollenanalyse', *Med. Fra. Dansk Geol. Forening.* 9, 253-5.

Troels-Smith, J. 1954 'Ertebøllekultur – Bondekultur', *Aarb. Nord. Oldkynd. Hist.* 1953, 5-62.

Troels-Smith, J. 1955a 'Pollenanalytischen Untersuchungen zu einigen schweizerischen Pfahlbauproblemen', in Guyan, W.U. (ed.), *Das Pfahlbauproblem*, Monograph, Ur-und Frühgesch. Schweiz. XI. Basle, 1-58.

Troels-Smith, J. 1955b 'Karakterisering af løse jordarter', *Danm. Geol. Unders.* IV 3 (10), 1-73.

Troels-Smith, J. 1956 'Neolithic period in Switzerland and Denmark', *Science* (N.Y.) 124, 876-9.

Troels-Smith, J. 1960a 'Ivy, mistletoe and elm: climatic indicators – fodder plants: a contribution to the interpretation of the pollen zone border VII-VIII', *Danm. Geol. Unders.* IV Series, vol. 4 (4), 1-32.

Troels-Smith, J. 1960b 'The Muldbjerg dwelling place: an Early Neolithic archaeological site in the Aamosen Bog, West-Zealand, Denmark', *Smithsonian Report for 1959.* Publication 4413, 577-601.

Troels-Smith, J. 1966 'The Ertebølle culture and its background', *Palaeohistoria* 12, 505-28.

Troels-Smith, J. 1975 'Knud Jessen. Nov. 29th 1884 – April 14th, 1971', *Med. Fra. Dansk. Geol. Forening.* 24, 99-111.

Turk, F.A. 1964a 'On some Bronze Age remains of the water-rat (*Arvicola terrestris amphibius* L.). *Proc. Zool. Soc. Lond.* 143, 345-9.

Turk, F.A. 1964b 'Blue and brown hares associated together in a Bronze Age fissure cave burial. *Proc. Zool. Soc. Lond.* 142, 185-8.

Turk, F.A. 1967 'Report on the animal remains from Nornour, Isles of Scilly, *J. Roy. Inst. Cornwall.* N.S. 5, 250-66.

Turner, C. 1970 'The Middle Pleistocene deposits at Marks Tey, Essex', *Phil. Trans. R. Soc. Lond.* (B) 257, 373-440.

·Turner, C. 1975 'The correlation and duration of middle Pleistocene interglacial periods in north-west Europe', in Butzer, K.W. and Isaacs, G. (eds), *After the Australopithecines: stratigraphy, ecology and culture in the middle Pleistocene.* The Hague.

Turner, C. and Kerney, M.P. 1971 'The age of the freshwater beds of the Clacton Channel', *J. Geol. Soc. London* 127, 93-5.

'Turner, C. and West, R.G. 1968 'The subdivision and zonation of interglacial periods', *Eiszeitalter und Gegen.* 19, 93-101.

Turner, J. 1962 'The *Tilia* decline: an anthropogenic interpretation', *New Phytol.* 61, 328-41.

Turner, J. 1964a 'Anthropogenic factor in vegetation history', *New Phytol.* 63, 73-89.

Turner, J. 1964b 'Surface sample analysis from Ayrshire, Scotland', *Pollen Spores* 6, 583-92.

Turner, J. 1965 'A contribution to the history of forest clearance', *Proc. R. Soc.* (B) 161, 343-54.

Turner, J. 1970 'Post neolithic disturbance of British vegetation', in Walker, D. and West, R.G. (eds), *Studies in the Vegetational History of the British Isles: essays in honour of Harry Godwin.* London, 97-116.

Turner, J. 1975 'The evidence for land use by prehistoric farming communities: the use of three-dimensional pollen diagrams', in Evans, J.G. *et al.* (eds), *The Effect of Man on the Landscape: the Highland Zone.* C.B.A. Research Report No. 11, 86-95.

Turner, J. *et al.* 1973 'The history of the vegetation and flora of Widdybank Fell and the Cow Green Reservoir basin, Upper Teesdale', *Phil. Trans. R. Soc. Lond.* (B) 265, 327-408.

Turner, W. 1895 'On human and animal remains found in caves at Oban, Argyllshire', *Proc. Soc. Antiq. Scot.* 29, 410-38.

Tutin, W. 1969 'The usefulness of pollen analysis in interpretation of stratigraphic horizons, both late-glacial and post-glacial', *Mitt. Internat. Verein. Limnol.* 17, 154-64.

Ucko, P. and Dimbleby, G.W. (eds) 1969 *The Domestication and Exploitation of Plants and Animals.* London.

Valentine, K.W.G. 1973 *The identification, lateral variation and chronology of three buried palaeocatenas in Lowland England.* Unpublished Ph.D. thesis, University of Reading.

Valentine, K.W.G. and Dalrymple, J.B. 1975 'The identification, lateral variation, and chronology of two buried palaeocatenas at Woodhall Spa and West Runton, England', *Quaternary Research* 5, 551-91.

Van der Werff, A. and Huls, H. 1958-74, *Diatomeeënflora van Nederland*. 8 parts published privately by van der Werff, A, Westzijde, 13a., De Hoef (U), The Netherlands.

Van Zeist, W. 1954 'A contribution to the problem of the so-called Grenzhorizont', *Palaeohistoria* 3, 220-4.

Vasari, Y. and Vasari, A. 1968 'Late- and post-glacial macrophytic vegetation in the Lochs of Northern Scotland', *Acta Bot. Fenn.* 80, 1-20.

Villaret-von Rochow, M. 1967 'Frucht- und Samenreste aus der neolithische Station, Seeberg, Burgäschisee-Süd', *Acta Bernensis* 2, 21-64.


Wade, A.G. 1928 'Ancient flint mines at Stoke Down, Sussex', *Proc. Prehist. Soc. East Anglia* 4, 82-91.

Waechter, J. d'A., and Conway, B.W. 1969 'Swanscombe 1968 (interim report on new excavations in the Barnfield Pit)', *Proc. Roy. Anthrop. Inst. Gr. Brit. Ireland for 1968*, 53-61.

Walker, D. 1965 'The post-glacial period in the Langdale Fells, English Lake District', *New Phytol.* 64, 488-510.

Walker, D. 1966 'The Late-Quaternary history of the Cumberland Lowland', *Phil. Trans. R. Soc. Lond.* (B) 251, 1-210.

Walker, M.F. and Taylor, J.A. 1976 'Post-Neolithic vegetation changes in the western Rhinogau, Gwynedd, north-west Wales', *Trans. Inst. Br. Geog.* N.S. 1, 323-45.

Wallace, A.R. 1876 *The Geographical Distribution of Animals (with a study of the relations of living and extinct faunas as elucidating the past changes of the earth's surface)*. London, 2 vols.

Washburn, H.L. and Lancaster, C.S. 1968 'The evolution of hunting', in Lee, R.H. and De Vore, I, (eds), *Man the Hunter*. Chicago, 293-303.

Watson, D.M.S. 1929 'The animal bones', in Curwen, C. 'Excavations in the Trundle, 1928', *Sussex Archaeol. Collections* 70, 68-9.

Watts, W.A. 1961 'Post-Atlantic forests in Ireland', *Proc. Linn. Soc. Lond.* 172, 33-8.

Watts, W.A. 1973 'Rates of change and stability in vegetation in the perspective of long periods of time', in Birks, H.J.B. and West, R.G. (eds) *Quaternary Plant Ecology*. 14th Symposium of the British Ecological Society. Oxford, 195-206.

Weber, C.A. 1900 'Uber die Moore, mit besonderer Berucksichtigung, der zwischen Unterweser und Unterelbe liegenden', *Jahres-Bericht der Männer von Morgenstern* 3, 3-23.

Wendland, W.M. and Bryson, R.A. 1974 'Dating climatic episodes of the Holocene', *Quaternary Research* 4, 9-24.

West, R.G. 1956 'The Quaternary deposits at Hoxne, Suffolk', *Phil. Trans. R. Soc. Lond.* (B) 239, 265-356.

West, R.G. 1957 'Interglacial deposits at Bobbitshole, Ipswich', *Phil. Trans. R. Soc. Lond.* (B) 241, 1-31.

West, R.G. 1964 'Inter-relations of ecology and Quaternary palaeobotany', *J. Ecol.* 52 (Suppl.), 47-57.

West, R.G., 1968 *Pleistocene Geology and Biology, with Special Reference to the British Isles*. London.

West, R.G. 1969 'Pollen analyses from interglacial deposits at Aveley and Grays, Essex', *Proc. Geol. Ass.* 80, 271-82.

West, R.G. 1970a 'Pleistocene history of the British Flora', in Walker, D. and West, R.G. (eds) *Studies in the Vegetational History of the British Isles: essays in honour of Harry Godwin.* Cambridge, 1-11.

West, R.G. 1970b 'Pollen zones in the Pleistocene of Great Britain and their correlation', *New Phytol.* 69, 1179-83.

West, R.G. 1971 'Studying the past by pollen analysis', *Oxford Biology Readers* 10, 1-16.

West, R.G. 1977 *Pleistocene Geology and Biology, with Special Reference to the British Isles.* London, (2nd ed.).

West, R.G. *et al.* 1964 'Interglacial deposits at Ilford, Essex', *Phil. Trans. R. Soc. Lond.* (B) 247, 185-212.

West, R.G. *et al.* 1974 'Late Pleistocene deposits at Wretton, Norfolk. II Devensian deposits', *Phil. Trans. R. Soc. Lond.* (B) 267, 337-420.

Westley, B. 1971 'The animal bones from Durrington Walls, 1970', *Wilts. Archaeol. Nat. Hist. Mag.* 66, 122-5.

Wheeler, A. 1977 'The origin and distribution of the freshwater fishes of the British Isles', *J. Biogeogr.* 4, 1-24.

Wheeler, A. 1978 'Why were there no fish remains at Star Carr?', *J. Arch. Sci.* 5, 85-9.

Whittle, A.W.R. 1978 'Resources and population in the British Neolithic', *Antiquity* 52, 34-42.

Whittle, A.W.R. 1979 'Scord of Brouster', *Current Archaeol.* 56, 167-71.

Wijngaarden-Bakker, L.H. 1974 'The animal remains from the Beaker settlement at Newgrange, Co. Meath: first report', *Proc. Roy. Irish Acad.* 74C, 313-83.

Willcox, G.H. 1977 'Exotic plants from Roman waterlogged sites in London', *J. Archaeol. Sci.* 4, 269-82.

Willerding, U. 1970 'Vor- und frühgeschichtliche Kulturpflanzenfunde in Mitteleuropa', *Neue Ausgrabungen und Forschungen in Niedersachsen* 5, 287-375.

Williams, D.E. 'Flotation at Siraf', *Antiquity* 47, 288-92.

Williams, D.E. 1976 'Preliminary observations of the use of flotation apparatus in Sussex', in Drewett, P. (ed.), 'Rescue archaeology in Sussex', *Bull. Inst. Arch. London.* 13, 51-9.

Williams, R.B.G. 1975 'The British climate during the Last Glaciation: an interpretation based on periglacial phenomena', in Wright, A.E. and Moseley, F. (eds), *Ice Ages: ancient and modern.* Geological Journal Special Issue No. 6, 95-120.

Willis, E.H. 1961 'Marine transgression sequences in the English Fenlands', *Ann. N.Y. Acad. Sci.* 95, 368-76.

Woodhead, T.W. 1929 'History of the vegetation of the southern Pennines', *J. Ecol.* 17 (1), 1-34.

Woodhead, T.W. and Erdtman, O.G.E. 1926 'Remains in the peat of the southern Pennines', *The Naturalist* 835 (609), 245-53.

Woodman, P.C. 1973-4 'Settlement patterns of the Irish Mesolithic', *Ulster J. Archaeol.* 36 and 37, 1-16.

Woodman, P.C. 1978 'The chronology and economy of the Irish Mesolithic: some working hypotheses', in Mellars, P.A. *The Early Postglacial Settlement of Northern Europe*. London, 333-69.

Wright, E.V. and Churchill, D.M. 1965 'The boats from North Ferriby, Yorkshire, England', *Prog. Prehist. Soc.* 31, 1-24.

Wright, E.V. and Wright, C.W. 1947 'Prehistoric boats from North Ferriby, East Yorkshire', *Proc. Prehist. Soc.* 7, 114-38.

Wright, H.E. Jr. 1976 'The dynamic nature of Holocene vegetation. A problem in palaeoclimatology, biogeography and stratigraphic nomenclature', *Quaternary Research* 6, 581-96.

Wymer, J.J. 1961 'The Lower Palaeolithic succession in the Thames Valley and the date of the ancient channel between Caversham and Henley', *Proc. Prehist. Soc.* 27, 1-27.

Wymer, J.J. 1964 'Excavations at Barnfield Pit, 1955-1960', in Ovey, C.D. (ed.), *The Swanscombe Skull. Roy. Anthrop. Inst. Occ. Paper* 20, 19-61.

Wymer, J.J. 1965 'Excavation of the Lambourn long barrow, 1964', *Berks. Archaeol. J.* 62, 16.

Wymer, J.J. 1968 *Lower Palaeolithic Archaeology in Britain, as Represented by the Thames Valley*. London.

Wymer, J.J. 1974a 'Clactonian and Acheulian industries in Britain – their chronology and significance', *Proc. Geol. Ass.* 85 (3), 391-421.

Wymer, J.J. 1974b 'Note on a hand-axe found at Mortimer', *Berkshire Archaeol. J.* 66, 7-9.

Wymer, J.J. *et al.* 1975 'Late Devensian and Early Flandrian barbed points from Sproughton, Suffolk', *Proc. Prehist. Soc.* 41, 235-41.

Wymer, J.J. and Rose, J. 1976 'A long blade industry at Sproughton, Suffolk', *E. Anglian Archaeol.* 3.

Zagwijn, W.H. 1975 'Variations in climate as shown by pollen analysis, especially in the Lower Pleistocene of Europe', in Wright, A.E. and Moseley, F. (eds) *Ice Ages: ancient and modern*. Geological Journal Special Issue No. 6, 137-52.

Zeuner, F.E. 1945 *The Pleistocene Period*. London.

Ziegler, A.C. 1973 'Inference from prehistoric faunal remains', *An Addison-Wesley Module in Anthropology* 43, 1-57.

# Index